Howard Van Fleet Furman

A Manual of practical assaying

Second Edition

Howard Van Fleet Furman

A Manual of practical assaying
Second Edition

ISBN/EAN: 9783337106102

Printed in Europe, USA, Canada, Australia, Japan

Cover: Foto ©ninafisch / pixelio.de

More available books at **www.hansebooks.com**

A MANUAL

OF

PRACTICAL ASSAYING.

BY

H. VAN F. FURMAN, E.M.,

*Late Chemist and Assayer of the Germania Lead Works, Salt Lake City, Utah;
Late Chemist and Assistant Metallurgist of the Rio Grande Smelting
Works, Socorro, N. M.; Late Chemist of the Globe Smelting and
Refining Co., Denver, Colo.; Member of the American
Institute of Mining Engineers; Member of the
Colorado Scientific Society; etc.*

SECOND EDITION, REVISED.

FIRST THOUSAND.

NEW YORK:
JOHN WILEY & SONS,
53 EAST TENTH STREET.
1894.

PREFACE.

SOME three years ago there was published in *The Mining Industry* of Denver, by the author of the present volume, a series of articles entitled "Notes on Technical Chemical Analyses." The articles were favorably received by the technical public, and in compliance with numerous requests their republication in the present book form was undertaken.

It is, however, proper to state that the original articles have been rewritten and much new matter has been added, embracing all the new technical methods which have been introduced and proved trustworthy since the publication of the series referred to, as well as many determinations not described there.

Greatest prominence has been given to the rapid methods in vogue in the technical laboratories of the United States, supplemented by a detailed description of some of the longer and more exact ones.

Although the plan of the work presupposes a knowledge of the general principles of chemistry, the endeavor has been to present the methods in a form that those having but a more limited experience in analytical chemistry could successfully perform the operations.

Chapter III of Part IV, while not strictly within the scope of a work of the present nature, was included to illustrate the practical application of the principles of stoichiometry and chemistry to metallurgy.

Reference has been made by footnotes to the original sources of information. Where, inadvertently, omissions have occurred and due credit has not been so given, the author would esteem it a favor to have his attention called to the neglect. He would also be pleased to receive criticisms on the work, so that he may be able to take advantage of them should a future edition be called for.

In conclusion the author begs to add that should this little volume fill even partially the wants of technical chemists and meet with their approval, he will feel amply repaid for the labor involved in the compilation and publication of the methods described.

H. VAN F. FURMAN.

DENVER, COLO., September 30, 1893.

TABLE OF CONTENTS.

PART I.

INTRODUCTORY.

CHAPTER	PAGE
I. Introduction	1
II. Sampling	5
III. Preliminary Examination	21
IV. Apparatus and Operations	49
V. Reagents	66

PART II.

DETERMINATIONS.

I. Silica	77
II. Sulphur	88
III. Phosphorus	100
IV. Carbon	106
V. Carbonic Acid	116
VI. Water	119
VII. Gold and Silver	122
VIII. Mercury	133
IX. Lead	136
X. Arsenic	144
XI. Antimony	147
XII. Tin	151
XIII. Copper	154
XIV. Bismuth	163
XV. Cadmium	165
XVI. Iron	168
XVII. Aluminium	181

	PAGE
XVIII. Chromium	188
XIX. Titanium	190
XX. Manganese	194
XXI. Zinc	205
XXII. Nickel and Cobalt	211
XXIII. Calcium	215
XXIV. Magnesium	220
XXV. Barium	224
XXVI. Sodium and Potassium	227

PART III.

SPECIAL ASSAYS AND ANALYSES.

I. Assay of Base Bullion	232
II. Assay of Silver Bullion	236
III. Assay of Gold Bullion	246
IV. Special Method for the Assay of Copper Matte, etc.	250
V. Assay of Silver Sulphides	252
VI. Chlorination-assay of Silver Ores	254
VII. Chlorination-assay of Gold Ores	256
VIII. Assay of Gold and Silver Ores containing Metallic Scales	258
IX. Amalgamation-assay	260
X. Analysis of Coal and Coke	263
XI. Analysis of Gases	269
XII. Analysis of Water	274
XIII. Acidimetry and Alkalimetry	282
XIV. Chlorimetry	289
XV. Analysis of White Lead	291
XVI. Specific-gravity Determinations	293
XVII. Analysis of Commercial Aluminium	298
XVIII. Analysis of Natural Phosphates	300
XIX. Analysis of Copper and Lead Slags	307

PART IV.

CALCULATIONS.

I. Writing of Chemical Equations	312
II. Stoichiometry	321
III. The Calculation of Lead Blast-furnace Charges	337
TABLES	353

A MANUAL OF PRACTICAL ASSAYING.

CHAPTER I.

INTRODUCTION.

ASSAYING as practised in the United States, and particularly as practised in the Far West, may be said to include all those operations of analytical chemistry which have for their object the determination of the value of ores and metallurgical products. Results are obtained by the following three methods: 1st. Fire-assay (dry method); 2d. Gravimetric analysis in the wet way; 3d. Volumetric analysis in the wet way. In this classification the colorimetric methods are included in the division of volumetric analysis.

Fire-assay determinations involve the separation of the metal sought from the other constituents of the ore by the aid of heat and suitable fluxes, and its estimation by weighing in a state of purity. For example, if the object is the determination of lead in an ore, the ore is mixed in a crucible with suitable fluxes and fused. The lead is reduced to the metallic state, in which condition it is readily detached from the slag for weighing.

Gravimetric determinations involve the separation of the substance from the other constituents of the ore, and its estimation by weighing either the substance itself in a state of purity or as a constituent of a chemical compound whose composition is accurately known. For example, if the object is the determination of lime in a mineral, the latter may be treated in such a manner that the ultimate product of such treatment is pure lime, which can be weighed direct; or the treatment may be such that the product is calcium sulphate, whose weight may be determined, and as this salt is of invarible composition the contained lime can readily be calculated.

Volumetric determinations are those which involve the separation of the substance to be determined from all interfering constituents of the ore, and the final measuring of the quantity of a solution necessary to complete a certain reaction; or, as in the case of colorimetric determinations, by measuring the color imparted to a definite quantity of the liquid by the constituent sought in comparison with the color imparted to the same quantity of water, or other suitable fluid, by a known quantity of the constituent sought. For example, if the object is the determination of iron in an iron ore, as the iron is capable of reduction from the ferric to the ferrous state, and of subsequent oxidation to the ferric state by the addition of a suitable oxidizing reagent, if the amount of oxidizing agent necessary to just convert the iron to the ferric state is known, the amount of iron in the substance can be readily calculated.

In fire-assaying generally but one constituent of the ore is determined in each assay,—except in the case of gold and silver determinations, where frequently both the gold and silver are determined in the same portion.

In gravimetric analysis frequently several or all of the constituents of the substance are determined in the one portion taken for analysis.

In volumetric work generally a separate portion is taken for each determination.

The following hints may be of benefit to the young and inexperienced chemist:

Cleanliness is absolutely essential to good work.

The work should be systematically arranged and carried out. The secret of accomplishing a large amount of work and avoiding errors depends largely upon being systematic. The apparatus and reagents should be adapted to the work, and should be systematically arranged. A system of labelling and keeping track of each sample through all stages of the analysis should be adopted. By this means mixing of samples will be impossible, and a glance will show at any time just how far the analysis has proceeded. A good system of labelling is to prepare some pieces of heavy paper about one and a half inches square. As the substance is weighed out mark the number or name of lot, the elements to be determined, and weight taken on one of these squares of paper, and carry the same along through the course of the analysis with the casserole, beaker, etc., containing the sample, making simple marks on the paper from time to time, as necessary, to show the stage of the analysis.

Where much work is to be done do not attempt to carry a few determinations through the different stages of the analysis to a finish at once, but start a number of determinations and carry them along through the different stages in series, as many as convenient at a time.

Use definite weights in weighing out a substance for analysis, as 0.5 or 1.0 gm.

Do not make up the reagents indiscriminately, but always try and have them of a definite strength. In this way the use of excessive quantities of reagents will be avoided. The use of excessive quantities of reagents not only unnecessarily prolongs the operations, but frequently spoils the results, or renders it impossible to obtain results. This applies to water as well as other reagents. The smallest quantity of a reagent which will thoroughly do the work required of it should be used.

In making up standard solutions for volumetric analysis care should be exercised to have them of the proper strength; they should be thoroughly mixed and accurately standardized. It is best to have these volumetric solutions of a definite, even strength. For example, the potassium-permanganate solution used in the determination of iron should be of such a strength that each cubic centimetre will equal 5 milligrammes or 10 milligrammes of iron. This saves a great deal of time, and possibly errors, in the calculation of results.

Use apparatus which is adapted to the work, and never use larger apparatus than is necessary. For example, if 0.5 gm. of slag is to be decomposed by acids, if introduced into a large casserole a greater quantity of acids will be necessary than if a small casserole is used and the operation will be prolonged.

Do not use larger filter-papers than are necessary. A large filter requires much more washing than a small one.

Be careful to avoid loss in boiling and other operations.

Never accept results where there is reason to believe that they may be incorrect, owing to faulty manipulation or accidents.

CHAPTER II.

SAMPLING.

ALL ores, furnace products, etc., which are to be assayed must be first accurately sampled. Accurate sampling is quite as essential as accurate assaying; for if the sample does not truly represent the lot or mass from which it was taken, the subsequent assay will be valueless.

The assayer or chemist will usually receive the sample already prepared; but as he will occasionally be called upon to take his own sample, a knowledge of the art of sampling and the different methods in vogue is essential.

The method to be adopted for obtaining a sample will depend upon the character of the material to be sampled and the use to which it is to be put after sampling: for example, in the case of a silver ore, whether the ore is high or low grade, whether it is wet or dry, etc. If the ore is to be smelted, it is not desirable to crush it finer than is necessary to obtain a correct sample, as fine ore is undesirable for smelting. If the ore is to be milled, fine crushing is not a disadvantage.

It is hardly necessary to say that in obtaining a sample the work should be fairly done, no discrimination as against any portion of the lot or mass being allowable.

There are many other methods of sampling besides those described in the following pages, but the methods as described are standard methods, and are in constant use in many of our large works, having been tried and found reliable.

For convenience the subject may be considered under the following headings:

1. Ore sampling.
2. Sampling of metallurgical products.

Ore Sampling.—A proper sampling requires adequate mixing, impartial selection of the sample, and proper relative comminution.

The different methods may be classified as follows:
1. Hand sampling.
2. Combined hand and mechanical sampling.
3. Mechanical sampling.

The first two methods may be subdivided into—

Fractional selection (tenth, fifth, etc., of a shovel).

Quartering (halving, etc.).

Split shovel (single, double, etc., scoop; assayer's riffles).

Channelling (driving one or more channels through a pile; driving a scoop or sampling rod through a pile of fine ore, etc.).

Mechanical sampling may be subdivided into—
1. Continuous sampling.
2. Intermittent sampling.

A combination of one or more of these methods is frequently adopted, as taking every tenth shovel from the car, crushing this sample, and reducing it by quartering or split shovelling.

Hand sampling consists of taking a sample by hand, the only tools necessary being a hammer, mortar, and buckboard. Hand or grab samples are frequently taken of the ores, fuels, slags, etc., at metallurgical works, as a check and control on the metallurgical operations. In taking such samples care should be exercised to select the proper relative amount of fine and coarse material. The coarse is selected by chipping pieces from the large lumps. Having obtained the sample, the whole should be further broken to the proper size and then reduced by quartering, passing over a split shovel or over assayer's riffles. The final sample should be ground on the buckboard until all will pass through an eighty-mesh sieve. At some works the practice is to pass all samples through a hundred-mesh sieve. The finer the sample is reduced the better. Accurate samples can be taken by hand, but to take an accurate sample of a large lot of ore in this way would involve an immense amount of labor; hence the second and third methods of sampling.

COMBINED HAND AND MECHANICAL SAMPLING.

This method of sampling can be carried on in several ways, as illustrated by the above classification. Just which method will be adopted will depend upon the requirements and the facilities in each individual case. Each of the methods gives good results, provided the proper precautions are observed. The method of fractional selection, followed by comminution and then by quartering or split shovelling, is a favorite method with many smelting-works, for the following reasons: It is desirable that the bulk of the ore as it is unloaded from the cars or ore-wagons should pass directly to the smelting beds or bins with a minimum amount of handling (most smelting-works make no charge for sampling), and also that the bulk of the ore should remain in as coarse a condition as is consistent with proper sampling.

This method is as follows: As the ore-cars are unloaded every tenth, fifth, third, or second shovelful, taken indiscriminately, is thrown into a wheelbarrow as a sample. In case the lot contains lumps of ore which are too large for the shovel, they should be broken with a sledge-hammer as encountered. The proportion which will be taken for a sample will depend upon the character of the ore. In the case of a high-grade silver or gold ore, ununiform in composition (where the silver and gold is unevenly distributed throughout the mass), proper sampling will require that the whole lot be taken for sampling. In the case of low-grade silver or gold ores, uniform in composition, and lead or copper ores, one tenth of the whole will generally give a fair sample. In the case of iron ores, other than ores which may be classed as silver and gold ores on account of their silver and gold contents, every twentieth or less may be taken. In the case of the limestone used as flux and the coal and coke, a much smaller proportion may be taken; in fact a fair hand sample will generally answer.

The portion taken for a sample is removed to the sampling works and passed through the crusher. Should the sample weigh about 10 tons, it can now be safely reduced to one ton by quartering, except in the case of very high-grade ores, which are ununiform in composition. In this latter case, or when the sample only weighs about one ton, it should be further comminuted to chestnut size by passing it through the rolls.

The sample can be reduced in bulk by any of the methods classified above, preference generally being given to quartering or split-shovelling. If quartering is chosen, the ore as it comes from the crusher or rolls is shovelled into a conical pile on the sampling-floor, each shovelful being thrown on the apex of the cone. When the cone is completed it is flattened out by commencing at its apex with a shovel and passing the shovel around in the path of a spiral until the whole is so flattened that it will be from 6 to 12 inches high, and present the appearance of a flat cake or pie. The point to be observed here is to not disturb the radial distribution of the coarse and fine ore. It is now divided into four equal quarters, and two of the diagonally opposite quarters removed to one of the bins in the sampling-works, where it remains until the lot is sampled and settled for. It is convenient to retain an original portion of the lot for resampling in case of a dispute between seller and buyer on the first sample. The remaining quarters are now formed into a conical pile by alternately shovelling from opposite quarters, each shovelful being thrown on the apex of the pile. This cone is flattened and quartered as before, the operation being continued until the remaining portion weighs about 200 pounds, provided the sample has previously been crushed to chestnut size. If the ore has not been previously reduced to chestnut size it should be so reduced before quartering down to 200 pounds. The 200-pound sample should now be further comminuted by passing it through a small set of rolls set close. It is now further reduced by quartering until it weighs about 5 pounds. This 5-pound sample should now be dried on a steam or hot-air bath, and when thoroughly dry is still further comminuted by passing through a coffee-mill grinder.

The product of the coffee-mill (about 20-mesh) is now reduced in bulk on the assayer's riffle or by quartering until we have a sample weighing from 1 to 3 pounds. This is now ground on the buckboard until it will all pass through an 80 or 100 mesh sieve. The fine pulp is then spread upon a piece of rubber oil-cloth in a thin layer, and the sample bottles or sacks filled by taking portions from all over the pile on the point of a steel spatula. The bottles are sealed and labelled, the works always retaining one sample as an umpire in case of dispute.

In case the split shovel is adopted the process is essentially the same, except that the ore should be crushed to a size finer than is possible in the crusher before using the split shovel. The following points are to be observed: The largest particles

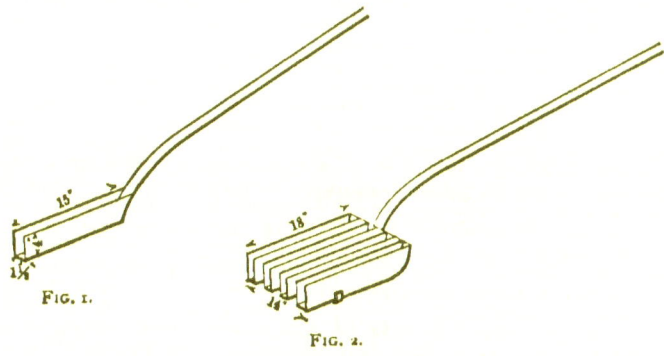

FIG. 1.   FIG. 2.

should not be wider than one fourth of the width of the scoop used; otherwise when they strike the edges of the scoop they may fly out. The scoop should be deep enough to render it impossible for pieces striking the bottom to fly out. The material should be thrown or delivered on the scoop squarely and in a wide flat stream. The split shovel may be one tenth as wide as the scoop shovel delivering the ore to it, or any other width which may be desired. The split shovels are made so as to take $\frac{1}{10}$, $\frac{1}{4}$, $\frac{1}{2}$, or any desired amount of the ore delivered to them, as is shown in the drawings.

The method of obtaining a sample by channelling is particularly adapted to obtaining a sample of a mine dump or a large pile of ore. It consists in running one or more channels or cuts through the pile, taking coarse or fine as it comes. This requires that the contents of the pile should have been pretty thoroughly mixed before channelling. If such is not the case several cuts or channels should be run. After the sample is obtained by channelling it should be crushed and cut down as described above. Channelling is sometimes adopted in place of quartering or split-shovelling after the ore sample has been reduced. It answers very well provided the pile is thoroughly mixed before channelling each time. Samples of fine ore, such as fine concentrates and mill tailings, are frequently obtained by driving a scoop or sampling-rod into the pile in several different places. The sampling-rod consists of a long steel rod with a semicircular depression in one side, being similar to the sampling rod used by sugar-samplers.

MECHANICAL SAMPLING.

A large number of different devices for obtaining samples mechanically have been invented. These all depend upon taking the sample from a stream of falling ore, a fractional portion being taken for the sample. The process may be continuous or intermittent. The main objections to all automatic samplers are: The difficulty of getting at the apparatus and cleaning it out after each lot is run through. This is a serious difficulty with some of the devices, as it will not do to run a low-grade galena, low in silver, through the apparatus which has just previously sampled a high-grade silver or gold ore, unless the apparatus has been previously thoroughly cleaned. Another objection is that the ore is not in full view during all stages of the process. Another objection amongst smelters is that it requires the whole sample to be crushed to a certain degree of fineness before it is run through the sampler. However, with proper care automatic samplers give good results, and have the great advantage that the work is done mechanically and indiscriminately. The general scheme with the continuous samplers is as follows: The ore is fed into a crusher, from which it passes through rolls. It is then elevated mechanically to a bin, from which it falls into a long vertical chute, where it is again mixed by rods or points in the chute. At a suitable point in the chute some device is introduced to take out a fractional portion of the falling stream. The fractional portion is frequently passed through a second set of rolls placed so as to crush finer than the first set, and again through some device, similar to the above, which takes out a fractional portion. This portion is then passed through a coffee-mill, bucked, and treated as before. This process requires that the ore should be quite dry before it is run through the mill. This method is a favorite one with some smelters for sampling low-grade sulphide ores and mattes which are roasted previous to smelting. In this case the fineness of the ore is no objection, as the ore would have to be reduced to a certain degree of fineness before roasting.

Intermittent samplers take a portion of the ore, fractional or otherwise, at intervals. The time between these intervals may be controlled mechanically, so that the intervals will be of equal duration. Many devices, such as intercepting-buckets, which intercept certain quantities at stated intervals, have been invented.

A modification of the method of taking a fractional portion from a continuous stream of falling ore has lately been introduced by The Denver Public Sampling Works which presents some advantages. The method as practised by these works is essentially as follows: All of the lot, or such fractional portion as is deemed necessary, is passed through the crusher and rolls. From the rolls it is raised to the upper floor of the mill by an elevator, which discharges into an iron hopper which is above the floor level and easily accessible for inspection and cleaning. This hopper is shown in Fig. 3.

The bottom of the hopper is connected with a vertical chute about 18 inches long, which is closed by a slide-gate (*a*). At the bottom of the chute is a sheet-iron chute (*b*) which diverts a portion of the ore to one side when the gate (*a*) is opened. Penetrating through this chute is a trough (*c*) similar to the scoop of a split shovel, the width of this trough being one tenth of the width of the chute. When the gate (*a*) is opened nine tenths of the ore is diverted to one side by the chute (*b*) into a car or wheelbarrow, and one tenth (the sample) to the opposite side by the trough (*c*). This sample is then reduced in bulk by split-shovelling to about 200 pounds, which is passed through a small set of rolls, after which it is reduced

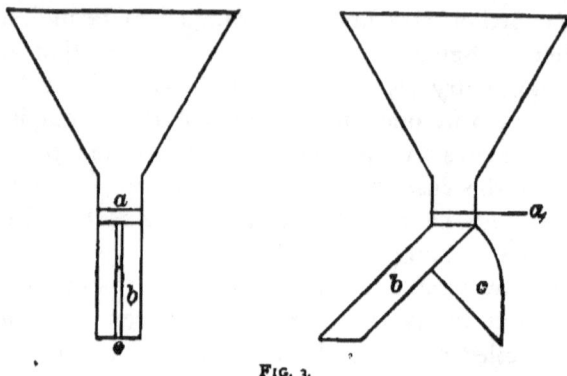

FIG. 3.

by the assayer's riffle, and is finally ground in the coffee-mill, bucked, etc., as before.

Many devices for the taking of intermittent samples, such as intercepting-buckets, which intercept certain quantities at stated times, have been invented. One of the best of the automatic samplers is that devised by D. W. Brunton, of Aspen, Colo.,* which is shown in Fig. 4. This device, in place of taking out a portion of the falling stream of ore, diverts the whole stream during certain intervals. These intervals may be regulated, as required, so as to obtain 10, 20, etc., per cent of the ore for a sample by a simple device. As the stream of ore is neither split nor divided, fine crushing on large samples is entirely unnecessary. After the ore has been crushed it is elevated a few feet above the level of the storage-bins and

---

* Transactions of the American Institute of Mining Engineers, Vol. XIII, p. 639.

discharged into the sampler, Fig. 4, in which C is a vertical or inclined chute, containing the falling stream of ore. B is a funnel for narrowing the width of the falling stream, so as to reduce to a minimum the necessary travel of the deflecting-chute A. This chute A is pivoted upon a rock-shaft. When it is deflected to the right the entire stream of ore is thrown into E, and when it is deflected to the left the entire stream is thrown into D. The driving-bar J receives its motion from the pins L in the face of the driving-wheel H, which is driven by the pulley G. The face of the wheel H is perforated by two rows of holes, the distance between the two rows being the same as the necessary movement of the crank. In these holes are inserted a number of pins L held in place by jam-nuts on the interior of the wheel-face. Preferably 20 holes are bored in each row, each hole or pin representing 5 per cent of the time necessary for a complete revolution of the wheel.

FIG. 4.

Now, if 50 per cent of the pins are placed in the right-hand row of holes, and 50 per cent in the left-hand row, then the revolution of the wheel H carrying the pins L through the guides NN on the driving-bar J will hold the deflecting-chute A on the right during one half revolution and on the left during the other half, thus dividing the stream into two equal portions. If 20 per cent of the pins are placed in the right-hand row and 80 per cent in the left, then the deflecting-chute A will be held on the right during one fifth of a revolution and on the left during four fifths, thus throwing 20 per cent of the ore into spout E and 80 per cent into spout D, etc. The ore falling into E passes into the storage-bins, whilst the ore falling into *D* is discharged through a spout into a set of rolls situated on the same level as the breaker.

After being fine-crushed by the rolls, the sample is raised by an elevator to the same level as at first, and drops through a second divider, similar to the first, set to any desired amount per cent.

The rejected ore falls into the bin with the ore from which it was first separated, and the final sample drops into a closed and locked bin on the working floor below.

All of these devices require thorough cleaning after each lot is run through and after one lot is finished. Before commencing on a new lot it is best to run through some of the new lot (this portion not to be mixed with the sample) in order to thoroughly cleanse the apparatus.

In handling wet or frozen ore it can generally be cut down to about one ton before drying. At this point it is best to dry the sample before proceeding further. Before grinding in the coffee-mill the sample should be thoroughly dried, the oven of an ordinary cook-stove being a very satisfactory piece of apparatus for this purpose.

Dr. S. A. Reed, in *The School of Mines Quarterly*, Vol. VI, No. 4, discusses the subject of ore-sampling mathematically, and deduces some interesting formulæ.

SAMPLING OF METALLURGICAL PRODUCTS.

Pig-iron.—The drillings are usually taken from the fractured end of a pig. In order to protect the sample from slag, sand, etc., the end of the pig is covered by wrapping around it a piece of heavy paper. As the

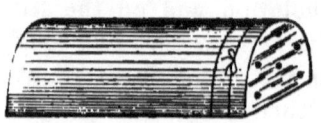

pigs are seldom perfectly homogeneous, especially if the iron contains much sulphur, phosphorus, or manganese, it is best to take several drillings, at the points indicated in the sketch, and thoroughly mix them together for the sample.

Base Bullion.—Base or silver-lead bullion, if pure, would be an alloy of lead with small quantities of silver and gold.

However, it is seldom pure, and may contain copper, zinc, bismuth, arsenic, antimony, sulphur, etc.

In many of our smelting-works the custom is to ladle directly from the lead-well of the blast-furnace into the bullion mould. If this method is adopted the resulting bars of bullion will necessarily contain nearly all the impurities of the lead. At some works the practice is to tap the lead-well, or ladle off the lead into a cooling kettle. This kettle is of cast-iron, heated underneath by a coal fire, and capable of holding from 600 to 1200 pounds of lead. When the cooling pot is used the following is the method of procedure: From 500 to 1000 pounds of lead is tapped or ladled into the cooling pot, which has previously been heated, and is kept at a proper temperature by the charcoal fire underneath the kettle. The bullion in the kettle is stirred and skimmed, the skimmings being returned to the blast-furnace, together with the ore charge. This is by far the best method of casting, as considerable of the dross of the bullion is removed, and the bars are cleaner and more uniform. The bullion is cast in moulds of such size that the resulting bars of bullion will weigh about 100 pounds.

It is a well-known fact that if an alloy of lead, silver, and gold be cast into a bar the different parts of the bar, owing to the sudden chilling, will contain different proportions of silver and gold.

This fact is illustrated by the "Pattison Process" of desilverization. If the alloy contains zinc, copper, sulphur, etc. (any or all of which most bullion contains), the percentage of silver and gold in different parts of the bar will vary to a much greater extent than in the previous case. The method of "zinc desilverization" is a partial illustration of this fact. These facts render the sampling of the bullion a difficult matter if it is at all rich in silver or gold.

The method of sampling as described below has been adopted by many of the large smelting and refining works of the United States, and it is believed that it obviates most of the difficulties heretofore experienced by smelters and refiners in arriving at a correct sample of the lot of bullion.

The pigs of bullion in series of five are weighed by the sampler, the weight being noted and the lot number being stamped on each pig as shown in Fig. 5. The pigs are unloaded on the sampling platform, as shown in Fig. 5.

The samples are taken by means of a steel punch similar to a belt punch, but larger, shown in Fig. 6. This punch is about 14 inches long, and is made of 1-inch to 1¼-inch steel, so arranged that when driven into the bar of bullion it will take out a core about ⅛ inch in diameter and in length equal to half the thickness of the bar of bullion. The head-sampler usually holds and directs the punch whilst his assistant strikes it with a sledge. In order to insure a uniform sample it is essential that the punch should be driven half through the bar in each case, so that the length of the core should be equal to half the thickness of the bar. The samples are taken from each pig at *a*, *b*, *c*, *d*, and *e*. The pigs are then turned over, and five

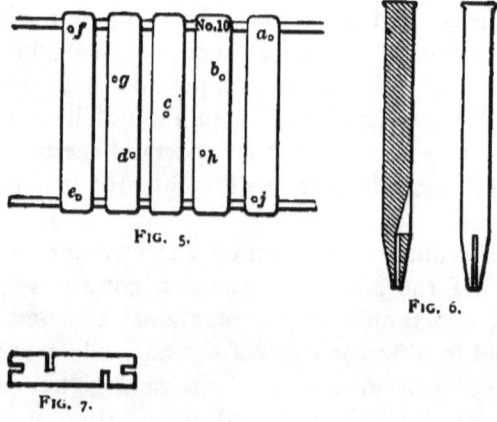

Fig. 5.

Fig. 6.

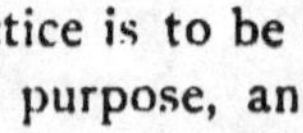

Fig. 7.

samples taken from the bottom side of each pig in the reverse order, as shown at *f*, *g*, *c*, *h*, and *j*. At some works it is the custom to dip the punch in oil, in order to make it drive easier. This practice is to be condemned, as dipping in water answers the same purpose, and oil greases the cores so that they are liable to take up any dirt or particles of dust (which are always present in a smelting-works), which are liable to affect the sample. Oil also makes a bad scum and has a tendency to affect the sample in melting.

A car-load of bullion generally contains 280 pigs. When the sampling of the lot is finished the 560 cores are taken to the assay office for melting and assay.

The cores are melted in a clean graphite crucible, which should not be more than two-thirds full when the sample is melted down. The melting should be carefully conducted, the temperature being gradually raised. It is essential that the temperature should be sufficiently high at the last, so that the mass will be perfectly fluid; but, on the other hand, the temperature should not be raised to such a point that the lead will cupel or scorify, as this would result in the loss of lead, and consequent enrichment of the sample in silver and gold.

When the sample is melted and perfectly fluid, the crucible is removed from the furnace, its contents thoroughly stirred with a clean iron rod, and poured into an iron mould. The mould should be of such a size that the resulting bar will be about 10 inches long, $2\frac{1}{2}$ inches wide, and $\frac{3}{4}$ inch thick. The sample should not be skimmed before pouring, as, if the melting is conducted at the proper temperature and not unduly prolonged, very little dross will rise upon the surface of the lead. When cool, the bar is removed from the mould and four samples are cut from it for assay, as shown in Fig. 7. The sample bar is stamped with the lot number of the bullion, and retained until the lot is settled for.

In the case of very rich and extremely impure bullion the following method may be necessary, although in several years experience the author has only had occasion to use this method a few times.

Special Method.—When a large amount of dross is formed it should be removed by skimming with a perforated skimmer, allowing the lead to drain back into the crucible. Place all the dross in an iron sample pan and reserve. Now pour the clean lead into the mould, and when cool remove the bar and weigh it. After weighing, sample the bar by taking four samples, as shown above.

Weigh the dross, and, after weighing, break it up on the bucking-board and thoroughly sample it, taking four samples of $\frac{1}{2}$ A. T. each, for assay. (For the assay and calculation, see Chapter I, Part III.)

Slags.—Lead and copper furnace slags may be sampled by any of the following methods :

First. After the slag-pot is removed from the furnace it is allowed to cool until a thin crust forms on the top of the slag. The crust is broken and removed with a bar. The end of a clean steel bar about one inch in diameter is then plunged into the hot slag to a depth of about three inches and in a few seconds withdrawn, and the end of the bar with the thin coating of slag adhering to it is plunged into water to cool or chill the slag quickly. The sample should be brittle and vitreous throughout. If not brittle and vitreous it should be rejected. Samples may be taken as frequently as desired, the separate samples being bucked down together and passed through a 100-mesh sieve.

Second. Some works prefer to take the samples in a small ladle as the slag runs from the spout of the furnace. These samples are usually taken at stated intervals, and just after the furnace has been tapped for matte. They may be poured into water from the ladle, in order to make them vitreous and granulated, which facilitates the subsequent pulverization.

Third. Some works prefer to take the sample from the cold cones of slag on the dump. The samples should be taken from the centre and above the matte, and about a third way from the edge towards the centre. These samples are taken with a small hammer, after breaking the cone up with a sledge.

The first method presents many advantages, as it lessens the labor required in pulverizing the sample, and also—at least in the case of lead and copper slags—converts the slag into a form which is soluble in acids.*

Silver Bullion.—If the silver is remelted before casting into bars, one of the following methods may be adopted :

---

* Determination of silica, Part II, Chap. I.

First. Just before pouring, the contents of the crucible are thoroughly stirred with an iron rod. The sample is now taken from the centre of the crucible by means of a sampling-cup, which consists of a small steel cup provided with a cover which fits tight when inserted in the cup. The cup and cover are provided with long iron handles. Before using, the cup and cover should be heated. The cover is now put on the cup and the apparatus inserted into the centre of the molten silver. The cover is now withdrawn and the cup allowed to fill with silver, when the cover is replaced by means of the handle, the apparatus removed from the crucible, and the silver which the cup contains poured into water in order to granulate it.

Second. Just after commencing to pour the silver out of the crucible into the moulds some of the silver is caught in a small ladle. This operation is repeated when about half the silver has been poured, and again when nearly all has been poured out. Each of the samples is granulated in water.

This method of sampling also answers where the silver is tapped directly from the cupel furnace into the moulds, a sample being taken just after the silver begins to run, another when about one half has run out, and a third just before all the silver has run out.

These are about the only methods which are to be recommended. The taking of a sample from the ends or corners of the bar by chipping will not give a fair sample unless the silver is very pure, nearly 1000 fine. If the silver has copper or other base metal alloyed with it, different portions of the bar will vary considerably in their composition.

Gold Bullion.—The weighed gold is melted in a graphite crucible with suitable fluxes, the slag skimmed off, after which it is thoroughly mixed by stirring and poured into a mould. Samples are now cut from the top and bottom of the bar. These samples should agree in fineness if the work of melting has been well done. In the U. S. mints and assay offices the practice is to weigh before and after melting, the difference in weight being reported as the loss in melting.

Mattes.—They can be sampled in the same manner as ore.

Automatic sampling answers very well, as the matte has to be finely pulverized prior to roasting.

Flue Dust.—Sampled the same as ore. As it is mostly in a fine state, the taking of every tenth shovelful as a sample, when cleaning out the flues, answers very well.

Concentrates.—Concentrates from milling operations are sampled in the same manner as ore. Being in a finely pulverized state, they present no difficulties.

Tailings.— Tailings from milling operations may be sampled the same as concentrates if there is a pile or heap. When the tailings are allowed to run into a neighboring stream samples should be taken from the tail-box at intervals. An automatic device may be arranged for this purpose.

Silver Precipitate.—The precipitated silver from a leaching works consists of sulphide of silver mixed with impurities, principally sulphides. To obtain a correct sample of this material, which runs from 4000 to 14,000 ounces of silver per ton, is a difficult matter. The following method answers very well, if carefully carried out: Spread the material upon a clean iron floor and divide into a number of squares about one foot square. From each square take five samples, putting all these samples in a pile. The pile should be thoroughly mixed, and then spread out and reduced as before. The final sample, of about five pounds, should be pulverized in the coffee-mill and still further reduced, the final sample being bucked on a bucking-board until it will all pass through an 80- or 100-mesh sieve.

Copper Ingots.—Pig-copper is usually sampled by drilling through the pigs from top to bottom. The top and bottom drillings being a mixture of slag and oxides come out as a powder, whilst the inside being malleable comes out in the form of strings. A good plan is to put the drillings in a glass bottle and then operate upon the strings with a pair of scissors until the large drillings are all chopped up fine, then quarter.

CHAPTER III.

PRELIMINARY EXAMINATION.

ALL material submitted to the assayer for analysis should first undergo a preliminary examination, to determine its character and principal constituents. A little time spent in this manner will frequently result in a great saving of time in the subsequent analysis. If the character of the material is not understood a wrong method of analysis may be adopted, or a substance may be analyzed for some constituent which is present in such small quantities that its determination is unnecessary. Sometimes this preliminary examination is unnecessary, as when a substance for analysis is submitted with a statement of its character and the constituents required to be determined. It frequently happens that the assayer receives a substance with the request that its chief constituents be determined, in which case a few qualitative tests will generally be a sufficient guide. In the case of an ore in lump form, the assayer will be able to determine its chief constituents by an eye examination and, possibly, a few tests with the blowpipe.

In most of our metallurgical works the assayer generally receives the sample for assay already pulverized. In this case the chief constituents and the character of the material can generally be determined readily by treating the sample as follows: Place about half a gramme of the sample on a large watch-glass, and van with a little water, by rotating and gently tapping the edge of the glass, so as to separate the lighter from the heavier particles. After thus separating the particles, an examination with the aid of a magnifying-glass will show the principal mineral constituents and their approximate amounts. The author has found this an invaluable aid in determining what the sample should be analyzed for, and also the method of analysis to be pursued. For example, the pulverized sample may show the ore to be oxidized, but upon vanning it will be found to contain small particles of sulphides.

For the preliminary testing of ores and furnace products and the testing of buttons and precipitates the blowpipe is extremely valuable. Any intelligent assayer, with a little practice, can become sufficiently familiar with the ordinary blowpipe tests.

The following list of blowpipe tests is taken from an article by Prof. A. J. Moses,* and gives all of the tests necessary for the preliminary examination, by means of the blowpipe, of ores, metallurgical products, etc.

BLOWPIPE TESTS.

The details in ordinary manipulations, such as obtaining beads, flames, coatings, and sublimates, are omitted, and the results alone stated. Unusual manipulations are described. The bead tests are supposed to be obtained with oxides; the other tests are in general true of all compounds not expressly excluded. The course to be followed in the case of interfering elements is briefly stated.

Aluminium, Al.

With Soda.—Swells and forms an infusible compound.
With Borax or S. Ph.—Clear or cloudy, never opaque.
With Cobalt Solution.—Fine blue when cold. (Certain phosphates, borates, and fusible silicates become blue in absence of alumina.)

Ammonia, NH_3.

In Closed Tube.—Evolution of gas with the characteristic odor. Soda or lime assists the reaction. The gas turns red litmus-paper blue, and forms white clouds with HCl vapor.

---

* Summary of Useful Tests with the Blowpipe. School of Mines Quarterly, Vol. XI, No. 1.

Antimony, Sb.

On Coal, R. F.—Volatile white coat, bluish in thin layers, continues to form after cessation of blast. (This coat may be further tested by S. Ph. or flame.)

With Bismuth Flux :—On Plaster.—Orange-red coat, made orange by $(NH_4)_2S$.

On Coal.—Faint yellow or red coat.

In Open Tube.—Dense, white, non-volatile, amorphous sublimate. The sulphide, too rapidly heated, will yield spots of red.

In Closed Tube.—The oxide will yield a white fusible sublimate of needle crystals; the sulphide, a black sublimate, red when cold.

Flame.—Pale yellow-green.

With S. Ph.—Dissolved by O. F., and treated on coal with tin in R. F. becomes gray to black.

Interfering Elements.

Arsenic.—Remove by gentle O. F. on coal.

Arsenic with Sulphur.—Remove by gently heating in closed tube.

Copper.—The S. Ph. bead with tin in R. F. may be momentarily red, but will blacken.

Lead or Bismuth.—Retards formation of their coats by intermittent blast, or by boracic acid. Confirm coat by flame, not by S. Ph.

Arsenic, As.

On Smoked Plaster.—White coat of octahedral crystals.

On Coal.—Very volatile white coat and strong garlic odor. The oxide and sulphide should be mixed with soda.

With Bismuth Flux :—On Plaster.—Reddish-orange coat, made yellow by $(NH_4)_2S$.

On Coal.—Faint-yellow coat.

In Open Tube.—White sublimate of octahedral crystals.

Too high heat may form brown suboxide or red or yellow sulphide.

In Closed Tube.—May obtain white oxide, yellow or red sulphide, or black mirror of metal.

Flame.—Pale azure-blue.

Interfering Elements.

Antimony.—Heat in closed tube with soda and charcoal, treat resulting mirror in O. F. for odor.

Cobalt or Nickel.—Fuse in O. F. with lead and recognize by odor.

Sulphur.—(*a*) Red to yellow sublimate of sulphide of arsenic in closed tube.

(*b*) Odor when fused with soda on coal.

Barium, Ba.

On Coal, with Soda.—Fuses and sinks into the coal.

Flame.—Yellowish green, improved by moistening with HCl.

With Borax or S. Ph.—Clear and colorless; can be flamed opaque white.

Bismuth, Bi.

On Coal.—In either flame is reduced to brittle metal and yields a volatile coat, dark orange-yellow hot, lemon-yellow cold, with yellowish-white border.

With Bismuth Flux (sulphur, 2 parts; potassic iodide, 1 part; potassic bisulphate, 1 part):—*On Plaster.*—Bright-scarlet coat surrounded by chocolate-brown with sometimes a reddish border. The brown may be made red by ammonia. (May be obtained by heating S. Ph. on the assay.)

On Coal.—Bright-red coat with sometimes an inner fringe of yellow.

With S. Ph.—Dissolved by O. F. and treated on coal with tin in R. F. is colorless hot, but blackish gray and opaque cold.

Interfering Elements.

Antimony.—Treat on coal with boracic acid, and treat the resulting slag on plaster with bismuth flux.

Lead.—Dissolve coat in S. Ph., as above.

Boron, B.

All borates intumesce and fuse to a bead.

Flame.—Yellowish green. May be assisted by: (*a*) Moistening with H_2SO_4; (*b*) Mixing to paste with water, and boracic-acid flux ($4\frac{1}{2}$ parts $KHSO_4$, 1 part CaF_2); (*c*) By mixing to paste with H_2SO_4 and NH_4F.

Bromine, Br.

With S. Ph., saturated with CuO.—Treated at tip of blue flame, the bead will be surrounded by greenish-blue flame.

In Matrass with $KHSO_4$.—Brown, choking vapor.

Interfering Elements.

Silver.—The bromine melts in $KHSO_4$ and forms a blood-red globule, which cools yellow and becomes green in the sunlight.

Cadmium, Cd.

On Coal, R. F.—Dark-brown coat, greenish yellow in thin layers. Beyond the coat, at first part of operation, the coal shows a variegated tarnish.

On Smoked Plaster with Bismuth Flux.—White coat made orange by $(NH_4)_2S$.

With Borax or S. Ph.—O. F. Clear yellow hot, colorless cold; can be flamed milk-white. The hot bead touched to $Na_2S_2O_3$ becomes yellow.

R. F. Becomes slowly colorless.

Interfering Elements.

Lead, Bismuth, Zinc.—Collect the coat, mix with charcoal dust, and heat gently in a closed tube. Cadmium will yield either a reddish-brown ring or a metallic mirror. Before collecting coat treat it with O. F. to remove arsenic.

Calcium, Ca.

On Coal, with Soda.—Insoluble, and not absorbed by the coal.

Flame.—Yellowish red, improved by moistening with HCl.

With Borax or S. Ph.—Clear and colorless, can be flamed opaque.

Carbonic Acid, CO_2.

With Nitric Acid.—Heat with water and then with dilute acid; CO_2 will be set free with effervescence. The escaping gas will render lime-water turbid.

With Borax or S. Ph.—After the flux has been fused to a clear bead, the addition of a carbonate will cause effervescence during further fusion.

Chlorine, Cl.

With S. Ph., saturated with CuO.—Treated at tip of blue flame the bead will be surrounded by an intense azure-blue flame.

On Coal, with CuO.—Grind with a drop of H_2SO_4, spread the paste on coal, dry gently in O. F., and treat with blue flame, which will be colored greenish blue and then azure-blue.

Chromium, Cr.

With Borax or S. Ph.—O. F. Reddish hot, fine yellow green cold.

R. F. In borax, green hot and cold. In S. Ph. red hot, green cold.

With Soda.—O. F. Dark yellow hot, opaque and light yellow cold.

R. F. Opaque and yellowish green cold.

Interfering Elements.

Manganese.—The soda bead in O. F. will be bright yellowish green.

Cobalt, Co.

On Coal, R. F.—The oxide becomes magnetic metal. The solution in HCl will be rose-red, but on evaporation will be blue.

With Borax or S. Ph.—Pure blue in either flame.

Interfering Elements.

Arsenic.—Roast and scorify with successive additions of borax. There may be, in order given: Yellow (iron), green (iron and cobalt), blue (cobalt), reddish brown (nickel), green (nickel and copper), blue (copper).

Copper and other Elements which Color Strongly.—Fuse with borax and lead on coal in R. F. The borax on platinum wire in O. F. will show the cobalt, except when obscured by much iron or chromium.

Iron, Nickel, or Chromium.—Fuse in R. F. with a little metallic arsenic, then treat as an arsenide.

Sulphur or Selenium.—Roast and scorify with borax, as before described.

Copper, Cu.

On Coal, R. F.—Formation of red metallic metal.

Flame.—Emerald-green or azure-blue, according to compound. The azure-blue flame may be obtained (sulphur, selenium, and arsenic should be removed by roasting; lead necessitates a gentle heat)—

(*a*) By moistening with HCl or aqua regia, drying gently in O. F., and heating strongly in R. F.;

(*b*) By saturating S. Ph. bead with substance, adding common salt, and treating with blue flame.

With Borax or S. Ph.—O. F. Green hot, blue or greenish blue cold. (By repeated slow oxidation and reduction, a borax bead becomes ruby-red.)

R. F. Greenish or colorless hot, opaque and brownish red cold. With tin on coal this reaction is more delicate.

Interfering Elements.

General Method.—Roast thoroughly, treat with borax on coal in strong R. F. (oxides, sulphides, sulphates, are best reduced by a mixture of soda and borax), and—

If Button Forms.—Separate the button from the slag, remove any lead from it by O. F., and make either S. Ph. or flame test upon residual button.

If No Visible Button Forms.—Add test lead to the borax fusion, continue the reduction, separate the button, and treat as in next test (lead alloy).

Lead or Bismuth Alloys.—Treat with frequently changed boracic acid in strong R. F., noting the appearance of slag and residual button.

Trace.—A red spot in the slag.

Over One Per Cent.—The residual button will be bluish green; when melted will dissolve in the slag and color it red upon application of the O. F., or may be removed from the slag and be submitted to either the S. Ph. or the flame test.

Fluorine, F.

Etching Test.—If fluorine be released it will corrode glass in cloudy patches, and in presence of silica there will be a deposit on the glass. According to the refractoriness of the compound the fluorine may be released—

(*a*) In closed tube by heat;
(*b*) In closed tube by heat and $KHSO_4$;
(*c*) In open tube by heat and glass of S. Ph.

With Conc. H_2SO_4 and SiO_2.—If heated, and the fumes condensed by a drop of water upon a platinum wire, a film of silicic acid will form upon the water.

Iodine, I.

With S. Ph., saturated with CuO.—Treated at the tip of the blue flame, the bead is surrounded by an intense emerald-green flame.

In Matrass with $KHSO_4$.—Violet, choking vapor and brown sublimate.

In Open Tube, with equal parts Bismuth Oxide, Sulphur, and Soda.—A brick-red sublimate.

With Starch Paper.—The vapor turns the paper dark purple

Interfering Elements.

Silver.—The iodide melts in $KHSO_4$ to a dark-red globule, yellow on cooling, and unchanged by sunlight.

Iron, Fe.

On Coal.—R. F. Many compounds become magnetic. Soda assists the reaction.

With Borax.—O. F. Yellow to red hot, colorless to yellow cold. (A slight yellow color can only be attributed to iron when there is no decided color produced by either flame in highly-charged beads of borax and S. Ph.)

R. F. Bottle-green. With tin on coal, violet-green.

With S. Ph.—O. F. Yellow to red hot, greenish when cooling. Colorless to yellow cold.

R. F. Red hot and cold, greenish while cooling.

State of the Iron.—A borax-blue bead from CuO is made red by FeO and greenish by Fe_2O_3.

Interfering Elements.

Chromium.—Fuse with nitrate and carbonate of soda on platinum, dissolve in water, and test residue for iron.

Cobalt.—By dilution the blue of cobalt in borax may often be lost before the yellow of iron.

Copper.—May be removed from borax bead by fusion with lead on coal in R. F.

Manganese.—(*a*) May be faded from borax bead by treatment with tin on coal in R. F.;

(*b*) May be faded from S. Ph. bead by R. F.

Nickel.—May be faded from borax bead by R. F.

Tungsten or Titanium.—The S. Ph. bead in R. F. will be reddish brown instead of blue or violet.

Uranium.—As with chromium.

Alloys, Sulphides, Arsenides, etc.—Roast, treat with borax on coal in R. F., then treat borax in R. F. to remove reducible metals.

Lead, Pb.

On Coal.—In either flame is reduced to malleable metal, and yields near the assay a dark lemon-yellow coat, sulphur-yellow cold, and bluish white at border. (The phosphate yields no coat without the aid of a flux.)

With Bismuth Flux :—On Plaster.—Chrome-yellow coat, blackened by $(NH_4)_2S$.

On Coal.—Volatile yellow coat, darker hot.

Flame.—Azure-blue.

With Borax or S. Ph.—O. F. Yellow hot, colorless cold. Flames opaque yellow.

R. F. Borax bead becomes clear, S.Ph. bead cloudy.

Interfering Elements.

Antimony.—Treat on coal with boracic acid, and treat the resulting slag on plaster with bismuth flux.

Arsenic Sulphide.—Remove by gentle O. F.

Cadmium.—Remove by R. F.

Bismuth.—Usually the bismuth-flux tests on plaster are sufficient. In addition the lead coat should color the R. F. blue.

Lithium, Li.

Flame.—Crimson, best obtained by gently heating near the wick.

Interfering Elements.

Sodium.—(*a*) Use a gentle flame and heat near the wick; (*b*) Fuse on platinum wire with baric chloride in O. F. The flame will be first strong yellow, then green, and, lastly, crimson.

Calcium or Strontium.—As these elements do not color the flame in the presence of baric chloride, the above test will answer.

Silicon.—Make into a paste with boracic-acid flux and water, and fuse in the blue flame. Just after the flux fuses the red flame will appear.

Magnesium, Mg.

On Coal, with Soda.—Insoluble, and not absorbed by the coal.

With Borax or S. Ph.—Clear and colorless; can be flamed opaque-white.

With Cobalt Solution.—Strongly heated, becomes a pale-flesh color. (With silicates this action is of use only in the absence of coloring oxides. The phosphate, arsenate, and borate become violet-red.)

Manganese, Mn.

With Borax or S. Ph.—O. F. Amethystine hot, reddens on cooling. With much, is black and opaque. (The colors are more intense with borax than with S. Ph.) If a hot bead is touched to a crystal of sodic nitrate an amethystine or rose-colored froth is formed.

R. F. Colorless or with black spots.

With Soda.—O. F. Bluish green and opaque when cold. Sodic nitrate assists the reaction.

Interfering Elements.

Chromium.—The soda bead in O. F. will be bright yellowish green instead of bluish green.

Silicon.—Dissolve in borax, then make soda fusion.

Mercury, Hg.

With Bismuth Flux:—On Plaster.—Volatile yellow and scarlet coat. If too strongly heated the coat is black and yellow.

On Coal.—Faint-yellow coat at a distance.

In Matrass, with Dry Soda or with Litharge.—Mirror-like sublimate, which may be collected in globules. (Gold-leaf is whitened by the slightest trace of vapor of mercury.)

Molybdenum, Mo.

On Coal.—O. F. A coat yellowish hot, white cold; crystalline near assay.

R. F. The coat is turned in part deep blue, in part dark copper-red.

Flame.—Yellowish green.

With Borax.—O. F. Yellow hot, colorless cold.

R. F. Brown to black and opaque.

With S. Ph.—O. F. Yellowish green hot, colorless cold. (Crushed between damp unglazed paper becomes red, brown, purple, or blue, according to amount present.)

R. F. Emerald-green.

Dilute ($\frac{1}{4}$) HCl Solutions.—If insoluble, the substance may first be fused with S. Ph. in O. F. Then, if dissolved in the acid and heated with metallic tin, zinc, or copper, the solutions will be successively blue, green, and brown. If the S.Ph. bead has been treated in R. F. the solution will become brown.

Nickel, Ni.

On Coal, R. F.— The oxide becomes magnetic.

With Borax.—O. F. Violet hot, pale reddish brown cold.

R. F. Cloudy, and finally clear and colorless.

With S. Ph.—O. F. Red hot, yellow cold.

R. F. Red hot, yellow cold. On coal with tin becomes colorless.

Interfering Elements.

General Method.—Saturate two or three borax beads with roasted substance, and treat on coal with strong R. F. If a visible button results, separate it from the borax and treat with S. Ph. in the O. F., replacing the S. Ph. when a color is obtained. If no visible button results, add either a small gold button or a few grains of test-lead. Continue the reduction, and—

With Gold.—Treat the gold alloy on coal with S. Ph. in strong O. F.

With Lead.—Scorify button with boracic acid to small size, complete the removal of lead by O. F. on coal, and treat residual button with S. Ph. in O. F.

Arsenic.—Roast thoroughly, treat with borax in R. F. as long as it shows color, treat residual button with S. Ph. in O. F.

Alloys.—Roast and melt with frequently changed borax in R. F., adding a little lead if infusible. When the borax is no longer colored, treat the residual button with S. Ph. in O. F.

Nitric Acid, HNO_3.

In Matrass with $KHSO_4$, or in Closed Tube with Litharge.—Brown fumes with characteristic odor. The fumes will turn ferrous-sulphate paper brown.

Phosphorus, P.

Flame.—Greenish blue, momentary. Improved by conc. H_2SO_4.

In Closed Tube with Dry Soda and Magnesium.—The soda and substance are mixed in equal parts and dried, and made to cover the magnesium. Upon strongly heating there will be a vivid incandescence, and the resulting mass, crushed and moistened, will yield the odor of phosphuretted hydrogen.

Potassium, K.

Flame.—Violet, except borates and phosphates.

Interfering Elements.

Sodium.—(*a*) The flame through blue glass will be violet or blue;

(*b*) A bead of borax and a little boracic acid made brown by nickel will become blue on addition of a potassium compound.

Lithium.—The flame through green glass will be bluish green.

Selenium, Se.

On Coal, R. F.—Disagreeable horse-radish odor, brown fumes, and a volatile steel-gray coat with a red border.

In Open Tube.—Steel-gray sublimate with red border, sometimes white crystals.

In Closed Tube.—Dark-red sublimate and horse-radish odor.

Flame.—Azure-blue.

On Coal, with Soda.—Thoroughly fuse in R. F., place on bright silver, moisten, crush, and let stand. The silver will be blackened.

Silicon, Si.

On Coal, with Soda.—With its own volume of soda, dissolves with effervescence to a clear bead. With more soda the bead is opaque.

With Borax.—Clear and colorless.

With S. Ph.—Insoluble. The test made upon a small fragment will usually show a translucent mass of undissolved matter of the shape of the original fragment.

When not decomposed by S. Ph., dissolve in borax nearly to saturation, add S. Ph., and re-heat for a moment. The bead will become milky or opaque-white.

Silver, Ag.

On Coal.—Reduction to malleable white metal.

With Borax or S. Ph.—O. F. Opalescent.

Cupellation.—Fuse on coal with one volume of borax-glass

and one to two volumes of test-lead in R. F. for about two minutes. Remove button and scorify it in R. F. with fresh borax, then place button on cupel and blow O. F. *across* it, using as strong blast and as little flame as are consistent with keeping button melted.

If the litharge is dark, or if the button freezes before brightening, or if it brightens but is not spherical, rescorify it on coal with borax, add more test-lead, and again cupel, until there remains only a white spherical button of silver.

Sodium, Na.

Flame.—Reddish yellow.

Strontium, Sr.

On Coal, with Soda.—Insoluble, absorbed by the coal.

Flame.—Intense crimson, improved by moistening with HCl.

With Borax or S. Ph.—Clear and colorless; can be flamed opaque.

Interfering Elements.

Barium.—The red flame may show upon first introduction of the sample into the flame, but it is afterwards turned brownish yellow.

Lithium.—Fuse with baric chloride, by which the lithium flame is unchanged.

Sulphur, S.

On Coal, with Soda and a little Borax.—Thoroughly fuse in the R. F. flame, and either,

(*a*) Place on bright silver, moisten, crush, and let stand. The silver will become brown or black. Or,

(*b*) Heat with dilute HCl (sometimes with powdered zinc); the odor of H_2S will be observed.

In Open Tube.—Suffocating fumes. Some sulphates are unaffected.

In Closed Tube.—May have sublimate red when hot, yellow cold, or sublimate of undecomposed sulphide, or the substance may be unaffected.

With Soda and Silica (equal parts).—A yellow or red bead.

To Determine whether Sulphide or Sulphate.—Fuse with soda on platinum foil. The sulphide only will stain silver.

Tellurium, Te.

On Coal.—Volatile white coat with red or yellow border. If the fumes are caught on porcelain, the resulting gray or brown film may be turned crimson when moistened with conc. H_2SO_4, and gently heated.

On Coal, with Soda.—Thoroughly fuse in R. F. Place on bright silver, moisten, crush, and let stand. The silver will be blackened.

Flame.—Green.

In Open Tube.—Gray sublimate fusible to clear drops.

With H_2SO_4 (conc.).—Boiled a moment, there results a purple-violet solution, which loses color on further heating or on dilution.

Tin, Sn.

On Coal.—O. F. The oxide becomes yellow and luminous.

R. F. A slight coat, assisted by additions of sulphur or soda.

With Cobalt Solution.—Moisten the coal in front of the assay, with the solution, and blow a *strong* R. F. upon the assay. The coat will be bluish green when cold.

With CuO in Borax Bead.—A faint-blue bead is made reddish brown or ruby-red by heating a moment in R. F. with a tin compound.

Interfering Elements.

Lead or Bismuth Alloys.—It is fair proof of tin if such an alloy oxidizes rapidly with sprouting and cannot be kept fused.

Zinc.—On coal with soda, borax, and charcoal in R. F., the tin will be reduced, the zinc volatilized; the tin may then be washed from the fused mass.

Titanium, Ti.

With Borax.—O. F. Colorless to yellow hot, colorless cold, opalescent or opaque white by flaming.

R. F. Yellow to brown, enamel-blue by flaming.

With Ph. S.—O. F. as with borax.

R. F. yellow hot, violet cold.

HCl Solutions.—If insoluble, the substance may first be fused with S. Ph. or with soda, and reduced. If then dissolved in dilute acid and heated with metallic tin, the solution will become violet after standing. Usually there will also be a turbid violet precipitate, which becomes white.

Interfering Elements.

Iron.—The S. Ph. bead in R. F. is yellow hot, brownish red cold.

Tungsten, W.

With Borax.—O. F. Flame colorless to yellow hot, colorless cold; can be flamed opaque white.

R. F. Colorless to yellow hot, yellowish brown cold.

With S. Ph.—O. F. Clear and colorless.

R. F. Greenish hot, blue cold. On long blowing or with tin on coal becomes dark green.

With Dilute HCl.—If insoluble, the substance may first be fused with S. Ph. The solution heated with tin becomes dark blue; with zinc it becomes purple and then reddish brown.

Interfering Elements.

Iron.—The S. Ph. in R. F. is yellow hot, blood-red cold.

Uranium, U.

With Borax.—O. F. Yellow hot, colorless cold; can be flamed enamel-yellow.

R. F. Bottle-green; can be flamed black, but not enamelled.

With S. Ph.—O. F. Yellow hot, yellowish green cold.
R. F. Emerald-green.

Interfering Elements.

Iron.—With S. Ph. in R. F. is green hot, red cold.

Vanadium, V.

With Borax.—O. F. Colorless or yellow hot, greenish-yellow cold.
R. F. Brownish hot, emerald-green gold.
With S. Ph.—O. F. Dark yellow hot, light yellow cold.
R. F. Brown hot, emerald-green cold.
H_2SO_4 Solutions.—Reduced by zinc becomes successively yellow, green, bluish-green, blue, greenish-blue, bluish-violet, and lavender.

Zinc, Zn.

On Coal.—O. F. The oxide becomes yellow and luminous.
R. F. Yellow coat, white when cold, assisted by soda and a little borax.
With Cobalt Solution.—Moisten the coal in front of the assay, with the solution, and blow a strong R. F. upon the assay. The coat will be bright yellow-green when cold.

Interfering Elements.

Antimony.—Remove by strong O. F., or by heating with sulphur in closed tube.
Cadmium, Lead, or Bismuth.—The combined coats will not prevent the cobalt-solution test.
Tin.—The coats heated in an open tube, with charcoal dust by the O. F., may yield white sublimate of zinc.

QUALITATIVE TESTS.

The following summary of characteristic qualitative tests in the wet way will be found useful in the preliminary examination of ores, furnace products, etc. :

Aluminium, Al.

1. Alkali hydroxides precipitate *grayish-white*, $Al_2(HO)_6$, soluble in fixed alkali-hydroxides, but only slightly soluble in NH_4OH if NH_4Cl is present.
2. Basic acetate of aluminium is precipitated by addition of $NaC_2H_3O_2$ to a warm and slightly acid solution.

Confirm.—By blowpipe test.

Antimony, Sb.

1. H_2S precipitates *orange-red* Sb_2S_3 from acid solutions. The precipitate is soluble in HCl, in alkalies, and in alkaline sulphides.
2. H_2S precipitates *orange* Sb_2S_5 from acid solutions. The precipitate is soluble in HCl, in alkalies, and alkaline sulphides.

To distinguish between Sb_2O_3 and Sb_2O_5, add solution of $AgNO_3$, in the presence of KOH or NaOH. Sb_2O_3 precipitates *black*, Ag_2O, which is insoluble in NH_4OH; and Sb_2O_5 precipitates *white*, $AgSbO_3$, which is soluble in NH_4OH.

Arsenic, As.

1. H_2S precipitates *yellow* As_2S_3 best from HCl solutions. Soluble in alkalies and alkaline sulphides, insoluble in HCl.
2. H_2S precipitates *yellow*, As_2S_5 from acid solutions after heating solution and passing gas for some time.
3. $AgNO_3$ precipitates *yellow* Ag_3AsO_3 or *reddish-brown* Ag_3AsO_4, soluble in dilute acids, ammonia, and ammonia salts.
4. $CuSO_4$ precipitates *yellowish-green* $Cu_3(AsO_3)_2$ or *greenish-blue*, $CuHAsO_4$, soluble in NH_4OH and NH_4Cl.
5. Ammonium magnesia mixture precipitates *white* $MgNH_4AsO_4$.

Barium, Ba.

1. Alkali carbonates precipitate *white* $BaCO_3$ soluble in HCl and HNO_3. Soluble in acids.

2. Soluble sulphates and H_2SO_4 precipitate *white* $BaSO_4$, which is practically insoluble in acids and water.
Confirm.—By blowpipe test.

Bismuth, Bi.

1. H_2S or $(NH_4)_2S$ precipitates *brownish-black* Bi_2S_3 insoluble in dilute acids, but soluble in strong HNO_3.
2. H_2O precipitates from the chloride *white* $BiOCl$, insoluble in an excess, but soluble in HCl and HNO_3.
3. $SnCl_2$ in the presence of NaOH or KOH precipitates *black* Bi_2O_2.
Confirm.—By blowpipe test.

Bromine, Br.

1. $AgNO_3$ precipitates *yellowish-white* AgBr; changes to gray, soluble in KCN, slightly soluble in NH_4OH, insoluble in HNO_3.

Separation of Cl, Br, and I.—Place a solution of the mixture in a test-tube with a little MnO_2 and water, add a drop of dilute H_2SO_4 (one in ten). A brown color indicates I. Boil; violet vapors are given off. When the secease add 2 cc. of H_2SO_4 and boil; *brown* vapors indicate Br. Boil until brown vapors cease and cool. When cold, add an equal volume of H_2SO_4 and heat; *green* vapors indicate Cl.

Boron, B.

1. $BaCl_2$ and $CaCl_2$ precipitate *white* $Ba_3(BO_3)_2$ and $Ca_3(BO_3)_2$.
2. $AgNO_3$ precipitates white Ag_3BO_3.
3. Free boracic acid turns turmeric paper *brownish red*, becoming more intense when the paper is dried. When mixed with HCl to acid reaction and dried it becomes *red*.

Cadmium, Cd.

1. H_2S or $(NH_4)_2S$ precipitates yellow CdS, insoluble in dilute acids, alkalies, alkali sulphides, or cyanides. Soluble in strong hot HCl, HNO_3, and H_2SO_4.

2. Zn precipitates from acid and ammoniacal solutions gray Cd.

3. KOH and NaOH precipitate *white* $Cd(OH)_2$, insoluble in excess; whilst NH_4OH precipitate *white* $Cd(OH)_2$, which is soluble in excess.

Confirm.—By blowpipe test.

Calcium, Ca.

1. H_2SO_4 precipitates *white* $CaSO_4$, soluble in a concentrated solution of $(NH_4)_2SO_4$; distinction from Ba and Sr.

2. Alkaline arseniates precipitate $CaHAsO_4$, soluble in acids and NH_4OH. Ba, Sr, and Mg give this precipitate only in concentrated solutions. Ammonia salts must be absent.

Confirm.—By blowpipe test.

Carbonic Acid, CO_2.

1. Add HNO_3 to substance in a test-tube, and pass gas through a solution of lime-water. A *white* precipitate of $CaCO_3$ indicates CO_2.

Chlorine, Cl.

1. $AgNO_3$ precipitates *white* AgCl, soluble in NH_4OH.

Chromium, Cr.

1. NH_4OH precipitates *bluish green* $Cr_2(OH)_6$, slightly soluble in excess.

2. From solutions of CrO_3 lead salts precipitate *yellow* $PbCrO_4$, soluble in HNO_3 and insoluble in acetic acid. Difficultly soluble in KOH.

3. A very delicate test for Cr as CrO_3 is by means of H_2O_2 (hydrogen peroxide) and ether, giving a fine *blue* color.

Cobalt, Co.

1. Fixed alkalies precipitate *blue basic salts*. This precipitate absorbs oxygen and becomes *olive-green* hydroxide. If

boiled before oxidation in the air becomes *rose-red* $Co(OH)_3$; does not dissolve in excess. HN_4OH produces the same precipitate, which is soluble in excess.

2. $K_3FeC_6N_6$ precipitates *dark brown* $Co_3(FeC_6N_6)_2$, insoluble in HCl. If to a solution of Co or Ni an excess of NH_4Cl and NH_4OH is added and then $K_3FeC_6N_6$, a *blood-red color* indicates Co. If Ni is present, and the solution is boiled, a *copper-red* precipitate forms; if any Co is present, a *dirty green*, on boiling.

3. To a dilute solution of cobaltous nitrate add tartaric or citric acid, then an excess of ammonia, and a few drops of potassium ferricyanide; a *deep-red color* appears, even if largely diluted.

Confirm.—By blowpipe test.

Copper, Cu.

1. HN_4OH produces a *deep-blue* solution.
2. NaOH and KOH when added to saturation precipitate *blue* $Cu(OH)_2$, insoluble in excess. When boiled the precipitate changes to *black* $Cu_2O_2(OH)_2$. Organic substances generally prevent the formation of this precipitate.
3. Fe and Zn precipitate metallic copper from cupric solutions.

Iron, Fe.

FeO.—1. $K_3FeC_6N_6$ precipitates *dark-blue* $Fe_3(FeC_6N_6)_2$, insoluble in acids.

2. NH_4OH precipitates *white* $Fe(OH)_2$.

Fe_2O_3.—1. NH_4CNS produces a *blood-red* solution.

2. NH_4OH precipitates brownish $Fe_2(OH)_6$.

Lead, Pb.

1. Zn precipitates crystals of Pb.
2. H_2SO_4 precipitates *white* $PbSO_4$, slightly soluble in excess, insoluble in alcohol, but soluble in ammonium acetate or citrate.

3. H_2S or $(NH_4)_2S$ precipitates *black* PbS, soluble in HNO_3 with formation of $PbSO_4$.

4. $K_4FeC_6N_6$ precipitates *white* $Pb_2FeC_6N_6$.

Lithium, Li.

1. Nitrophenic acid forms a *yellow* precipitate.
2. Na_2CO_3 precipitates *white* Li_2CO_3, slightly soluble in H_2O.

Confirm.—By blowpipe and spectroscope.

Magnesium, Mg.

1. Na_2HPO_4 precipitates, in presence of NH_4OH and NH_4Cl, *white* $MgNH_4PO_4$. Fine crystals.

Confirm.—By blowpipe.

Manganese, Mn.

1. Boil with HNO_3, and add peroxide of lead. A *reddish-violet* solution (color of potassium permanganate) indicates Mn.

Mercury, Hg.

1. A piece of bright metallic copper is coated with a precipitate of metallic Hg, upon insertion in a solution of Hg.
2. $SnCl_2$ precipitates first *white* Hg_2Cl_2 and then *gray* Hg.

To distinguish between mercurous and mercuric compounds HCl precipitates *white* Hg_2Cl_2, soluble in aqua regia, HNO_3, and NH_4Cl, and blackened by NH_4OH, from mercurous compounds. No precipitate on addition of HCl to mercuric compounds.

Molybdenum, Mo.

Upon heating the acid solution with metallic zinc it will turn successively *blue, green, and brown.*

Confirm.—By blowpipe test.

Nickel, Ni.

1. Alkaline carbonates precipitate *green basic carbonate* $2NiCO_3$, $3Ni(OH)_2$, soluble in $(NH_4)_2CO_3$ or, in excess of re-

agent, with *blue or greenish-blue* color. Again precipitated by KOH or NaOH as *pale-green* $Ni(OH)_2$.

2. NH_4OH in excess gives *blue* color.

3. KCN precipitates *pale-green* NiC_2N_2, soluble in excess. Upon boiling with NaClO, *black* $Ni(OH)_2$ is precipitated. Distinction from Co, which gives a *dirty-white* precipitate with KCN, soluble in excess, but no precipitate being formed on boiling with NaClO.

Nitric Acid, HNO_3.

1. To the solution, in a test-tube, add a saturated solution of ferrous sulphate, and then concentrated sulphuric acid (free from HNO_3); a brown ring between the $FeSO_4$ and H_2SO_4 indicates HNO_3.

Phosphorus, P.

Orthophosphates.—1. Magnesia mixture precipitates *white* $MgNH_4PO_4$.

2. $AgNO_3$ precipitates *light-yellow* Ag_3PO_4, soluble in HNO_3 and NH_4OH.

3. $(NH_4)_2MoO_4 + HNO_3$ precipitates *yellow* ammonium phospho-molybdate; composition variable. The precipitate is soluble in NH_4OH, in excess of phosphoric acid, and is prevented by organic substances, such as tartaric acid.

Pyrophosphates.—1. $MgSO_4$ precipitates *white* $Mg_2P_2O_7$, soluble in an excess of either solution. NH_4OH fails to precipitate it from these solutions. On boiling it separates again. By this reaction *pyro* can be detected in the presence of phosphoric acid.

2. $(NH_4)_2MoO_4 + HNO_3$ does not give a precipitate until orthophosphate is formed. Most of the pyrophosphates of the heavy metals (Ag an exception) are soluble in alkali pyrophosphates (distinction from orthophosphates).

3. $AgNO_3$ precipitates *white* $Ag_4P_2O_7$, soluble in HNO_3 and NH_4OH. Addition of an alkali aids the precipitation.

Metaphosphoric Acid.—1. Magnesia mixture gives no precipitate.

2. $(NH_4)_2MoO_4 + HNO_3$ gives no precipitate.

3. $AgNO_3$ precipitates *white* $AgPO_3$, soluble in alkali metaphosphate solutions (distinction from pyrophosphates).

4. Albumen gives a precipitate (distinction from *ortho* and pyrophosphates).

5. Fusion with Na_2CO_3 converts meta and pyro into orthophosphates.

Potassium, K.

1. $PtCl_4$ with HCl precipitates *yellow* crystalline $(KCl)_2PtCl_4$. Evaporate to dryness. The precipitate is not dissolved by alcohol.

Confirm.—By blowpipe and spectroscope.

Selenium, Se.

1. H_2S precipitates *yellow* sulphide of selenium, soluble in $(NH_4)_2S$. Upon heating the precipitate turns *reddish yellow*.

2. $SnCl_2 + HCl$ produces a *red* precipitate of Se, which turns *gray* at a high temperature.

3. Metallic copper, when placed in a warm solution of selenious acid, containing HCl, becomes *black;* if the fluid remains long in contact with the copper, it turns bright *red* from separation of selenium.

Confirm.—By blowpipe tests.

Silicon, Si.

Silicates are determined by the separation of SiO_2. Fuse with $Na_2CO_3 + NaNO_3$, dissolve in HCl, and evaporate to dryness. Upon evaporation gelatinous silica will separate out. Upon heating and dissolving with HCl insoluble SiO_2 remains behind.

Confirm.—By blowpipe test.

Silver, Ag.

1. HCl precipitates *white* AgCl, insoluble in HNO_3, soluble in NH_4OH.

2. Cu precipitates metallic Ag.

3. KI precipitates *yellow* AgI, insoluble in NH_4OH, soluble in excess of reagent.

Confirm.—By blowpipe test.

Sodium, Na.

1. $(NaCl)_2PtCl_4$ crystallizes from its concentrated solutions in *red* prisms.

2. $KSbO_3$ (in neutral or alkaline solutions) precipitates *white* $NaSbO_3$. The reagent should be dissolved as wanted, as it is unstable in solution.

Confirm.—By blowpipe and spectroscope.

Strontium, Sr.

1. $NaOH$, NH_4OH, Na_2CO_3, $(NH_4)_2CO_3$, and Na_2HPO_4 form precipitates which closely resemble those produced by these reagents with Ba salts.

Confirm.—By blowpipe tests.

Sulphur, S.

1. $BaCl_2$ gives a *white* precipitate, $BaSO_4$, when added to sulphuric-acid solutions. Practically insoluble.

2. On addition of HNO_3 to sulphides H_2S is given off.

Tellurium, Te.

1. H_2S precipitates *brown* TeS_2 from acid solutions. Soluble in $(NH_4)_2S$.

2. Boiled with concentrated H_2SO_4 there results a *purple-violet* solution, which fades upon further heating or dilution.

Confirm.—By blowpipe tests.

Tin, Sn.

Stannous Oxide (SnO).—1. H_2S precipitates *dark-brown* SnS, soluble in HCl, in alkalies; moderately soluble in yellow $(NH_4)_2S$.

2. $HgCl_2$ precipitates *white* Hg_2Cl_2, with excess *black* Hg (distinction from stannic compounds).

3. $AuCl_3$ with free HCl or HNO_3, a *purple* precipitate.

4. Zn precipitates spongy Sn.

Stannic oxide (SnO_2).

1. H_2S precipitates yellow SnS_2, soluble in HCl, in alkalies and alkaline sulphides.

2. $HgCl_2$ no precipitate.

3. $AuCl_3$ no precipitate.

4. Zn precipitates spongy Sn.

Confirm.—By blowpipe tests.

Titanium, Ti.

1. NH_4OH gives a bulky *white* precipitate, $Ti(OH)_4$, insoluble in excess.

2. Sn or Zn boiled in acid solutions after some time give *pale-violet or blue solutions*, subsequently a *blue* precipitate, which gradually becomes *white*.

Confirm.—By blowpipe.

Tungsten, W.

1. $SnCl_2$ produces a *yellow* precipitate on acidifying with HCl, and applying heat the precipitate acquires a beautiful *blue* color.

2. Heated with HCl and Zn the solution becomes *purple*, and then *reddish brown*.

3. $K_4FeC_6N_6$ + HCl gives a deep *brownish-red* color; after some time a precipitate of the same color is produced.

Uranium, U.

1. NH_4OH, KOH, and NaOH produce a *yellow* precipitate of uranic hydroxide and alkali.

2. $K_4FeC_6N_6$ *produces a reddish-brown* precipitate.

Confirm.—By blowpipe test.

Vanadium, V.

1. $K_4FeC_6N_6$ produces a green flocculent precipitate, insoluble in acids.

2. Dissolved in H_2SO_4 and Zn added the solution becomes successively *green, blue, bluish violet,* and *lavender*.

3. An acidified solution of vanadates upon being shaken with hydrogen dioxide acquires a *red* tint; if ether is then added, and the solution shaken, its retains its color, the ether remaining colorless.

Zinc, Zn.

1. Alkali hydroxides precipitate *white* $Zn(OH)_2$, soluble in excess of precipitant.

2. H_2S precipitates (from neutral or acetic acid solutions) *white* ZnS.

3. $K_4FeC_6N_6$ precipitates *white* $Zn_2FeC_6N_6$, insoluble in very dilute solutions of HCl.

4. $(NH_4)_2S$ precipitates *white* ZnS, insoluble in KOH and $HC_2H_3O_2$.

Confirm.—By blowpipe test.

CHAPTER IV.

APPARATUS AND OPERATIONS.

THE general apparatus used in the ordinary course of an analysis or assay is all that will be discussed here. The special pieces of apparatus, such as the apparatus used in the analysis of gases, will be discussed under the head of the different determinations.

Crushing and Pulverizing.—A small hand-crusher, or a small power-crusher, where power can be obtained, will be found very convenient for crushing small samples of ore, slag, etc. If such a crusher is not at hand, the crushing can be done in an iron mortar; but in a laboratory where much work is done a small jaw-crusher will save a great deal of time and labor.

A cast-iron bucking-plate and muller are indispensable for fine pulverization of ore samples. The ordinary plate is 2×2 feet and 1 inch thick, cast with flanges about 1 inch high on the two sides. The surface should be planed perfectly smooth. The muller or grinder is of cast iron, about 6 inches long, 4 inches wide, $1\frac{1}{2}$ inches thick in the middle and 1 inch thick at the two ends, so that the surface is convex. The surface should be planed smooth and true at all points.

The crushed ore is spread upon the plate, a few ounces at a time, the left hand being placed on the muller so as to throw the weight of the body on it, whilst the right hand grasps the handle. The muller is moved back and forth, depressing the handle as it is brought forward and raising it when pushing the muller back.

A small agate mortar and pestle will be found indispensable, where wet determinations are to be made, for finely pulverizing ores, etc., which are decomposed with difficulty. As the pulverizing in the mortar is a tedious operation, a quantity of the substance only slightly in excess of the amount required for analysis should be taken. Of course this small sample should be carefully taken from the general pulverized sample, so that it accurately represents the whole.

Screening.—After the sample is cut down and pulverized on the bucking-plate it should be passed through a screen or sieve. What refuses to pass through the sieve is again bucked and screened until all has passed through. The usual sieve is one of 80 or 100 meshes. This is sufficiently fine for samples which are to be assayed by fire-assay, but samples which are to be treated in the wet way will frequently have to be still further pulverized in the agate mortar. The sieves come in nests comprising 20, 40, 60, 80, and 100 meshes, each nest being provided with a tin box and cover. Such a nest of sieves will be found very convenient and useful in a laboratory doing metallurgical work.

Storing Samples.—Small paper sacks, or, preferably, envelopes made of heavy brown paper and provided with patent end-fasteners, are very convenient for keeping the pulverized samples. Small wide-necked sample-bottles holding about four ounces each are sometimes used for this purpose. All samples should be properly labelled and filed away for a reasonable length of time.

Moulds.—Cast-iron ingot moulds for casting bars of base bullion or silver bullion will be necessary where assays of bullion or alloys are to be made.

Cupel-moulds and pestles are required for making cupels. They are made of both brass and steel, the brass moulds being preferable. They come in different sizes, those most used being moulds which will make cupels weighing about 8 grammes and 18 grammes, respectively.

Moulds for pouring scorification and crucible charges are necessary. These should be of cast-iron, the depression being conical in shape, with the apex of the cone slightly rounded off. They should be of two sizes, the smaller for scorification and the larger for crucible assays.

Rolls.—A set of small steel hand-rolls for flattening out samples of gold and silver bullion, and gold cornets in the gold-bullion assay, will be found convenient.

Weighing.—For a laboratory doing general work (both wet and dry assays) five balances will be found useful. Each of these balances should be provided with the proper set of weights. It is best to have separate weights for each balance.

A. A rough scales for weighing large samples of ore, metals, etc. An ordinary grocers' scales answers very well for this purpose. This balance should be provided with avoirdupois weights.

B. A pulp-balance for weighing out ore for fire-assay. This balance should take 120 grammes in each pan, and should be sensitive to within 5 milligrammes. It should be provided with a set of gramme weights from 5 mgs. to 20 gms. It should also be provided with a set of assay-ton weights from 0.05 A. T. to 4 A. T.

The system of assay-ton weights was devised by Prof. C. F. Chandler, of Columbia College. These weights are not only very convenient, but their use results in the saving of considerable time in the calculation of the results of gold and silver assays. As ores of the precious metals, as well as those of the base metals, are weighed in pounds avoirdupois, whilst gold and silver are weighed in ounces Troy, the basis of the system is the number of Troy ounces in one ton avoirdupois (2000 pounds), which is 29,166.66 ounces. The assay-ton contains 29,166.66 milligrammes; hence if one assay-ton of ore is taken for assay and a silver button weighing 100 milligrammes is obtained, the ore will assay 100 ounces of silver per ton, as each milligramme in 1 assay-ton is equivalent to 1 ounce Troy per ton avoirdupois. If ½ assay-ton were taken for assay, it would be necessary to multiply the result (in milligrammes) by 2 to obtain the assay value, etc.

C. An analytical balance for weighing out ore, etc., for analysis and weighing the results of wet determinations. This balance is also used for weighing out ore for scorification-assay in the case of rich ores and the buttons obtained by fire-assay for base metals. The balance should take at least 30 grammes in each pan, and should be sensitive to within 0.5 milligramme. It should be enclosed in a glass case, and should be kept free from moisture, fumes, etc. It should be provided with a set of gramme weights from 1.0 mgm. to 30 gms., and also with a beam-rider for weighing milligrammes and fractions of milligrammes. The best balances are provided with agate knife-edges.

D. A button-balance, for weighing the gold and silver beads and for weighing out samples of gold and silver bullion for assay. This balance should take at least 1 gm. in each pan, and should be sensitive to within $\frac{1}{20}$ mgm. It should be provided with a set of gramme weights from 1 mgm. to 1 gm., and a beam-rider for weighing fractions of a milligramme. It should be provided with a glass case and agate knife-edges, and should be kept free from dust, fumes, etc. The balance should not be exposed to the direct rays of the sun, as they cause expansion of the metal-work and throw it out of balance.

E. A gold button-balance, for weighing the gold beads from the assay of gold ores. This balance should take at least 0.5 gm. in each pan, and should be sensitive to within $\frac{1}{100}$ mgm. It should be provided with a set of weights from 1 mgm. to 0.5 gm., and a beam-rider for weighing fractions of a milligramme. It should be kept in a glass case, free from dust, etc., and should be provided with agate knife-edges.

The last three balances should be set up on a perfectly firm support, and should be cleaned and adjusted from time to time.

The balance should always be tested before weighing, to see if it is in perfect adjustment.

The analytical balance should be provided with two watch-glasses, one for each pan. These watch-glasses are made with a glass lip or handle for convenience in removing. If they are not of equal weight, one can be filed on the bottom until they counterbalance, or the balance can be brought into adjustment by means of a small piece of platinum foil or wire.

Accurate weighing is absolutely essential to accurate work. The most expeditious way of ascertaining the exact weight of a substance is to avoid trying the weights at random, but to proceed in a methodical manner. Suppose, for example, we wish to ascertain the weight of a precipitate whose weight subsequently turns out to be 0.535 gm. The precipitate is transferred to the left-hand pan of the analytical balance, and a 1-gm. weight is placed in the right-hand pan. The weight is found to be too much; so it is replaced by a 0.5-gm. weight, which is found to be too little. A 0.1-gm. weight is now added, and is found to be too much; so it is replaced by a 0.05-gm. weight, which is found to be still too much. The 0.05-gm. weight is replaced by the 0.02 and the two 0.01-gm. weights, which is found to be still too much. One of the 0.01-gm. weights is removed, when the weight is found to be too little; hence the 0.005-gm. weight is added. The balance is found to exactly balance; hence this is the correct weight. It is best, in order to have a check on the weight, to add up the different weights on the pan and set down the total. As the weights are removed from the pan each weight is set down, and the sum taken after all are removed.

The balance should be arrested each time a change is contemplated, such as removing weights, substituting one weight for another, etc.

Substances liable to attract moisture from the air should always be weighed in closed vessels—as between two watch-glasses, in covered crucibles, or in a closed glass tube. The same applies to substances liable to lose moisture upon exposure to the air.

Fluids should be weighed in small bottles provided with glass stoppers, or occasionally in accurately counterpoised beakers.

A vessel should never be weighed whilst warm, as in that case its weight will invariably be too low. This is due to two circumstances: highly heated bodies are constantly communicating heat to the surrounding air; the heated air expands and ascends, and the denser and cooler air flowing toward the space which the heated air leaves produces a current, which tends to raise the scale-pan. Every body condenses on its surface a certain amount of air and moisture, which amount depends upon the temperature and the hygroscopic state of the air and the temperature of the body.

In weighing out a substance for assay or analysis it is generally best to take a certain definite quantity, as 0.5 A. T., 0.1 A. T., 1.0 gm., 0.5 gm., for example, rather than to weigh out an indefinite quantity, as 0.946 gm. Whilst this takes longer in the weighing out, the extra time expended in weighing is more than made up by the time saved in the subsequent calculations. Moreover, when a definite even quantity is taken, errors in the subsequent calculations are much less liable to occur.

Furnaces.—For fusions in fire-assaying either the wind- or muffle-furnace may be used. As the muffle-furnace is cleaner, and allows of a more perfect control of the heat, it is preferable to the wind-furnace. Where samples of bullion, etc., are to be melted, it will be necessary to have a wind-furnace; otherwise not.

Both wind- and muffle-furnaces are built to use either solid or gaseous fuel. The gas-furnaces have several advantages, inasmuch as they allow of a more perfect control of the temperature, are cleaner, are readily started, and only consume fuel when the work is going on. On account of the facility with which the temperature can be controlled the U. S. Government have adopted gas-furnaces in many of the Government mints and assay-offices. Gas-furnaces can only be used where power is handy, as they require a pressure-blower to furnish the necessary blast. They are no more economical in fuel than furnaces using coal or coke, but are to be recommended where power and gas are at hand, for the above reasons. Many excellent forms are kept in stock by the dealers.

Where solid fuel is used coke or charcoal is the usual fuel

in the wind-furnace, and coke or bituminous fuel in the muffle-furnace, although charcoal is also used in the muffle-furnace.

The ordinary type of wind-furnace built for coke or charcoal is shown in Fig. 8. This furnace is built of red brick, and lined with one course of fire-brick. It should be firmly bound with angle-iron, and tied with **tie-rods**. The top of the furnace

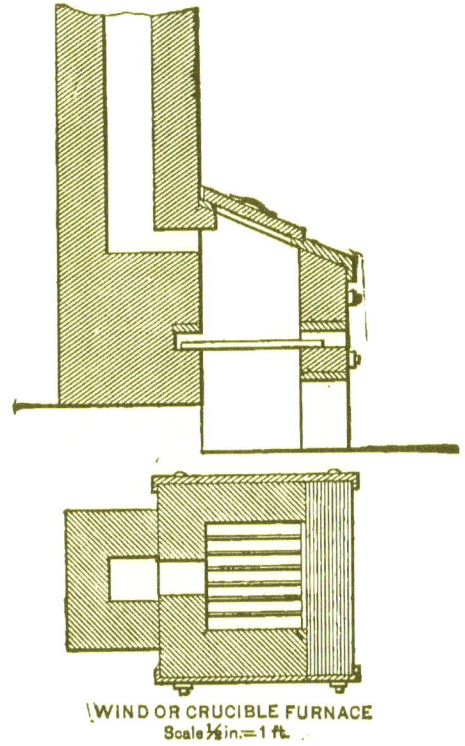

WIND OR CRUCIBLE FURNACE
Scale ½ in.=1 ft.

Fig. 8.

is covered with a cast-iron plate, the cover or lid also being of cast iron. The dimensions of the furnace shown in the sketch can be increased to any desired extent, but the same relative dimensions between the parts should be maintained when increasing the size. Where large amounts of silver bullion are to be melted the furnace will necessarily have to be considerably larger than shown in the sketch. Where bullion is to be melted it is also well to provide the furnace with a chain-tackle for lifting the crucibles out of the furnace. Where retort silver from a pan-amalgamation mill is to be melted, the furnace should be provided with a sheet-iron hood, connected with the stack, for carrying off the fumes.

There are many different styles of muffle-furnace in use. The furnace shown in Figs. 9 and 10 is designed to burn

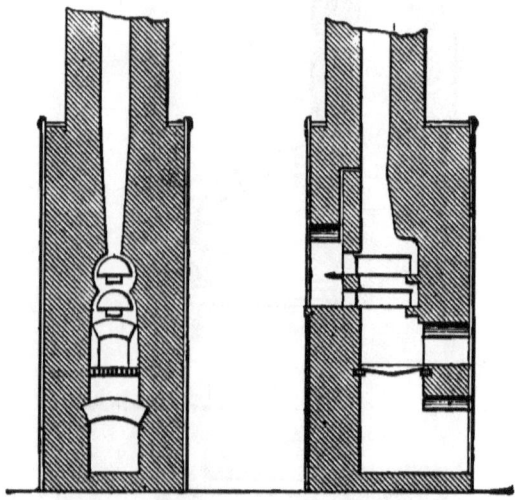

MUFFLE FURNACE FOR BITUMINOUS COAL.
Scale ½ in.=1 ft.

FIG. 9.   FIG. 10.

bituminous coal. Where good bituminous coal can be obtained, this is as satisfactory a furnace as can be built. The furnace is built of red brick, and lined throughout with one course of fire-brick. It should be firmly bound with angle-iron, tied with iron tie-rods. Where good bituminous coal can be obtained, this furnace is preferable to a coke-furnace for the following reasons: It is quickly started, the temperature is readily controlled, the consumption of muffles is much less than in a coke-furnace, the consumption of fuel is less (in cost) at the ordinary prices of coal and coke, and the furnace has a longer life.

Figs. 11 and 12 show a furnace constructed to burn coke.

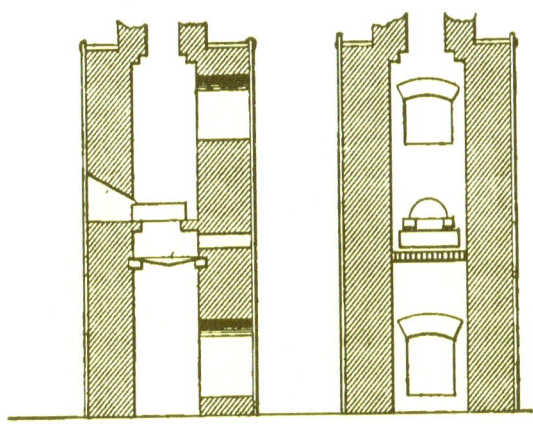

MUFFLE FURNACE FOR COKE OR CHARCOAL.
Scale ¼ in.=1 ft.

FIG. 11.   FIG. 12.

This furnace is lined throughout with fire-brick, and bound with angle-iron and tie-rods.

Heating Apparatus.—The fusion of substances with carbonate of soda or mixed carbonates can be performed in the muffle-furnace or over a blast-lamp. Fletcher's gas blast-lamp will be found almost indispensable in a laboratory provided with gas, for both fusions and the ignition of precipitates. Where gas is not at hand, Fletcher's petroleum blast-lamp or an alcohol blast-lamp may be used for fusions, etc. However, if gas is not at hand, the muffle-furnace best answers the purpose, and in a metallurgical laboratory where a great number of determinations are made daily the muffle is preferable, as it allows of a number of fusions or ignitions to be made at one time.

For fusions which do not require a very high temperature, as the fusion with caustic potash or the fusion with potassium bisulphate, the Bunsen burner or a good alcohol-lamp is all that is required.

For heating solutions, evaporations, etc., the gas-stove (Fletcher's) is an excellent piece of apparatus. When gas is not at hand a petroleum-stove can be substituted. Where a high temperature is not detrimental the top of the stove can be covered with a piece of wire-gauze. Where a high heat is not wanted the wire-gauze can be covered with a piece of asbestos paper or asbestos cardboard.

A most excellent piece of apparatus for evaporations, etc., consists of a sheet-iron plate, supported on four legs. This plate can be heated by gas- or petroleum-stoves or Bunsen burners. The temperature can be controlled by placing under the vessels containing the solutions pieces of asbestos paper of different thicknesses.

Large vessels which are liable to be broken by the ebullition during heating are best supported on a sand-bath. A convenient form of sand-bath is an ordinary tin pie-plate partially filled with fine, clean sand.

A water-bath will be essential for evaporations, which should not be heated above the boiling temperature of water. A good form of water-bath is a water-tight box of sheet copper 18 inches long, 12 inches wide, and 4 inches deep. The top should have several round holes of different diameters, so that vessels of different sizes may be used on the bath. The openings should be provided with covers, so that they may be closed when not in use. The water-bath is partially filled with water, and the heat turned on. As soon as the water reaches the boiling-point it is ready for use.

Where solutions require to be heated at a definite fixed temperature, either higher or lower than that of boiling water, a solution of calcium chloride, salt, etc., can be substituted for the water in the bath, or the solution may be evaporated in a hot-air bath which is kept at a fixed temperature.

A hot-air bath will be found convenient for drying precipitates, evaporation of solutions, and determinations of moisture in certain substances. It should be provided with a thermometer, so that the temperature may be controlled.

In a laboratory where gas is not at hand a very good

apparatus for evaporations, etc., is an ordinary cook-stove. The evaporations can be performed on the top of the stove, the temperature being controlled by means of pieces of asbestos paper. In case quite high temperatures are necessary, the lids of the stove can be removed and asbestos cardboard substituted for them. The oven can be used for the drying of precipitates, samples, etc. The stove should be provided with a hood connected with a good draught to carry off the fumes. This hood can be conveniently made of wood lined on the inside with asbestos paper. The conduit of the hood may be connected with the same flue as the stove, thus insuring a good draught.

Crucibles.—In an assay-office doing general work several different kinds of crucibles will be necessary.

A. *Graphite Crucibles.*—These are used for the melting of samples of base bullion, silver bullion, gold bullion, etc. The best crucibles are made by the Dixon Crucible Co., and come in different sizes, holding from 4 ounces up to 5000 ounces. The melting is performed in the wind-furnace as follows: A good fire is started in the furnace, and when burning well the crucible and its contents are introduced, the spaces around the outside of the crucible being filled in with fresh coke or charcoal. The cover is then put on the furnace, and the damper opened. After each melt the crucible should be thoroughly cleaned whilst hot by means of a scraper. With proper care a crucible will serve for a large number of melts.

B. *Clay and Sand Crucibles.*—These are used for the fusion in the crucible assay of gold and silver ores, and also for the fusion- or fire-assay of ores of the base metals. They come in a great variety of shapes and sizes, those most used being rated as 5, 10, 20, and 30 grammes (capable of holding charges for the assay of 5, 10, 20, and 30 grammes of ore). The best makes are the Colorado clay (made by the Denver Fire-clay Co.), the French clay, the Battersea (English make), and the Hessian sand (German make). In the western portions of the United States the Colorado-clay crucible has generally replaced the other makes, owing to the less cost of these crucibles and their general excellence.

C. *Porcelain Crucibles.*—These are used for the ignition of precipitates, fusions which cannot be made in platinum or silver crucibles, and for the parting and annealing of the gold beads obtained in the assay of gold and silver ores, etc. They come in a great variety of sizes, the best makes being royal Berlin china and royal Meissen porcelain.

D. *Platinum Crucibles.*—These are used for the fusion of ores, furnace products, etc., with carbonate of soda, etc. They come in a variety of sizes, and are sold by the gramme, the present price being about 65 cents per gramme. They weigh, with the cover, about as many grammes as they hold cubic centimetres. As they are expensive they should be handled carefully. They should never be squeezed in the fingers to remove the fused mass. The best way to remove a fusion is to remove the crucible from the heat and quickly pour its contents out on a piece of clean platinum (the cover of a large crucible answers very well), or just before the fused mass solidifies insert a stout piece of platinum wire in it. The end of the wire should be bent in the form of a h... the mass is cool, introduce a little hot wate... in a few minutes the mass may be lifted out by means of the wire. The crucibles may be cleaned by heating with a little nitric acid (free from chlorine) or by scouring with a little finely pulverized red iron oxide.

E. *Rose Crucibles.*—These are used for the ignition of certain precipitates, which require to be ignited in an atmosphere of hydrogen, sulphuretted hydrogen, etc. They are made of porcelain, with a perforated porcelain cover and tube. The tube is attached to the supply of hydrogen or other gas. A very good substitute for a Rose crucible is an ordinary porcelain crucible, and a clay tobacco-pipe for the cover and tube.

F. *Silver Crucibles.*—These are used for fusions where caustic soda or caustic potash is the flux. The crucibles with a gold lining are preferable. An alcohol-lamp should be used to heat these crucibles.

Scorifiers.—These are used in the scorification-assay of gold or silver ores. They come in the following sizes: $2\frac{1}{4}$, $2\frac{1}{2}$, 3, and 4 inches diameter. The best makes are the Colorado (Denver Fire-clay Co.) and the Battersea.

Cupels.—The cupels used for the cupellation of the lead buttons carrying the gold and silver are made of bone-ash, the bones of horses or sheep being considered the best. It is better to make the cupels than to buy them ready-made. The bone-ash is mixed with sufficient warm water to hold it together without being too moist. By adding a little wood-ash or pearl-ash (potassium carbonate) to the water used in moistening the bone-ash the cupels will be more firm. The cupels are prepared by filling the mould with the moistened bone-ash, and driving the pestle with two or three light blows of a wooden mallet. They should be dried carefully by standing them in a warm place or in a place exposed to the rays of the sun, and all moisture and organic matter should be expelled previous to using by heating them in the muffle.

Casseroles.—Casseroles and evaporating dishes are used for the decomposition of ores, etc., with acids and other liquid reagents, and for the evaporation of solutions. They are of porcelain and platinum, the porcelain being most generally used. They come in a variety of sizes holding from $\frac{1}{2}$ ounce up to $\frac{1}{2}$ gallon. A very convenient size is the $\frac{1}{2}$-ounce casserole, which is 2 inches in diameter. The best makes are royal Berlin china, royal Berlin porcelain, and German porcelain.

Beakers.—Beakers serve for a variety of uses in the laboratory. Lipped beakers are always preferable. Bohemian-glass beakers are the best. They come in a number of sizes, ranging from $\frac{1}{2}$ ounce up to 200 ounces in capacity.

Beaker covers of convex glass (watch-glasses) will be found indispensable.

Funnels and Filtering.—The best funnels are made of the best Bohemian or the best German glass. They come in a variety of sizes, ranging in capacity from 1 ounce to 1 gallon. They are also made in a variety of different forms for special purposes.

There are a number of different makes of filter-paper, of which Schleicher & Schuell's and Munktell's best Swedish are the best for quantitative work.

The best form of glass rods for filtering are made by cutting glass tubing into suitable lengths, and sealing the ends by means of the blast-lamp. They are light, and there is less liability of fracturing the beakers than in the case of solid-glass rods.

In preparing a funnel for filtration the paper should always fit tight to the sides, and should be moistened with water after placing it in the funnel. In pouring a stream from the beaker on to the filter the stream should always be poured against a glass rod. The under side of the lip of the beaker should always be dry. In filtering, the rods should not have rubbers on the end, as they are liable to introduce organic matter into the solutions. Rubbers on the rods are used in cleaning the beakers, and sometimes in removing the last particles of a precipitate from the beaker or casserole.

Always use as small a filter as will allow of the proper washing of its contents. In washing allow all the solution to run through the filter before adding any wash-water. Fill up the filter with the water, and allow that to run through before adding any more. By this means excessive quantities of wash-water may be avoided. In washing by decantation, which is sometimes necessary, allow the precipitate to settle, decant as closely as possible, pouring the solution on the filter; add water, stir well, allow to settle, and decant again closely before adding more wash-water.

A filter-pump will be found a great convenience in a laboratory where many bulky precipitates are to be washed. Richards' filter-pump, for water-pressure, is the best where water-pressure can be obtained. Where water-pressure cannot be obtained Bunsen's filter-pump is the best.

After a precipitate is thoroughly washed the funnel should be removed with the filter from the filter rack, and the precipitate thoroughly dried with the filter before ignition. When a filter-pump is used the precipitate and filter can be partially dried rapidly by drawing air through by means of the pump.

Flasks.—The best flasks are made of the best Bohemian glass. A number of flasks of different sizes and different kinds will be found useful. Flat-bottom flasks of 8, 16, and 24 ounce capacity, provided with double perforated rubber stoppers, are useful for making wash-bottles. Pear-shaped flasks of 4 and 6 ounce capacity will be found useful for copper determinations and for decomposing ores, etc. Filtering flasks of 1 and 2 pints capacity, and of heavy glass, are useful, especially where the filter-pump is used. A set of volumetric flasks, accurately graduated, and provided with ground-glass stoppers, will be indispensable for volumetric analysis. The following makes a convenient set: 50 cc., 100 cc., 250 cc., 500 cc., and 1000 cc. They should not only be accurately graduated, with two marks on the neck of each, one called the holding-mark (the capacity of the flask when filled to that mark), and the other called the delivery-mark (the number of cubic centimetres the flask will deliver when filled to that mark), but, which is most important, they should be graduated so that they will bear the same relative ratio to each other; that is, the 100-cc. flask should hold just half as much as the 200-cc. flask, and the 1000-cc. flask should hold just four times as much as the 250-cc. flask when each is filled to the holding-mark. This is of the utmost importance in volumetric analysis where aliquot portions are frequently taken.

If it is desired to standardize a flask with great accuracy it can be done by counterpoising the flask on the balance with any convenient weight, adding weights to those on the balance to an amount corresponding to the desired capacity of the flask, adding the proper amount of water, and marking the neck of the flask with the aid of a diamond or a good steel file. If an accurately standardized flask or pipette is at hand, others of twice, thrice, etc., its capacity can readily be prepared.

Pipettes and Burettes.—These are constantly used in volumetric analysis. They are best purchased already graduated, but their capacity should always be tested, especially as against the other measuring apparatus on hand, and as against each other.

To test the capacity of a pipette, fill it to the proper mark with distilled water of 16° C., run this water into a weighed flask or beaker, and weigh the amount delivered. This weight should nearly correspond in grammes to the capacity of the pipette in cubic centimetres. A slight difference should be allowed for the expansion of water between 0° and 16° C. One cc. of distilled water at 16° C. weighs 0.9988 gramme. In like manner the accuracy of a burette may be verified by weighing the amount delivered, taking any even number of cubic centimetres.

A pipette should always be filled by suction to a little above the mark; then, by closing the top with the finger, the liquid may be allowed to run slowly out until the lower part of the meniscus is at the line. It will then (if correct) deliver the number of cubic centimetres marked upon it. Pipettes may have both a holding- and delivery-mark, but if used for delivery only the holding-mark is unnecessary.

There are many different forms of burettes made, but those of Mohr and Gay-Lussac are the most convenient, and generally preferred. Mohr's burette, provided with Geissler's glass stop-cock or the Gay-Lussac burette, should always be used for solutions liable to decompose rubber.

In a laboratory where the volumetric solutions are in constant use it is a good plan to have a separate burette for each standard solution, and attach it, by means of a siphon, of glass tubing, and a glass stop-cock, to the bottle holding the standard solution. By this means the burettes are readily filled, and do not have to be emptied and cleaned after each set of determinations.

As the success of volumetric analysis depends largely upon accurate measuring, too much care cannot be given to accurately graduating and reading the flasks, pipettes, and burettes.

Tools.—A number of small tools will be required as follows: A set of three hammers, for pounding lead buttons, flattening silver-gold buttons for parting, and cutting out samples of bullion, etc.;

Shovels and pokers, and scrapers for cleaning out the muffle;

Crucible tongs, scorifier tongs, and cupel tongs, for fire-work. Small crucible tongs, for crucibles used in wet assays;

Cold-chisels, for cutting out samples of bullion;

A small anvil or steel plate, for hammering lead buttons and separating the buttons from the slag;

Spatulas, for sampling, weighing out, mixing charges, etc.;

A set of small steel dies, from 0 to 9 inclusive, for marking bars and samples of bullion;

A pair of cutting shears and nippers, for cutting samples of bullion, etc.;

A pair of scissors, for cutting filter-papers, and a set of filter patterns;

Files, for cutting glass rods and tubing, marking flasks, etc.;

An assorted lot of rubber stoppers, both perforated and plain;

An assorted lot of glass tubing and glass rods;

An assorted lot of rubber tubing;

Platinum-wire and platinum-foil.

Whilst most of the apparatus used in the analytical work can be purchased of the dealers, a great deal of it can be made in the laboratory with a little patience and ingenuity. The student should accustom himself to make such odd pieces of apparatus as he requires, as the chemist frequently needs apparatus, and cannot wait until it can be obtained from some distant dealer.

In purchasing apparatus and supplies always buy the best, as cheap apparatus is dear at any price. Do not be extravagant in your purchases, as it is not necessary to have an immense amount of costly apparatus on hand in order to do good work.

CHAPTER V.

REAGENTS.

THE reagents used in both wet and dry assaying may be divided into the following general classes:

Fluxes.—This class includes a large number of bodies, but generally they are substances which render others to which they are added more fusible, either by acting as solvents or as decomposing agents. They are either acid, basic, or neutral in their action.

The following are the principal fluxes used in wet assaying or chemical analysis:

Carbonate of Soda (Na_2CO_3). This acts as a decomposing agent, and is used for the decomposition by fusion, either alone or in conjunction with other reagents, of silicates, etc. It should be pure, and free from moisture.

Carbonate of Potassium (K_2CO_3). This acts the same as sodium carbonate, with which it is frequently mixed. A mixture of the two carbonates in the proportion of their molecular weights is a most excellent flux for the decomposition of certain silicates, clays, etc., which are difficultly decomposed by either carbonate when used alone. The potassium carbonate should be pure and free from moisture.

Potassium Bisulphate ($KHSO_4$). This acts both as a decomposing agent and as an acid flux. Silica is not rendered soluble by fusion with this reagent, whilst iron oxide, alumina, etc., are converted into a form which is soluble.

Sodium Hydrate (NaOH). This acts both as a decomposing agent and a basic flux. It is used principally for the decomposition of sulphides and sulphates in the determination of sulphur. It is occasionally used for the decomposition of certain silicates and oxides, and is particularly adapted to the decomposition of certain organic compounds, converting them into compounds which are soluble in water.

Potassium Hydrate (KOH). This acts the same as sodium hydrate, and is used for the same purposes.

Sodium Nitrate ($NaNO_3$). This acts as a decomposing agent, and also as an oxidizer. It should be pure, and free from moisture. The corresponding potash salt (KNO_3) is also used for the same purposes.

Hydrofluoric Acid (HFl). This is one of the most powerful decomposing agents, and by its means many silicates are decomposed, the silica being volatilized.

The following are the principal fluxes used in dry or fire-assaying:

Sodium Bicarbonate ($NaHCO_3$), or the corresponding potassium salt. These act as desulphurizing agents, as basic fluxes, and in some cases as oxidizing agents. They should be free from moisture and coarse particles. As they are readily fusible, they can retain in suspension a large proportion of pulverized infusible substances without losing their fluidity.

Borax, crystallized ($2NaBO_2$, B_2O_3, $10H_2O$). This acts as an acid flux, and is sometimes used as a cover in place of salt. As it contains a large amount of water, it is usually used in a vitrified condition. It loses its water readily upon fusion. To prepare the vitrified borax (borax-glass), fuse it in an iron- or chalk-lined clay crucible, pour the fused mass out on a clean surface, and pulverize when cold.

Litharge (PbO). Acts as a basic flux, an oxidizing and desulphurizing agent, and supplies the necessary lead in the gold and silver crucible assay. It should be free from red oxide of lead. White lead is sometimes used in its place. As it always contains silver, its silver contents should be determined and deducted from the results of all silver assays.

Silica (SiO$_2$). This acts as an acid flux. Sometimes powdered glass is substituted for silica. Lime-glass makes the best flux, and when used for lead assays should be free from lead.

Lead Flux. This is a mixture of sodium bicarbonate (16 parts), potassium carbonate (16 parts), flour (4 parts), and borax-glass (8 parts). This acts as a flux, reducing agent, and desulphurizing agent. It is especially useful in the lead assay, and frequently forms the basis of the charge in the crucible assay of gold and silver ores.

Black Flux. This consists of one part nitre and three parts argol (deflagrated). It is not much used.

Black Flux Substitute. This consists of a mixture of flour (3 parts) and sodium bicarbonate (10 parts). It is sometimes used in place of lead flux.

Potassium Cyanide (KCN). Acts as a powerful reducing and desulphurizing flux. It is frequently used for the determination of lead, tin, bismuth, and antimony by fire-assay. For this purpose it should be quite pure, and free from sulphides and sulphates.

Argol (KHC$_4$H$_4$O$_6$). Commercial bitartrate of potash. This acts as a powerful reducing agent, and also as a basic flux. Its reducing power should be determined by fusion with litharge and sodium bicarbonate.

Charcoal (C). Acts as a reducing agent and desulphurizer. Its reducing power should be determined.

Salt (NaCl). Is used principally as a cover in crucible assays.

Nitre (KNO$_3$). This acts as a basic flux and powerful oxidizing agent. Its oxidizing power should be determined. To determine its oxidizing power, make up the following charge, place it in a clay crucible, and fuse in a hot fire. Remove, pour cool, and weigh the lead button. The difference between the weight of the button obtained and that given in the determination of the reducing power of the charcoal, divided by 1.5, gives the oxidizing power of the nitre per gramme.

Charge.—Litharge .... 30 gms.
Soda bicarb .... 15 "
Charcoal .... 0.5 "
Nitre .... 1.5 "

Metallic Iron (Fe). Acts as a basic flux and desulphurizing agent. Nails or iron wire about $\frac{1}{8}$ inch in diameter are the most convenient form.

Metallic Lead (Pb). This acts as a basic flux and as a solvent or collector of the precious metals in the assay of gold and silver ores. It is used in the form of granulated lead in the scorification assay and in the form of sheet lead in the bullion assay. As it is never free from silver, its silver contents should be determined and the proper deduction made from the results of all silver assays.

All of the above fluxes should be dry and pulverized.

Solvents.—Whilst many of the fluxes described above act as solvents during fusion, only such solutions as act as solvents in wet analysis will be discussed.

Water (H_2O). Water used in quantitative analysis for solution, dilution, etc., should always be distilled.

Hydrochloric Acid (HCl). This acts as a powerful solvent either alone or in conjunction with other acids. Aqua regia ($2HCl + HNO_3$) is one of the most powerful solvents, and the only acid in which gold and platinum are soluble to any great extent. It should be pure, and kept on hand of two strengths, concentrated and dilute. The specific gravity of dilute hydrochloric acid should be 1.2.

Nitric Acid (HNO_3). Is a powerful solvent and oxidizing agent. It should be pure, and kept on hand in concentrated and dilute state. Fuming nitric acid is a most powerful oxidizing and desulphurizing agent. The specific gravity of the dilute nitric acid should be 1.2.

Sulphuric Acid (H_2SO_4). Is a powerful solvent, and is extensively used both as a solvent and a precipitant. The specific gravity of the concentrated acid is 1.84. The dilute acid is prepared by adding one volume of the concentrated acid to five volumes of water.

Acetic ($HC_2H_3O_2$), Oxalic ($H_2C_2O_4$), Citric ($H_3C_6H_5O_7$, H_2O), and Tartaric Acids ($H_2C_4H_4O_6$) are weak solvents, and are much used for special purposes. Acetic acid comes in solution either as commercial, c. p. ordinary, c. p. glacial (99 p. c.), or c. p. anhydrous. The other acids come in the crystalline form, either commercial or c. p. In making up solutions of these acids it is best to use an excess of the reagent and make a saturated solution.

Ammonium Acetate ($NH_4C_2H_3O_2$). Is a powerful solvent of lead salts, especially lead sulphate. The reagent is best made by adding strong acetic acid to strong ammonia-water until the solution is just acid, and then add a few drops of ammonia to render the solution alkaline. The corresponding salts of ammonia with citric or tartaric acids answer the same purpose, but are more expensive and no better than the acetate.

Ammonia (NH_4OH). Acts as a powerful solvent of chloride and bromide of silver.

Sodium Hyposulphite ($Na_2H_2S_2O_4$). Is a solvent of silver chloride, and is used largely in the lixiviation of silver ores.

Potassium Cyanide (KCN). Is a solvent of gold and silver, and is extensively used in the leaching of gold ores.

Ammonium Sulphide [$(NH_4)_2S$]. Is a powerful solvent of the sulphides of arsenic, antimony, and tin.

Precipitants.—There are a great number of precipitants used in wet analysis. Only a few of the more important will be discussed.

Barium Chloride ($BaCl_2$). Is used principally as a precipitant for sulphuric acid. In making up the solution one gm. of the crystalline salt is added to 10 cc. of water. One cc. of this solution will precipitate 0.0327 gm. SO_3.

Hydrodisodic Phosphate (Na_2HPO_4). Is used principally as a precipitant for magnesia. In making up the solution 1 gm. of the crystalline salt is added to 10 cc. of water. One cc. of this solution will precipitate 0.0112 gm. of MgO.

Ammonium Oxalate [$(NH_4)C_2O_4$]. Is used principally as a precipitant for calcium. In making up the solution 1 gm. of the salt is added to 10 cc. of water. One cc. of this solution will precipitate 0.0145 gm. CaO.

Magnesia Mixture. Is used as a precipitant for phosphorus and arsenic. In making up the solution 1 gm. of $MgSO_4$ (salt), 1 gm. of NH_4Cl (salt), and 4 cc. of ammonia are added to 8 cc. of water. One cc. of this solution will precipitate 0.024 gm. of P_2O_5.

Molybdate Solution. Is used as a precipitant for phosphorus and arsenic. In making up the solution 1 gm. MoO_3 is dissolved in 4 cc. of ammonia and the solution is poured into 15 cc. of HNO_3 (sp. gr. 1.2). One cc. of this solution will precipitate 0.0013 gm. of P_2O_5.

Silver Nitrate ($AgNO_3$). Is used principally as a precipitant for chlorine. In making up the solution 1 gm. of salt is added to 20 cc. of water. One cc. of this solution will precipitate 0.0104 gm. of Cl.

Potassium Permanganate ($K_2Mn_2O_8$). Is used as a precipitant of MnO_2 in the volumetric estimation of manganese. The solution is made up in the manner described in Part II, Chapter XVI.

Ammonia (NH_4OH). Is used as a precipitant of iron, alumina, etc., and is an indispensable reagent in the laboratory.

The strongest concentrated ammonia has a sp. gr. of 0.88. This diluted with two volumes of water has a sp. gr. of 0.96, which is the reagent commonly used.

Ammonium Carbonate [$(NH_4)_2CO_3$]. Is used as a precipitant of Zn, Mn, Fe, Ca, Ba, etc. Is an invaluable reagent. In making up the solution 1 gm. of the salt and 1 cc. of ammonia are added to 4 cc. of water.

Ammonium Sulphide [$(NH_4)_2S$]. Is used as a precipitant of Fe, Zn, Mn, Ni, and Co. To prepare the solution pass a rapid current of pure sulphuretted hydrogen through a solution of ammonia in the reagent bottle. Should be kept corked, and in a dark, cool place. As it loses its strength rapidly, it is best to prepare freshly from time to time.

Ammonium Chloride (NH_4Cl). Is used in conjunction with ammonia as a precipitant of iron, etc. It is best to prepare a saturated solution.

Sodium Carbonate (Na_2Co_3). Is used as a precipitant of Zn, Fe, Mn, Ca, Ba, etc. A saturated solution is usually used.

Sodium Sulphide (Na_2S). Is used principally as a precipitant of the heavier metals and as a solvent for sulphides of arsenic, antimony, and tin. To prepare the solution add 1 gm. of salt to 10 cc. of water.

Sodium and Potassium Hydrates (NaOH and KOH). Are used as precipitants of Cu, $Fe_2Al_2O_3$, etc. To prepare the solution dissolve 1 gm. of the salt in 10 cc. of water.

Sodium Acetate ($NaC_2H_3O_2$). Is used as a precipitant of iron and alumina in the basic-acetate separation of these metals. The salt is generally used.

Sodium Chloride (NaCl) and *Sodium Bromide* (NaBr). Are used as precipitants of silver in the volumetric estimation of silver (Part III, Chap. II) and in the special method for copper mattes (Part III, Chap. IV).

Platinic Chloride ($PtCl_4$). Is used as a precipitant of potassium. To prepare the solution dissolve 1 gm. of the metal in aqua regia, evaporate to dryness and dissolve in 1 cc. HCl and 9 cc. of water. One gramme of this solution will precipitate 0.048 gm. of K_2O.

Hydric Sulphide (Sulphuretted hydrogen, H_2S). Is used principally as a precipitant of the heavy metals. To prepare the gas add dilute sulphuric acid to pure iron sulphide. The gas should be washed by passing it through water before using. If pure iron sulphide is not at hand it can be prepared by fusing iron nails with sulphur in the proportion of about 1 part iron to 2 parts sulphur, by weight. A very convenient generator is shown in Figure 13.

Sulphuric Acid (H_2SO_4). As a precipitant, is used principally to precipitate barium. One cc. of the dilute acid will precipitate 0.4291 gm. Ba.

Metallic Zinc (Zn). It is used for the precipitation of Pb,

Cu, As, Sb, Ag, and Au (from cyanide solutions). The zinc should be free from these metals, and free from iron when used for the reduction of iron solutions. It is used in the form of sticks, sheets, or as granulated, zinc. To granulate, melt some bar zinc in a clay crucible, skim off the surface, and pour into cold water from a considerable height.

Metallic Copper (Cu). Is used as a precipitant of mercury. Comes in the form of thin foil and sheets.

Metallic Aluminium (Al). Is used as a precipitant of Cu and Bi. Comes as foil.

Metallic Lead (Pb). Is used as a precipitant for copper. Either sheet lead, or preferably granulated test-lead, is used.

Pure materials should always be used. In making up the solutions distilled water should be used. The salts obtained from the dealers and labelled "chemically pure" are seldom absolutely so, and often afford a sediment or precipitate when the solutions are allowed to stand. Hence it is best to prepare the solutions in bulk and filter them off after they have been allowed to stand for some time. Tests should always be made for such impurities as are liable to interfere, or cause error in the analyses. If such impurities are found, the amount will have to be determined and an allowance made for it in the work, either by carefully measuring the amount of reagent used and making the proper deduction from the result of the analysis, or by running a blank analysis. The latter course is generally preferable where really accurate results are required. In running a blank analysis the same amounts and kinds of reagents are added to the proper amount of water as are used in the regular analysis. The solution is boiled, filtered, etc., as in the regular analysis. The weight of the final precipitate obtained in the blank analysis should be deducted from the weight of the precipitate obtained in the regular analysis.

Reducing Reagents.—To this class belong those bodies which have the power of removing oxygen from its compounds. They are the reverse of oxidizing reagents.

The principal reducing reagents used in fire-assaying are as follows: Charcoal, Argol, Flour, Starch, Sugar, Potassium Ferrocyanide, and Potassium Cyanide. They have been discussed under the head of "Fluxes."

The following are the principal reducing reagents used in wet analysis:

Hydrogen (H). This is the most powerful reducing agent. Is used in the form of a gas, which should be dry and free from impurities, such as arseniuretted hydrogen. It is best prepared by treating zinc, or iron filings, with dilute sulphuric acid. Sometimes dilute hydrochloric is substituted for the sulphuric acid. The gas is frequently generated in the solution to be reduced as in the case of the reduction of a solution of ferric sulphate to ferrous sulphate in the determination of iron. (See Part II, Chap. XVI.)

Sulphuretted Hydrogen (H_2S). Is a powerful reducing agent. The gas is generated in the manner described under the head of "Precipitants."

Sodium Sulphite (Na_2SO_3). This is a good reducing agent. It is frequently used for the reduction of ferric solutions. It separates Arsenious Sulphide, which is soluble in it, from the sulphides of antimony and tin, which are insoluble in it.

Stannous Chloride ($SnCl_2$). This is frequently used for the reduction of iron solutions for the volumetric estimation of iron. (See Part II, Chap. XVI.)

There are many organic compounds, as solutions of sugar, tartaric acid, etc., which serve as reducing agents.

Oxidizing Reagents.—Under this heading are comprised all bodies which readily yield up their oxygen.

The principal oxidizing reagents used in fire-assaying are Nitre, Litharge, Sodium Bicarbonate, and Ferric Oxide.

The principal oxidizing reagents used in wet analysis are the following:

Oxygen (O). This is the most powerful oxidizing agent, and is generated or produced in various different ways.

Chlorine (Cl). Is a powerful oxidizer, and is readily generated by treating bleaching-powder with sulphuric acid.

Bromine (Br). Is a powerful and very convenient oxidizing agent. It is purchased in the liquid form, and is generally used as bromine water (water saturated with bromine).

Potassium Permanganate ($K_2Mn_2O_8$). Is a powerful oxidizing agent, which is largely used in volumetric analysis. The standard solutions are made up as described for the determination of iron (Part II, Chap. XVI).

Potassium Bichromate ($K_2Cr_2O_7$). Is a powerful oxidizing agent, which is largely used in volumetric analysis. The standard solutions are made up as described for the determination of iron (Part II, Chap. XVI).

Nitric Acid (HNO_3). Is a very powerful and convenient oxidizing agent, and is largely used for the oxidation of precipitates. Fuming nitric acid is the most powerful. It should be kept in a cool dark place and should be handled carefully.

Potassium Chlorate ($KClO_3$). Is a powerful oxidizer, yielding its oxygen with facility. Is largely used as an oxidizer in fusions and for solutions.

Sodium Nitrate ($NaNO_3$). Is largely used as an oxidizing agent in fusions. The corresponding potassium salt (KNO_3) may be substituted for the sodium salt.

Hydrogen Peroxide (H_2O_2). Is a very powerful oxidizing agent. The objection to the use of this reagent is the difficulty of obtaining it in the pure state and its liability to undergo decomposition, it soon losing its strength.

Ammonium Nitrate (NH_4NO_3). The salt is readily decomposed upon heating, and is a good oxidizing agent.

Indicators.—There are a number of color indicators which are extremely useful in volumetric analysis. These are fully discussed in Chapter XIII, ACIDIMETRY AND ALKALIMETRY.

To the above classes of reagents might be added those which act as sulphurizing and desulphurizing agents. These are mostly included in the above, the principal sulphurizing reagents being sulphur and sulphuretted hydrogen, and the principal desulphurizing reagents used in the wet way being the oxidizing reagents. In the dry way the principal desulphurizing reagents have been discussed under the head of FLUXES.

For a complete discussion of reagents, their preparation, etc., see Fresenius' "Qualitative Analysis."

PART II.

CHAPTER I.

SILICA (SiO_2).

THE method to be pursued in the determination of silica will depend on the character of the substance on which the determination is made. The following methods are extensively used in many of our metallurgical works:

Iron Ores.—Most oxidized iron ores are decomposed by heating in a beaker with concentrated hydrochloric acid. Evaporation to dryness is not necessary, and is to be avoided except where the ore gives up gelatinous silica on heating. When evaporation to dryness is necessary, the evaporation should be finished at comparatively a low temperature, preferably on the water-bath, otherwise some of the iron is liable to be converted into an insoluble form. After evaporation to dryness the mass is taken up with a small amount of hydrochloric acid and boiled. It is then diluted with distilled water and filtered, transferring the silica to the filter-paper with the successive additions of wash-water. When the washings are free from chloride of iron, which can be determined either by the yellow color of the filtrate or by testing with a solution of ammonium sulphocyanate, which should turn red if iron is present, a few drops of dilute hydrochloric acid are dropped around the edges of the filter-paper, and the paper and contents washed a few times with boiling distilled water. This addition of hydrochloric acid to the filter-paper and subsequent washings is a precaution necessary to dissolve any trace of iron, calcium sulphate, etc., which may have remained on the filter with the silica. The filter and its contents are then removed from the funnel, the paper being folded so as to thoroughly envelop its contents. It is then placed in a small porcelain crucible and ignited in the muffle furnace or over the blast-lamp. Previous drying of the paper and its contents is unnecessary. One gramme of the ore is the amount usually taken. A very convenient vessel for the solution and evaporation of the ore is a porcelain casserole, of about 100 cubic centimetres capacity, provided with a handle. Some ore, such as chromic iron ore, and magnetites carrying considerable titanium, will not be thoroughly decomposed by simple treatment with acids. In such a case the best method of procedure is to fuse the insoluble residue, after previous ignition, with c. p. carbonate of soda* in a platinum crucible, one to two grammes of carbonate being generally sufficient where one gramme of ore has been taken, or the ore may be fused directly with sodium carbonate and the silica determined as usual where a fusion is made.

The fusion can be made over a blast-lamp or in the muffle. It should be complete, which will be indicated by the mass being perfectly liquid and quiet. Ten to twenty minutes will generally be sufficient time to bring the fusion to completion. During the last few minutes the crucible and its contents should be raised to a high temperature.

When the fusion is complete the crucible is removed from the source of heat, and its bottom is dipped in cold water in order to chill the mass quickly. The fused mass is removed from the crucible by boiling water added from a wash-bottle. Slightly bending the crucible a few times with the fingers will greatly facilitate the removal, and will not injure the crucible if proper care is exercised. The washings and mass are poured off into a casserole provided with a convex glass cover, and hydrochloric acid added in slight excess. The solution is then evaporated to dryness, the evaporation being completed at

---

* Many chemists prefer a mixture of equal parts of sodium and potassium carbonate.

temperature not much above that of boiling water, otherwise the mass is likely to spit, and consequently there will be a loss. The mass is then heated at a temperature of about 120° C. until all the free hydrochloric acid is driven off. It is then taken up with water and a few cubic centimetres of hydrochloric acid, boiled, filtered, washed, ignited, and weighed.

Silver-Lead Ores.—One gramme of ore is usually taken. If the ore is oxidized, this is dissolved in seven cubic centimetres of hydrochloric acid and treated in the same manner as in the case of iron ores, the precaution being taken to remove the lead and silver in the manner described below. If the ore is a sulphide, it is best to dissolve in four cubic centimetres of strong hydrochloric acid, three cubic centimetres of strong nitric acid, and evaporate to dryness.

It is then taken up with a few cubic centimetres of hydrochloric acid, boiled, and diluted with distilled water. The solution is then filtered off on to a filter-paper by decantation, and after all the chloride of iron, etc., is removed, about six or seven cubic centimetres of a warm solution of ammonium acetate added to the casserole, and its contents stirred with a glass rod provided with a rubber on the end. The ammonium acetate dissolves the sulphate and chloride of lead present, and the stirring serves to break up any clots of these salts which might not otherwise go into solution. Two additions of ammonium acetate are generally sufficient to dissolve all of the lead, although a third washing may sometimes be necessary.

The ammonium acetate is usually prepared as follows: Some ammonia is poured into a beaker, and then acetic acid is added until the solution has an acid reaction, which is determined by a piece of litmus-paper. The solution prepared in this way is quite warm, owing to the heat generated by the combination of the acetic acid and ammonia, and is ready for immediate use.

After all the lead is removed the silver may be removed by treating with a few drops, or cubic centimetres if much silver is present, of ammonia.

The insoluble residue remaining in the casserole is now

washed on the filter with warm water, the filter washed once more, and a few drops of dilute hydrochloric acid poured around its edges. The filter and its contents are now washed again with warm water, and are then ready for ignition and subsequent weighing.

For technical work the insoluble residue will generally be sufficiently close to the true amount of silica present to be considered as such. When an ore contains silicate of alumina or other insoluble compounds, if an accurate determination is required it can be made by fusion with sodium carbonate, as in the case of iron ores.

On many ores a direct fusion of the ore with acid sulphate of potassium ($KHSO_4$) yields very good results. To make this fusion one gramme of ore is mixed with five grammes of potassium bisulphate in a porcelain crucible. The ore and flux should not fill the crucible much more than one-third full. The contents are then heated over the flame of a Bunsen burner or spirit-lamp until the fusion becomes quiet. The heat should be low at first in order to prevent loss by rapid boiling, and should be gradually increased until it is at a dull red. The fusion will usually take about fifteen minutes. When it is completed the crucible is removed from the source of heat and allowed to cool. When sufficiently cool the mass is removed from the crucible by boiling water and about thirty cubic centimetres of water added, and the whole brought to a boil in order to thoroughly disintegrate the mass. The solution is then ready for filtration and subsequent ignition, which is performed as before, more careful or longer washing with ammonium acetate being required if lead is present, as the lead is all in the form of sulphate.

Slags.—In the case of lead slags the method to be pursued will depend on the manner in which the sample was taken. If the sample was taken on a rod* and chilled suddenly the silica may be determined by treating half a gramme in a small casserole of about 100 cubic centimetres capacity, with about two

---

* See Part I, page 18.

cubic centimetres of water, and stirring with a glass rod, then adding two or three cubic centimetres of strong hydrochloric acid and stirring again. This addition of water and stirring prevents the slag coagulating and sticking to the bottom of the casserole, which it would otherwise do, and consequently would be difficult to decompose. A few drops of strong nitric acid are now added, the casserole being covered with a convex glass to prevent loss by effervescence, and the contents stirred again. Sufficient nitric acid should be added to decompose whatever sulphides are present and oxidize the iron, leaving a slight excess of nitric acid in solution. A considerable excess of acid is to be avoided, as this would only prolong the evaporation, and cause loss of time. The mass is then evaporated to dryness, care being taken not to raise to such a temperature as to cause the gelatinous silica to spit. The subsequent driving off of the free hydrochloric acid may be facilitated by breaking up the lumps with a glass rod, and also by moistening with a few drops of water once or twice, and heating to dryness again. It is essential that all of the free acid and water should be driven off, in order that all of the silica may be rendered insoluble. After the first evaporation to dryness the casserole can be removed to a warmer place, care being taken not to heat to such a degree that the iron will be rendered insoluble. If iron is to be determined in the filtrate from the silica, the mass should not be heated to a temperature much over 110° C., as chloride of iron is volatile at quite a low temperature. After the free hydrochloric acid is driven off the casserole is removed from the source of heat, and the mass moistened with a little water, and about two cubic centimetres of hydrochloric acid added. The contents of the casserole are then brought to a boil. After diluting with water the silica can be filtered off, dried, ignited, and weighed, as in the case of silver-lead ores.

The silica should be white, and there should be no gritty particles in the bottom of the casserole after solution. In the analysis of something over a thousand different samples of lead blast-furnace slags the writer has never yet encountered a slag which did not yield to this method of treatment, except in the case of slags containing barium. If the slags contain barium, some sulphate of barium, which is insoluble, will invariably be formed when the sulphides are oxidized with the nitric acid, and be precipitated with the silica.

This method of decomposing lead slags has been tested by the writer and others, a number of times, by fusing the insoluble residue, obtained as above, with carbonate of soda, and determining the silica in the regular manner, with results agreeing so closely with those obtained by weighing the insoluble residue as to prove the accuracy of the method—at least for all technical purposes.

A determination may be made in this way in less than forty minutes. In case the slag contains barium, a good method of procedure is to weigh the insoluble residue, and fuse it with about a gramme and a half of carbonate of soda in a platinum crucible. The fused mass is then removed from the crucible, and dissolved in water by boiling. It is then filtered through a small filter, and washed thoroughly with warm water to remove all the silicate and sulphate of sodium. This can be determined by acidifying the washings with a few drops of hydrochloric acid, heating, and adding a few drops of barium-chloride solution. The carbonate of barium is then dissolved on the filter-paper with dilute hydrochloric acid, and several subsequent washings with warm water into a clean beaker, and after bringing the solution to a boil the barium is precipitated by the addition of a few drops of sulphuric acid, and determined as barium sulphate, as described in Part II, Chapter XXV.

The weight of the barium sulphate thus determined may be deducted from the weight of the insoluble residue, the difference being considered as silica. This determination of the silica by difference is generally considered sufficiently accurate. If greater refinement is necessary, the silica may be determined directly in the filtrate by acidifying with hydrochloric acid, and evaporating to dryness, as in the case of an ordinary fusion for silica. This evaporation takes considerable time on account of the bulk of the liquid, and liability to loss through spitting, unless the evaporation takes place slowly. (See determination of silica in slags, etc.) An excellent method for technical purposes is described in Chapter XXV, page 225.

The same method may be used for the determination of silica in ores containing barium sulphate. The chemist will sometimes be called upon to analyze slags where the sample has not been taken in the manner described, as, for example, a piece of lump slag broken from a cold pot or cone. In this case the slag will very rarely be decomposed by direct treatment with acids. A direct fusion of the slag in platinum is not safe, as there is a liability of the lead, which the slag contains, attacking the crucible. This difficulty can generally be obviated in the following manner: Mix one half a gramme of the slag with about one and a half grammes of sodium carbonate, and transfer to a small platinum dish (of about 25 cc. capacity). Place in the muffle, and heat till the mass cinters together, care being exercised not to heat sufficiently long or to a sufficiently high temperature to fuse the mass, or else the lead is liable to be reduced and injure the platinum. As soon as the mass has cintered, remove from the muffle and cool. If the cintering has been properly performed the mass will almost invariably be decomposed by the addition of water and hydrochloric and nitric acids, when the silica may be determined in the manner described above. A platinum crucible may be used in place of a dish, but a dish is preferable, inasmuch as if a crucible is used the mass is liable to fuse around the edges before it has begun to cinter. When barium is present fuse the insoluble residue as before.

Iron Blast-furnace Slags.—The first method described above does very well for the determination of these slags for technical purposes, the sample when taken being suddenly chilled. According to some authors, the decomposition is not as good as in the case of lead-slags, but from all the results which the author has seen he would say that they were sufficiently close to check the workings of the furnace, for which the determinations are usually made. When the sample has not been suddenly chilled on taking, the best method is to fuse one half a gramme of finely pulverized slag with about three grammes of sodium carbonate. Remove fused mass from the crucible, and determine as in the case of fusion of iron ores.

Copper-furnace Slags.—These may be treated in the same manner as lead slags.

Fused Ore.—This may be sampled and treated in the same way as lead slags. Whether the chilled sample of ore will be decomposed in acids or not, depends upon its composition and the completeness of the fusion before the ore was drawn from the furnace. Very frequently it will not decompose. Under these circumstances, the insoluble residue which is free from lead, must be fused with sodium carbonate and the silica determined as before.

Mattes.—These will seldom decompose completely in acids, owing to the slag which is mixed with them mechanically. Generally the insoluble residue will have to be fused with sodium carbonate if an accurate silica determination is required.

Limestones.—As the silica of most limestones is present in the form of slate or quartz, the insoluble residue will generally represent the amount of silica present. The limestone should be dissolved in hydrochloric acid, using about 6 to 7 cc. of acid for 1 gramme of limestone,—the amount generally taken,—and a few drops of nitric acid to decompose any pyrite that may be present. In the case of a limestone carrying clay, the insoluble residue will have to be fused with sodium carbonate, as above.

Fire-clays, Marls, etc.—As these substances contain silicate of alumina, which is not decomposed by acids, 1 gramme of the substance is fused direct with about 5 or 6 grammes of carbonate of soda, and the silica determined as usual. When the alumina is also to be determined, the insoluble residue can first be determined by evaporation with acids, as in the case of iron ores. The silica is then determined by fusion with sodium carbonate as before, the difference between the percentage of silica and the percentage of insoluble residue being the percentage of alumina (Al_2O_3). When barium is present, the method of procedure after fusion of the insoluble residue is the same as in the case of the determination of silica in lead slags containing barium.

Note.—In nearly all cases where an ore or product does not contain lead and a fusion is necessary to decompose it, the fusion may be made directly, thus frequently saving time. Where an ore is known to contain silicate of alumina, and the alumina is to be determined, it is best to obtain the insoluble residue, weigh it, and then fuse, determining the silica as before and the alumina by difference, or directly in the filtrate, from the silica.

Pig-iron, Steel, etc.—The following method, proposed by Dr. Drown,[*] for the determination of silicon in pig-iron, etc., is used in some of our largest metallurgical works, and is as accurate and rapid as any:

Treat 1 gramme of finely pulverized iron or steel in a covered casserole with 10 cc. of water and about 8 cc. of concentrated nitric acid, until action ceases. Add 4 cc. of sulphuric acid and heat on an iron plate or sand-bath until the nitric acid is all expelled. This evaporation can be facilitated by conducting it in a platinum dish with a strong-flamed Bunsen burner below and another from a blast-lamp above, the latter flame being directed downward upon the surface of the solution in the dish.

When the evaporation is complete, which will be indicated by dense white fumes of sulphuric anhydride, the silica will all be insoluble. Remove from the source of heat and cool. When the contents of the dish are cold, add cold water, about 40 cc., carefully, to prevent spitting, and a few cubic centimetres of hydrochloric acid. Heat, filter, wash, ignite, and weigh as usual. The addition of considerable water and hydrochloric acid is necessary to dissolve the ferrous sulphate formed during evaporation. After the silica is transferred to

---

[*] Transactions of the American Institute of Mining Engineers, Vol. VII, p. 346.

the filter, it should be thoroughly washed with hot water and hydrochloric acid, as in iron ores. In the case of ferro-silicons where the percentage of silicon is high, this treatment with acids will fail, except by repeated additions of fresh acid and repeated evaporations. In this case a shorter method is to fuse 1 gramme of the pulverized metal with sodium carbonate in a covered platinum crucible. The silicon is converted into a sodium silicate and the spongy iron remains in a finely-divided condition, and is readily attacked by acids. After fusion is complete, remove from heat, cool, and dissolve in hot water and hydrochloric acid. Evaporate to dryness, and determine silica as in fusion of iron ores.

The silicon is determined as silica and weighed as such. From the weight of the silica calculate the percentage of silicon as follows: Multiply the weight of the silica found by 7 and divide the result by 15; the quotient will be the weight of the silicon in the amount of substance taken.

Note.—The purity of silica can always be tested in the following manner: Brush the insoluble residue into a weighed platinum crucible, moisten with pure concentrated sulphuric acid, and add one gramme of ammonium fluoride. Place the lid on the crucible and incline it in its support; then heat gently by a burner or spirit-lamp, allowing the flame to play around the top of the crucible. Continue this heating (it should always be performed under a hood with a good draught) until all the sulphuric acid is expelled. Then heat the crucible strongly, removing the cover towards the last of the operation, cool and weigh the crucible, and repeat the operation, if necessary, until the crucible ceases to lose weight. The loss in weight represents the silica expelled as silicon fluoride, and if the silica as previously determined was pure, should equal its weight. Whatever remains in the crucible, if anything, may be alumina, barium sulphate, ferric oxide, etc. If these constituents are to be determined, they may be obtained in solution, with the exception of barium, by fusing with acid potassium sulphate.

Titaniferous Ores.—Many iron ores, especially magnetites, contain considerable quantities of titanium. None of the above methods will serve to thoroughly decompose such ores. The following method, proposed by Dr. Drown,* is in general use: Fuse 1 gramme of ore in a platinum crucible with sodium carbonate. Dissolve in warm water and hydrochloric acid, and after solution is effected add an excess of sulphuric acid (40 cc.) and evaporate until all the hydrochloric acid is driven off, thus rendering the silica insoluble. Dissolve the ferrous sulphate in water and hydrochloric acid, heat to effect solution, filter, wash with warm water and hydrochloric acid, ignite, and weigh the silica.

Note.—The best Swedish and German filter-papers, such as Schleicher & Schuell's c. p. paper, leave such a small quantity of ash after ignition that the weight of the filter-ash may be disregarded when this paper is used. Should pure filter-paper not be at hand, the ash of the paper should be determined as follows: Place about six pieces of the paper to be used in a glass funnel, and wash with warm water containing several cubic centimetres of hydrochloric acid. After washing, roll the paper together, place in a crucible, dry, ignite, and weigh. From the total weight calculate the weight of one piece of paper. The weight thus obtained should be deducted from the combined weights of the silica and filter-ash in each determination.

Bauxite.—As this mineral frequently contains titanium, a method for its separation must be adopted in determining the value of an ore and its silica contents. Fuse 0.5 gm. of the finely pulverized mineral with potassium bisulphate in a covered platinum crucible. Dissolve the fused mass in hot water, filter, wash, dry, ignite, and weigh. Treat this residue with hydrofluoric acid, and should a residue remain after expelling the silica, weigh it and deduct this weight from the weight of the insoluble residue as obtained, the difference being the weight of the silica.†

---

* Transactions of the American Institute of Mining Engineers, Vol. X, p. 143.
† Mineral Resources of the U. S. 1892. Washington, 1893.

CHAPTER II.

SULPHUR (S).

WHILST there are a great many methods in use for the determination of sulphur in ores, furnace products, etc., the author must confess, after having tried a great number of different methods, that he has not as yet found a method which is accurate and at the same time rapid.

Fahlberg-Iles' Modified Method.—This method was first proposed by M. W. Iles * for the determination of sulphur in certain organic compounds which are extremely difficult to decompose by ordinary means, such as treatment with acids or an ordinary fusion. It consists in decomposing the substances by fusion with caustic alkali, subsequent solution of the fused mass in water, oxidation of the sulphur, and determination as barium sulphate. The method is largely used for the determination of sulphur in ores and furnace products,† and is accurate if the precaution is taken to remove all of the silica which the solution may contain before addition of the barium solution. This is a precaution which is not mentioned by the author of this method or by any of the text-books, but is a precaution which the writer has found by numerous experiments to be essential, owing to the fact that if the silica is not removed a large portion of it will be precipitated together with the barium sulphate and be weighed as such. The method as modified by the writer is as follows:

Fuse 1.0 gramme of substance with from one to two sticks of potassium hydrate (the c. p. caustic potash by alcohol should

---

* School of Mines Quarterly; American Chemical Journal; etc.
† School of Mines Quarterly.

be used, as any other generally contains sulphur. It should always be tested for sulphur, to be sure that it contains none) in a silver crucible (a crucible lined with gold is preferable, as the alkali generally attacks the silver of the crucible to a slight extent) over a spirit-lamp. The best method of making the fusion is to place the potassium hydrate in the crucible and heat over the spirit-lamp (gas cannot be used, as it always contains sulphur compounds) to quiet fusion. Then remove the lamp from underneath the crucible, brush the substance into it, and heat for from 5 to 30 minutes until the substance is thoroughly decomposed. Remove the crucible and allow it to cool; as soon as cold dissolve the mass out with warm water into a beaker, and when it is all transferred to the beaker bring its contents to a boil and filter through a ribber filter-paper. Wash with boiling water until the washings come through free from sulphides or sulphates. Add from 20 cc. to 40 cc. of bromine water to the filtrate and heat to about 90 degrees C., and then acidify with hydrochloric acid. If the substance contains silica, it will now be in solution, and must be removed by evaporating the solution to dryness, heating and dissolving with water and hydrochloric acid, and filtering off the silica thus rendered insoluble. (See Chapter I.)

To the filtrate from the silica, after boiling, add a solution of boiling barium chloride until all of the sulphur is precipitated as barium sulphate. By heating the solution of barium chloride, before adding it to the solution, the barium sulphate is precipitated almost immediately, which is not the case if a cold solution of barium salt is used. After the addition of the barium chloride the solution is brought to a boil and then removed to a warm place and allowed to settle. After settling, it is filtered, washed thoroughly with boiling water, and then with a few drops of dilute hydrochloric acid dropped around the edge of the paper and again twice with hot water. It should be washed until the washings no longer give a precipitate with silver-nitrate solution.

The precipitate is now dried, together with the filter-paper, and when dry transferred to a crucible by inverting the filter-paper in the crucible and gently rolling in the fingers. (See Chapter XXV, Barium.) The crucible should be placed on a large clean watch-glass so that any particles which may fly outside of the crucible can be recovered. After all that is possible is removed from the filter-paper, it is rolled up and placed on the lid of a platinum crucible and burned by holding the platinum over the flame of a burner or spirit-lamp. The ash of the filter-paper is then added to the contents of the crucible, and the whole ignited in the muffle or over the blast-lamp. The crucible is then cooled and its contents should be found perfectly white. The precipitate is now transferred from the crucible to the watch-glass of the balance and weighed. The weight of the barium sulphate, less the known weight of the filter-ash, multiplied by 0.13734, will be the weight of the sulphur present in the amount of substance taken.

When silica is not present the evaporation to dryness of the filtrate from the solution of the fusion can be omitted, thus greatly shortening the method. This method is universal in its application, but unfortunately requires considerable time, owing to the time required to evaporate the solution to dryness, and drive off the free hydrochloric acid for the precipitation of the silica, which must be conducted slowly on account of the large amount of salts present. When evaporation to dryness is not necessary, a determination may be made in less than an hour and a half.

Second Method.—The following method is frequently used in lead- and copper-smelting works for the determination of sulphur, and whilst it is not as accurate as the method previously described, it has the advantage of being rapid, and consequently would be used where time for an accurate determination is not available:

Treat one gramme of ore in a flask (about 200 cc. capacity) with three to four grammes of potassium chlorate and 7 cc. of nitric acid, the acid being added as follows: About 3 cc. at first, and then 1 cc. from time to time. When all the acid has been added, heat to boiling on a sand-bath and evaporate off the excess of acid. All but about 2 cc. of acid should be expelled. The potassium chlorate and nitric acid oxidize the sulphur in the ore, and in the case of a heavy sulphide more potassium chlorate may be necessary. The solution, after boiling, should show no undecomposed particles of sulphides and no globules of yellow sulphur, which will sometimes form if the oxidation has been imperfect. Remove from the source of heat, dilute with about 50 cc. of water, and add a saturated solution of sodium carbonate in excess. The sodium carbonate precipitates the lead, iron, etc., and the excess is added to decompose the sulphates of lead and calcium which may have formed during solution. Boil for from thirty minutes to one hour, adding water from time to time to keep the bulk of the solution about the same. Filter through a fluted filter into a beaker, and wash until the washings no longer show the presence of sulphuric acid. Acidify the filtrate with hydrochloric acid, and boil to expel the carbonic acid. When the carbonic acid is all expelled the solution is ready for the precipitation of the sulphuric acid with barium-chloride solution, and the determination of the barium sulphate as before. If the ore contains barium sulphate it will remain undecomposed with the precipitate of mixed carbonates.

Matte Fusion.—The writer has frequently had occasion to make use of this method to obtain data upon which to calculate a furnace charge when time was wanting in which to make an accurate sulphur determination.

This assay is made in order to determine the amount of sulphur, or matte-forming material, which an ore contains. It is at best only an approximation, but generally gives a result which is a sufficiently close approximation to the actual amount of matte which an ore will produce in the blast-furnace to be of value for metallurgical purposes. It has the advantage of being a rapid method, which is frequently of the utmost importance in a smelting-works. This method takes about 20 minutes, whilst a sulphur determination in the wet way, even within reasonably close limits, cannot be made in much less than an hour and a quarter.

A charge which will generally give very good results is as follows:

Ore.............................	5	grammes.
Borax glass.....................	15	"
Charcoal........................	3	"

One or two nails, points down.

The charge is thoroughly mixed in an ordinary clay crucible and placed in the furnace, the time of fusion with a hot fire being about 15 minutes. After the fusion is complete the crucible is removed from the furnace, the nails drawn out, and the assay poured. As soon as the cone is cool it is removed from the mould and the slag broken off from the matte button, which is then weighed and the percentage calculated. In the case of a lead ore a lead button will also be found below the matte, but this is easily separated from the matte button. The matte button may be generally considered as containing about 30 per cent sulphur, although the amount of sulphur which it will contain will vary somewhat, according to the nature of the ore. Theoretically the button should contain 36.3 per cent sulphur, matte being considered as FeS. However, a pure matte is seldom produced, as the ores generally contain impurities such as zinc, copper, lead, arsenic, antimony, etc. A number of analyses of matte buttons produced in this way show that an average of 30 per cent sulphur is reasonably close.

Volumetric Method.—The following volumetric method was suggested by Alexander's method for the determination of lead (see Part II, Chapter VIII). The method requires a standard solution of ammonium molybdate, which is prepared by dissolving 30.7 gms. of ammonium molybdate in water and diluting to 1000 cc. Each cc. of this solution should be equivalent to 0.005 gm. of sulphur. To standardize the solution weigh out two portions of from 0.3 to 0.5 gm. of pure sheet lead, dissolve in a few cc. of dilute nitric acid, add a slight excess of sulphuric acid, and boil to drive off the nitric acid. Cool, add a slight excess of ammonia, and then strong acetic acid in excess. Heat to dissolve the lead sulphate and dilute with hot water to about 180 cc., when the solution is ready for titration with the molybdate solution. The molybdate solution is run in from a burette with constant stirring, and a drop of the solution tested from time to time on a porcelain plate with a drop of a solution of tannin. As soon as the molybdate solution is in slight excess the drop of the solution added to the tannin solution will turn it yellow, when the titration is finished. From the amount of lead taken and the number of cc. of molybdate solution used, the value of the solution in terms of sulphur may be calculated as follows: Suppose 0.3 gm. of lead was taken and 10 cc. of molybdate solution was used to precipitate the lead. Then 1 cc. of molybdate solution is equivalent to 0.03 gm. of lead, or to 0.043913 gm. of lead sulphate, and as lead sulphate contains 10.56 per cent sulphur, its equivalent in S may be calculated by the factor 0.1056; the equivalent in this case being 1 cc. = 0.004637 +.

To determine sulphur in an ore or metallurgical product by this method the ore may be decomposed and the sulphur obtained in solution by fusion with caustic potash as described, by treatment with nitric acid and chlorate of potash and subsequent treatment with sodium carbonate as described, or by fusion in a porcelain or platinum crucible with a mixture of sodium carbonate and potassium nitrate.

Where fusion with caustic potash is the method employed the fused mass is dissolved in hot water and filtered, hydrogen peroxide being added to the filtrate to oxidize the potassium sulphide. The solution is then heated and acidified with a *slight* excess of nitric acid. To the hot solution add an excess of a solution of lead nitrate, allow to stand until the precipitated lead sulphate settles and filter, retaining as much as possible of the lead sulphate in the beaker. Wash by decantation with cold water until the washings no longer give a reaction for lead. Dissolve the lead sulphate in hot ammonium acetate, acidify with acetic acid and titrate with the standard ammonium molybdate solution.

In case the nitric acid-potassium chlorate method is used,

acidify the filtrate from the precipitated carbonates with a slight excess of nitric acid, boil out the carbonic acid, precipitate the sulphuric acid with lead nitrate, and proceed as above.

In case fusion with mixed carbonate of soda and potassium nitrate is the method adopted, to each gramme of substance taken add about 10 gms. of the mixed salts and fuse until the mass is liquid. Cool and dissolve the fused mass in hot water. Filter, acidify the filtrate with nitric acid, boil to drive out carbonic acid, precipitate the sulphuric acid with lead nitrate, and proceed as above.

In all cases the reagents used should be examined for sulphur, as they are liable to contain sulphates. If pure reagents cannot be obtained a blank analysis should be run, using the same quantity of reagents as in the regular analysis, and deducting the amount of sulphur found in the blank analysis from that found in the regular analysis.

In the case of ores, etc., containing but a small percentage of sulphur, it is advisable to use a more dilute solution of ammonium molybdate. Having made up the solution and standardized it as described, a solution of any desired strength can be readily prepared by drawing off a definite quantity of the standardized solution and diluting it with water to any desired strength.

Iron and Steel.—The following rapid method for the determination of sulphur in iron and steel is quite accurate, and is extensively used in metallurgical works for technical determinations. Many modifications of the method have been proposed, but the two following are believed to be as good and rapid as any. The method was originally suggested by Karsten, and depends upon the principle that, if iron or steel is dissolved in dilute hydrochloric or sulphuric acid, H_2S is evolved. The evolved H_2S may subsequently be absorbed in a solution of a metallic salt.

The cut, Fig. 13, shows the usual arrangement of apparatus for carrying out the decomposition and absorption. The wash bottle A contains an alkaline solution of lead nitrate.

The generator *G* is used for generating hydrogen gas. The funnel-tube *C* is tightly connected with *A*. The small flask *E* serves as a condenser, and is supplied with an inlet-tube reaching

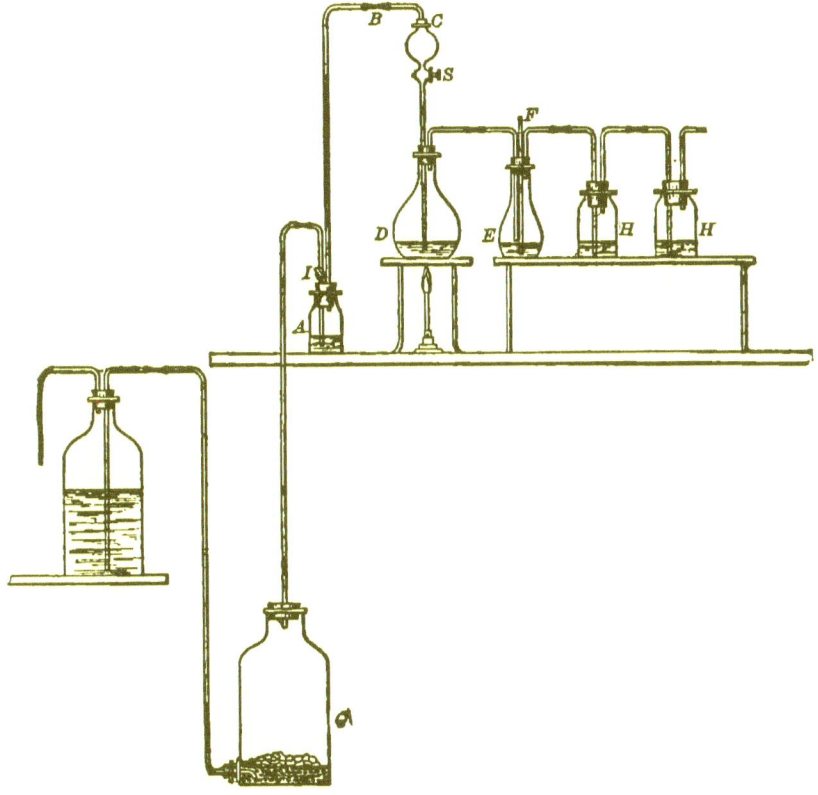

FIG. 13.*

almost to the surface of a small amount of water in the bottom of the flask, a safety-tube *F* reaching just below the surface of the water, and an exit-tube connected with the first of the wide-mouthed bottles *H*. In each of the bottles *H* is poured from 20 cc. to 30 cc. of the absorbent solution, and sufficient water to fill them more than half full.

Into the previously dried flask *D* are introduced 10 gms. of the drillings, free from lumps. The apparatus is now con-

* From Blair's Chemical Analysis of Iron and Steel.

nected up, and a slow stream of hydrogen run through it until all the air is expelled, when the glass stop-cock S is closed and the supply of hydrogen is shut off by closing the glass stop-cock L. If the connections are all right the water in the safety-tube F will keep its level. When this is assured, disconnect the tube C and fill the bulb with 50 cc. of strong hydrochloric acid and 50 cc. of water. Replace the tube C, turn on the hydrogen, and open the stop-cock S so as to allow the acid to flow into the flask D, drop by drop. When the acid has all run into D regulate the supply of hydrogen so that the gas will continue to pass through the solutions in the bottles H at the rate of 6 to 8 bubbles a second, and heat the contents of the flask D cautiously. Finally, heat the solution in the flask D to boiling, and boil for a few minutes. When the metal in the flask is completely dissolved, remove the source of heat and continue the current of hydrogen for about ten minutes, regulating its flow by means of the stop-cock L, to prevent any reflux of the liquid in H, which might be caused by the cooling of D. Shut off the hydrogen, disconnect the apparatus, and wash the contents of the bottle H into a beaker.

Many methods of proceeding with the analysis, according to the absorbent used, have been proposed, for which see " The Chemical Analysis of Iron and Steel," by Blair.

Absorption by Ammoniacal Solution of Cadmium Sulphate.—T. T. Morrell [*] proposes to absorb the H_2S in a solution of cadmium sulphate prepared by adding ammonia to a solution of sulphate of cadmium until the precipitate formed redissolves and the solution is clear. This solution is placed in the bottles H, H, and the analysis conducted as described. The precipitated cadmium sulphide is filtered off, and washed with water containing a little ammonia. The filter containing the precipitated cadmium sulphide is now placed in a beaker containing a little cold water, and sufficient hydrochloric acid to dissolve the precipitate is added. The sulphur may now be determined by titration with standard iodine solution.

---

[*] Chemical News, Vol. XXVIII, p. 229.

The method of determining the sulphur by standard iodine solution was first suggested by Elliott* and requires the following solutions:

Iodine Solution.—Dissolve 6.5 gms. of pure iodine in water with 9 gms. of potassium iodide, and dilute to 1000 cc.

Hyposulphite of Sodium Solution.—Dissolve 25 gms. of sodium hyposulphite in water, add 2 gms. of ammonium carbonate, and dilute to 1000 cc. The addition of ammonium carbonate retards the decomposition of the sodium hyposulphite.

Starch Solution.—Place 1 gm. of pure wheat starch in a porcelain mortar and rub into a thin cream with water. Pour into 150 cc. of boiling water, allow to stand until cold, and decant the clear solution. A fresh solution should be prepared every few days.

Bichromate of Potassium Solution.—Dissolve 5 gms. of pure potassium bichromate in water and dilute to 1000 cc.

The bichromate solution is standardized as described in the determination of iron (Part II, Chapter XVI). When a solution of potassium bichromate is added to a solution of potassium iodide containing free hydrochloric acid, iodine is liberated as follows:

$$K_2Cr_2O_7 + 6KI + 14HCl = 8KCl + Cr_2Cl_6 + 7H_2O + 6I.$$

Or, 1 equivalent of $K_2Cr_2O_7$ ($= 294.5$) liberates 6 equivalents ($= 761.1$) of iodine. When a solution of hyposulphite of sodium is added to a solution containing free iodine the following reaction takes place:

$$2NaHS_2O_3 + 2I = 2HI + Na_2S_4O_6.$$

By adding a few drops of starch solution to a solution containing iodine, blue iodide of starch is formed, and colors the solution as long as it contains free iodine. When sufficient hyposulphite is added to such a solution to exactly combine with the iodine, the blue color disappears. Conversely, upon

---

* Chemical News, Vol. XXIII, p. 61.

the addition of a solution of iodine to a solution containing hyposulphite of sodium and a little starch, the blue color of the iodide of starch will disappear as fast as formed until all the triosulphate has been converted into tetrathionate, and then the slightest excess of iodine will give the solution a permanent blue color. The same is true of a solution containing free H_2S, the reaction being $H_2S + 2I = 2HI + S$. To standardize the hyposulphite solution proceed as follows: Dissolve 1 gm. of pure potassium iodide in 300 cc. of water, add 5 cc of hydrochloric acid, and then 25 c.c. of the standardized bichromate solution, which will liberate a known amount of iodine. Now add from a burette the hyposulphite solution until the blue color nearly disappears, add a few drops of starch solution, and continue the addition of the hyposulphite solution until the blue color disappears entirely. The amount of iodine being known, the value of the hyposulphite solution is readily calculated from the reading of the burette. Now measure off into a beaker 25 cc. of the hyposulphite solution, dilute to 300 cc., add a few drops of starch solution, and run in, from a burette, standard iodine solution until the blue color is permanent. The value of the hyposulphite solution being known, that of the iodine solution can be readily calculated. (See Part IV, Chapter II.)

Having prepared and standardized the solutions the actual determination is performed by titrating the solution containing the sulphur with the standard iodine solution in the manner just described.

Absorption by Alkaline Solution of Lead Nitrate. —To prepare the solution pour a cold solution of nitrate of lead into a solution of potassium hydrate (1.27 sp. gr.), stirring constantly to dissolve the oxide of lead, which precipitates. Continue the addition of lead nitrate until a permanent precipitate is formed. Allow the precipitate to settle, and siphon the clear liquid into a glass-stoppered bottle. To prevent the stopper sticking, coat it with a little paraffine.

From 20 to 30 cc. of this solution is poured into the bottles H, H, and water added until the bottles are more than half full. The decomposition and absorption are conducted as previously described. When the operation is completed rinse out the bottle H (should the second bottle contain a precipitate this must be added to the contents of the first) into a beaker and filter, washing with hot water until the washings no longer give a reaction for lead when treated with a drop of acetic acid and potassium-chromate solution. Transfer the lead sulphide to a beaker, and dissolve in a little dilute nitric acid, being careful to use as little acid as possible. Add a slight excess of sulphuric acid and boil. Dilute with hot water, add a slight excess of ammonia, and then a slight excess of strong acetic acid. The lead sulphate will be dissolved, when the solution is ready for titration with standard solution of ammonium molybdate, after dilution to about 180 cc. with hot water. The lead is precipitated as a molybdate, and the end reaction obtained by means of a solution of tannin, in the manner described in the volumetric determinations of sulphur and lead. Having the standard of the molybdate solution in terms of lead, its standard for sulphur may be obtained by the factor 0.1548.

Generally the carbonaceous residue left after treating pig-iron with hydrochloric acid will contain sufficient sulphur to seriously affect the results of the analysis. Hence where an accurate determination of sulphur in pig-iron is required the examination of the carbonaceous residue should never be neglected when the evolution method is employed. To determine the sulphur in this residue transfer the contents of flask D to a beaker and filter, using the filter-pump and platinum cone and a strong filter-paper; wash thoroughly, first with a little dilute hydrochloric acid, and finally with water. Dry the residue on the filter, and determine the sulphur by some of the methods previously described, preferably by fusion.

CHAPTER III.

PHOSPHORUS (P).

A number of different methods have been proposed for the determination of phosphorus in iron ores, pig-iron, steel, etc., but the volumetric method, as described below, and the standard gravimetric method are the only ones in general use at present in the United States.

Volumetric Method.—This method, as originally described by Mr. B. B. Wright,* and improved by Mr. F. A. Emmerton,† is applicable for phosphorus determinations in ores, steel, etc., and the writer believes is as rapid and accurate, provided the necessary precautions are observed, as any method which we have. It is rapidly being adopted by our iron and steel chemists as a standard method.

Steels, Pig and Wrought Iron.—Dissolve 5 grammes of drillings in a dish (about 6 inches in diameter) in 75 cc. of nitric acid of 1.20 sp. gr., cover the dish with a watch-glass, placed on a glass triangle so that there is a space between the rim of the dish and the watch-glass, and boil down to dryness on the sand-bath or hot iron plate. Heat on the plate or bath for about 30 minutes after the mass has gone to dryness, at the end of which time all the free acid should have been expelled. Remove from the source of heat, cool, and add 40 cc. of concentrated hydrochloric acid, and place the watch-glass on the casserole. Heat gently until the iron goes into solution, and then boil down until all but about 15 cc. of the acid is driven off. The boiling down of the solution requires attention, as it

---

* Transactions of American Institute of Mining Engineers, Vol. X, page 197.
† Ibid., Vol. XV, page 93.

is necessary that the solution should be very concentrated, and at the same time there should be very little ferric chloride dried on the sides of the casserole, as this will be difficult to redissolve. Let the casserole cool, wash off the watch-glass with 40 cc. of concentrated nitric acid, allowing the acid to run down into the casserole. Cover the casserole with a glass funnel, and boil down to about 15 cc. in bulk. Remove the casserole from the source of heat, and move its contents so as to moisten whatever crust may have formed on the sides. The solution is now practically free from hydrochloric acid, and should be diluted with water and washed into a 400-cc. flask, bringing the bulk of it to about 75 cc. Add strong ammonia, shaking thoroughly after each addition. Continue to add ammonia until the mass sets to a stiff jelly, and add a few cc. more. There should be a strong smell of ammonia in excess after shaking. Then add concentrated nitric acid, shaking well after each addition, until the solution begins to get thinner. After the precipitate has all dissolved, and the solution shows a very dark color, add sufficient nitric acid to bring the solution to a clear amber color. The solution should now have a bulk of about 250 cc. Immerse a thermometer into the solution, and heat or cool carefully until it has a temperature of $85°$ C. When the solution has a temperature of $85°$ C. add 40 cc. of ammonium-molybdate solution (prepared by dissolving 100 grammes of molybdic acid in a mixture of 300 cc. of strong ammonia and 100 cc. of water, and pouring this solution into 1250 cc. of nitric acid of 1.20 sp. gr.). Close the flask with a stopper, wrap it in a thick-warm cloth, and shake violently for 5 minutes. This covering with a cloth is necessary, as the temperature of the solution must not vary much from $85°$ C. Collect the yellow precipitate on a filter, using the filter-pump to filter rapidly, and wash the flask and precipitate with a solution of ammonium sulphate [$(NH_4)_2SO_4$ crystals, 25 grammes; H_2SO_4 conc., 50 cc.; H_2O, 2500 cc.]. Dissolve the washed precipitate in ammonia. If a small portion of the precipitate should adhere to the sides of the flask it may be dissolved with a portion of the ammonia used to dissolve the yellow precipitate on the filter. Place about 10 grammes of granulated zinc (the same as is used in the determination of iron; see Chapter XVI) in a 500-cc. flask, place the funnel containing the yellow precipitate in the neck of the flask, and wash the precipitate into the flask with dilute ammonia (1 in 4), using about 30 cc. A larger amount of ammonia than is absolutely necessary is to be avoided. After having washed with ammonia wash twice with water, and suck dry by means of the filter-pump. Pour the ammonia solution into a small beaker, reinsert the funnel in the flask, and pour the solution in the beaker through the filter again, washing the paper thoroughly with water after the ammonia solution has all run through, finally sucking the filter dry with the pump. Pour into the flask about 80 cc. of warm dilute sulphuric acid (1 in 4), and heat quickly until rapid solution of the zinc commences, and then gently stir for 10 to 15 minutes, at the end of which time the reduction of the molybdic acid is complete. Filter the liquid from the undissolved zinc through a large fluted filter, rinse the flask with cold water, pouring on to the filter. After these washings have run through, rinse the flask once more with cold water, pouring on to the filter again. The filtration should be rapid, so as to expose the solution to the air as short a time as possible.

The filtrate is now ready for titration with a standard solution of potassium permanganate. The permanganate solution is run in until the solution is colorless, it having been of a dark olive-green color before oxidation. One drop of permanganate solution should now produce a pink tint when the titration is stopped and the reading of the burette taken. A convenient strength to have the permanganate solution is 1 cc. $= 0.0001$ gramme of phosphorus. Such a solution may be made by diluting the solution used for iron (Chapter III) with distilled water until 1 cc. $= 0.006141$ gramme iron. As 0.9076 time this value gives its strength in terms of molybdic acid $= 0.005574$, and 1.794 per cent of this is its value in phosphorus $= 0.0001$.

In order to insure good results with this method the above conditions as to temperature, etc., must be carried out.

Dr. Drown* has proposed a method of effecting the solution of a pig-iron or steel which greatly lessens the time required. His method is as follows: Dissolve the weighed drillings in nitric acid of 1.135 sp. gr., and allow to boil one minute; then add potassium-permanganate solution until a precipitate of MnO_2 appears. Now add a few crystals of ferrous sulphate (should be tested for phosphorus, as the usual c. p. salt contains more or less. The phosphorus free salt can be purchased of Baker & Adamson, Easton, Pa.) to dissolve the precipitated MnO_2. Filter the solution into the flask, and add sufficient ammonia. When the solution clears up, add a few drops of permanganate solution to insure complete oxidation, again dissolving with ferrous sulphate if necessary. Precipitate with ammonium-molybdate solution, proceeding as above, and using the same precautions.

A modification of the above method has been proposed by Handy,† which consists in the determination of the acidity of the molybdate precipitate in place of reducing the molybdic acid and titrating with permanganate. The following solutions are required:

Standard Sodium Hydrate.—Dissolve 15.4 grammes of NaOH in 100 cc. of water, stir in saturated barium-hydrate solution until a precipitate of barium carbonate is no longer formed. Filter immediately, and dilute to two litres.

Standard Nitric Acid.—Make a stock solution of 200 cc. of acid (sp. gr. 1.42) in two litres of water. For approximate standard dilute 200 cc. of this solution to two litres.

These two solutions should be made to agree cc. for cc., and had also best be brought to a strength of 1 cc., equal to 0.0002 gramme of phosphorus.

The sodium-hydrate solution is standardized by 0.1 gramme of pure molybdate precipitate obtained from acidified ammo-

---

* Transactions of American Institute of Mining Engineers, Vol. XVIII.
† Journal of Analytical and Applied Chemistry, Vol. VI, p. 204.

nium or sodium phosphate, washed with one per cent nitric acid, and thoroughly dried at 100° C. The precipitate contains 1.63 per cent phosphorus.

As an indicator, 0.5 gramme of phenolphthalein in 200 cc. of 95 per cent alcohol is used. Three drops of this solution are taken for each titration.

The method is as follows: Dissolve 2 grammes of steel in a 12-ounce Erlenmeyer flask in 75 cc. of nitric acid (sp. gr. 1.13), and add 15 cc. of potassium-permanganate solution (5 grammes in 1000 cc.) to the boiling solution. Boil until the pink color disappears. If brown MnO_2 separates, the oxidation is complete. Some irons and steels will require more permanganate, especially those high in carbon. Remove momentarily from the heat, add about $\frac{1}{30}$ gramme of granulated sugar, and heat until the solution clears. Allow to cool for a few minutes and then add 13 cc. of ammonia (sp. gr. 0.90), pouring carefully down the sides. Agitate until the ferric hydrate is dissolved, and cool or heat to 85° C. Add 50 cc. of the molybdate solution, cork, wrap the flask in a towel, and shake for five minutes. Filter immediately, wash five times with a one per cent solution of nitric acid, and then five times with a one per cent solution of potassium nitrate. Place the filter and its contents in the flask, add 10 to 20 cc. of the standard sodium-hydrate solution, and shake a few times to dissolve the precipitate. Add three drops of the indicator solution and titrate back with the standard nitric-acid solution. The titration must be performed quickly, and as soon as the precipitate is completely dissolved.

Iron Ores.—Dissolve from 2 to 10 grammes of ore in hydrochloric acid (sp. gr. 1.12), and proceed as above. The insoluble residue can be filtered off and fused with sodium carbonate (see Part II, Chapter I) if necessary, the fused mass being dissolved in dilute sulphuric acid, and the solution added to the nitric-acid solution.

Coal and Coke.—The phosphorus will be found in the ash. Weigh out 10 grammes of the coal or coke, and ignite it over the blast-lamp or in the muffle-furnace until nothing but ash remains. Fuse the ash with sodium carbonate, and proceed as above.

In the case of ores or pig-iron containing arsenic the arsenic will be precipitated, together with the phosphorus, upon the addition of the molydate solution, as above. In this case if the temperature of the solution is not above $25°$ C.,[*] when the molybdate solution is added the arsenic will remain in solution, whilst the phosphorus will be completely precipitated. As the steel metallurgists consider arsenic quite as detrimental to the quality of the pig as phosphorus this precaution is not usually taken.

Gravimetric Method.—Proceed as above until the yellow precipitate is obtained, filtered, and washed, such care in regard to the temperature of the solution before adding the molybdate solution being unnecessary in this case. Dissolve the yellow precipitate with ammonia as before, filtering into a beaker; make the solution acid with dilute hydrochloric acid and then alkaline with ammonia in excess; cool, and when cold add 5 cc. of magnesia mixture. Allow to stand in a cool place for several hours with frequent agitation (see Part II, Chapter XXIV); finally filter, wash, ignite, and weigh as in the case of the determination of magnesia.

The weight of the magnesia pyrophosphate obtained, multiplied by 0.27928, equals the weight of phosphorus in the amount of substance taken.

---

[*] Transactions of the American Institute of Mining Engineers, Feb., 1893.

CHAPTER IV.

CARBON (C).

FOR the determination of carbon in organic substances the reader is referred to works that treat of such determinations.

The determinations of carbon in steel, pig-iron, etc., are about the only determinations of carbon which the metallurgical chemist will be called upon to make, except the determination of carbon in fuels, for which the reader is referred to Part III, Chapter X.

The carbon in steel, pig-iron, etc., usually exists in two conditions; that is, combined (as a carbide) and uncombined (graphite). Usually the combined carbon is all that is required. When the percentage of carbon in both conditions is required, the total carbon is determined in one portion and the combined carbon in another. The difference between the total amount of carbon and the combined carbon gives the graphite. Or the graphite may be determined, the difference between the amount of graphite found and the total carbon being the combined carbon.

Many methods for these determinations have been proposed, but only those that are known to be good and are in general use will be given.

Total Carbon.—The following method, which was first proposed by Arthur Elliot,[*] is a modification of Rodger's and Ullgren's methods. It is believed to be among the best in use.[†] Add to 2 or 3 grammes of borings or filings in a small beaker 50 cc. of a solution of neutral copper sulphate, prepared

---

[*] Chemical News, May, 1869.
[†] American Chemist, October, 1871. Also Cairns, page 105.

by dissolving the recrystallized copper sulphate (as sold by dealers) in water, adding a small quantity of copper oxide, boiling until the copper sulphate begins to crystallize, filtering out the excess of oxide, and concentrating the solution until it is completely crystallized. Dry the crystals by draining off the water, and pressing them between layers of bibulous paper, and dissolve them in water in the proportion of 1 part of salt to 5 parts of water.

After heating the solution of copper sulphate containing the iron about 10 minutes, by which means the iron is dissolved and the copper precipitated, add 20 cc. of a solution of cupric chloride (containing one part of salt in two parts of water) and 50 cc. of concentrated hydrochloric acid, and heat to a point just below boiling, with frequent stirring until the precipitated copper is dissolved, leaving the carbon free. Filter out the carbon through a funnel made of glass tubing about five eighths of an inch in diameter, and drawn to a point at one end. Fill the point of the funnel up to the shoulder with broken glass, and place upon this a thin layer of ignited asbestos, pressing it gently against the walls of the funnel. Care should be taken not to make the layer of asbestos too thick or compact, as it is liable to become clogged by the carbon and render the filtration very tedious. Filter off into a clean beaker, and should any carbon run through, as it is liable to at first if the asbestos layer is too thin, pour back the first filtrate into the filter. Transfer all of the carbon to the filter, and wash with hot water until the washings no longer give a precipitate with silver nitrate. After washing all of the carbon down from the sides of the tube, cut it off about an inch above the layer of carbon, by scratching the glass with a file, and pressing a red-hot glass against the cut. Then invert the part containing the carbon into the mouth of the decomposing flask of an apparatus similar to that described for determining carbonic acid * (see Part II, Chapter V), and blow the contents into the flask, avoiding the use of water by wiping out any carbon that may adhere to

---

* See Cairns' Quantitative Analysis, page 35.

the glass with a little piece of ignited asbestos, and throwing this also into the flask. To the filtrate from the carbon add 4 or 5 cc. of concentrated hydrochloric acid to prevent the formation of any precipitate of basic copper salt, and dilute with water until the fluid is transparent. If any carbon should have passed through the asbestos it can readily be seen in the transparent fluid. Should there be any filter it out through another filter of ignited asbestos and transfer it also to the flask. Connect the apparatus, and start the aspirator very slowly. After the aspirator has been working about 12 minutes, disconnect the absorption-tube and weigh it. Then connect again and start the aspirator very slowly again. After the aspirator has run a few minutes in order to partially exhaust the air in the apparatus, introduce through the funnel-tube about 40 cc. of the chromic-acid solution.

This solution is prepared by dissolving 3 gms. of chromic acid in a little water and adding 30 cc. of pure concentrated sulphuric acid. This should be heated to incipient boiling and then cooled. When cold it is ready for use.

After adding this solution close the stop-cock of the funnel-tube and heat slowly up to boiling. After the acid boils remove the heat, put on the guard-tube, open the stop-cock of the funnel-tube, and aspirate slowly until the absorption-tube is cool. After it is thoroughly cooled weigh it, and from the increase in weight due to the carbonic acid (CO_2) calculate as follows: The weight of the carbonic acid multiplied by 0.27273 equals the weight of carbon.

In place of the copper sulphate and copper chloride, the double chloride of copper and ammonium may be used. The same precautions should be observed as in the determination of carbonic acid by direct weight. Some chemists prefer to burn the carbon obtained in the above manner in a current of oxygen in a piece of combustion-tubing, absorbing the resulting carbonic acid in an absorption-tube similar to the one used above, or in a potash bulb.* (See Part III, Chapter X.)

---

* American Chemist, Vol. VI, September, 1875.

Graphite.—The best and safest method is that described by Cairns * as follows: Dissolve from 2 to 3 grammes of gray pig-iron or from 4 to 5 grammes of white iron, steel, etc., in dilute hydrochloric acid and boil for half an hour, filter through asbestos as described for total carbon, wash with hot water until all acid is washed out, then with a strong solution of potassium hydrate, which will remove silica; afterwards with hot water to wash out any potassium carbonate, of which the potassium hydrate is apt to contain some; then with alcohol (which will remove hydrocarbons), until the alcohol runs through the funnel colorless. Again wash with a little hot water, then with ether, until it runs through colorless, in order to displace the water and remove another class of hydrocarbons which the alcohol may have failed to reach. It is well, finally, to wash with a little hot water (particularly if the ether used is not perfectly pure), in order to keep the graphite from adhering to the walls of the funnel, when blown into the decomposing flask, being careful to remove any excess of water by gently blowing through the funnel. After the graphite is thoroughly washed it is transferred to the decomposing flask, and oxidized with chromic and sulphuric acids, in precisely the same manner as in the determination of total carbon.

The objection to this method is the time required to filter and wash, the washings with potassium hydrate being extremely tedious.

Eggerz's modified method † is as follows: In a beaker of 100 cc. capacity mix 4 cc. of sulphuric acid and 20 cc. of water, and when the heat produced by the combination of the water and the acid has entirely disappeared, shake 2 grammes of the finely powdered pig-iron into the dilute acid, and boil for half an hour. (For steel and wrought iron not less than 3 grammes should be taken, and the acid for solution should be increased in proportion.) The solution is then evaporated until it measures 18 cc., allowed to cool to the temperature of 50° C., and 4 cc. of nitric acid (of 1.20 sp. gr.) added; boil for a

---

* Cairns' Quantitative Analysis, edition 1881, page 114.
† Crook's Select Methods, pages 79 and 80.

quarter of an hour, and allow to evaporate on a water-bath until on holding a watch-glass over the beaker there occurs on it no perceptible condensation. To the dry mass add 30 cc. of water, and 5 cc. of hydrochloric acid 1.16 sp. gr.; boil for a quarter of an hour, and add more hydrochloric acid if there appears to be anything besides silica and graphite undissolved. The insoluble silica and graphite are thrown on a filter (which has been dried at 100° C. and carefully weighed), washed with cold water until the washings give no reaction for iron when tested with potassium ferrocyanide, then washed with boiling water containing 5 per cent of nitric acid. The silica and graphite are then dried on the filter at 100° C. and weighed, ignited in a porcelain crucible, and the weight carefully taken. The difference between the weighings before and after ignition gives the amount of graphite.

Combined Carbon.—Dr. Eggerz, of the Swedish School of Mines, first proposed a method of determining the combined carbon in steel, etc., by comparing the color of a solution of the iron or steel under examination with that of a solution of another sample of which the carbon percentage was known. This method is based upon the fact that when steel is dissolved in dilute nitric acid, and heated until the separated flocculent carbonaceous matter goes into solution, the liquid assumes a brown color proportionate to the amount of combined carbon present. This method has been modified from time to time by different chemists so that we have at present a method which is not only rapid, but extremely accurate provided the proper precautions are observed. A number of standard solutions for comparison have been proposed, but the best and safest method is to run a standard, together with each set of determinations, using a steel or iron in which the percentage of combined carbon has previously been accurately determined. This standard steel should be as nearly like the samples to be treated as possible, both as to chemical composition and mechanical treatment. Treat the standards and samples to be tested exactly alike in working, the same amounts being taken.* Drillings are preferable to filings, as they are less liable to contain foreign matter, and, being coarser, dissolve more slowly. Fine particles of steel, rich in carbon, dissolve so rapidly that, unless special precautions are taken to keep the solution cold, some of the carbon is oxidized and given off as a gas. From 0.1 to 0.2 gramme are taken for analysis, one tenth being the usual amount in the case of steels.

The weighed portions are best dissolved in perfectly dry (so that no particles will stick to the sides) test-tubes six inches long and about five eighths of an inch internal diameter, the sample being placed in the test-tube, which is then immersed in cold water and the dilute nitric acid then slowly and steadily poured on. A very convenient form of apparatus is a beaker or other vessel about 7 inches high, which is half filled with cold water and covered with a perforated tin plate, through the holes of which the tubes are placed and thus steadied. Nitric acid (free from organic matter, nitrous fumes, and chlorine) of about 1.20 sp. gr. is used to effect solution. The ordinary c. p. nitric acid is 1.40 sp. gr., and by diluting this one half with distilled water an acid of very nearly 1.20 sp. gr. is obtained. It should be kept in a dark glass-stoppered bottle and in a dark place. The following amounts of dilute acid for one-tenth gramme of steel give good results: up to 0.20 per cent carbon, 2 cc. of acid; from 0.20 up to 0.50 per cent carbon, 3 cc.; from 0.50 per cent up to 1.00 per cent carbon, 4 cc.; 1.00 per cent up to 1.75 per cent, 6 cc.; over 1.75 per cent of carbon, 8 cc. The most convenient method of adding the acid is to let it run in from a graduated burette provided with a glass stop-cock.

The solution must not be heated until all action has ceased in the cold, when the cold water in which the tubes are immersed is rapidly brought to a boil and boiled for 15 minutes for soft steels under 0.15 per cent carbon, for 20 minutes if

---

* Transactions of American Institute of Mining Engineers, Vol. XII, page 303.

between 0.15 and 0.30 per cent carbon, for 30 minutes if between 0.30 and 0.80 per cent carbon, and 45 minutes if above 0.80 per cent carbon. The boiling temperature is usually maintained, although for special reasons other temperatures are often used, the essential point being to always maintain the same temperature in all cases where fixed standards are used, and to treat the standard and the steel under examination at exactly the same temperature where standard steels are used for comparison, as is recommended here. Sometimes a reddish-yellow deposit of nitric acid and ferric oxide forms on the sides of the tubes and renders the solution turbid; in such cases a low temperature of about 70° C. is preferable. The water-bath in which the tubes are heated may be provided with a thermometer, and the evaporation of the water may be prevented by the addition of paraffine. The ceasing of the evolution of the fine bubbles of gas from the clear solution is an indication of the completion of the solution. The tubes should be shaken from time to time during the heating, and the iron salt should not be allowed to dry on the walls of the tubes. The color solutions during the entire operation must be kept out of the direct rays of the sunlight, as it rapidly fades them. The color fades more rapidly after dilution with water than it does in the strong acid solution. After heating, the tubes may be cooled rapidly by plunging into cold water. If the percentage of carbon is high (about 1.00 per cent) the solution should not be allowed to stand any length of time before comparison; if the carbon is low they may be allowed to stand at least two hours. However, it is best to cool quickly. After the solution is completed it must be diluted with at least its bulk of water to get rid of the tint of oxide of iron. The color solution, after heating, cooling, and diluting with distilled water, can be filtered from the graphite, etc., through an ordinary dry filter-paper. The quantity of water added, including the distilled water used for cleaning the test-tube, must be at least equal to the quantity of nitric acid used, and the total volume must never be less than 8 cc. when it is to be compared with the standard solution. The solution is filtered directly into a burette or tube for comparison. Tubes of about one half an inch in internal diameter and 30 cc. capacity are preferable, and it is generally preferable to calibrate the tubes by means of an accurately calibrated burette, as those which are purchased calibrated often show errors of considerable importance. The tubes used for the standard and the different determinations should be of exactly the same internal and external diameters, and of colorless glass, and provided with mouth-pieces at the upper ends. The method of procedure is as follows: Suppose the standard steel contains 0.75 per cent carbon; if we dilute the solution in the tube (thoroughly mixing after each addition of water) to 15 cc., then each cc. will contain 0.05 per cent of carbon. We now dilute the solution of the steel in which the carbon is to be determined with distilled water until its color exactly corresponds with that of the standard steel, and then take the reading of the height of the liquid. One minute should be allowed for the liquid to run down the walls of the tube before taking the final reading. Suppose it reads 16 cc.; then, as each cc. contains 0.05 per cent carbon, 16 will contain 0.80 per cent. In comparing the colors it is usual to hold a piece of thin, clear, white paper behind the tubes. To most eyes the left-hand tube will appear slightly the darkest. A good plan is to match the colors so that either tube, as it is reversed, will appear darkest when it is placed to the left. This appearance can be corrected by holding the tubes a little to the right. A. E. Hunt recommends the use of a camera-shaped box, painted black inside, open at one end to look into, and having a frame hinged at the bottom which is covered with thin white paper to form a background for the tubes. Near this end have an opening in the frame and a gutter in the bottom to allow the tubes to be placed. Hunt says: "This arrangement I have found especially useful in the night-time, when I used a fixed Bunsen gas-burner in which a bead of carbonate of soda on a platinum wire gives a monochromate flame. It is placed in such a position as to have the rays reflected, by means of the hinged frame of paper at the back, upon the tubes. I have been enabled in this way to read color carbons with much ease. In fact, I prefer this means of comparison to daylight, as the light is always under control, and no outside rays interfere with lights and shadows." It is preferable, especially where color-carbon analyses are only occasionally made, to use color standards of steel with each set of analyses in the manner described. Where many samples are to be tested every day, as in a Bessemer-steel works, it is much more conveniently and rapidly done by simply matching the diluted test with a rack of permanent standards representing different percentages of carbon. Permanent standards of organic substances, as burnt sugar, burnt coffee, etc., are not satisfactory.* Eggerz describes a mixture of chlorides of iron, cobalt, and copper, which is highly recommended by a number of chemists for the preparation of permanent standards. By adding to the neutral chlorides water containing 1.5 per cent hydrochloric acid for the chloride of iron and 0.5 per cent hydrochloric acid for the two other chlorides, solutions can be prepared of a strength corresponding to 0.01 gramme of metal per cubic centimetre. Then 8 cc. of the iron solution are mixed with 6 cc. of the cobalt solution and 3 cc. of the copper solution, and about 5 cc. of water containing 0.5 per cent hydrochloric acid are added to the mixture. At a temperature of 18° C. this solution shows the same color as a solution of steel in dilute nitric acid corresponding to 0.1 carbon per cubic centimetre. The solution may be afterwards diluted with water containing 0.5 per cent hydrochloric acid to any standard color required. The addition of water is almost directly proportional to the percentage of carbon. The standards thus proposed should always be standardized by comparison with solutions of steel containing a known amount of carbon. Frequently, as in the case of the open-hearth steel process, only a few minutes can be allowed for the determination of the carbon in tests taken from the furnace. For samples where the carbon is below 0.25 per cent a quite accurate determination can be made by dissolving 0.10 gramme of the fine drillings in 2 cc. of 1.20 nitric acid in a test-tube, and by treat-

---

* Transactions Institute of Mining Engineers, Vol. X, p. 186.

ing the standard in the same manner and at the same time in a similar tube as regards diameter, color, and thickness of glass, and then judging of the variations of color at the moment of complete solution and before the carbon begins to separate out. The drillings should be of about the same degree of fineness, so that they will dissolve in about the same time. When the carbon is above 0.25 per cent the drillings are dissolved in 4 cc. of dilute nitric acid, which has previously been heated in the water-bath to a point below boiling, and as soon as the violent ebullition has ceased, boiled by holding the tubes over a burner protected by a piece of wire-gauze. It takes about 4 or 5 minutes' boiling to effect complete solution, and a few minutes to cool sufficiently in cold water. When the solutions are ready to decant into the calibrated tubes, dilute and compare. The color solutions prepared in this way are much darker than when prepared in the usual way and boiled for several minutes. For this quick work a number of weighed portions of standard drilling are prepared beforehand.

CHAPTER V.

CARBONIC ACID (CO_2).

CARBON dioxide (usually called carbonic acid) may be determined by loss of weight upon heating, provided no other volatile matter (such as water) is present, loss upon treatment with acids, or it may be determined by direct weight. The latter method is preferable, and is more satisfactory in all cases.

The determination by direct weight consists in driving off the carbonic acid, by means of heat or decomposition of the substance by acids, conducting it over into a weighed absorption apparatus. The increase in weight of the absorption apparatus represents the weight of the carbonic acid driven off. When heat is used as the decomposing agent the apparatus described for the determination of water by direct weight (Chapter VI) may be employed. The apparatus is the same as before, with the exception that between the calcium-chloride tube and the last U-tube (the one connected with the aspirator) is connected a suitable apparatus for the absorption of the carbonic acid. A calcium-chloride tube filled with small lumps of freshly prepared soda lime is a very good form of absorption apparatus, or a Liebig potash bulb containing a strong solution of caustic potash may be used. The left-hand end of the combustion-tube should also be connected with a similar absorption apparatus in order that all air which enters the combustion-tube may be free from carbonic acid. The substance is introduced into the combustion-tube and the analysis performed in the same manner as described for water, the increase in weight in the absorption apparatus representing the carbonic acid (CO_2) absorbed. In the case of white-lead and similar substances the water and carbonic acid may be determined in this way by one operation. When acids are used as the decomposing agent the form of apparatus will be slightly different. In place of the combustion-tube a decomposing flask is used. A wide-necked glass flask of about 300 cc. capacity, provided with a tight rubber stopper with three perforations, answers the purpose. In one of the holes is fitted a piece of bent-glass tubing, provided with a glass stop-cock or a piece of rubber tubing and a pinch-cock. The tube should enter the neck of the flask about one inch. This will be designated a. A funnel-tube provided with a glass stop-cock should enter the flask through the second hole. The bottom of the funnel-tube should reach to within about an inch of the bottom of the flask so that its end will be covered by the fluid in the flask. This will be designated b. Through the third hole pass a piece of bent-glass tubing so that its end is flush with the bottom of the rubber stopper. To a attach a chloride of calcium tube filled with soda-lime, close the stop-

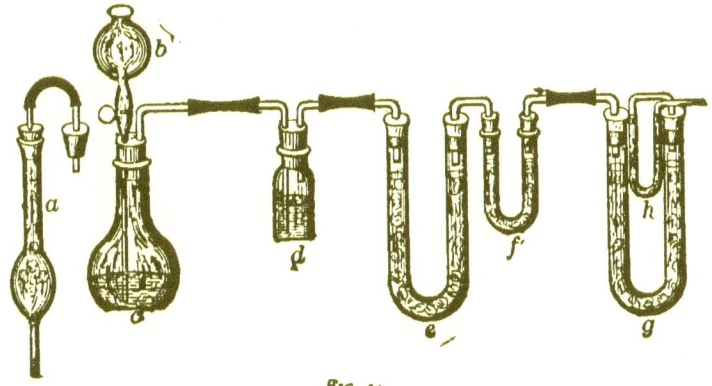

FIG. 14.

cock of b, and attach to c a series of three U-tubes partially filled with pumice and sulphuric acid, as before. To the last U-tube of the series attach a calcium-chloride tube filled with soda-lime, or similar absorption apparatus, and to the right-hand end of the tube attach another U-tube filled with pumice and soda-lime to prevent moisture finding its way back. To this last U-tube attach the aspirator, and start slowly so as to pass a current of air through the apparatus. To perform the analysis, disconnect the absorption-tube, and after carefully weighing reconnect it. Into the decomposing flask introduce about 25 cc. of water and then a weighed amount of the substance. Replace the stopper and close the stop-cock of a and b. Start the aspirator and introduce into the funnel at b some strong sulphuric acid, turning the stop-cock of b gradually, so as to allow a small amount of acid to run into the flask. The aspirator should be run slowly so as to pass a slow current through the apparatus, and the acid should be added slowly by means of the stop-cock b. After sufficient acid has been added and all ebullition of gas has practically ceased, gradually heat the contents of the flask by means of the flame of a lamp or burner. Open the stop-cock a and continue to run the aspirator until the volume of air in the apparatus has been changed four or five times. Disconnect the absorption-tube and weigh. The increase in weight represents the carbonic acid driven off and absorbed.

CHAPTER VI.

WATER (H_2O).

WATER may exist in two states in ores, etc., uncombined (moisture) and combined (water of crystallization).

Moisture.—To determine the moisture in an ore, heat a weighed amount of the pulverized sample at 100° to 105° C. in a weighed porcelain crucible to constant weight. The loss in weight represents the moisture expelled in drying. A hot-air bath provided with a thermometer is the most convenient apparatus in which to perform the drying.

In the case of coal, coke, etc., it is advisable to raise the temperature of the bath to about 115° C.

In a metallurgical works the sample will usually be given to the chemist with the moisture expelled, it having been previously dried by steam at the sampling-works, where the percentage of moisture in the lot or shipment of ore is determined. A good method to be pursued at a sampling-works is as follows: One or more samples of a little over a pound each are taken from each car or wagon load of ore as it comes into the yard, care being exercised to take for a sample the fine and coarse ore in about the same proportions as they exist in the car or wagon load, and to take the sample from different parts of the load. The lumps of ore are then broken up and one pound of the sample weighed out into the ordinary assay-pan. A good plan of keeping track of the samples is to write the number of the car on a piece of wood and stick it in the sample. A convenient drier can be made of boiler-iron. It should be several feet in length and at least 3 feet in width, if many determinations are to be made in the course of the day as is the case in most smelting-works, and about 6 inches in depth. The joints should be steam-tight. The exhaust-steam from the engine is conducted into the box and heats the iron plate upon which the sample-pans are placed. A good plan is to take the samples in the afternoon, and, after weighing out, let them dry over night on the dryer. The Fairbanks Scales Company make a very convenient scales for this purpose. The top of the beam is graduated into ounces and the bottom into percentages. When the weight is on the end of the beam the scales will weigh one pound. After drying, transfer the sample to the pan of the scales and weigh; the indicator of the weight will show the percentage of moisture lost. From the percentages thus found calculate the total pounds of moisture in the lot of ore.

Combined Water.—The method to be pursued will depend on the character of the substance. When the substance contains no volatile matter which is driven off by heating except water, and does not undergo oxidation upon heating, heat to redness over the flame of a burner or in the muffle-furnace and weigh. Heat and weigh again, and repeat the operation until the crucible and contents no longer lose weight by being heated.

When volatile matter other than water is present, as for example white-lead, which contains both water and carbonic acid, a direct determination of the water is necessary. The following method will serve for most substances:

Prepare a piece of combustion-tubing, about 12 inches in length, and to the left-hand end attach a suitable drying apparatus so that all air entering the tube will be perfectly dry. A very good form of drying apparatus can be made of three U-tubes about 5 inches in length, and nearly filled with small lumps of pumice. Then pour into each tube sufficient concentrated sulphuric acid to fill the tubes about one third, pouring the acid over the pumice, so as to saturate it. The U-tubes are connected together and to the combustion-tube by perforated rubber stoppers and pieces of glass tubing. All joints can be made perfectly tight with paraffine. To the right-hand end of the combustion-tube attach a calcium-chloride tube filled with small lumps of freshly prepared calcium chloride. To prepare the calcium chloride, break it into small lumps and heat to redness in a clay crucible. After cooling in a dry place it is ready for use. To the other end of the calcium-chloride tube attach a U-tube filled with pumice and sulphuric acid, as before, to prevent any moisture finding its way back. When the apparatus is all connected attach the last U-tube to the aspirator (the filter-pump makes a very convenient aspirator) and start a slow current of air through the apparatus. Gently warm the combustion-tube, by holding the flame of a burner under it, to expel any moisture there might be in the tube. After the current of air has passed through the apparatus for about 15 minutes, disconnect the calcium-chloride tube and weigh it carefully. Now introduce one or more grammes of the substance into the combustion-tube by means of a weighed platinum or porcelain boat, reconnect the calcium-chloride tube, and start the aspirator slowly. Heat the substance in the boat by means of a good burner, gradually bringing to redness, and continue to heat for some time, finally moving the flame along the combustion-tube to expel any moisture that may have condensed on its sides. Cool and whilst cooling continue to run the aspirator. Disconnect the calcium-chloride tube and weigh it. Its increase in weight will be due to the moisture absorbed by the calcium chloride. From the amount of substance taken calculate the percentage of water.

CHAPTER VII.

GOLD (Au) AND SILVER (Ag).

As gold and silver are generally associated together in ores, and as their methods of assay are similar, they will be treated of together in the following pages.

Gold is universally determined and weighed as metallic gold. In ores it is universally determined by fire-assay, the assay occasionally being preceded by treatment of the ore with acids (Part III, Chap. IV), and occasionally being preceded by roasting of the ore. Silver is determined in the same manner, the ore or furnace-product sometimes undergoing treatment with acids or roasting previous to assay. Alloys, such as silver bullion, are treated by special methods, either fire-assay or volumetric assay in the wet way (Part III, Chapters II and III).

The fire-assay is general in its application, and is the method universally adopted for estimating the gold and silver contents of ores, mattes, slags, etc. The results are not absolutely accurate, as there is necessarily a loss of both gold and silver in fusion, scorification, and cupellation. The most serious loss takes place in cupellation, the precious metals being carried into the cupel and off in the fumes. On the other hand, the gold and silver buttons may be contaminated with certain impurities of the ores under treatment, and the silver buttons with oxides of silver and lead, and the final gold beads with silver. When necessary, corrections may be made for these differences, but such corrections are not usual in commercial work, except in the assay of gold bullion and silver bullion.

The fire-assay consists essentially in the collection of the gold and silver in a button of metallic lead either by scorification (scorification method) or by fusion (crucible method). The lead button is then freed from the adhering slag by hammering on an anvil, and is finally hammered into the form of a cube when it is ready for cupellation.

Both the scorification and crucible methods are extensively used, the general practice in Colorado being to determine the silver in two or more portions of the ore by scorification and the gold in two or more portions by crucible assay. On the Pacific coast the crucible method is the favorite one for both gold and silver. Both methods have their advocates, but we believe the Colorado practice is preferable, as most ores will yield higher silver results by scorification and higher and more uniform gold results by crucible assay. The reason that the crucible method gives better results on gold is owing to its allowing larger quantities to be taken for assay, and hence a larger button of gold is obtained for weighing than in the scorification-assay, where only a small quantity can be taken, resulting in a small button, which introduces a source of error in the weighing and calculation of results. This can be obviated by running a number of scorifications and combining the buttons in parting.

Scorification-assay.—The quantity of ore taken for assay will depend upon the grade and character of the ore and the size of the scorifiers on hand. The amounts usually taken are $\frac{1}{10}$ or $\frac{2}{10}$ assay-tons. The table on the next page gives the charges upon the basis of $\frac{1}{10}$ A. T. ton.

Litharge added to the assay as a cover, in the case of pyrites and mattes, helps the assay. A mixture of equal parts of sodium bicarbonate and nitre effects the same results.

Arsenical and copper pyrites, speiss, and copper mattes containing a high percentage of copper are preferably assayed by special method.

On most ores a charge consisting of ore $\frac{1}{10}$ A. T., test-lead 40 grammes, and borax-glass as required, after scorification commences, gives good results.

In case an insufficient quantity of lead or borax-glass has

Ore.	Grammes of Test lead.	Grammes of Borax-glass.	Remarks.
Galena............	15–18	up to 0.5	
Galena with blende and pyrite......	20–35	0.4–0.8	
Iron pyrite........	30–45	0.3–0.8	
Arsenical pyrite...	45–50	0.3–1.5	High temperature. Addition of litharge helps assay.
Gray copper.......	35–48	0.3–0.5	Low temperature.
Blende............	30–45	0.3–0.6	High temperature. Addition of oxide of iron helps assay.
Copper ores and mattes..........	35–40	0.3–0.5	Low temperature. If necessary, the button should be rescorified with lead.
Lead mattes.......	25–35	0.5–1.0	
Furnace accretions.	25–50	0.3–1.5	
Tellurides.........	50	0.3	Add a cover of litharge and re-scorify the button.
Silicious..........	25–30		
Basic.............	25–30	0.5–2.0	If the ore contains much lime or magnesia the addition of sodium carbonate helps the assay.
Basic with Barium sulphate........	25–30	0.5–1.5	Addition of sodium carbonate helps the assay.
Lead carbonate....	10–15	up to 0.5	
Speisse............	30–60	0.3–0.5	High temperature. Rescorify the button with lead if necessary.

been added, the deficiency can be made up by adding, after the scorification has commenced, lead in the form of sheet-lead rolled into a compact piece, or borax-glass wrapped in a small piece of tissue-paper. If the test-lead or sheet-lead contains silver (some silver is always present), the amount which it contains should be determined, and the amount present in the weight of test-lead or sheet-lead used in the assay should be deducted from the weight of the resultant button.

To determine the silver in the test-lead, scorify 100 grammes of test-lead with borax and cupel the resulting button.

Care should be exercised to use the proper amount of fluxes, so that the resulting button will be of the proper size (8 to 12 grammes in weight). If the button is too large, it may be reduced to the proper size by further scorification with test-lead and borax-glass. This will frequently happen with ores containing much copper. It is better to reduce too large a button by scorification rather than to cupel the button directly, as the loss of precious metals is less in scorification than in cupellation. In case the button is hard or brittle, it should be rescorified, with the addition of test-lead. In this case care should be exercised in removing the button from the slag that no particles of the button be lost. The fluxes are usually measured in place of weighing them out. A very convenient tool for measuring out the test-lead is the adjustable measure which sportsmen use for measuring the charges of shot with which they load shells. After some experience the assayer will be able to guess at the weight of the borax-glass sufficiently close.

One half of the test-lead is placed in the scorifier, the carefully weighed ore added and mixed with the lead by means of a steel spatula. The balance of the test-lead is now added as a cover and the borax-glass placed on top. The scorifiers are placed in the muffle and the door closed. The door is kept closed until scorification commences, which is indicated by the mass subsiding and a ring of slag forming around the surface of the metallic lead. As the scorification proceeds the ring of slag grows larger, until it finally closes over the surface of the lead. The muffle should now be closed and the heat raised for a few minutes, in order to insure the slag being perfectly fluid ; the scorifier is then removed from the muffle and its contents poured into the scorifier mould. As soon as the assay is cool, which takes but a few minutes, it is removed from the mould and the slag removed by pounding on the anvil with a light hammer. The lead button is hammered into the form of a cube, when it is ready for cupellation. The slag should be perfectly fluid. The lead should collect in one malleable button. The buttons should be weighed separately, and should not differ by more than 0.5 oz. per ton on ore assaying 100 ozs. per ton.

The calculation of results is as follows: Suppose $\frac{1}{10}$ A. T. taken for each scorification, four scorifications being made. The combined weights of the four buttons before parting is 42.5 milligrammes. The weight of the gold button from the four assays is 3.8 milligrammes: then $42.5 - 3.8 = 38.7 =$ weight of silver, and $38.7 \times \frac{10}{4} = 96.75$ oz. silver, and $3.8 \times \frac{10}{4} = 9.5$ oz. gold per ton of 2000 lbs. If the gold is determined separately by crucible-assay it is unnecessary to part the buttons from the scorification-assay, except as a check. In order to obtain the weight of the silver, the amount of gold as found by crucible-assay is deducted from the amount of silver and gold as shown by the scorification-assay.

Crucible-assay.—The amounts of ore usually taken for assay is $\frac{1}{2}$ A. T. or 1 A. T., depending upon the grade of the ore, the size of the crucibles, and whether the fusion is performed in the wind-furnace or the muffle-furnace. If the fusion is performed in the muffle-furnace $\frac{1}{2}$ A. T. will usually be taken, as a larger quantity would involve the use of an awkward-sized crucible for the muffle. In Colorado the fusion is usually performed in the muffle, and this practice is to be recommended on account of the cleanliness and the greater facility with which the heat can be regulated as compared with fusion in the wind-furnace.

In making up a charge the object to be attained is to produce a fluid slag which will permit of a perfect separation of the lead into a button of the proper weight (10 to 20 grammes), to drive the impurities in the ore into the slag and not into the lead, and to collect all the gold and silver in the lead button. The proper fluxes and the amounts of each to be added will depend upon the mineral composition of the ore.

If the ore is in lump form its mineral composition can be determined by simple eye-inspection or a few blowpipe tests. If in the form of powder, place about 0.2 gramme of the ore on a large watch-glass, add water, and van by rotating and tapping the glass to separate the different minerals. An inspection of the vanned sample with a magnifying-glass will usually show the mineral composition.

In making up a charge it must be remembered that sulphur, arsenic, and antimony act as reducing agents, and that ferric oxide and carbonate act as oxidizing agents. Nitre acts as an oxidizing agent, but its use is objectionable for the following reasons: Unless a large-sized crucible is used, and care is exercised to heat the crucible and its contents gradually, during fusion loss is liable to occur from deflagration and the contents of the crucible boiling over. The use of nitre also requires that the reducing power of the ore be known. If the composition of the ore is known (as regards S, As, and Sb), its reducing power can be calculated. If its composition is unknown, its reducing power may be determined by making a fusion, using the following charge: Ore, 2 gms.; litharge, 15 gms.; sodium bicarbonate, 10 gms. Fuse in a hot fire, and when the fusion is quiet remove the crucible from the fire, pour its contents into a mould, and when cool detach the lead button from the slag and weigh it. From the weight of the lead button calculate the amount of nitre necessary to add to the assay to obtain a lead button of the proper weight.

Most assayers prefer the use of iron nails in the assay of sulphides and arsenides rather than the use of nitre. Powdered argols, flour or powdered charcoal are the usual reducing agents used. The fusion is performed in either the wind- or muffle-furnace, and requires from 25 to 40 minutes. When the fusion is quiet, the assay should be allowed to remain in the furnace for a few minutes at a strong heat before it is withdrawn. When the assay is cool, the lead button is extracted from the slag in the same manner as in the scorification-assay.

The lead button should weigh from 8 to 18 grammes when $\frac{1}{2}$ A. T. to 1 A. T. of ore is taken, the weight depending somewhat upon the richness of the ore. Should the lead button be hard (due to copper) or brittle (due to As, Sb, Te, etc.), or should a button of matte or speiss be formed, it should be scorified, with the addition of test-lead or borax, if necessary, before cupellation. The lead button is finally cupelled, the silver-gold button weighed, and parted as described before.

In the case where gold only is determined by the crucible-assay, it is usual to add silver to the charge before fusion, either in the form of pure silver foil or a small crystal of silver nitrate, unless the ore is known to contain sufficient silver to insure parting. The charge should always contain an excess of litharge, as it serves as an excellent flux and renders the slag fluid. The litharge used should be thoroughly sampled and the silver which it contains determined. A good charge for this purpose is: Litharge, 2 A. T.; sodium bicarbonate, 1 A. T.; argol, 1 gm. The amount of silver which the litharge used in each assay contains should be deducted from the result of the assay. The crucibles should never be more than three-fourths filled, and in case nitre is used not over two-thirds.

The assays are usually made in duplicate, and the buttons should agree within 0.5 oz. silver per ton on ore assaying 100 oz. per ton. The results in gold should agree almost exactly. For gold assays by this method the general practice is to run two assays of $\frac{1}{2}$ A. T. of ore each, and part the buttons together. In the case of rich ores the buttons are parted separately as a check. The table on the following page gives the charges for different ores.

In the case of copper, iron, and arsenical pyrites it is preferable to roast the ore previous to assay. After roasting, the ore is treated as an oxidized ore. To roast, weigh out $\frac{1}{2}$ A. T. of the ore, introduce into a clay roasting-dish and roast in the muffle, stirring from time to time. The addition of ammonium carbonate (commercial salt) facilitates the roasting.

The special method (see Part III, Chapter IV) is especially adapted to the assay of pig copper, copper mattes, copper and arsenical pyrites, etc.

Cupellation.—Cupellation is performed in a small cupel made of powdered and sifted bone-ash. In making up the cupels the addition of a small amount of potassium carbonate to the water used to moisten the bone-ash aids in making it

GOLD AND SILVER.

TABLE OF CRUCIBLE CHARGES.

Ore.	Character of the Gangue.	A.T. Ore	Gms. of Lead Flux.	Gms. of Soda Bicarbonate.	Gms. of Litharge.	Gms. Potassium Ferrocyanide.	Gms. Nitre.	Gms. Silica.	Gms. Argol.	Loops of Iron Wire.	Gms. Borax Glass.	Cover.	Remarks.
Oxidized	Neutral no Pb	½	50		20							borax	If cover of salt is used in place of borax add 3 to 5 gms. borax glass.
Quartz	No bases	½			75								Special method. If oxide iron is present add soda in proportion.
Quartz	No bases	½	30	30	20								
Oxidized	Basic no Pb	½	50		20							borax	
Oxidized	Basic with BaSO₄	½	50	10–20	25			15	2			salt salt	If gangue is oxide or carbonate of iron add 2 to 3 gms. of argol. Borax-glass may be substituted for some of the silica.
Galena	Lead 84 per cent	½	20		15		10	15				salt	Heat gradually until mass subsides.
Galena	Silicious Pb 42 per cent	½	20	5–10	10		5					salt	Litharge is added according to the lead contents of the ore.
Lead carbonate	Neutral Pb 40 per cent	½	40		20							salt	Litharge added according to the lead contents of the ore.
Iron pyrites	None	½	15	30	30			15		3–4		salt	Collect matte, if any, and scorify with lead button.
Copper pyrites	Iron pyrites	½	15	30	30			15	2	3–4		salt	Collect matte and scorify with lead button. If button is hard add test-lead.
Lead matte		½ ½	15 15	30 30	20 30		5 5	15 15		3–4 3–4	2	salt salt	Special method is preferable. If button is hard or brittle scorify with lead. Scorification preferable.
Copper matte		½	50	20	40–80	17						salt salt	Special method. Scorify button. Scorification-assay is preferable.
Tellurides	Silicious	½ ½		15	75 30				2			salt salt	
Arsenical	Silicious				10								
Slag		1	50								8		If slag contains matte add loop of iron wire.

adherent. The cupel should always weigh a little more than the lead button to be cupelled. A very convenient size is a cupel weighing 18 gms. The cupels should be dried for a few days before using.

The cupels are placed in the muffle and allowed to become hot before introducing the lead button. The cube of lead is dropped into the cupel and the door of the muffle closed until cupellation commences. As soon as cupellation begins, indicated by the surface of the lead becoming bright and fumes arising from the cupel, the door of the furnace is opened. The temperature should be controlled within rather narrow limits. If the temperature is too low there will be a considerable loss of silver and a liability of the button "freezing" (solidifying), when the assay is ruined, as it is not safe to accept the results from a frozen button. If the temperature is too high there will be a considerable loss of silver by oxidation and also probably a mechanical loss in the lead fumes. The proper control of the temperature can be learned only by experience. A safe rule is to have the cupels show a slight ring of litharge crystals (feather litharge) around the edges. As the cupellation proceeds the lead is oxidized, part being absorbed by the cupel and part passing off in fumes. Just before the last traces of lead are removed the button will exhibit a play of colors, owing to a thin film of litharge on the surface. At this point the temperature should be quite high in order to insure the removal of all the lead. This is usually accomplished by pushing the cupel back in the muffle. When the lead is all removed the play of colors ceases, the button "brightens" or "winks" and solidifies. The cupel should be allowed to remain in the furnace for a few minutes (there is no loss of silver after the button solidifies), when it is removed and cooled previous to weighing. If the button of silver is large it is best to cover it with a hot cupel before removing from the muffle, and remove it gradually, otherwise the button is liable to spit or sprout, which may occasion loss. It is never safe to accept a sprouted button.

The button, when cold, is removed from the cupel by a

pair of nippers, squeezed slightly in the nippers, and its bottom brushed with a stiff bristle- or wire-brush, when it is ready for weighing.

The weighing of the gold-silver button is performed on a button-balance, which should weigh accurately to within 0.10 milligramme. In the case of small buttons and where $\frac{1}{10}$ A. T. is taken for assay, the balance used should be the gold balance, and should weigh to within 0.01 milligramme. The weight of the gold-silver button being noted, the button is ready for parting.

Parting.—Prior to parting it is best to flatten the button by a few light blows, especially if it contains much gold. In order that the button will part it should contain at least two and one half times as much silver as gold. If the button does not contain sufficient silver to insure parting, pure silver in the shape of foil is added on a cupel and fused by means of the blowpipe flame. After alloying, the button is flattened and is ready for parting. The button is placed in a small porcelain crucible and c. p. nitric acid of 1.16 sp. gr. is added.* The crucible and its contents are now warmed on an iron plate until all action of the acid has ceased, when the solution is brought to a boil. The crucible is now removed from the plate and the gold collected in one mass by gently rotating and tapping the crucible. The solution is then poured off and fresh acid of 1.26 sp. gr. is added. The contents of the crucible are now boiled for three minutes, the gold collected in one mass, and the acid poured off. The gold is now washed three times with hot water, and the last drops of water removed from the crucible. A convenient piece of apparatus for removing the last drops of water is a piece of glass tubing drawn to a fine point at one end. The water is removed by suction on the large end of the tube. The crucible is now warmed on the iron plate until thoroughly dry, when it is ignited over a lamp or in the muffle. The gold should be bright, and have the characteristic color of pure gold The gold is now ready for weighing on the gold balance.

---

* Most western assayers use acid of only one strength having a sp. gr. of about 1.20.

Some assayers prefer to part in a test-tube or small parting matrice. If the parting is done in a test-tube or matrice the tube is rinsed out twice with warm distilled water, and then filled with water and inverted over a small porcelain crucible. When the gold has all settled to the bottom of the crucible the tube is removed, the water poured off, and the gold dried, ignited, and weighed as before.

The only exception to the above methods is in the case of an ore containing metallic scales. Such ores should be assayed by the special method described in Part III, Chapter VIII.

On the Pacific coast the fusion for the assay of low-grade gold ores is usually performed in the crucible or wind-furnace, from 2 A. T. to 4 A. T. of ore being taken. This method presents the advantages that large quantities of ore are taken for assay, and that only one fusion is necessary for each assay.

CHAPTER VIII.

MERCURY (Hg).

THE wet methods for the determination of mercury are extremely tedious, and at the same time far from accurate, unless extreme precautions are observed.

The distillation methods, as described by Fresenius, Ricketts, Mitchell, etc., are good, and are to be recommended where the percentage of mercury present is large.

The two following methods have been tested and proved to be accurate, and, as they are simple and rapid, are to be recommended, especially when the percentage of mercury present is small. They both depend upon the distillation of the mercury and catching it on gold in the form of amalgam.*

First Method.—Mix from 0.2 to 2.0 grammes of ore with from 1 to 4 grammes of iron filings (iron filings are preferable to lime, as they render the mass porous and facilitate the distillation) in a porcelain crucible of sufficient size. Prepare a cover for the crucible of sheet gold. This cover should be made in the form of a dish, so that it can be kept cool by keeping it filled with water. It should be of a diameter somewhat larger than the diameter of the crucible, so that its sides project over the outer rim of the crucible. The weight of such a cover will be from 7 to 10 grammes.

Place the crucible in the ring-stand, fit on the cover, and fill it with cold water. Now heat the crucible gradually with the

---

* Silver suggests itself as a substitute for gold, but as the author has never tried silver he cannot recommend it.

flame of a Bunsen burner, care being taken to keep the upper part of the crucible cool, and to especially keep the gold cover cool. The first can be accomplished by allowing the flame to play only around the bottom of the crucible, care being taken to never allow it to reach the upper sides; and the second by adding cold water to the cover from time to time. It will require from 10 to 30 minutes to distil off all the mercury. When the distillation is completed remove the gold cover, pour off the water, dry carefully, and weigh. The increase in weight of the gold cover (it having been dried and weighed before the operation) represents the mercury.

Second Method.—This method is essentially the same as the above, the form of apparatus used only being different.

Prepare a piece of combustion-tubing about 14 inches long and closed at the left-hand end. Introduce a weighed quantity of the ore, which should be mixed with iron filings and lime, into the tube, shaking it down into the closed end. On top of the ore place a plug of ignited asbestos. Into the right-hand end of the combustion-tube introduce a spiral of gold-foil of which the weight has previously been determined, and a rubber cork connected with a small glass tube. This small tube should be about 18 inches in length, and should be bent up in the form of an L at the open or right-hand end. It can be kept cool by wrapping around it a cloth saturated with cold water. This second small tube is to catch any mercury which might pass the gold-foil and not be caught by it.

After the apparatus is connected up, heat the left-hand end of the tube containing the ore, to drive off the mercury, gradually raising the temperature, but keeping the right-hand end of the tube containing the gold spiral cool. Should any mercury condense in the combustion-tube it can be driven forward by moving the flame of the burner towards the right. After all of the mercury is distilled off, which will require from 10 to 30 minutes' heating, remove the heat, and allow the tube to cool. When cool disconnect the apparatus, examine the small tube, and if it contains no mercury remove the gold spiral, and weigh. The increase in weight of the gold will represent the mercury. Should there be any mercury collected in the small tube, which will seldom happen if the operation was properly conducted, it must be collected and weighed, its weight being added to the weight of mercury caught by the gold spiral.

This process properly performed will give excellent results.

CHAPTER IX.

LEAD (Pb).

NUMEROUS methods have been proposed for the determination of lead, both volumetrically and gravimetrically, but the following are the only ones which are extensively used:

1. Fire-assay;
2. Gravimetric determination as lead sulphate, and weighing as such;
3. Volumetric determination with a standard solution of potassium ferrocyanide;
4. Volumetric determination with a standard solution of potassium permanganate;
5. Volumetric determination with a standard solution of ammonium molybdate.

The first method is generally used in the United States and elsewhere for the determination of lead in purchasing ores. Its advantages are: Rapidity, ease of execution, and the large number of assays which may be made in a given time. Its disadvantages are: All the lead is seldom reduced, and the buttons are seldom pure. If the ore contains Sb, Sn, Bi, Cu, Fe, and Zn, the button is liable to contain more or less of these impurities. A recent analysis of the buttons resulting from several hundred lead determinations at one of our large smelting works showed the buttons to only contain 96 per cent lead, as an average. The method, and with good reason, is gradually giving way to the more accurate volumetric methods. Some chemists now use the volumetric methods on mattes and all but pure ores.

The advantages of the second method are that the results obtained are extremely accurate. Its disadvantages are: Time and nicety of manipulation required.

The advantages of the third, fourth and fifth methods are rapidity and ease of execution. The disadvantage of the fourth method is that the results are apt to be a trifle low on account of the incomplete precipitation of the lead as oxalate, but for technical purposes it leaves but little to be desired. The fifth method answers all requirements for technical purposes and is at present extensively used in the West. As this method fails where much lime is present, owing to the precipitation of calcium molybdate, in such cases it will have to be slightly modified. A good method to follow where lime is present is to proceed according to Knight's method up to the point of precipitation of the lead on zinc. Dissolve the precipitated lead in dilute nitric acid, using as small a quantity as possible, render the solution alkaline with ammonia, neutralize with acetic acid, and proceed with the titration as usual.

1. **Fire-assay.**—The general practice in Colorado is as follows: 5 grammes of pulverized ore are mixed with from 15 to 20 grammes of lead flux in a clay crucible, a cover of borax is added, and the fusion made in a muffle-furnace. The time of fusion with a good fire is from 15 to 20 minutes. In the case of sulphide or base ores one or two iron nails or a few loops of iron wire are added to the charge. When the fusion has become quiet the crucible is allowed to remain in the muffle from 1 to 5 minutes, when it is drawn out and its contents poured into a scorifier-mould. As soon as cold the button and slag are removed from the mould, and the button extracted from the slag by pounding with a hammer. The button is pounded out thin on the anvil, and should be soft and malleable. If brittle it contains Sb, S, etc. If hard it probably contains Fe, Cu, etc. The slag should be vitreous and brittle, and should not contain shots or globules of lead. Duplicate assays should agree to within about 0.5 per cent.

2. **Gravimetric Method, weighing as $PbSO_4$.**—Lead may be determined in its ores and furnace-products by treating 1.0 gramme of ore with 7 to 10 cc. of strong nitric acid in a flask or beaker of about 250 cc. capacity, covered with a watch-glass, and heating until the violent action ceases and the sul-

phur is oxidized. Then add 10 cc. of dilute sulphuric acid (50 per cent strong sulphuric acid and 50 per cent water), and boil until the nitric acid is expelled and dense white fumes of sulphuric anhydride appear. Then cool, dilute cautiously with about 50 cc. of water, and shake in the flask to break up any clots which may have formed, and also to cause the basic sulphate of iron to go into solution. If very much iron is present, as in the case of mattes, it may be necessary to heat the solution in order to dissolve the basic sulphate of iron. Then cool, filter, and wash the residue, containing lead sulphate and gangue, with water containing 1 per cent of sulphuric acid, and then with about 40 cc. of alcohol. Dissolve the lead sulphate on the filter, also what may stick to the sides of the flask, with a slightly acid solution of ammonium acetate, made by adding acetic acid to strong ammonia until the solution is slightly acid, then bringing back to an alkaline state with dilute ammonia, and then back to an acid state with a few drops of acetic acid. The solution should be warm when used. From two to three washings with ammonium acetate will be necessary to dissolve all of the lead sulphate. After washing with the acetate solution, wash with warm water. The lead will now all be in solution in the filtrate, whilst the silica, calcium sulphate, etc., will remain behind on the filter. Acidify the filtrate with an excess of sulphuric acid, cool, and filter off the sulphate of lead, washing as before with a 1 per cent solution of sulphuric-acid water and afterwards with alcohol in order to displace the sulphuric acid. The filtrate may be tested for lead by adding a few drops of hydrochloric acid and passing a current of sulphuretted hydrogen gas through it. Should any lead sulphide be precipitated, it should be filtered off and dissolved in a small quantity of nitric acid. Sulphuric acid should then be added, and the nitric acid be driven off by boiling. The lead sulphate thus recovered from the filtrate should be added to the other precipitate. The filter and its contents are then dried at a moderate temperature (not above 100° C.), and when dry transfer the contents of the filter-paper as completely as possible to a clean watch-glass by inverting it over the glass and working it with the fingers. Then burn the filter in a weighed porcelain crucible, and after it is burned and ignited add to the ash a few drops of nitric acid (to dissolve the lead reduced to metallic lead by the carbon of the filter-paper) and warm, then add two or three drops of sulphuric acid, evaporate off the excess of acid, brush the precipitate into the crucible from the watch-glass, and ignite all. Cool, and weigh the crucible and its contents. This weight, less the known weight of the crucible and filter-ash, will be the weight of the lead sulphate. To calculate the weight of the lead, multiply the weight of the lead sulphate by 0.68317.

3. **Volumetrically, by Means of Standard $K_4FeC_6N_6$.**—This method, while not new,* has lately come into prominence,† and is highly recommended. Treat 0.5 to 1 gm. of ore in the same manner as with Alexander's method, and filter off and wash the precipitated lead sulphate. Wash this precipitate back into the flask or beaker with a minimum amount of water, and add 30 cc. of a saturated solution of ammonium carbonate. Heat quickly to boiling, and boil at least one minute in order to decompose any calcium sulphate which may have formed. It is essential that any calcium sulphate present should be converted into a carbonate, as otherwise the sulphate would react upon the dissolved lead and thus cause low results. Filter and wash thoroughly with hot water containing a little ammonium carbonate. Dissolve the washed carbonate of lead in strong c. p. acetic acid, dilute to about 180 cc., and titrate with the standard ferrocyanide solution in the same manner as described for zinc (p. 207). The ferrocyanide solution should be of such a strength that each cc. will precipitate 0.01 gm. of lead. It is prepared by dissolving 14 gms. of c. p. potassium ferrocyanide in one litre of water.

4. **Volumetrically, by Means of Standard $KMnO_4$.**—For ores and furnace-products the method of procedure is as follows: Treat from 0.5 to 1.0 gramme of the material, according to its richness, with from 8 cc. to 15 cc. of strong nitric and

---

* Eng. and Min. Jour., Vol. XLIX, p. 178, Feb. 8, 1890. Mining Industry, Vol. VI, No. 16, Apl. 1890.

† Jour. Am. Chem. Society, Oct. 1893.

from 8 cc. to 15 cc. of strong sulphuric acids in a casserole, cover with a watch-glass, and heat until decomposition is effected and fumes of sulphuric anhydride appear. Remove the casserole from the heat and cool; when cool, gradually add about 50 cc. of cold water, heat to boiling, and immediately filter. Wash well with boiling water acidified with sulphuric acid, and finally with plain hot water. Rinse the insoluble residue into a beaker of about 200 cc. capacity, using not more than 50 cc. of water; add 5 cc. of concentrated hydrochloric acid, cover with a watch-glass, and boil for 5 minutes. The sulphates of lead and lime pass into solution.

If much silica and barium sulphate is present, it is best to filter and wash well with boiling water. The filtration must be done rapidly. Small quantities of silica do not interfere, but larger quantities prevent the subsequent precipitation of the lead in one spongy mass.

Dilute the solution with water to about 100 cc., keeping it hot but not boiling. Add two grammes of granulated zinc (free from lead) to the solution, when the lead will immediately begin to be precipitated as a metallic sponge. When the action of the acid on the zinc has apparently ceased add 0.5 gramme more of zinc and allow to stand for 5 minutes. Now boil the solution, and add 10 cc. of concentrated hydrochloric acid. This dissolves the remainder of the zinc very quickly, and when the reaction is completed the lead sponge will be found floating on the surface of the liquid. Decant the solution, wash the lead sponge with cold water, and press it out flat with the finger. Dissolve it in 1 cc. of concentrated nitric acid and 20 cc. of hot water. Add a slight excess of sodium carbonate (salt), and redissolve the precipitated lead carbonate by the addition of 5 cc. of strong acetic acid. Add 20 cc. of 95 per cent alcohol, heat the solution to 65° C., and precipitate the lead with a saturated solution of pure crystallized oxalic acid. The lead comes down immediately as a dense white crystalline precipitate. Stir briskly until the precipitate settles, leaving a perfectly clear supernatant liquid. Filter and wash the precipitate three times with a hot mixture of alcohol and water (1 alcohol, 1 water), and then four times with hot water alone. In washing the precipitate it is well to use a fine jet, keeping the stream on the filter and not allowing it to flow on the glass, as otherwise the precipitate is liable to creep up on the funnel and thus occasion loss. When thoroughly washed, the precipitate is rinsed into a flask or beaker with about 50 cc. of hot water, add 5 cc. of concentrated sulphuric acid and determine the oxalic acid which was combined with the lead in the same manner as in the estimation of lime volumetrically, using a standard solution of potassium permanganate. (See Part I, Chap. XXIII.)

A quite dilute solution of permanganate should be used—not stronger than 1.58 grammes of $KMnO_4$ to 1000 cc. of water. One cc. of such a solution will be equal to about 0.05 gm. of lead. The standard of the solution in terms of lead is obtained by multiplying the standard in terms of oxalic acid by 1.6428.

Bismuth and antimony are the only impurities of the ores which are liable to affect the results. By adding a large excess of sulphuric acid to the nitric-acid solution, so that when the evaporation takes place and the sulphuric-acid fumes appear the mass will be in a fluid and not a pasty condition, and allowing the mixture to cool and adding cold water gradually to avoid heating, all of the bismuth goes into solution, and remains in solution for a sufficient length of time to allow filtration and a separation of the sulphate of lead to be effected. If sufficient sulphuric acid is used, most of the antimony will likewise be held in solution. Should some antimony remain with the lead sulphate, it will be reduced to the metallic state by the zinc, and when the solution of the lead is effected with the nitric acid it will remain behind as the insoluble oxide, and thus be eliminated.

A determination may be effected in from 35 to 40 minutes. This method is due to F. C. Knight.[*]

According to Mr. Knight's results, about 99.6 per cent of the lead present is obtained.

A. H. Low[†] proposes a modification of Knight's method which presents some advantages.

---

[*] Proceedings of the Colorado Scientific Society, Nov. 7, 1892.
[†] Journal of the Am. Chem. Society, Oct. 1893.

5. Volumetrically by Means of a Standard Solution of Ammonium Molybdate.—This method is based upon the fact that ammonium molybdate when added to a hot solution of lead acetate will produce a precipitate of lead molybdate ($PbMoO_4$) which is insoluble in acetic acid. Any excess of ammonium molybdate will give a yellow color with a freshly prepared solution of tannin. The solution of tannin is made by dissolving one gramme of tannin in 300 cc. of water, and is used as an indicator on a porcelain plate. The standard solution of ammonium molybdate is prepared by dissolving 9 grammes of the salt in 1000 cc. of water. This should give a solution of which 1 cc. is equal to about 0.01 gm. of lead. If the solution is not clear, it can be clarified by adding a few drops of ammonium hydrate.

To standardize the molybdate solution weigh out 0.3 gm. of pure lead sulphate and dissolve it in hot ammonium acetate; acidify the solution with acetic acid and dilute with hot water to 250 cc. Heat to boiling, and add from a burette the molybdate solution until all the lead is precipitated as a white precipitate. This is ascertained by placing the drops of tannin solution on a porcelain plate and adding drops of the solution in the beaker to the tannin drops from time to time. As long as the lead is in excess no color is produced, but as soon as the molybdate is in excess a yellow color is produced (0.3 gm. $PbSO_4 \times 0.68317 = 0.20495$ gm. Pb). This operation should be repeated, and from the number of cc. of the molybdate solution used in each case the value of one cc. is calculated in the usual way.

To determine the lead in an ore- or furnace-product by this method 0.5 or 1.0 gm. of substance is weighed out (according to the percentage of lead: if 30 per cent or over, 0.5 gm. will be sufficient) and decomposed in a casserole by heating with 15 cc. of strong nitric and 10 cc. of strong sulphuric acids. When the nitric acid is completely expelled, which is indicated by fumes of sulphuric anhydride, the casserole is removed from the heat and its contents cooled. Dilute with cold water, stir thoroughly, and boil until all soluble sulphates are dissolved.

Now filter, leaving as much of the precipitate in the casserole as possible, and wash twice with hot dilute sulphuric acid and once with cold water. Now add to the sulphate of lead remaining in the casserole hot ammonium acetate, pour the hot solution on the filter, and allow it to run through into a clean beaker. This operation is repeated until the sulphate of lead is completely dissolved. Now wash out the casserole thoroughly with hot water into the filter. Acidify the solution in the beaker with acetic acid,* dilute up to 250 cc. with hot water, and heat to boiling. Run in from the burette the standardized solution of ammonium molybdate until all the lead is precipitated, stirring thoroughly after each addition of the molybdate, and testing a drop of the solution from time to time on the porcelain plate with the tannin solution. From the number of cc. of the molybdate solution used calculate the per cent of lead.

Arsenic, antimony, and phosphorus do not interfere with the method as they pass through the filter into solution.

A determination can readily be made in thirty minutes.

The method is largely used in Colorado for the determination of lead in ores containing copper, and in both lead and copper mattes. The results are excellent.†

This method is due to H. H. Alexander. ‡

---

* The acidification is unnecessary.—L. G. EAKINS, *communication to the author.*

† State School of Mines Scientific Quarterly, Vol. I, No. 4.

‡ The Engineering and Mining Journal, Vol. LV, No. 13, April 1, 1893.

CHAPTER X.

ARSENIC (As).

FOR the technical estimation of arsenic in ores and metallurgical products, the following method, which was devised and published by Dr. Richard Pearce, of Denver, Colo.,* is the most rapid and at the same time one of the most accurate methods which we have :

The finely powdered substance for analysis is mixed in a platinum crucible with from six to ten times its weight of a mixture of equal parts of sodium carbonate and potassium nitrate. The mass is then heated with gradually increasing temperature to fusion and allowed to remain for a few minutes in that state. It is then allowed to cool, and the mass removed by the addition of warm water. It is best to remove the mass by warm water, pouring in to a casserole, and, after the whole is transferred to the casserole, to heat to a boiling temperature and filter. The arsenic is in the filtrate as an alkaline arseniate, which is then acidified with nitric acid and boiled to expel carbonic acid and nitrous fumes. It is then cooled and almost exactly neutralized as follows: Place a small piece of litmus-paper in the liquid, which should show an acid reaction, and then gradually add ammonia until the litmus-paper turns blue, avoiding a great excess. Again make slightly acid with a drop or two of concentrated nitric acid, and then, by means of very dilute ammonia and nitric acid, added drop by drop, bring the solution to a condition that the litmus-paper, after having previously been reddened, will in the course of half a minute begin to turn blue. If the neutralization has caused much of a pre-

---

* Proceedings of the Colorado Scientific Society, Vol. I.

cipitate (alumina, etc.) the solution is best filtered at once in order to render the subsequent washing and filtration of the arseniate of silver more rapid. If this filtration is unnecessary, the litmus-paper is drawn up the sides of the beaker, leaving a portion, however, yet immersed in the liquid. A neutral solution of nitrate of silver is now added in slight excess, and after stirring the color of the immersed portion of the litmus-paper is noted, and if necessary the neutralization is repeated. The second neutralization is always necessary when the amount of arsenic present is large, as nitric acid is set free in the reaction between the alkaline arseniate and silver nitrate, according to one or both of the following equations, or those of the corresponding potassium salts:

$$3AgNO_3 + NaH_2AsO_4 = Ag_3AsO_4 + NaNO_3 + 2HNO_3,$$

and

$$3AgNO_3 + Na_2HAsO_4 = Ag_3AsO_4 + 2NaNO_3 + HNO_3.$$

The precipitated arseniate of silver, which is of a brick-red color, is finally collected on a filter and well washed with cold water. As a further precaution, the filtrate may be tested with silver nitrate, dilute nitric acid, and ammonia to see if the precipitation is complete. The object is now to determine the amount of silver in the precipitate of arseniate of silver, and from this to calculate the arsenic. This may be accomplished in two ways: First, the precipitate may be dried in a scorifier, test-lead and borax added, and a scorification-assay made to determine the amount of silver. If this method is adopted any soluble chloride must be removed earlier in the process. Generally but few ores will be encountered in which any soluble chloride is present. Another and shorter method of determining the silver is as follows: Dissolve the arseniate of silver on the filter with dilute nitric acid (which leaves undissolved any silver chloride) and titrate the filtrate, after addition of about 5 cubic centimetres of a saturated solution of ferric ammonium sulphate, with a standard solution of ammonium sulphocyanate (about 5 grammes of the salt to the litre of water), run in until a faint-red tinge is obtained, which remains after considerable shaking. The shaking breaks up any clots of sulphocyanate of silver, and frees any solution held mechanically.

From the formula $3Ag_2O, As_2O_5$ we find that 648 parts of silver represent 150 parts of arsenic, or 108 parts of silver 25 parts of arsenic.

In determining arsenic in ores very rich in arsenic, such as arsenopyrite, niccolite, etc., it is desirable to add a few drops of fuming nitric acid to the weighed sample in the platinum crucible prior to the usual fusion. This oxidizes the arsenic and sulphur present, and prevents subsequent loss by deflagration; this precaution should also be adopted in the determination of arsenic in sulphide of arsenic obtained in the ordinary course of analysis. Molybdic and phosphoric acids, which behave similarly to arsenic under this treatment, interfere, of course, with the method. Antimony, by forming antimoniate of sodium, or potassium, remains practically insoluble and without effect. A determination can be made in 30 minutes by this process. A modification of the above method has been proposed by R. C. Canby,[*] in which he neutralizes the solution with an emulsion of c. p. zinc oxide. The zinc oxide is added in slight excess (see Chapter XX: manganese), no delicate testing with litmus-paper and alternate adding of dilute ammonia and nitric acid becomes necessary, thus saving time. The slight excess of zinc oxide also tends to render the subsequent filtration and washing of the arseniate of silver more rapid, as it holds the gelatinous silica which is precipitated on neutralization. The writer has tried this method of neutralization, and regards it as an improvement on the method as originally given.

---

[*] Transactions of the American Institute of Mining Engineers, Vol. XVII, p. 77.

CHAPTER XI.

ANTIMONY (Sb).

ANTIMONY in ores, mattes, etc., is best determined by one of the following gravimetric methods. The first method is the most accurate, and is to be recommended in scientific work and where great accuracy is required. The second method is more rapid and simpler than the first, and answers all purposes for technical work.

First Method.—Precipitation of the antimony as sulphide, conversion of the sulphide into antimony tetroxide (Sb_2O_4), and weighing as such. Method due to Bunsen.*

Second Method.—Precipitation of the antimony as metallic antimony, and weighing as such. This method is due to Carnot.†

First Method.—Treat 1.0 gm. of finely pulverized ore in a flask, similar to the flask used in the determination of copper, with 5 cc. of concentrated nitric acid, 10 cc. of concentrated hydrochloric acid, and 3 gms. of crystallized tartaric acid. Heat until the substance is nearly dry, in order to expel most of the free acid. To the nearly dry mass add 100 cc. of water, make alkaline with ammonia, add 10 cc. of yellow ammonium sulphide, and warm gently for one hour. Sufficient ammonium sulphide should be added to render the fluid yellow. Filter, and wash with hot water until the filtrate runs through colorless. The antimony will be in the filtrate as ammonium sulphantimonate. Acidify the filtrate with hydrochloric acid, and allow the precipitate to settle. Should the ore be not thoroughly decomposed by the above treatment with acids, dry

---
* Fresenius, Quant. Anal., § 125, p. 243.
† Comptes, Rendus, CXIV, p. 587.

the residue remaining on the filter, and fuse it with 5 gms. of sodium carbonate and 1.0 gm. of sodium nitrate. Treat the fused mass with an excess of hydrochloric acid and 1.0 gm. of tartaric acid, evaporate off the excess of acid, add 25 cc. of water, render alkaline with ammonia, and treat with yellow ammonium sulphide. Filter, wash, and acidulate the filtrate with hydrochloric acid. Allow the precipitated antimony sulphide to settle, and filter off the precipitate on the same filter as before washing with hot water. Wash finally with alcohol to displace the water adhering to the precipitate, dry it at a low heat, wash with carbon disulphide to dissolve the free sulphur, and dry at a temperature of not over 100° C. As soon as the precipitate is dry enough to remove it from the filter, brush it into a watch-glass, cleaning the paper as thoroughly as possible, and place the filter in a large covered porcelain crucible which has been previously weighed. Moisten it with concentrated nitric acid, add 4 to 5 cc. of red fuming nitric acid, and evaporate on a water-bath to dryness. Now transfer the precipitate to the crucible and add a little concentrated nitric acid by means of a pipette, inserting the point of the pipette under the edge of the lid. When the violent action has ceased add 10 times the volume of the precipitate of red fuming nitric acid, and evaporate to dryness on the water-bath, removing the cover as soon as all danger of loss by spirting is past. Finally ignite cautiously over a Bunsen burner to expel the sulphuric acid and convert the antimony into tetroxide. Weigh the tetroxide and calculate the antimony. The weight of the precipitate multiplied by 0.78947 equals the weight of antimony.

In very accurate work all the filtrates should be treated with sulphuretted hydrogen to recover any traces of antimony which may have possibly escaped.

A determination requires from three to four hours.

Second Method.—This method consists essentially in obtaining the antimony in a hydrochloric-acid solution, in precipitating it with tin and weighing it in the metallic state. The method varies somewhat, according to whether the ores are oxidized or sulphide ores, and according to whether they contain lead or not.

Sulphides.—Take from 2 to 5 gms. of ore, according to its supposed percentage of antimony, so that we may operate on about 1.0 gm. of antimony. Treat in a small flask, as before, with 50 to 60 cc. of concentrated hydrochloric acid, and heat on a sand-bath. When the acid appears to have no further action and the ore is decomposed, decant the clear liquid through a filter and add a fresh quantity of acid. Heat again, and continue until the sulphides are thoroughly decomposed. Decant through the filter and renew the acid once more, adding 1 or 2 drops of nitric acid to complete the attack; heat at 100° C., filter, and wash the insoluble gangue with hydrochloric acid diluted with water.

The combined filtrates are diluted with an equal volume of water, a blade of tin is introduced and the solution heated to 80° or 90° C. The precipitation begins immediately, and for 1.0 gm. of antimony is completed in about 90 minutes.

The precipitate is washed by decantation, replacing the liquid with dilute hydrochloric acid to remove salts of tin and any other salts which may be present. The metallic antimony is brought upon a weighed filter, washed thoroughly with hot water, and finally with alcohol. The metallic antimony is then dried at 100° C. and weighed together with the filter.

If the operation is conducted as above there is neither appreciable loss nor oxidation.

Oxidized Ores.—The oxides of antimony are frequently attacked with extreme difficulty by hydrochloric acid. We are then exposed either to notable losses by volatilization or to an incomplete solution of the antimony.

The method of procedure is as follows: The ore is placed in a small flat-bottomed flask, in which the quantity of from 2 to 5 gms. forms a light layer permeable to gases. Place an elbow-tube in the flask, by means of a cork in the neck, so that its lower end descends almost to the level of the ore. Through the tube pass a current of dry sulphuretted hydrogen, placing the flask upon a piece of wire-gauze at the height of a few inches above the flame of a Bunsen burner, so that the temperature shall not exceed 300° C., producing no volatilization of the antimony sulphide. The ore remains pulverulent and is permeated by the hydrogen sulphide, which acts at the same time as a reducing and sulphurizing agent. The surface of the ore is renewed from time to time by shaking the flask. The conversion is complete in about one hour. When cold the ore is treated with hydrochloric acid in the same flask. The precipitation and weighing are then effected as described above. Experience shows that the quantity of antimony remaining undissolved is quite insignificant.

Ores containing Iron or Lead.—Neither the presence of iron nor of zinc, even in considerable quantities, interferes with the method.

Lead, if present, will be precipitated with the antimony by the tin. Its presence can easily be detected. If present weigh the combined precipitates of antimony and lead, and after weighing heat to 50° or 60° C. in a solution of yellow sodium sulphide (prepared by boiling the monosulphide with flowers of sulphur). The antimony is rapidly dissolved, the lead being converted into a sulphide which is insoluble.

Filter off the lead sulphide, wash thoroughly, and dry. Finally ignite the precipitate in a Rose crucible in a stream of sulphuretted hydrogen, and weigh. Eighty-five per cent of the weight of this lead sulphide represents the corresponding weight of the metallic lead, which is to be deducted from the combined weight of the antimony and lead.

CHAPTER XII.

TIN (Sn).

A GREAT many methods have been proposed for the separation and estimation of tin, for which see Fresenius, Rose, Cairns, Crooks, etc. It is the opinion of the author that the following methods are the best in use :

First Method.—Fuse 1.0 gm. of *very finely pulverized* rich ore with 3 gms. of sulphur and 3 gms. of dry sodium carbonate in a large porcelain crucible over a Bunsen burner for about one hour. The ore and flux should be thoroughly mixed. The heat should not be too great, nor should the fusion be too greatly prolonged, as the sulphide of tin may become oxidized, and consequently be insoluble when the fusion is treated with water. The fusion results in the production of sodium and tin sulphides. If the fusion has been properly conducted the tin sulphide should go into solution, upon addition of water, as sodium sulpho-stannate.

Allow the fusion to cool, place the crucible in a casserole, add hot water, and digest on the water-bath until the mass is disintegrated and removed from the crucible. Filter, wash thoroughly with hot water, and acidulate the filtrate with sulphuric acid to precipitate the tin sulphide. Allow the sulphide to settle, keeping the solution warm ; pour the clear solution on a filter, wash four or five times by decantation, and finally on the filter, using hot water. Should the precipitate run through the filter wash with ammonium acetate. Place the filter and its contents in a weighed porcelain crucible, and apply a very gentle heat, with free access of air until the odor of sulphurous acid is no longer perceptible. Gradually increase the heat to a high degree, and finally add ammonium carbonate to insure the complete elimination of the sulphuric acid. The treatment with ammonium carbonate should be repeated several times. A high heat at the beginning is to be avoided, as fumes of stannic sulphide are liable to escape if the heat is too high.

The residue from the first fusion and solution invariably contains tin; hence it must be refused. Before fusion, if much iron is present it should be removed with a little dilute hydrochloric acid. If but little iron sulphide is present the treatment with acid can be dispensed with. The residue is now dried, burned, mixed with sodium carbonate and sulphur, and fused as before. The fused mass is dissolved in water, filtered, and the tin precipitated as before. The weight of tin recovered from this second fusion is to be added to the weight obtained from the first fusion. If the fusions were properly conducted a third fusion will generally be unnecessary.*

After weighing the stannic oxide, it should be examined for silica as follows: Fuse a weighed portion with three or four parts of a mixture of equal parts of sodium and potassium carbonates, treat the fused mass with hot water, filter, and wash. Acidulate the filtrate with hydrochloric acid, and should any silica separate out, filter it off, reserving the filter and its contents. Acidulate the filtrate with hydrochloric acid and pass sulphuretted hydrogen, to precipitate the tin. Filter out the precipitated sulphide and treat the filtrate as usual for silica, finally filtering through the reserved filter. Calculate the silica thus found to the whole weight of stannic oxide, and, after deducting this weight from the weight of the stannic oxide and silica, calculate the metallic tin. This method is due to Rose.†

Second Method.—Of all the different methods proposed for the dry or fire assay of tin ores it is believed that the following is the best. This is the German method, and is essentially as follows:‡ Mix 5 grammes of ore with 1.0 gramme of

---
* School of Mines Quarterly, Vol. XIII, No. 4, p. 370.
† Quantitative Analysis, p. 393.
‡ Miller, School of Mines Quarterly, Vol. XIII, No. 4, p. 372.

finely ground charcoal, and place in the bottom of an ordinary Hessian or clay crucible. Over this place 15 grammes of black-flux substitute mixed with 1 gramme of borax-glass. The black-flux substitute is made by mixing ten parts of sodium bicarbonate with three parts of flour. On top of the charge is placed a cover of salt, and on this several lumps of charcoal. The fusion is performed in the wind-furnace, using a coke fire, or in the muffle-furnace. The crucibles should be left in the fire for from one hour to one hour and twenty minutes. The fire should be hot—between a bright red and a white heat, but not as hot as a white heat. The crucibles are removed from the furnace and allowed to cool. When cold they are broken open and the slag removed from the buttons, which are then ready for weighing. The slag should be clear and well fused.

This method requires that the ore should be quite pure, and should contain a high per cent of tin. If the ore is low-grade, it should be first concentrated by washing in a gold-pan or by coarse jigging. In this case the sample should be weighed, then washed until most of the silica, iron, etc., is removed. The concentrates are now dried and weighed. From the dry concentrates two portions of 5 grammes each are taken for assay.

The method of calculating results is illustrated by the following example:

Sample weighed	500 grammes.
Concentrates weighed	55 "
Assay of 5 grammes concentrates gave tin	3.5 "
" " 5 " " " "	3.4 "
Average	3.45

Hence $\dfrac{3.45 \times 55}{5} = 37.95$ gms. tin in the 55 gms. of concentrates; and $\dfrac{37.95 \times 100}{500} = 7.59$ per cent tin in the ore.

CHAPTER XIII.

COPPER (Cu).

Two wet methods for the determination of copper in ores and furnace-products are generally used in the United States, as follows: The volumetric assay, by a standard solution of potassium cyanide, and the battery-assay. In addition to these, the colorimetric method and the volumetric iodide method are sometimes used.

Volumetric Assay by Means of Standard Potassium-cyanide Solution.—The best and most rapid method for making this assay is the method developed by Mr. A. H. Low, late chemist to the Boston and Colorado Smelting Company at Argo, Colorado.* The method is essentially that of Dr. Steinbeck, but so modified as to save considerable time, while insuring equal if not greater accuracy. Treat 1 gramme of the pulverized ore in a flat-bottomed flask (250 cc. capacity), or casserole, with 7 cc. of nitric and 5 cc. sulphuric acid. Commercial acids will answer all purposes. Heat till the nitric acid is all expelled and the sulphuric acid is boiling freely. Sulphur, if present, is usually partially, sometimes entirely, volatilized, a portion recondensing on the neck of the flask. What is in the bottom of the flask should be melted into globules, which are yellow when cold and free from copper. Allow the flask and contents to cool sufficiently, and add 6 grammes of commercial sheet zinc cut into small strips of about 3 grammes each. Shake the contents of the flask in order to break up any cake formed in the bottom, and allow to stand

---
* Transactions of the Colorado Scientific Society, Vol. I.

five minutes. Then add 50 cc. of water and 20 cc. of sulphuric acid to rapidly dissolve the excess of zinc, which usually takes about five minutes more. When solution of the zinc is complete, fill up to the neck with water, allow to settle, and decant the clear supernatant liquid. This may be tested for copper, if desired, with sulphuretted-hydrogen water, bearing in mind that antimony, bismuth, etc., may be present and give discolorations likely to be mistaken for copper. As a rule, no discoloration or only an extremely faint one will be observed, and consequently the test is usually omitted. Fill up with water and decant twice more. The residue in the flask may consist of gangue and copper, besides various other constituents of the ore and the impure reagents used, such as silver, gold, lead, arsenic, antimony, etc., of which only silver is likely to interfere with the assay. Now add 5 cc., pretty exactly measured, of pure concentrated nitric acid, and boil, to expel the red fumes. Now add a single drop of strong hydrochloric acid, and if much silver (1 per cent or more) is thus indicated, add a second drop of hydrochloric acid, which is usually quite sufficient, and, after dilution with a little water, filter. A simple cloudiness or very slight precipitate of silver may be disregarded. To the somewhat dilute acid solution add 10 cc. of strong ammonia-water and cool.

One of two courses is now to be chosen. If the color of the solution indicates that not more than 3 per cent of copper is present, add about 125 cc. of water and filter, using a filter of about 6 inches in diameter and folded into corrugations. It filters rapidly, and the small amount of dilute solution remaining in the pores of the filter generally need not be washed out. If a larger amount of copper is present, the 125 cc. of water is added and the titration with potassium cyanide is proceeded with, until all but about 2 or 3 per cent of the copper has been neutralized, and then the liquid should be filtered as before. The object of this filtration is to remove the gangue, lead, ferric hydrate, etc., which may be present, and afford a clear solution with which to complete the titration. The cyanide solution is run into the filtered liquid, and when within a few cubic centimetres of the end the bulk of the solution should be noted and distilled water added, if necessary, so that the final bulk will be about 180 cc. This is about the bulk which should be attained, without any dilution, in the assay of a substance containing about 80 per cent copper, which is the maximum amount considered in the present scheme, starting with one gramme of substance. The final addition of the cyanide should be made drop by drop, the flask being well shaken each time, until the blue or lilac tint can scarcely be discerned at the upper edges of the liquid when viewed against a white background. Many chemists titrate to a faint rose or pink tint. The cyanide solution should be of such a strength that 1 cc. will correspond to 5 milligrammes of copper. Accordingly, it will contain from 55 to 60 grammes of commercial cyanide of potassium to the litre. It should be kept in a closed bottle, preferably of dark-green glass, covered with black paper, and be protected with a layer of coal-oil. To standardize, dissolve from three to five tenths of a gramme of pure copper-foil in 5 cc. of pure concentrated nitric acid; boil off red fumes, dilute slightly, add 10 cc. of strong ammonia-water, cool, and titrate. When near the end add distilled water, to bring the final bulk up to about 180 cc., and finish as described above.

Although most ores yield to the above treatment with nitric and sulphuric acid, the addition of a little hydrochloric acid is sometimes necessary and advantageous. When the amount of silver present is known, it need not be removed, but a correction can be applied to the final result instead. $2Ag = Cu$, or 1 per cent $Ag = 0.3$ per cent Cu, about.

When large amounts of arsenic, etc., are present, they may be only partially precipitated by the treatment with zinc, and may consequently, when the zinc is dissolved, react on the precipitated copper and cause the solution of a small portion. With such ores more time should be allowed for the zinc to act before dissolving the excess, and also the first decantation should be made as soon as possible after the zinc has all been dissolved. An accurate assay can be made by this method in from 20 to 30 minutes.

Battery-assay.—The amount of ore or substance to be taken will depend on the amount of copper which it contains. For the assays of a substance containing 5 per cent or less of copper 3 grammes should be taken, while for a substance containing over 60 per cent of copper 0.25 of a gramme will be sufficient. The usual amount is 1 gramme, but the assayer should use his judgment according to the amount of copper he thinks the substance contains.

The substance is dissolved in the same manner described under the head of the cyanide-assay. It is then diluted with a little distilled water and in order to remove silver, if present, one or two drops of hydrochloric acid (in extreme cases the amount necessary may be larger, but care should always be exercised to avoid an excess, as this interferes with the results) are added, and the liquid filtered into a platinum dish of about 60 to 70 cc. capacity. This dish is best made of the lightest platinum which will admit of ordinarily careful handling when filled with the solution. The platinum dish is then placed on a piece of copper or brass, connected with the negative or zinc element of the battery (a very good battery for this purpose is the ordinary Bunsen cell), while the liquid in the dish is connected with the positive pole either by a platinum wire attached to the positive pole and coiled in a horizontal spiral, or by a copper wire on which is hung a strip of platinum-foil the ends of which are immersed in the liquid. About 8 hours is the time usually required to complete the assay, the time of course depending on the amount of copper present and the activity of the electrical action. In order to determine if all the copper has been precipitated, a drop of the solution is removed from the dish by means of a pipette and tested with sulphuretted-hydrogen water.

If this test shows all the copper to have been precipitated, the liquid is best removed from the dish by siphoning off by means of a bent-glass tube, the solution being replaced by distilled water as fast as it siphons off, until it is washed sufficiently. When washed sufficiently the wires are removed and the dish is washed with alcohol, which is poured off and the contents dried by setting fire to the alcohol, which adheres to the sides, after which the dish with its brilliant coating of rose-red copper is weighed. The difference between the weight of the dish and its weight after the precipitation of the copper upon it represents the weight of copper precipitated, from which the percentage of copper can be calculated. The precipitated copper should always be of a rose-red color, otherwise the result cannot be relied upon. Many of the different elements, if in solution, will be liable to be precipitated together with the copper, and will affect the result, sometimes to a very great extent. Messrs. Torrey and Eaton of New York[*] have made a large number of tests with the cyanide and battery methods, and the results of their tests and the conclusions which they draw from them are that in all cases the cyanide method is more reliable than the battery method. When much arsenic, antimony, bismuth, etc., are present, a very good method of procedure is to treat the ore according to the method described under the head of cyanide-assay, and after dissolving the precipitated copper with nitric acid, add sulphuric acid and evaporate to expel the nitric acid, filter if necessary, and proceed to precipitate the copper by the battery. This method is preferable to the method described by Cairns,[†] and some other authors, of precipitating the metals of groups VI and VII by means of sulphuretted hydrogen and then dissolving the sulphides of arsenic, antimony, and tin by the addition of caustic potash, on account of its greater speed and the less liability of loss of copper in manipulation. The use of sulphuretted hydrogen is not only a source of annoyance and discomfort to the chemist, but, without very careful manipulation, introduces a liability of error owing to the difficulty of handling and washing the precipitate.

Taking all of the liabilities of error into consideration, the writer agrees with Messrs. Torrey and Eaton that the cyanide method is generally more accurate and preferable to the battery method.

---
[*] See Engineering and Mining Journal for May and June 1885.
[†] See Cairns' Quantitative Analysis.

A very ingenious and simple apparatus for the estimation of copper by electrolytic deposition has been devised by Mr. A. H. Low of Denver, Colo.,* and is for sale by Eimer & Amend of New York. This apparatus not only shortens the time required for the determination of the copper, but considerably lessens the expense of apparatus, requiring no expensive batteries and platinum dishes. It is consequently to be highly recommended for use in a laboratory where a large number of determinations are required to be made daily by means of electrolytic deposition. This method fails when a large quantity of ferric sulphate is contained in the solution.

Colorimetric Method.— This method is to be recommended for the estimation of copper in substances containing less than 2 per cent, as, for example, in slags from copper-smelting operations and in tailings from concentrating-works. The method was first suggested by Heine.† The method given here is a modification of Heine's method. Where the amount of iron and alumina present is small, previous precipitation of the copper is not necessary, but in the case of slags and tailings, for which this method is particularly adapted, it would be impossible to wash out all of the copper salts with the small amount of wash-water which can be used; hence in this case previous precipitation of the copper is necessary.

The method consists essentially in converting the copper in the substance to be tested into ammonium cupric nitrate, and comparing the blue color produced with that produced by dissolving a known amount of copper in the same amount of acid and using the same amount of ammonia as is used in the regular assay. With each set of assays a separate standard should be run, as the blue color is not constant, but fades. For the standard either an accurately weighed amount of pure copper can be taken, or the same amount of slag or tails as is used in the regular assay may be taken. Where the latter method is adopted, and it is generally preferable, as there

---

* Proceedings of the Colorado Scientific Society, Vol. I.
† See Mitchell on Practical Assaying; Kerl's Metallurgy of Copper.

is less liability to error in weighing than where a small amount of pure copper is taken, and it also introduces the same conditions into the standard as are present in the regular assay, of course the copper must have been previously accurately determined in the sample from which the standard is weighed out. A few ounces of the material will last for a large number of assays. In order to make the assay, the amount of material for assay and of the standard are weighed out and treated in the same manner as described under the head of the cyanide-assay. When the precipitated copper has been thoroughly washed by decantation it is dissolved in a small amount of nitric acid (about 2 cubic centimetres is sufficient), and an excess of strong ammonia added (about 4 cubic centimetres), the acid and ammonia being pretty accurately measured. The solution after slight dilution with water is then filtered into a graduated tube for comparison, and washed. Two of these graduated tubes are necessary,—one for the regular assay and one for the standard. They should be of thin colorless glass and of the same internal and external diameter, and should also be provided with a stopper, so that the solution may be thoroughly mixed by shaking. The assayer can prepare and graduate these tubes for his own use.

The method of determining the percentage of copper present is best illustrated by an example: Suppose the material used for making the standard assay contained exactly 1 per cent of copper; then if a half gramme was taken, and after filtering into the tube and washing, the contents of the tube were diluted up to the 25-cc. mark with distilled water, each cc. of the solution would contain $\frac{5}{25}$ milligramme of copper, or 0.2 milligramme. The regular assay is then run, and after filtering into the tube the color of the solution is noted, and it is diluted with distilled water, shaking after each addition of water until the tint or color in the two tubes is the same when compared together against a white background. The height of the liquid in the tube is then noted. Suppose it reads 22 cc. Now, as each cubic centimetre of the standard solution contains 0.2 milligramme of copper, each cubic centimetre of the solu-

tion in the other tube contains the same amount; hence
22 × 0.2 = 4.4 milligrammes.

500 mgs. ore taken: 4.4 mgs. Cu = 100 : x; $x = 0.88\%$ Cu.

Volumetric Iodide Method.—A new volumetric method which presents many advantages has recently been proposed. This is a modification of Berringer's* iodide method, and, as described by Mr. G. E. Jewell,† is essentially as follows: Treat 1 gramme of the substance in a flask with from 10 to 15 cc. of strong nitric and 3 to 5 cc. of strong hydrochloric acids; run down over a strong flame or on the sand-bath until the substance is decomposed; cool, add from 5 to 8 cc. of concentrated sulphuric acid, and heat until white fumes of sulphuric anhydride are given off. Cool, dilute with 25 cc. of water, boil to disintegrate the mass, and filter off the residue, in which the lead and silica may be determined if necessary.

Filter into a 250-cc. copper flask, add one or two strips of heavy aluminium-foil (where only small amounts of copper are present the foil may be replaced to advantage with a coil of aluminium wire), and boil for from 10 to 15 minutes, which will generally be sufficient time to insure the complete precipitation of the copper. Pour off the solution, wash three times by decantation with hot water, add 3 cc. of nitric acid to the contents of the flask, allowing the acid to flow over the aluminium. The fine adherent particles of copper dissolve readily. Boil to expel nitrous fumes, decant into another flask and rinse the aluminium with a few cc. of water, adding the washings to the second flask. Cool, and add gradually a concentrated solution of sodium carbonate until a slight precipitate remains after shaking; now add 3 cc. of acetic acid to redissolve the precipitate and render the solution slightly acid. Cool, and add 5 to 10 grammes of potassium iodide; if the solution is not cold there is danger of volatilizing some of the liberated iodine. The copper is reduced to cuprous iodide, and an equivalent of iodine is liberated. This liberated iodine

---

* Text-book of Assaying.

† "The Determination of Copper by the Iodide Method," State School of Mines Scientific Quarterly, Vol. I, No. 4.

gives to the solution a brown color which varies in depth according to the amount present. Dilute to 100 cc. with cold water, when the solution will be ready for titration with the standard sodium-thiosulphate solution. Add the standard solution gradually from a burette until the brown color is almost discharged. At this point add 2 or 3 cc. of freshly prepared starch solution, and continue the titration carefully until one drop of the standard sodium solution suddenly charges the blue color of the solution to a cream color, which is the end point in the reaction. From the number of cc. of the standard sodium solution used calculate the percentage of copper.

The standard sodium solution is prepared by dissolving 19.59 grammes of pure sodium thiosulphate in 1000 cc. of distilled water. One cc. of this solution should be equivalent to 0.005 gramme of copper. To standardize weigh out 0.3 or 0.4 gramme of c. p. copper, and proceed exactly as in the case of an ore from the point at which the copper is precipitated by the aluminium.

Bismuth is the only element which is likely to be present which will interfere with the results. Comparatively small amounts of bismuth will give the solution a brown color and mask the end reaction.

CHAPTER XIV.

BISMUTH (Bi).

THE following method will answer for the determination of bismuth in ores, alloys, furnace-products, etc.

In the case of an alloy, if malleable, it should be rolled out thin and cut into thin strips; if not malleable it should be pounded up as fine as possible on the anvil.

When lead is present it should be removed before the bismuth is precipitated. It can be removed by the addition of sulphuric acid.

Dissolve 1 or 2 grammes (depending upon the amount of Bi present) of substance in from 7 cc. to 15 cc. of nitric acid. Evaporate until most of the excess of acid is driven off, and add from 2 cc. to 4 cc. of conc. hydrochloric acid and some water. Nearly neutralize the excess of acid with ammonia, and add a large quantity of water. After allowing the precipitate of basic chloride of bismuth to settle, test a portion of the clear supernatant fluid by the addition of water. If the fluid is rendered turbid add water to the whole until the precipitation is complete. Now filter off the precipitate of BiOCl, and wash completely with cold water.

One of two methods can now be followed:

1. **Determination as Bismuth Trioxide (Bi_2O_3).**—Dissolve the precipitate of basic chloride in nitric acid, and dilute with water, paying no attention to any precipitate of basic nitrate that may form. Add ammonium carbonate in *very slight* excess, and heat nearly to boiling for from 15 to 30 minutes. Filter, wash with cold water, dry the precipitate, and when dry transfer it to a watch-glass, removing as completely as possible

from the filter; burn the filter in a weighed porcelain crucible. After the combustion of the filter-paper is complete and nothing but ash remains, moisten it with a few drops of nitric acid (to convert any bismuth which adhered to the filter-paper, and was reduced to metallic bismuth by it, into nitrate), evaporate, and ignite gently until all the carbonic acid is driven off. Weigh the bismuth trioxide and ignite gently again, repeating this operation until the weight is constant, care being exercised not to ignite too strongly.

To obtain the weight of the metallic bismuth multiply the weight of the precipitate (Bi_2O_3) by 0.89744.

2. **Determination as Metallic Bismuth.**—Fuse the precipitate of basic chloride of bismuth in a porcelain crucible with six times its weight of c. p. potassium cyanide, proceeding as follows: Place one-half the cyanide in the crucible, then introduce the precipitate rolled up in the filter-paper, and on top of it add the remainder of the cyanide. The fusion should be conducted carefully, the heat being gradually raised. It should be completed in about 15 minutes at a comparatively gentle heat. The fused mass is now dissolved in water, when grains or shots of metallic bismuth should separate. These grains are now washed rapidly and completely with water, and finally with strong alcohol, dried, and weighed.

Sometimes the crucible may be attacked, and particles of porcelain will be found with the metallic bismuth. In such a case Rose recommends that the crucible, together with a small dried filter, be weighed before the fusion. Collect the insoluble matter on the filter, dry, and weigh the crucible with the filter and bismuth again.

CHAPTER XV.

CADMIUM (Cd).

CADMIUM may be determined gravimetrically by precipitation as $CdCO_3$, ignition to CdO, and weighing as such, or it may be determined volumetrically by means of a standard solution of potassium ferrocyanide.

There are several other methods, both gravimetric and volumetric, for which see Fresenius, Rose, etc.

Gravimetric Determination.—Decompose the ore with nitrohydrochloric acid, evaporate nearly to dryness to drive off the nitric acid, leaving but a small quantity of free hydrochloric acid present. Dilute with warm water, filter, and wash thoroughly with hot water. Through the filtrate pass a rapid current of sulphuretted hydrogen until all members of the sulphuretted-hydrogen group are completely precipitated. The solution should not contain a large excess of hydrochloric acid; if it does the cadmium will fail to precipitate. Filter off the precipitated sulphides, and wash with sulphuretted-hydrogen water. Dissolve the precipitated sulphides in hot hydrochloric acid, and boil. If lead is present some will pass into solution, and can be removed by precipitation with sulphuric acid. Filter and wash. The filtrate will contain the cadmium as a chloride. Precipitate the cadmium with a slight excess of potassium carbonate (pure), filter, and wash precipitate thoroughly with warm water. Dry the precipitate, and when dry remove carefully from the filter-paper, introducing it into a weighed crucible. Moisten the filter-paper with a strong solution of ammonium nitrate, wrap it in a spiral of platinum wire, and ignite over an alcohol flame, allowing the ash to fall into the crucible. The cadmium carbonate adhering to the filter-paper is liable to be reduced by the carbon of the filter, and volatilized; hence the addition of ammonium nitrate, and the care required in ignition. Transfer all the ash to the crucible, and ignite to constant weight. Care should be exercised during ignition that the cadmium oxide is not reduced. If reduced some will be volatilized and lost. Weigh the cadmium oxide, and calculate the percentage of cadmium. The results are liable to be a little low.

Volumetric Determination.—This requires a standard solution of potassium ferrocyanide of about two-thirds the strength of the solution used for the determination of zinc. If its standard for zinc is known its standard for cadmium may be calculated as follows: Let $a = $ mgs. of zinc, which 1 cc. of ferrocyanide solution is equivalent to, and $x = $ mgs. of cadmium, which 1 cc. of the solution should precipitate; then

$$130 \text{ (mol. wt. } 2Zn) : 224 \text{ (mol. wt. } 2Cd) :: a : x.$$

It is best to standardize the solution with a solution of cadmium known to contain a certain weight of cadmium.

The titration is performed in the same manner as in the determination of zinc, using uranium acetate as an indicator. The solution should not contain a large excess of hydrochloric acid, as cadmium ferrocyanide is soluble in hydrochloric acid. The analysis is performed as follows: Treat 1 gramme of ore in the same manner as in the determination of zinc (see Chapter XXI), and filter off the precipitated oxides. Neutralize the filtrate with hydrochloric acid, and add a slight excess of acid. Dilute with warm water, and pass a rapid current of sulphuretted hydrogen. Filter off the precipitated sulphides, wash with sulphuretted-hydrogen water, and dissolve the precipitate in dilute hot hydrochloric acid. Dilute, and if copper is present precipitate it with test-lead or aluminium-foil. The solution is now ready for titration with the standard solution of potassium ferrocyanide.

The filtrate from the precipitated sulphides may be used for the determination of zinc, and the copper (if precipitated on aluminium-foil) may be determined as described in Chapter XIII.

The method is rapid, and gives results which answer all requirements for technical purposes.

CHAPTER XVI.

IRON (Fe).

WHILST many different methods have been proposed for the determination of iron, the three following are the only ones in general use in the United States:

1. By precipitation with ammonia, filtration and ignition to ferric oxide, weighing as such;
2. Volumetrically, by means of a standard solution of potassium permanganate (Marguerite's method);
3. Volumetrically by means of a standard solution of potassium bichromate (Peeny's method).

The chemist may have occasion to use all of these methods, as one very frequently gives good results where the others fail. Sometimes a combination of the first and second or first and third may be employed to advantage. When the iron is to be determined by the first method the solution from which the iron is precipitated should first be freed from alumina, chromium, manganese, titanium, lead, arsenic, etc., which are wholly or in part precipitated together with the ferric hydrate. As this is not always possible, especially in technical determinations, a combination of this method with one of the volumetric methods may be employed as follows: The iron, either in a hydrochloric- or sulphuric-acid solution (sometimes it may be an acetic-acid solution when a basic-acetate precipitation has been made as described under the head of Alumina), is precipitated by adding ammonia in excess to the warm solution and the solution brought to a boil. It is then filtered through a ribbed filter-paper and washed. As this precipitate is exceedingly bulky and difficult to wash, a filter-pump may here be used to advantage. It should be washed with warm water until the washings show only a faint trace of chlorides or sulphates, as the case may be. It is then dissolved on the filter-paper directly into a flask with warm diluted hydrochloric or sulphuric acids. It may then be reduced and determined volumetrically by either the second or third methods, as the case may be. If dissolved with sulphuric acid, it may be determined by either of these methods; if dissolved by hydrochloric acid, preferably by the bichromate method.

The second method depends upon the fact that when a solution of potassium permanganate, which has an intense color, is dropped into a solution of ferrous oxide it gives up a portion of its oxygen, being decomposed into salts of manganese and potassium, until the ferrous oxide is completely converted into ferric oxide. The moment this conversion is complete the permanganate imparts a pink color to the solution. The reaction which takes place is as follows:

$$10FeSO_4 + 8H_2SO_4 + K_2Mn_2O_8 =$$
$$5Fe_2(SO_4)_3 + 2MnSO_4 + K_2SO_4 + 8H_2O.$$

From this it will be seen that in order to determine the amount of iron in solution it will only be necessary to know what amount of iron one cubic centimetre of the permanganate solution will oxidize from the ferrous to the ferric form.

A normal solution of permanganate is a solution of which 1 cubic centimetre is equal to or converts 10 milligrammes of iron from the ferrous to the ferric state. To prepare such a solution, dissolve 12 grammes of pure crystallized potassium permanganate in 2030 cc. of distilled water. The amount of water will vary slightly with different permanganates, so that the chemist will have to determine for himself the exact amount with each new bottle of permanganate he uses. This solution should be placed in a stoppered bottle and shaken from time to time until ready for use. It is best to make up the solution at least forty-eight hours before standardizing. This solution may be standardized in two ways:

1st. By means of metallic iron.

The iron employed for the purpose is usually fine pianoforte wire, which contains 99.7 per cent iron. This should be rubbed with sand-paper until bright, in order to remove dust and shellac, with which it is sometimes covered, etc., before weighing out. It is best to weigh it out on the button-balance, two portions being taken of about 150 and 200 milligrammes, respectively. These portions are each introduced into a flat-bottomed flask (250 cc.) and dissolved with dilute sulphuric acid by gently warming. Many chemists (see Fresenius, Cairns, etc.) use a valve-flask for this purpose, to prevent the oxidation of the iron during solution. The writer prefers to dissolve without going to the trouble of preparing a valve-flask, and afterwards reduce the small amount of iron which may have been oxidized, by the addition of some pure granulated zinc. This reduction takes but a few minutes. When the iron is all reduced, which may be determined by removing a drop of the solution on a glass rod and testing it on a porcelain plate with a drop of ammonium-sulphocyanate solution (if the iron is all reduced to the proto state the drop will remain colorless, whilst if any ferric oxide is present the drop will turn red, the depth of the color depending on the amount of ferric iron present), the contents of the flask are diluted, by the addition of cold distilled water, and the solution decanted off from the zinc into a large beaker, or preferably an ordinary glass battery-jar, the jar being much less liable to breakage in subsequent stirring of the solution. The flask and zinc are well washed, the washings being transferred to the jar. The solution is then diluted up to about 700 cc. (it is a good plan to scratch a mark on the side of the jar at this point), and about 20 cc. of dilute sulphuric acid are added. In making subsequent determinations it is better to use the same or a similar jar, and always fill to the same point so as to have the same bulk of solution. Sometimes minute particles of zinc will be decanted over with the washings, but these will quickly be dissolved by the excess of sulphuric acid. As soon as all effervescence of gas has ceased,—the solution should not be allowed to stand too long, as some iron is liable to be oxidized by contact with the air,—the solution is ready to titrate with the previously prepared permanganate solution which is run in drop by drop from a burette, with constant stirring, until the color (which disappears rapidly at first, and then more slowly) finally becomes permanent, and remains so for one minute. The final color should be a light pink, and the chemist should note this color and bring his subsequent titrations to the same tint. The titrations should be performed in a good light and with a white surface (piece of paper) underneath the jar. Note carefully the quantity of permanganate solution used, and calculate its value or standard as follows: Suppose 0.200 gramme of iron were taken and 19.5 cc. of the permanganate solution was used: then

$$0.1994 \div 19.5 = 0.010225 +.$$

Hence 1 cc. of permanganate solution corresponds to .01022 gramme of iron.

The results obtained on the two samples of iron wire taken should not differ more than one tenth of a cubic centimetre. If the difference is greater than this more trials should be made.

The other method of standardizing the solution is by means of oxalic acid. The objection to this method is the uncertainty of procuring a normal acid. When oxalic acid is used the crystals should be kept in a tight-stoppered colored-glass bottle, and each bottle should be tested with some permanganate solution, the standard of which has been previously determined, to determine if it is normal. The oxalic method has the advantage that it is more rapid than the iron-wire method. To standardize the solution by this method weigh out about 250 milligrammes of oxalic acid on the button-balance, the exact amount taken being immaterial, so that the exact weight is known. Dissolve in water (about 100 cc.), and add 6 to 8 cc. of pure concentrated sulphuric acid. Heat to about 60° to 70° C., and add permanganate solution until the color is permanent. The color will disappear very slowly at first, but after a few cubic centimetres of the permanganate solution have been added, it will disappear rapidly. After the first faint permanent tint has formed, add one or two drops of permanganate in excess (one or two drops having previously been determined to be the amount required to impart a faint tint to 600 cc. of distilled water) on account of the greater bulk of solution used when standardizing by iron wire.

By comparing the equation previously given with the following equation, which represents the oxidation of oxalic acid,

$$5(H_2C_2O_4 \cdot 2H_2O) + 3H_2SO_4 + K_2Mn_2O_8 =$$
$$10CO_2 + 2MnSO_4 + K_2SO_4 + 18H_2O,$$

it will be seen that the same quantity of potassium permanganate is required to oxidize one molecule of oxalic acid whose molecular weight is 126, or two atoms of iron (in the form of monoxide) whose molecular weight is 112. Consequently we have the equation assuming 0.250 gramme of oxalic acid were taken:

$$126 : 112 :: .250 : .222 +.$$

In other words, the 250 milligrammes of oxalic acid taken represented .222 + grammes of metallic iron. Suppose that 21.7 cc. of permanganate solution were used, then one cubic centimetre of permanganate solution would correspond to .01023 + grammes of iron.

In practice the writer has usually standardized the solution once with iron wire and then checked the result with oxalic acid, using an acid which was known to be normal.

Provided the proper precautions are observed, iron may be determined in a hydrochloric-acid solution by means of standard potassium-permanganate solution, although most authors claim that this method is not accurate on account of the following reaction, which takes place if the solution is at all warm:

$$K_2Mn_2O_8 + 16HCl = 2KCl + 2MnCl_2 + 8H_2O + 10Cl.$$

Some of the chlorine set free will convert the ferrous iron present into ferric; but some will usually escape, and the results obtained will consequently be too high.

The writer has found by experience that if only a small quantity of hydrochloric acid is present and the solution is extremely dilute (700 cc.) and cold, and moreover contains a large excess of sulphuric acid (usually 20 cc. concentrated acid), that the results obtained are as reliable as when sulphuric acid has been used as the solvent. As a further precaution some chemists add a few cubic centimetres of a saturated solution of manganous sulphate before titration. The writer has generally found this latter precaution unnecessary, provided the above conditions were carried out; but as the addition of manganous sulphate can do no harm, it is well to use it when the operator is in doubt or when a considerable amount of hydrochloric acid has been used.

The third method depends on the fact that if potassium bichromate is added to a solution of a ferrous salt in the presence of a strong free acid, the ferrous oxide is converted into ferric oxide, as is shown by the equation

$$6FeCl_2 + K_2Cr_2O_7 + 14HCl = 3Fe_2Cl_6 + 2KCl + Cr_2Cl_6 + 7H_2O,$$

which shows that 1 or 295.18 parts of potassium bichromate will convert 6 equivalent or 336 parts of iron to the ferric state (295.18 being the molecular weight of $K_2Cr_2O_7$ and 336 being 6 times the atomic weight of Fe). In practice a half-normal solution, or a solution of which one cubic centimetre is equal to 0.005 gramme of iron, is usually used. To prepare this solution dissolve 8.785 grammes of pure potassium bichromate in two litres of water. The solution is best standardized by means of iron wire, dissolving the wire either in hydrochloric or sulphuric acids. The solution is then reduced and transferred to a suitable vessel for titration, some free acid being added. The bichromate solution is dropped in from a burette, the liquid being constantly stirred with a glass rod. The liquid, which is at first nearly colorless, speedily acquires a pale-green tint, which changes gradually to a darker green. A small drop of the liquid is now from time to time taken out by means of the stirring-rod and tested on a porcelain plate with a drop of potassium ferricyanide (free from ferrocyanide), which should not be too strong or it will give a red precipitate. When the blue color produced by the action of a ferrous salt on the ferricyanide begins to lose the intensity which is exhibited on the first trials and becomes quite faint, the addition of bichromate solution is proceeded with more carefully. When the test no longer produces a blue color the oxidation is complete. From the remarkable delicacy of the reaction the exact point may be easily hit to a drop. After a little practice a large number of tests will seldom have to be made, as the operator may determine, from the manner in which the green color of the solution deepens, about how much bichromate it will be safe to add before testing. Many authors (Fresenius, Cairns, etc.) recommend the use of a solution one tenth as strong as the regular solution for finishing the titration. In ordinary practice this is found to be unnecessary where a solution as dilute as the one recommended is used.

After the titration is completed, take the reading of the burette and determine the value of one cubic centimetre of the solution in the same way as described for the permanganate solution. It is best to weigh out two portions of the iron wire and standardize the solution in duplicate, as is done in the case of the permanganate solution.

For determining the iron by this method it may be reduced to the ferrous state either by means of zinc or by means of a solution of stannous chloride added in slight excess, the excess being taken up by means of mercuric chloride. This latter method has the advantage that the reduction may be performed in a few moments, thus greatly reducing the time required to make a determination. It may also be employed to advantage when zinc free from iron and arsenic cannot be obtained, which may sometimes happen. If proper care is used in the reduction the result will agree perfectly with those obtained by reduction with metallic zinc. The only point to be observed is that the solution of stannous and mercuric chloride should not be too strong, and only a slight excess should be used. The operator, after a little practice, will have no difficulty in observing these conditions. The best form, and, on the whole, that which gives the most rapid reduction, when zinc is used to reduce the iron, is pure granulated zinc. The granulations should be quite heavy, otherwise small portions will become detached and pass over with the solution for titration into the jar. The granulated zinc may be made from pure bar zinc by melting in a crucible, placing a few lumps of charcoal on the surface of the zinc, and pouring into cold water after skimming.

The solution may also be reduced by boiling in a flask with granulated zinc which has previously been amalgamated with mercury. In order to amalgamate the zinc place it in sulphuric acid for a few moments, remove, and wash with water; then place in a bottle containing clean mercury and sulphuric acid, and shake. This method of reduction has the advantage that less zinc is consumed than in the case where raw zinc is used, and also that if, in transferring the solution from the flask, some pieces of zinc pass over, they need not be removed before the titration is proceeded with, as hydrogen is not evolved from the amalgamated zinc in a cold dilute solution. It has the disadvantage that more time is required to reduce the solution. Where zinc free from impurities cannot be obtained, the solution may be reduced in the following manner: Prepare some cubes of zinc about one-half inch square, and thoroughly amalgamate them with mercury. In each of the flasks containing the solution of iron to be reduced place a strip of platinum-foil about three inches long and three quarters of an inch in width, and on this place a cube of the amalgamated zinc. In order to have the foil work well it should be cleaned and its surface roughened. A strong current of gas should be induced by contact between the zinc and platinum. A convenient form of apparatus for this reduction is described in Vol. XV, Transactions of the American Institute of Mining Engineers. A good vessel to perform this reduction in is the ordinary pound bottle that caustic potash and other reagents are put up in by the manufacturers. It has been found by experiment that amalgamated zinc will not give up its iron until it is nearly dissolved. The disadvantage of this method is the length of time it requires to reduce a solution—from 6 to 20 hours generally being necessary. Several other methods of reduction are described by different authors, but the above are sufficient for every case likely to occur in practice, and are among the best.

The exact method to be pursued in making a determination will depend on the character of the substance.

Iron Ores.—Most iron ores will yield their iron by simple boiling with acids. Hydrochloric acid is the acid usually employed. Nitric acid is to be avoided, and this is especially the case where the iron is to be determined volumetrically by either of the above methods, for, if any nitric acid (which is an oxidizing agent) is present, reduction and subsequent titration will be impossible. If an ore is not decomposed by simple boiling with hydrochloric acid it may be treated with all three acids in the manner described for sulphide ores.

Usually from 0.5 to 1.0 gramme of ore is dissolved in a small casserole or beaker, a small vessel always being desirable, as it avoids the use of a large excess of acid; and when all the iron is in solution, which may be determined by the appearance of the insoluble residue, the contents of the vessel are washed into a flask and reduced by some one of the methods described above, and the iron determined volumetrically by either of the standard solutions in the manner described above.

For the determination of the iron the filtrate from the silica can be taken, always provided nitric acid has not been used in dissolving.

In some rare cases an ore may be encountered which will not yield all of its iron by treatment with acids. In such a case a very good method of procedure is to filter off and fuse the insoluble residue with potassium bisulphate (see Silica, Chapter I), and add the product of the fusion, after solution in water, or water together with a few drops of hydrochloric acid, to the filtrate containing the greater portion of the iron.

In the case of chromic and titaniferous iron ores which will not readily dissolve by treatment with acids, fuse the insoluble residue as described in Chapter I, combine the filtrate from the insoluble residue and the iron, determine the iron as above in the combined filtrates.

Manganese Ores.—Determine iron in the same manner as in iron ores.

Limestone, Clay, Cement, etc.—The iron is best determined in the filtrate from the silica (when the insoluble residue has been fused, the filtrate from it should be added to the filtrate from the fusion) by heating it and precipitating the iron with ammonia as ferric hydrate. If the iron alone is required this precipitate should be boiled in the beaker for a few minutes and then filtered and washed with boiling water. When the washings no longer show the presence of chlorides (this can be determined by obtaining a small portion of the washings in a test-tube, acidifying with nitric acid, and adding a drop of silver-nitrate solution, which should not give a white precipitate if the chlorides are all removed), the precipitate can be dissolved with warm dilute sulphuric acid directly into a flask, the iron being reduced and determined as before. Where lime, magnesia, etc., are not to be determined in the filtrate, the precipitate need not be washed to the extent of removing the last traces of chlorides.

When alumina is to be determined, proceed in the manner described in Chapter XVII, on Alumina.

Sulphide Ores, Mattes, etc.—The same method may be pursued in the case of all sulphide ores, no distinction being made between copper ores, lead ores, iron ores, etc., except that, when the amount of iron present is small, larger quantities should be taken. Dissolve 0.5 gramme of ore in a small casserole with 2 cc. of strong hydrochloric, 5 cc. strong nitric, and about 8 cc. dilute sulphuric acids added in the order named. The sulphuric acid should be about 60 per cent concentrated acid and 40 per cent water. A flat-bottomed flask can also be used for the solution, the subsequent reduction being performed in the same flask. Heat on a sand-bath or iron plate until dense white fumes of SO_2 are evolved. Continue to heat for about two or three minutes, in order to be sure of removing the last traces of nitric acid; remove from the source of heat, cool, and dilute to about 30 cc. If a casserole was used for solution, wash the contents into a flask, reduce, and determine volumetrically. In the case of lead ores the solution is best reduced by means of metallic zinc, on account of the sulphate of lead which is formed. The zinc reduces this lead sulphate to metallic lead, resulting in the liberation of any small amount of ferric sulphate which it might have held mechanically so that it would not have been reduced, thus giving too low a result. When an ore contains arsenic or antimony the reduced solution cannot be safely titrated by means of potassium permanganate. In this case it is best to first precipitate the arsenic or antimony with sulphuretted hydrogen, filter off the precipitated sulphides, and determine the iron in the filtrate. In the case of copper ores containing large percentages of copper, it is best to first precipitate the iron with ammonia and determine as in the case of iron in limestones, as copper will interfere with the titration and give too high results.

Oxidized Ores of Lead, Silver, Copper, etc.—Treat in the same manner as an oxidized iron ore.

Slag.—If the sample has been taken by suddenly chilling it (see Chapter I, on Silica), it may be treated as follows: Weigh out one half gramme of finely pulverized slag into a casserole of about 100 cc. capacity, moisten with about 7 cubic centimetres of water, and stir with a glass rod. Then add about 5 cc. hydrochloric acid and stir again with a glass rod in order to break up any clots which form and stick to the bottom. Heat to boiling, and stir from time to time, if necessary. When the slag is decomposed, which may be determined by moving the glass rod around the bottom of the casserole to see if any gritty substance is encountered. If no grit is encountered and the insoluble portion appears like flocculent silica when the solution is stirred with the rod, the slag is decomposed. Usually there will be some black specks seen floating on the surface of the liquid, but they may be disregarded, as they consist principally of lead sulphide. The contents of the casserole are now diluted with water and a few cubic centimetres of dilute sulphuric acid added, and then some pure zinc to reduce the iron, the casserole being covered with a convex watch-glass. After the iron is reduced, which will only require a few minutes, as most of the iron was originally present as ferrous iron, and if the solution is performed rapidly, but a small portion of it will have become oxidized ; it can be determined by either of the methods of titration given,—standard bichromate or permanganate of potassium solution. Or the iron may be reduced by means of stannous chloride as before described, and determined with standard bichromate solution. A determination may be made in from ten to fifteen minutes, according to the method employed. When the sample was not so taken that the slag will decompose in hydrochloric acid a cintering fusion may be made on 0.5 gramme (see Chapter I), the fusion being dissolved in water and hydrochloric acid, and the iron determined as above, or the iron may be determined in the filtrate from the silica. If the iron is determined in the filtrate from the silica, care should be taken not to heat the mass, after evaporation to dryness, much above 110° C., otherwise chloride of iron will be volatilized. Objection may be taken to the above rapid method on the ground that it is not absolutely accurate. However, with ordinary care in manipulation duplicates will agree within two tenths of a per cent, and the method certainly gives results sufficiently accurate for the control of the workings of the furnace in a metallurgical works. The writer has frequently examined the insoluble residue from the silica determination for iron by fusing, without finding more than a trace, and generally without being able to detect any ferrous oxide. On account of the rapidity of this method it is invaluable to the lead or copper metallurgist for the control of the workings of the furnace.

Fused Ores, Fused Flue-dust, etc.—These will frequently decompose as perfectly as a slag if sampled by the rod (see Part II, Chapter I). In such a case the iron may be determined as above. When the insoluble residue is gritty and contains iron it should be fused either with acid sulphate of potassium or carbonate of soda, the determination then being proceeded with as described under the head of Iron Ores, the filtrate from the insoluble residue and the silica being combined.

Pig-iron, etc.—Most pig-irons, steels, etc., will give up their iron by simple heating with dilute sulphuric acid. The iron may then be determined as easily as in the case of pianoforte wire, it however being a good plan where 0.5 gramme is taken to dilute the solution up to 500 cc. with distilled water, draw off two or three portions of 100 cc. each with a pipette, reduce each portion, and determine. A very good plan is to titrate one portion, then add the next portion to the same solution and titrate, then add the third portion, and take the total reading of the burette, making the calculation of the percentage on the basis of three fifths of a gramme of substance taken.

In the case of ores, etc., containing arsenic and antimony the following rapid method will serve for all technical determinations: Decompose as described above, and reduce the iron with granulated zinc. When the iron is all reduced filter rapidly, and wash thoroughly with water. The arsenic and antimony will be precipitated by the zinc and remain on the filter. The filtrate containing the iron can now be safely titrated as above.

CHAPTER XVII.

ALUMINIUM (Al).

ONLY two methods are in general use for the determination of aluminium (Al) or alumina (Al_2O_3): 1st. Precipitation of the alumina as hydroxide with ammonia, filtration of the precipitate, ignition to Al_2O_3, and weighing as such; 2d. Direct determination as aluminium phosphate ($Al_2P_2O_8$).

First Method.—This method presents the disadvantages common to all indirect methods, and is quite tedious, especially in the case of a substance containing iron, phosphorus, chromium, titanium, etc.

The method of procedure is as follows: The silica, and all metals of the sulphuretted-hydrogen group (As, Sb, Sn, Pb, Hg, Cu, Bi, and Cd), if present, must be removed from the solution. The silica is removed by any of the methods described in Part II, Chapter I. The metals of the sulphuretted-hydrogen group can be removed by passing a rapid current of sulphuretted-hydrogen gas through the filtrate from the silica, the precaution being observed that nitric acid is not present. After the sulphides are all precipitated, the solution should be rapidly filtered, and the beaker and precipitate on the filter should be thoroughly washed with distilled water, to which has been added some sulphuretted-hydrogen water. Should a precipitate of sulphides form in the filtrate, the solution should be again treated with sulphuretted-hydrogen gas until a precipitate no longer forms. The filtrate from the precipitated sulphides is heated to boiling, and the sulphur is oxidized by the addition of potassium chlorate or bromine-water, which should be added from time to time until the solution is perfectly clear. Should a precipitate form upon boiling (if much sulphuretted hydrogen was used yellow sulphur will separate), it should be filtered off.

The solution is now ready for the precipitation of the aluminium as hydroxide with ammonia, which is effected as follows: Ammonia in slight excess is added to the solution, and the contents of the beaker are boiled until the free ammonia is driven off. This can be determined by holding a piece of glass, previously moistened with dilute hydrochloric acid, over the beaker; should no white fumes form the free ammonia has been expelled. It is essential that the free ammonia should be expelled, as aluminium hydroxide is slightly soluble in an excess of ammonia. It is also essential that ammonium chloride be present; sufficient will be formed when the ammonia is added if the solution contains much hydrochloric acid. The contents of the beaker are now ready for filtration, which is performed as usual, washing the precipitate thoroughly with hot water. Add a little ammonia to the filtrate, and boil. Should a precipitate form, filter it off, and add it to the first precipitate. This is essential, as when the amount of alumina present is large it may not all be precipitated the first time.

The precipitate will consist of aluminium hydroxide, ferric hydroxide, if any iron was present in the solution (iron is generally present); chromium hydroxide, provided chromium was present in the solution (except in the case of chromic iron ores and chrome iron and steel, chromium will rarely be encountered); and also of phosphoric acid, which is present in all iron ores. The precipitate is now dried in an air-bath or by placing the funnel with the filter in a ring-stand over a sand-bath or hot plate. When dry the precipitate is transferred to a weighed platinum crucible by removing the filter from the funnel, inverting it over the crucible, and rolling it between the fingers. The filter is rolled into a ball, and placed upon the lid of the crucible, where it is burned and ignited over the flame of a burner. The contents of the lid are now added to the contents of the crucible, and the whole moistened with a few drops of nitric acid, the addition of nitric acid being necessary in order to oxidize any iron to the ferric form which might have been reduced by the carbon of the filter-paper. A second addition of nitric acid, and a second ignition, is necessary where much iron is present and a large filter-paper has been used. The crucible and its contents are now ignited over the blast-lamp or in the muffle-furnace at a bright-red heat, cooled, and weighed. The increase in weight of the crucible represents the weight of the combined alumina (Al_2O_3), ferric oxide (Fe_2O_3), phosphoric acid (P_2O_5), and chromic acid (Cr_2O_3).

From the weight of the combined oxides calculate the percentage. From this percentage deduct the percentages of the different oxides, as determined, in separate portions. Except in the case of chromic titaniferous and phosphoric iron ores, the difference between the percentage of the combined oxides and the percentage of ferric oxide will be the percentage of alumina present. The percentage of ferric oxide present in the combined oxides may be determined as follows: Transfer the combined oxides, after weighing, to an agate mortar, and grind to an impalpable powder. Weigh out a portion of the powder, and fuse it with acid potassium sulphate in the manner described in Chapter I. Dissolve the fused mass in hot water, add an excess of sulphuric acid, reduce, and determine the iron as described in Chapter XVI. From the weight of the ferric oxide, as thus determined, calculate the total weight of the ferric oxide present in the combined oxides, and deduct it from the weight of the combined oxides, the difference being the weight of alumina in the amount of substance taken for analysis. When extreme accuracy is required the author prefers this method to the determination of the iron in a separate portion, and deducting that result from the weight of the combined oxides.

Iron Ores.—Dissolve as in Chapter XVI. The treatment with sulphuretted hydrogen can usually be omitted, as metals of the sulphuretted-hydrogen group are seldom present. To the filtrate from the silica add ammonia and proceed as above. When titanium and chromium are present they will be precipitated with the alumina. In this case proceed as described in Chapters XVIII and XIX, or by the second method.

Manganese Ores.—Same treatment as with iron ores, except that it is necessary to dissolve the first precipitate of hydroxides with a little hydrochloric acid and reprecipitate with ammonia, in order to insure the separation of the manganese.

Limestones, Clays, Cements, etc.—Same treatment as in the case of iron ores, taking the filtrate from the silica obtained as described in Chapter I. When a fusion of the insoluble residue has been necessary, combine the filtrates from the insoluble and the silica. As the alumina is generally present as a silicate, it can be determined in these substances, with a sufficient degree of accuracy for technical purposes, as follows: Determine the insoluble residue (see Chapter I), and after weighing it fuse and determine the silica. The difference between the weights of the insoluble residue and silica obtained will be the weight of alumina present. When barium is present the weight of the barium sulphate should also be determined and deducted from the weight of the insoluble residue.

Silver and Lead Ores.—It will generally be sufficient to determine the insoluble residue (Chapter I) and the alumina by difference as in the case of clays. When the ore contains compounds of alumina which are soluble in acids, the filtrate from the silica, obtained by fusion, should be added to the filtrate from the insoluble residue, and the alumina determined in the combined solutions as above. In the case of lead ores which do not contain any members of the sulphuretted-hydrogen group, except lead, the following method may be adopted: Determine the insoluble residue by treating with hydrochloric, nitric, and sulphuric acids and evaporation to fumes of sulphuric anhydride. The lead will all be converted into sulphate, and can be removed from the insoluble residue with ammonium acetate. The filtrate from the insoluble residue and lead sulphate will now be free from lead, and the treatment with sulphuretted hydrogen can be omitted.

Slags, Mattes, etc.—Determine the alumina in the filtrate from the silica as above. In the case of lead and copper slags and mattes these metals will have to be removed by treatment with sulphuretted hydrogen. When much manganese or zinc is present, it will be necessary to redissolve the first precipitate of hydroxides in a little hydrochloric acid and reprecipitate with ammonia. If this precaution is omitted the results will be high, on account of the manganese and zinc carried down with the iron and alumina. A better method is to make a basic-acetate precipitation, dissolve the filtered and washed precipitate with a little hydrochloric acid, and reprecipitate with ammonia as above.

Second Method.—This method, which was proposed by Dr. Drown,* depends upon the principle that if a slightly acid solution of aluminium and iron is electrolyzed with an anode of platinum and a mercury cathode, the iron will be precipitated on the mercury, and the solution, after precipitation of the iron, will contain all the aluminium, from which it (the Al) may be readily precipitated as a phosphate. This method is particularly adapted to the analysis of alloys containing comparatively small quantities of aluminium and considerable iron. The method of procedure in the case of an iron or steel is as follows: Dissolve from 5 to 10 grammes of the substance in sulphuric acid, evaporate until white fumes of sulphuric anhydride appear, add water, heat to bring the iron into solution, filter off the silica and carbon, and wash with water acidulated with sulphuric acid. Render the filtrate nearly neutral with ammonia, and add to the beaker, in which the electrolysis is to be made, about one hundred times as much mercury as the weight of iron or steel taken. The bulk of the solution should be from 300 to 500 cc. Connect with the battery or dynamo current so that about two amperes will pass through the solution over night. The connection with the mercury is best made by means of a platinum wire fused into a piece of glass tubing which passes through the solution. The glass tube should be filled for about one inch with mercury in order to

---

* Transactions of The American Institute of Mining Engineers Vol. XX, page 242.

weight it and make a perfect connection with the mercury in the beaker. In the morning the solution is tested for iron, and if necessary the electrolysis is continued after adding sufficient ammonia to neutralize the acid set free by the deposition of the iron. The progress of the operation may be observed by the change in color of the solution. At first it becomes darker in color near the anode; after five or six hours it is nearly colorless, and finally becomes pink, from the formation of permanganate.

When the solution gives no reaction for iron, upon testing, it is removed from the beaker by means of a pipette while the current is still passing. When as much as possible has been removed without breaking the current, water is added and drawn off by the pipette as before. When the solution has been treated in this manner until there is no longer danger of resolution of the precipitated iron, the current is broken and the mercury is thoroughly washed with water until the last traces of the solution have been removed. Should the solution not be perfectly clear, sometimes there will be a separation of oxide of manganese; it should be filtered. The solution is now made nearly neutral with ammonia, sodium phosphate in excess, and about 10 grammes of sodium acetate are added, and the solution is boiled for at least forty minutes. The aluminium will be precipitated as a phosphate, which precipitate is filtered, washed, dried, ignited, and weighed. The ignited aluminium phosphate should be white. If it has more than the faintest shade of color (due to iron), it should be fused with acid potassium sulphate, the fused mass being brought into solution with water and a little sulphuric acid, the solution finally being electrolyzed for 2 or 3 hours. The solution now free from iron is drawn off and the aluminium is precipitated as a phosphate as before. This second precipitate will be pure. Drown states that he has generally found the first precipitate of such purity that this treatment and second precipitation are unnecessary. Drown states the ignited precipitate to have the composition $7Al_2O_3$, $6P_2O_5$, in place of $AlPO_4$, and consequently gives 24.14 as the percentage of aluminium.

This method also answers for the determination of iron. If the iron is to be determined the mercury is weighed before proceeding with the electrolysis, and after electrolyzing washing and decanting, it is dried for a few minutes at a temperature of 100° to 110° C. and weighed again. The increase in weight of the mercury represents the weight of iron in the amount of substance taken. As mercury loses weight upon drying, even at such a low temperature as 100° C., and there is generally a loss in weight owing to the impurities in the mercury which pass into solution, it is best to run a blank beaker, containing about the same weight of mercury as is used in the analysis, and water slightly acidulated with sulphuric acid, in the circuit with the analyses. The loss in weight of the mercury used in the blank should be added to the results in the case of each iron determination.

This method may also be used for the determination of iron and aluminium in ores, etc.

CHAPTER XVIII.

CHROMIUM (Cr).

CHROMIUM is always determined as chromic oxide (Cr_2O_3), dark green in color.

The only determinations of chromium which the metallurgical chemist will be called upon to make are in iron ores (especially chromic iron ore, known as chromite, or magnetite, which sometimes contain chromium), pig-iron, and steel.

Ores.—Fuse from 1.0 to 2.0 grammes of ore with 5 to 10 grammes of mixed carbonates of sodium and potassium and 1 gramme of sodium nitrate (see Part II, Chapter I). Dissolve the fused mass in water and hydrochloric acid in slight excess, evaporate to dryness, and determine the silica in the usual way. To the filtrate from the silica add sodium carbonate until it is strongly alkaline, and then, without filtering out the precipitate, bromine water until the solution is deeply colored, stirring continually. Now add 3 cc. of pure bromine and heat for one hour, with frequent stirring, keeping the solution alkaline and gradually increasing the heat until it boils. Allow to boil for an hour, when the chromic oxide should all be oxidized to chromic acid. Now filter (precipitate A) and wash thoroughly with hot water, washing first by decantation and then on the filter until the filtrate runs through colorless. Should the ore contain a large amount of chromium, in order to insure its complete separation, wash the precipitate on the filter back into the beaker with the wash-bottle, bring the bulk of the solution up to about 100 cc. with water, add 2 cc. of bromine, and proceed as before, filtering through the same filter. The filtrate will now contain all of the chromium as alkaline chromate, and probably some of the manganese. The precipitate will contain all of the other constituents of the ore. Partially neutralize the filtrate with nitric acid, add from 1 to 3 grammes of ammonium nitrate, and evaporate until no odor of ammonia is perceptible. Dilute with water, and should a precipitate form (precipitate B, probably MnO_2, SiO_2, Al_2O_3, and TiO_2), filter, and wash with warm water. Acidify the filtrate with hydrochloric acid, and saturate it with sulphuretted hydrogen to reduce the chromic acid to sesquioxide. Filter out the precipitated sulphur and wash. In the filtrate precipitate the chromic hydroxide with ammonia, filter, wash, dry, ignite, and weigh the chromic oxide (Cr_2O_3). To obtain the weight of the chromium multiply the weight of the precipitate by 0.68586.

Pig-iron, Steel, etc.—Dissolve the alloy in nitric and hydrochloric acids, evaporate to dryness, dry, and ignite the insoluble residue. Fuse the insoluble residue with mixed carbonates and proceed as above.

Titaniferous Ores containing Chromium.—Proceed as described in Part II, Chapter XIX (Titanium), for the determination of the silica. Treat the filtrate from the silica as described above for the determination of the chromium. For the determination of the iron and titanium combine precipitate B (should one form) with the sodium-carbonate precipitate A. Dissolve the combined precipitates in hydrochloric acid, and proceed to determine the titanium as described in Chapter XIX (Ti).

Determine the iron in the filtrate as described in Chapter XIX (Ti) and Chapter XVI (Fe).

CHAPTER XIX.

TITANIUM (Ti).

TITANIUM is generally determined by the gravimetric method as titanic oxide, but may also be determined by the colorimetric method.

About the only determinations of titanium which the metallurgical chemist will be called upon to make are the determinations in iron ores (especially some magnetites), in pig-iron, and occasionally steel.

When titanium is present the method of determining the iron and silica in iron ores, pig-iron, etc., will have to be modified, and the titanium first separated according to the gravimetric method described below.

Colorimetric Method.—This method is due to Weller,[*] and the improvements to H. L. Wells[†] and W. A. Noyes.[‡]

Mix 0.1 gramme of ore with 0.2 gramme of sodium fluoride, both finely powdered, in a platinum crucible. Add 3 grammes of sodium pyrosulphate without mixing. Fuse carefully and heat gently until the effervescence ceases and copious fumes of sulphuric acid are evolved. This should take two to three minutes. When cold the mass in the crucible is dissolved in from 15 to 20 cc. of cold water, and the solution filtered and washed slightly. If a residue remains it can be treated again by the same method after burning it on the filter, but the amount of titanium usually found by a second fusion is small.

To the solution, as obtained above, 1 cc. of hydrogen per-

---

[*] Berichte d. Chem. Ges., 1882, p. 2592.
[†] Trans. Am. Inst. of Mining Engineers, Vol. XIV, p. 763.
[‡] Journal of Analytical and Applied Chemistry, Jan. 1891.

oxide and a few cc. of dilute sulphuric acid are added, when the solution is ready for comparison with a solution containing a known amount of titanium. For a standard solution titanic oxide is dissolved in hot concentrated sulphuric acid, and the solution diluted with dilute sulphuric acid at first (to prevent the precipitation of titanic oxide), and then with water until 1 cubic centimetre contains 1 milligramme of TiO_2.

As iron affects the color of the solution, ferric sulphate, approximately in the same proportion as iron is present in the ore, should be added to the standard solution. A solution of iron-ammonium alum answers well for this purpose, and, if the amount of iron in the ore is not known, all that is necessary is to match the color of the solution of the mineral before adding the hydrogen peroxide to it. Small quantities of titanium in the presence of large quantities of iron can be readily determined by this method, which is especially adapted for technical determinations.

Gravimetric Method.—For the technical estimation of titanium in iron ores, pig-iron, etc., the following method is as rapid and accurate as any : *

Iron Ores.—Fuse 1.0 gramme of finely pulverized ore with 10 grammes of pure potassium bisulphate in a large platinum crucible, heating the covered crucible over a very low flame until the bisulphate is melted. This operation must be carefully conducted, as there is danger of the bisulphate boiling over, and also loss from spirting. Raise the heat very gradually, keeping the mass just liquid and the temperature at the point at which slight fumes of sulphuric anhydride are given off when the lid is slightly raised, until the bottom of the crucible is dull red. When the ore is completely decomposed, remove the heat, take off the crucible lid, and incline the crucible at such an angle that the fused mass will run together on one side of the crucible and as near the top as possible. Allow it to cool in this position; when cold it is easily detached from the crucible. Place the crucible and lid in a beaker (No. 4) half full of cold water, and the fused mass in a

---
* Blair's "Chemical Analysis of Iron." Tenth Census U. S., Vol. XV, p. 512.

small platinum tray or basket suspended in the beaker. Pour into the beaker sufficient strong aqueous solution of sulphurous acid to raise the liquid to the top of the basket, and allow the fusion to dissolve, which may require twelve hours. Remove the crucible, lid, and basket, washing off with a jet of cold water. Stir the solution, which should smell strongly of sulphurous acid, and allow the insoluble matter to settle. Filter, wash, dry, ignite, and weigh the insoluble residue. Treat with hydrofluoric acid and a few drops of sulphuric acid, evaporate to dryness, ignite, and weigh, the loss being silica. Should any appreciable residue remain, fuse it with sodium carbonate, dissolve the fusion in water and sulphuric acid, heat, and add to the main filtrate. To the combined solutions, which should be colorless and smell strongly of sulphurous acid, add a clear filtered solution of sodium acetate (20 gms.) and one sixth its volume of acetic acid (1.04 sp. gr.), heat to boiling, and continue to boil for a few minutes. Allow to settle, filter on an ashless filter; wash thoroughly with hot water containing 17 per cent acetic acid, and finally with hot water; dry, ignite, and weigh as TiO_2. This precipitate is seldom quite pure, as it is liable to contain small amounts of Fe_2O_3 and Al_2O_3. Hence it is best to fuse it with sodium carbonate, dissolve in water, filter, wash, dry, and fuse the insoluble sodium titanate with sodium carbonate, dissolving the fusion, when cool, in the crucible with sulphuric acid, and precipitate and determine the TiO_2 as above.

To obtain the weight of titanium, multiply the weight of the titanic oxide found by 0.60976.

Pig Iron, etc.—Decompose according to Drown's method for the determination of silicon (Part I, Chapter I, page 85), dry, and ignite the residue of silica, graphite, etc. Treat this residue with hydrofluoric acid and sulphuric acid to expel silica and evaporate the fumes of sulphuric anhydride Finally, evaporate to dryness and fuse with sodium carbonate. Dissolve the fusion in water and sulphuric acid, heat, and add the solution to the main filtrate. Proceed with this solution as with iron ores.

Slags.—Treat 2 gms. of finely pulverized slag in a large platinum crucible with an excess of hydrofluoric acid and 5 cc. of conc. sulphuric acid. Evaporate off the hydrofluoric acid, and heat carefully until the greater part of the sulphuric acid is driven off. Allow the crucible to cool, add 10 gms. of sodium carbonate, fuse for half an hour, finally at a high heat, and remove the crucible, running the fused mass well up on its walls. Dissolve the fused mass in water, transfer to a beaker, and filter. Wash the insoluble matter, dry, ignite, and re-fuse it with sodium carbonate. Dissolve in water as before, and filter. By this method alumina will be entirely separated from the titanium. Fuse the insoluble matter on the filter with sodium carbonate, dissolve the fusion, when cool, with sulphuric acid, and determine the titanium as above.

CHAPTER XX.

MANGANESE (Mn).

A NUMBER of methods for the determination of manganese have been proposed, and a number of different methods are in use. There seems to be considerable difference of opinion between many of our best chemists as to which are the best methods. However, the methods described below are all in use in some of our largest metallurgical works and by some of our most reliable technical and commercial chemists.

Ford's Method.*—This method was first proposed for the determination of manganese in spiegels, irons, and steels, but is applicable to slag, ores, etc., if slightly modified. From 0.5 to 2.0 grammes of substance, depending on the percentage of manganese it contains, are dissolved in from 25 to 50 cc. of strong nitric acid (1.4 sp. gr.) perfectly free from chlorine. Evaporation to dryness is not necessary, except where the amount of silicon is large, as in the case of certain pig-irons. Then, as a clogging of the filter in the subsequent filtration is apt to follow, dissolve first in a dish in hydrochloric acid, using as small an amount of acid as possible, and quickly evaporate to dryness. Take up with nitric acid and evaporate again to dryness. This second evaporation is necessary in order to remove all the hydrochloric acid, which, if present, would interfere with the subsequent precipitation of the manganese. Slag, ores, and such other material as contains much silica, should also be treated in this way. Redissolve for the second

---

* Transactions of the American Institute of Mining Engineers, Vol. IX, p. 397.

time in strong nitric acid, and boil until the red fumes cease coming off, and while boiling throw in crystals of potassium chlorate from time to time. Violent action ensues, yellow fumes are driven off, and binoxide of manganese is precipitated, since it is insoluble in strong nitric acid. As soon as all of the manganese has been oxidized the fumes will cease coming off, with a slight explosion. After this has occurred, add a few more crystals of potassium chlorate, boil for a minute or two, remove from the lamp, and filter through an asbestos filter. The most convenient apparatus is a small funnel-shaped tube in which is fitted an asbestos plug, the filter-pump being used to facilitate filtration. The asbestos should be free from soluble lime, magnesia, and manganese. It is best to prepare it by treating it successively with boiling hydrochloric acid, boiling water, boiling nitric acid, and then boiling water until the washings no longer show a trace of these elements when treated with the proper reagents. The asbestos should then be ignited to free it from organic matter. This is of the utmost importance, as the writer has known of more than one chemist who condemned this method as giving too high results, when upon investigation it was found that they had not taken the precaution to purify the asbestos used, which probably accounted for the high results obtained.

After filtering the nitric-acid solution through the asbestos filter, rinse the dish or beaker in which the substance was dissolved with strong nitric acid, pour it upon the filter, and wash with strong nitric acid until the washings come through colorless. The funnel-tube is then removed from the filtering apparatus, the filter with its contents placed back into the dish in which the solution was made, hydrochloric acid added, and the substance boiled until the manganese binoxide is dissolved as chloride. The asbestos is then removed by filtration, using the same tube and filter-pump, and finally washing with hot water. Nearly neutralize the filtrate with ammonia, adding a few crystals of sodium acetate, and boil, filter, wash slightly with hot water, redissolve the small precipitate of iron oxide in hydrochloric acid, again nearly neutralize with ammonia, add a crystal or so of sodium acetate, boil, and filter. The solution and reprecipitation of the iron is necessary as a small amount of manganese is always contained in the first precipitate. Add the second filtrate to the first, heat nearly to boiling, and add an excess of microcosmic salt. Then make slightly ammoniacal, and boil, stirring until the precipitate assumes the characteristic appearance of the phosphate of ammonia and manganese. Allow it to settle, and filter, wash with hot water, dry, ignite, and weigh as pyrophosphate of manganese.

It is best to use some filter-paper which is pure, such as Schleicher & Schuell's c. p., for both filtrations, as many of the qualitative papers contain appreciable quantities of manganese.

In the case of slags or other substances containing lime and magnesia, it is necessary to wash the binoxide precipitate more thoroughly with nitric acid in order to remove all of these elements.

Evaporation to dryness in the case of steels or spiegels is not necessary. They may be immediately dissolved in strong nitric acid, and potassium chlorate added. A determination may be made in two hours by this method.

Williams's Method.[*]—Mr. H. Williams has proposed a modification of the above method which shortens it somewhat, and simplifies it, especially in the case of a substance which contains lime or magnesia, as, for example, slag.

The substance is treated, as before, with nitric acid, and potassium chlorate (in the case of a pig-iron, slag, etc., the silica and carbon must first be removed by filtration through asbestos) added to precipitate the manganese. After filtering off this precipitated manganese binoxide, wash with strong nitric acid, and then well with water. Blow the contents of the funnel into the beaker in which the precipitation was made, which should previously be well washed, and rinse the funnel with a little water.

---

[*] Transactions of the American Institute of Mining Engineers, Vol. X, p. 100.

Run into the beaker an accurately measured quantity of a standard solution of oxalic acid (a moderate excess over what the manganese binoxide is capable of oxidizing), add water to bring the bulk of the solution up to about 75 cc., and then 3 or 4 cc. of concentrated sulphuric acid, and heat to about 70° C. The solution of the binoxide is readily effected by the aid of a little stirring. Finally, titrate the solution with a standard solution of potassium permanganate. (See Part II, Chapter XVI.) The presence of the asbestos does not obscure the final reaction. Two standard solutions are necessary, viz., a permanganate solution and an oxalic solution.

It is best to use a decinormal permanganate solution, i.e., 1 cubic centimetre equal to 1 milligramme of iron. By using such a dilute solution the accuracy of the method is greatly increased. The permanganate solution may be prepared by dissolving 1.2 grammes of potassium permanganate in 2030 cc. of distilled water. It should be prepared and standardized as described in Part II, Chapter XVI.

The oxalic solution may be of almost any strength, but if it is made so that 1 cc. will require about 3 cc. of the permanganate solution to oxidize it, it will answer well. It should be kept in a tight-stoppered bottle in a dark place, and should be standardized from to time with the standard permanganate solution.

The method of calculating the result is best shown by the following example: Suppose we have taken 1 gramme of steel, in which we suspect about 1 per cent of manganese. Having separated the binoxide, we add 15 cc. of the standard oxalic-acid solution of the strength already mentioned, and effect the the solution as described. This 15 cc., by itself, would require 45 cc. of the permanganate, but on titrating we use, say, 25 cc.; the difference, 20 cc., is equivalent to 0.020 gramme of iron. Since 1 equivalent of manganese binoxide converts 2 equivalents of a proto-salt of iron to the state of a sesqui-salt, as shown by the formula

$$2FeSO_4 + MnO_2 + 2H_2SO_4 = Fe_2(SO_4)_3 + MnSO_4 + 2H_2O,$$

the solving of the proportion 112 : 55 :: 0.020 : x gives the weight of the manganese equivalent to the 0.020 gramme of iron. The value of x is 0.00982 and the per cent is 0.982. It will be seen from the above that in operating on ores or products which contain a high percentage of manganese it will be necessary to take smaller quantities of the substance.

Sometimes when the percentage of manganese is high it may be advantageous to use a stronger solution of oxalic acid and also a stronger solution of permanganate,—say a half-normal solution.

The results obtained by this method agree very closely between themselves, and also with the results obtained by Ford's method.

The following modification of Ford's method the writer has used for the determination of manganese in ores and slags with very good results: Dissolve the precipitated binoxide with just sufficient hydrochloric acid to cause the precipitate to go into solution, and add a little sulphuric acid. An emulsion of pure zinc oxide is now added, a little at a time, shaking or stirring the solution until the hydrochloric acid is neutralized and the zinc oxide is in slight excess. Care should be exercised not to add too large an excess of zinc oxide, as if too large an excess is present it will obscure the reaction, and filtration will be necessary before the solution can be titrated. The solution is now ready for titration with standardized permanganate solution in the manner described under the head of Volhard's Method.

Volhard's Volumetric Method.—This method, which is generally used in the Western lead, and copper-smelting works, may be used for the determination of manganese in iron, manganese, lead, copper, silver, and gold ores, etc., and also for the determination of manganese in other substances, such as spiegel, steel, etc.

Dissolve 1 gramme of substance in 2 cc. of hydrochloric, 4 cc. of nitric, and 6 cc. of dilute sulphuric acids in a flask or casserole, as in the determination of iron, and evaporate to copious fumes of sulphuric anhydride. Transfer the contents of the flask or casserole to a graduated 500-cc. flask, washing into the flask with boiling water. Then add an emulsion of zinc oxide to the contents of the flask until the acid is neutralized and the iron is all precipitated as sesquioxide, violent shaking of the contents of the flask facilitating the precipitation of the iron. After the precipitation is complete the oxide of zinc should be in slight excess. The contents of the flask are then diluted with distilled water to the holding mark, and after thorough shaking allowed to settle. After the oxides have settled so that the supernatant liquid is comparatively clear, 100 cc. is drawn off by means of a pipette and transferred to a flask (about 250 cc. capacity), rinsing out the pipette with distilled water into the flask. The contents of the small flask are then brought to a boil by heating over a flame, and are then ready for titration with a standard solution of permanganate of potassium. The titration is performed as follows: The permanganate solution is dropped into the liquid in the flask from a burette, the contents of the flask being shaken after each addition of permanganate solution in order to facilitate the settling of the precipitated manganese dioxide. From the amount of the precipitate and the rapidity with which the precipitate is formed after each addition of permanganate solution, the operator after a little practice will be able to determine in what quantities it is safe to add the permanganate solution. The addition of permanganate should be continued until a faint pink color appears around the edges of the clear liquid after shaking, when held against a white background. The precipitation of the manganese is then complete, although it is safest, especially if the precipitation has occupied some time, to bring the contents of the flask again to a boil, and notice, after allowing the precipitate to settle, if the pink tint remains. If the color should have disappeared another drop of permanganate is added, the flask shaken, and the precipitate allowed to settle. If the color is permanent after settling the titration is completed.

The same solution of potassium permanganate used for the determination of iron may be used for this determination. In order to determine how much manganese one cubic centimetre of the permanganate solution is equal to, it is only necessary to multiply its value for iron by 0.2946 to obtain its value for manganese. Hence if the 1 cc. of the permanganate solution was equal to 0.010 gramme of iron, it would be equal to 0.002946 gramme of manganese. The reaction which takes place is as follows: $3MnO + Mn_2O_7 = 5MnO_2$.

Many chemists prefer to filter off the precipitated oxides before diluting to 500 cc.; but this is unnecessary, as the precipitate occupies such a small bulk, although in the flocculent state its bulk appears to be large, that it may be disregarded. Moreover, the precipitate is difficult to wash, and filtration generally gives low results. The method gives closely agreeing results, and results which are as good as if not better than those obtained by the other methods with the same degree of proficiency in practice. The zinc oxide should be tested, and, if it contains manganese or organic matter, purified. If commercial zinc is used it will be necessary to purify it.

Colorimetric Method.—This method was first used in this country by Mr. Samuel Peters,[*] and is especially applicable to the estimation of manganese in steels, and such substances as contain less than 1½ to 2 per cent of manganese. The method, as used in iron and steel laboratories, is essentially as follows, for steels: Dissolve 0.1 gramme of the steel in 20 cc. nitric acid (1.20 sp. gr.) in a test-tube about nine inches long by one inch in diameter, by the aid of heat, boiling the solution until the carbonaceous matter is entirely in solution and all nitrous fumes are evolved. This usually takes about five minutes at a gentle ebullition. Then add, with a platinum spatula, about 0.4 gramme of pure peroxide of lead to the boiling solution, adding first a small portion of the lead, and as soon as the violent action ceases, an instant later, the remainder of the salt, boiling gently but continuously for exactly two and a half minutes longer, then removing from

---

[*] Crooks' Select Methods. Transactions of the American Institute of Mining Engineers, Vol. XV, p. 104.

the heat, and placing the test-tube in a beaker of cold water, out of contact with the direct rays of sunlight, and allowing the solution to cool and to settle for about an hour. The clear supernatant solution is then ready to decant off from the lead into the graduated tube, and to match, by dilution with distilled water, with the standard solution containing 0.0001 gramme of manganese as permanganate in each cc. of solution; so that, using 0.1 gramme of steel for the analysis, each cc. of the solution to be determined will represent 0.01 per cent of manganese when the shades of color match.

The standard solution for comparison may be made in several ways, but the best are to use either a standard solution of potassium permanganate or, preferably, the standard may be prepared by using 0.1 gramme of a standard steel containing a known percentage of manganese, treating it exactly as the unknown sample, and decanting the solution into a similarly graduated tube, and diluting with water until the solution has a volume of which the number of cc. is an equivalent or multiple of the percentage of manganese in the steel, applying the same principle as is used with the standard steels in the Eggertz method for the estimation of carbon (see Part II, Chapter IV). This method is preferable to the other methods of making a comparison, and it is also preferable to run a standard with each set of analyses.

A. E. Hunt[*] says: "This method, when properly used, is at least sufficiently accurate for all practicable purposes within, say, 0.02 per cent manganese for steels within the range of from 0.15 to 1.50 per cent manganese. It is fully as accurate, and can be as safely guarded from error, as the Eggertz color-method for the estimation of carbon in steel." The method, however, has many sources of error that must be carefully avoided.

Mr. Hunt recommends the following precautions:

First. The drillings of steel must have no oil or other extraneous matter with them. Owing to the ease with which

---

[*] Transactions of the American Institute of Mining Engineers, Vol. XV, p. 106.

permanganate solutions are reduced, it is necessary that no organic matter be present which will not be entirely destroyed by the boiling nitric acid before the addition of the peroxide of lead.

Second. The nitric acid must be pure, and especially free from chlorine or nitrous fumes. The acid must be of very nearly 1.20 sp. gr. throughout the process, and must not be allowed to become much more concentrated by boiling. It is best to cover the mouths of the test-tubes with clean covers of porcelain crucibles during the ebullition. If the acid becomes too concentrated during the boiling, as it is very liable to do if the ebullition becomes too violent and the test-tube is a large one, on the addition of the peroxide of lead some of the manganese is transformed into the insoluble manganese binoxide and precipitated.

Third. The peroxide of lead must be free from color on boiling with the dilute nitric acid, and must be so free from lead nitrate that it will oxidize all the manganese in the steel into a reasonably permanent permanganic acid. This is a very important point, which, not properly guarded, has occasioned failures, and has caused many chemists to condemn the method. In commencing the use of any new lot of peroxide of lead it is a necessary precaution to mix up the salt thoroughly and then to test it by making an analysis with a steel of known composition, comparing it with a standard solution of potassium permanganate, and obtaining a concordant result. Most of the peroxide of lead found in the markets and sold as c. p. is non-homogeneous, and contains considerable quantities of nitrate disseminated through it. It is best to purify your own peroxide of lead.

Fourth. The ebullition must not be too violent, and must not last over two and one half minutes. It is necessary to stand by the tubes with watch in hand and to remove them when the time is up. Too long boiling invariably gives bad results. The boiling is best done in a water-bath in which chloride of calcium is added to the water to raise its boiling-point.

Fifth. There must not be hydrochloric acid, sulphuretted hydrogen, or other fumes in the air of the room in which the tubes are allowed to stand to cool. It is best not to allow the solution to stand too long—never two hours—before comparison.

Sixth. Mr. Hunt says: "I have had no trouble in getting good, reasonably permanent colors, but have never had uniformly satisfactory results by filtering the solution from the peroxides through asbestos, and have consequently preferred to decant off the solution from the lead. When a standard steel is used, having nearly the same percentage of manganese as the sample to be determined, equal amounts of solution and treatment exactly the same so far as practicable, the error due to the amount of the liquid remaining with the lead in the bottom of the tube is comparatively trifling, never over 0.02 per cent, when the precautions mentioned above are carefully observed."

Seventh. The water used in diluting must be free from organic matter. The ordinary distilled water used in chemical laboratories often contains considerable organic matter, which will rapidly reduce the permanganate solution.

Eighth. The mixing of the color solutions for comparison can best be done by having the graduated tube provided with a glass stop-cock, or it can be satisfactorily performed by pouring the solution out into a clean beaker and then decanting back into the graduated tube.

This method is especially applicable, owing to its simplicity and rapidity, for checking and controlling the converting and mill work in a steel-works. When great rapidity is necessary, as it sometimes may be in this latter case, the solution need not be allowed to stand so long after the addition of the peroxide of lead, but may be filtered through asbestos, using the filter-pump.

The above methods will serve for the estimation of manganese in almost any substance. Volhard's method is the one generally used in the West, and is the simplest and most rapid. In the case of oxidized ores, soluble in hydrochloric acid, the addition of nitric and sulphuric acids may be dispensed with, the ore being dissolved directly in a small quantity of hydrochloric acid, and the manganese determined by Volhard's method as above. In the case of slags, when the sample has been suddenly chilled (Chapter I), treat with water and hydrochloric acid, as in the determination of silica, add a few crystals of potassium chlorate, heat to oxidize the iron, etc., and determine by Volhard's method. When the sample has not been suddenly chilled, make a cintering fusion (Chapter I), dissolve fused mass as above, evaporate to dryness and heat. Redissolve in hydrochloric acid, and proceed by Volhard's method.

Mr. A. H. Low* proposes a method for the determination of manganese in ores which is a combination of Volhard's and William's methods, and which is said to give excellent results.

The method is essentially as follows; Dissolve 0.5 gm. of ore in hydrochloric acid, or nitrohydrochloric acids, in a flask. Heat until most of the free acid is expelled, dilute with 75 cc. of water, add an excess of zinc oxide, and boil. Now add a saturated solution of bromine-water (not over 50 cc.), and boil out the excess of bromine. The solution should still contain an excess of zinc oxide. Filter, and wash the precipitate thoroughly with hot water. Return the washed precipitate to the flask and add 50 cc. of dilute sulphuric acid (1 in 9). Warm to dissolve the iron, and run in an excess of oxalic-acid solution from a burette, heat, dilute with warm water, and titrate the excess of oxalic acid with a standard solution of potassium permanganate.

The permanganate solution should be about one-tenth normal. The oxalic-acid solution is prepared by dissolving 11.46 gms. of pure crystallized oxalic acid in 1000 cc. of water. The solutions are standardized in the usual manner, and their relations to each other determined.

---

*Journal of Analytical and Applied Chemistry, Vol. VI, p. 663.

CHAPTER XXI.

ZINC (Zn).

SEVERAL methods have been proposed for the determination of zinc both gravimetrically and volumetrically. Only one, the volumetric estimation by a standard solution of potassium ferrocyanide, will be given. For the standard gravimetric methods see Fresenius, Cairns, Rose, etc.

This method, provided the proper precautions are used, gives results which agree as closely with the results obtained by any of the standard gravimetric methods as two gravimetric determinations of the same sample will agree among themselves, provided the percentage of zinc present is not very low (less than 4 per cent). The accuracy of the method has been fully demonstrated. See Proceedings of the Colorado Scientific Society, June 1892, and The School of Mines Quarterly, Vol. XIV, No. 1, p. 40.

It is the opinion of the writer, after numerous experiments, that once the zinc is obtained in solution in the proper form its percentage may be more safely determined by this titration method than it can be by precipitation and subsequent ignition and weighing. It, moreover, has the advantage of being rapid, and consequently would be used in metallurgical works in many instances, even if the results were not quite up to the standard of accuracy.

This method requires a standard solution of potassium ferrocyanide. A solution of which one cubic centimetre is equal to 0.010 gramme of zinc is the solution generally preferred by most chemists using this method. To prepare such a solution 90 grammes of pure potassium ferrocyanide (free from potassium ferricyanide) are dissolved in two litres of water and kept in a tightly-stoppered green-glass bottle. The solution will keep for some time without alteration, provided the bottle is well stoppered, and need not be tested more frequently than once every two or three weeks. It is best to make up the solution at least one day before using. To standardize the solution, dissolve two portions of about 0.250 gramme each of pure zinc oxide (the zinc oxide should previously be ignited to convert any carbonate of zinc into oxide, and kept in a stoppered bottle so that it may not absorb carbonic acid or water from the air) in 5 cc. of pure hydrochloric acid, and add 50 cc. of water in a beaker of about 300 cc. capacity. In order to have the same conditions present as near as possible as in the actual analysis, it is well to add ammonia in slight excess and then neutralize with hydrochloric acid, using a small piece of litmus-paper as an indicator. When the solution has been brought to the point where it is just slightly acid, add an excess of 10 cc. of pure strong hydrochloric acid, and dilute to 250 cc. with cold distilled water. The solution is now ready for titration with the ferrocyanide solution, which may be run in from a burette, rapidly at first, stirring from time to time. If 0.2493 gramme of pure oxide of zinc were weighed out, it would require just 19.99 cc. or practically 20 cc. of the ferrocyanide solution to precipitate the zinc, provided the solution was normal; hence in this case about 18 cc. may be run in before testing. In order to test, the solution is thoroughly stirred with a glass rod, and a drop removed and added to a drop of a solution of pure uranium acetate on a porcelain plate. The uranium-acetate solution is prepared by dissolving sufficient uranium acetate in water to give a pretty strong solution, and clarified by adding a few drops of acetic acid. This solution should be kept in a small stoppered bottle in a dark place, as it is decomposed by the action of sunlight. As long as there is not an excess of ferrocyanide in the solution the drop of uranium acetate will retain its yellow color; as soon as the ferrocyanide is in slight excess it will turn a light brown, the shade being darker according to the amount of ferrocyanide in excess. The titration should be proceeded with, testing after the addition of each drop of ferrocyanide towards the last of the operation, and stirring well before testing, until a slight brownish tint is produced on the drop of uranium acetate. The amount of ferrocyanide used is then noted, and the value of one cubic centimetre calculated. The duplicates should not differ by more than one tenth of a cubic centimetre.

The precautions to be observed are : to have about the same bulk of solution in all subsequent titrations; to have the same amount of hydrochloric acid present; to have the standard solution at about the same temperature, and to have the zinc solution comparatively cool. If too large an excess of acid is present, or if the zinc solution is too warm, a decomposition will ensue, resulting in the liberation of chlorine. This may be seen by the solution turning yellow or a yellowish green. The precipitate should always be white, and the solution colorless or nearly so. This method is due to Fahlberg.

To determine the zinc in an ore by this method, the zinc solution must first be freed from such elements as copper, iron, manganese, etc., which are also precipitated in an acid solution with the ferrocyanide, or react on it. The three elements named above are the ones most likely to be encountered in zinc ores. Should cadmium be present (its presence in ores of zinc is rare) it must be removed before proceeding with the titration.

The following method will serve for the determination of zinc in all ores and furnace-products, except in the special cases mentioned below.

Method of Von Schulz and Low modified.*—Treat 1 gm. of finely pulverized ore with 15 cc. of aqua regia, and evaporate nearly to dryness. Should the ore be incompletely decomposed, which will seldom happen, evaporation to dryness, dehydration of the silicic acid, and fusion of the insoluble res-

---

* The Mining Industry, Denver, Colo., Vol. VI, No. 13 ; Proceedings of the Colorado Scientific Society, June 1892; School of Mines Quarterly, Vol. XIV, No. 1.

idue with carbonate and nitrate of soda, after solution and filtration of the silica, will be necessary. In this case the first and second filtrates are combined, nitric acid is added, and the solution is evaporated nearly to dryness. To the ore or nearly dry mass add 25 cc. of a solution of potassium chlorate in nitric acid, prepared by shaking an excess of the crystals with strong pure nitric acid in a flask. Add the solution gradually and do not cover at first, but warm gently until all violent action has stopped and greenish fumes cease coming off. Then cover with a watch-glass and boil on a hot iron plate to dryness, —overheating or baking should be avoided,—a drop of nitric acid adhering to the cover doing harm. Cool sufficiently and add 7 gms. of ammonium chloride, 15 cc. of strong ammonia-water, and 25 cc. of hot water. Replace the cover on the casserole and boil for one minute, stirring with a rubber-tipped glass rod to break up all particles or clots of solid matter on the sides and bottom of the casserole and the cover. Filter into a flask of about 250 cc. capacity, and wash several times with a hot solution of ammonium chloride prepared as follows: Dissolve 10 gms. of ammonium chloride in 1000 cc. of water, and before using heat to boiling in a wash-bottle and render slightly alkaline with ammonia. Should a considerable precipitate be produced it will carry down zinc hydrate with it. In the case of a small precipitate the amount of zinc which it retains may be disregarded. If a large precipitate forms it should be transferred from the filter to the original decomposing vessel by means of a spatul, and wash-bottle, using as little water as possible. The excess of water is evaporated off and the precipitate finally treated with the mixture of chlorate and nitric acid as before. The second precipitate is treated with ammonia, ammonium chloride, and water, filtered and washed as before, the second alkaline filtrate being combined with the first. A blue coloration in the filtrate indicates the presence of copper, which must be removed before proceeding with the titration. Add hydrochloric acid to neutralization (indicated by the gradual disappearance of the blue color), and then 10 cc. of hydrochloric acid in excess. If the solution is not sufficiently warm (about 70° C.) it should now be heated to that point. Now add from 20 to 40 gms. of test-lead and shake vigorously until all the copper is precipitated. The amount of test-lead and the amount of shaking necessary will of course depend upon the amount of copper present, which will be indicated by the depth of the blue color before neutralization. Aluminium-foil may be used for the precipitation of the copper in place of test-lead. In case aluminium is used it should be cut into strips of a convenient size, the strips being removed and washed after the copper is all precipitated. The copper can be removed from the foil when it is ready for use again, it being serviceable until it becomes too thin for further use. If test-lead is used it is best to use fresh lead for each determination. In case copper is absent the above treatment with test-lead or aluminium may be dispensed with. In this latter case it is best to add a piece of litmus-paper, two drops of methyl orange, or some suitable indicator to the alkaline solution, then hydrochloric acid until the solution is neutral, and finally an excess of 10 cc. of acid. The solution is now ready for the determination of the zinc with the standard solution of potassium ferrocyanide, as described above in standardization of the solution. A very good plan in titrating, when the per cent of zinc is not approximately known, is to pour off about half of the solution into a beaker and titrate roughly. This will give the approximate per cent of zinc, when the balance of the fluid in the flask is added to the contents of the beaker and the titration proceeded with, a considerable, or such, quantity of the standard solution being added as the per cent of zinc, as approximately determined, will allow. The flask is finally thoroughly rinsed out with water, the rinsings being added to the beaker, and the titration finished by adding a few drops of the standard solution at a time, testing a drop of the solution, after each addition, with the uranium-acetate solution. At the first indication of a brown color the addition of the ferrocyanide is stopped and the reading of the burette taken. If we have approximately the same bulk of solution and the same amount of free acid present in the regular assay as we have in the standardization of the ferrocyanide solution, no allowance need be made for the quantity of excess of ferrocyanide (about two drops) necessary to color the indicator.

Slags.—In the case of slags it is necessary to evaporate the solution of the slag (if the sample is obtained by sudden chilling, the acid solution; or, if fusion was necessary to decompose the slag, the solution of the fusion) to dryness, heat to dehydrate the silicic acid, and finally dissolve the dry mass in a little water and nitric acid. Now add the chlorate mixture and proceed as above. Unless this precaution be taken the results will invariably be low, probably owing to the gelatinous silica retaining a portion of the zinc solution.

Ores containing Cadmium.—The acid solution, before adding test-lead or aluminium, is subjected to the passage of a rapid current of sulphuretted hydrogen. This precipitates the cadmium as well as the copper. When the precipitation is complete the sulphide precipitate is filtered off and washed, when the filtrate is ready for titration as before, it being unnecessary to expel the excess of sulphuretted hydrogen by boiling before proceeding with the titration.

With many ores, especially the sulphide ores of the west, treatment with aqua regia is unnecessary in order to effect complete decomposition, simple treatment with the nitric-acid potassium-chlorate mixture being sufficient.

A determination, except when a fusion is necessary to effect decomposition, or cadmium is present, may be made in 30 minutes.

CHAPTER XXII.

NICKEL (Ni) AND COBALT (Co).

NICKEL and cobalt are almost invariably associated with each other in ores and metallurgical products, and consequently a determination of either metal generally involves their separation. A number of different methods for the separation and determination of nickel and cobalt have been proposed, but the writer believes the following to be as rapid and accurate as any:

The material should first be examined for members of the sulphuretted-hydrogen group. If any members of this group are found to be present, it will be necessary to remove them before proceeding with the analysis. To remove the members of the sulphuretted-hydrogen group dilute the filtrate from the silica with water to about 60 cc., warm to about 70° C., and pass a rapid current of sulphuretted-hydrogen gas, allowing the solution to cool during the passage of the gas. Filter out the precipitated sulphides, wash thoroughly with dilute sulphuretted-hydrogen water, and boil the filtrate, adding hydrochloric acid and chlorate of potash to oxidize the iron and sulphur. The solution is now ready to proceed with the analysis in the usual way. If no members of the sulphuretted-hydrogen group are present, this treatment is not necessary.

Treat from 1 to 5 grammes of ore (according to the amount of Ni and Co which the ore contains) with pure concentrated sulphuric, nitric, and hydrochloric acids in a small flask similar to the flask used in the copper-assay. For 1 gramme of ore use about 5 cc. of sulphuric, 5 cc. of nitric, and 3 cc. of hydrochloric acid. Heat until copious fumes of sulphuric anhydride are given off, adding more sulphuric acid, if necessary, to avoid reducing the mass to dryness. Cool, dilute with cold water, filter, and wash thoroughly with hot water.

Dilute the filtrate or the oxidized filtrate from the precipitated sulphides, if sulphuretted hydrogen was used, with water, and gradually add ammonia-water, with constant stirring, until the solution is decidedly alkaline. Filter out the precipitated ferric hydrate and wash slightly with hot water. Dissolve the precipitate with dilute hydrochloric acid, dilute with water, add pure sodium carbonate until a slight cloudiness is perceptible, and then add a drop of dilute hydrochloric acid to clear the solution. Now add from 7 to 15 grammes of pure sodium acetate, and boil to precipitate basic acetates. Filter whilst hot, using the filter-pump if the precipitate is bulky. Wash with hot water, and dissolve the precipitate with dilute hydrochloric acid, and reprecipitate as basic acetates, as before. This second basic-acetate precipitation is unnecessary if the amount of iron and alumina is small; but if the first basic-acetate precipitate is large, it is necessary in order to insure all the nickel and cobalt passing into solution. Combine the three filtrates and concentrate to 400 or 500 cc. by evaporation, acidify slightly with acetic acid, and boil. When boiling saturate the solution with sulphuretted hydrogen, continuing the boiling whilst passing the gas. Filter off and wash the precipitated sulphides of nickel and cobalt, and wash thoroughly with sulphuretted-hydrogen water. To recover any possible traces of nickel or cobalt which may have escaped, acidify the filtrate with a little acetic acid and boil. Should any precipitate of sulphides be recovered by this treatment wash it and the main precipitate from the filter into a casserole, dry and burn the filters, add the ashes to the precipitates, and dissolve with nitrohydrochloric acid. Evaporate nearly to dryness to expel the excess of acid, dilute with water and add a solution of pure potassium hydrate, heat for some time, keeping the solution near the boiling-point, and then filter and wash. Wash the precipitated oxides from the filter into a beaker, place the beaker under the funnel, and dissolve what remains on the filter with a saturated solution of pure potassium cyanide, allowing the solution to run through the filter into the beaker containing the oxides. Warm the beaker and its contents until the oxides are dissolved, and heat to boiling to expel the free hydrocyanic acid. Now add to the hot solution finely pulverized and elutriated red mercuric oxide, and boil. The whole of the nickel will be precipitated, partly as cyanide and partly as sesquioxide, the mercury combining with the free cyanogen. Filter off this precipitate, wash, dry, and ignite. The ignited precipitate is oxide of nickel (NiO). To obtain the weight of nickel, multiply the weight of this precipitate by 0.78667.

The filtrate from the precipitated nickel contains the cobalt in solution. Carefully neutralize it with nitric acid, so that the solution is not acid and not strongly alkaline. Now add a solution of mercurous nitrate as long as it produces a precipitate of mercury-cobaltocyanide. Filter, wash, and dry the precipitate, finally igniting in a strong current of hydrogen in a Rose crucible so as to reduce the precipitated cobalt to the metallic state. Weigh the metallic cobalt.

Another good method is to concentrate the combined filtrates from the ammonia and basic-acetate precipitations to about 100 cc., render the solution decidedly alkaline by the addition of a little ammonia, transfer to a weighed platinum dish, and precipitate the nickel and cobalt together by passing a strong galvanic current, keeping the solution alkaline with ammonia. The battery used for the generation of the current is the same as that used in the precipitation of copper electrolytically, two or three Bunsen cells making a very good battery.

The nickel and cobalt are thrown down on the platinum in the form of a metallic coating. When they are completely precipitated remove the dish, wash it thoroughly with hot water, dry, and weigh it. The increase in weight of the dish is the combined weights of the metallic nickel and cobalt. If it is necessary to determine them separately dissolve, the precipitate in nitric acid and effect the separation and determination as above. This is a very neat and accurate method.

The ignited oxide of nickel is liable to contain impurities. To determine these, transfer the ignited oxide to a beaker, add water, and boil. Filter, and wash thoroughly with boiling water. Dry, and ignite the oxide of nickel again. The loss in weight is probably due to some adhering alkali. Now dissolve the oxide of nickel in nitrohydrochloric acid, boil, dilute, filter, wash, dry, ignite, and weigh any undissolved silica. Deduct this weight from the weight of the oxide of nickel. Dilute the filtrate and add a large excess of ammonia, and filter out any precipitate of alumina or ferric hydrate which may form. Wash, dry, and ignite this precipitate and deduct its weight from the weight of the nickel oxide. From the true weight of the nickel oxide, as thus determined, calculate the weight of the metallic nickel.

CHAPTER XXIII.

CALCIUM (Ca).

LIME (CaO) is usually determined gravimetrically by precipitating it as calcium oxalate, converting the precipitate into a sulphate, and weighing as calcium sulphate; or volumetrically by precipitating it as calcium oxalate, and determining, after filtering and washing, the oxalic acid combined with the calcium by means of a standard solution of potassium permanganate. The second method is much more rapid than the first, and is fully as accurate, if proper care be observed. (See Fresenius, Wiley & Sons' edition of 1881, page 828.)

The solution of permanganate used may be the same as is used for the determination of iron, and may be standardized in the same manner. A comparison of the following equation with the one for the oxidation of ferrous iron to ferric iron by permanganate of potassium (see Part II, Chapter XVI) will show that one cc. of the permanganate solution is equal to exactly half as much lime (CaO) as iron, the molecular weight of lime and the atomic weight of iron being the same:

$$5CaC_2O_4 + 8H_2SO_4 + K_2Mn_2O_8 =$$
$$5CaSO_4 + 2MnSO_4 + K_2SO_4 + 2CO_2 + 8H_2O.$$

Consequently, if 1 cubic centimetre of permanganate solution equals 0.010 gramme of iron it will equal 0.005 gramme of lime.

Limestones.—One gramme of the limestones is treated as described in Chapter I, on Silica. The iron and alumina are precipitated out of the filtrate from the silica, as described in Chapter XVII, on Alumina. The filtrate from the precipitated hydrates of iron and aluminium is then ready for the precipitation of the calcium, provided its bulk is not much over 100 cc. If much iron or alumina is present it is safer to dissolve the precipitated hydroxides in a few cc. of hydrochloric acid, and reprecipitate with ammonia, combining the filtrate from this precipitate with the first filtrate for the determination of the lime. A cubic centimetre of ammonia should be added, and the solution brought to a boil. If a precipitate other than aluminium or ferric hydrate forms (such a precipitate should be filtered out, and added to the previous precipitate of hydrates), acidify slightly with hydrochloric acid, and make alkaline with ammonia. This is done to introduce sufficient ammonium chloride to prevent the precipitation of magnesium hydrate. The lime is then precipitated as an oxalate by the addition of ammonium oxalate or oxalic acid. If oxalic acid is used there should be a considerable excess of ammonia present in order that the solution may be alkaline after the addition of the oxalic acid. If magnesia is present the ammonium oxalate should be in considerable excess. [According to Cairns, 40 cc. of a solution of ammonium oxalate prepared by dissolving one part of oxalate in twenty-four of water.] This is not only to precipitate all of the lime as oxalate, but to convert all of the magnesia into oxalate, which is soluble. Heat nearly to boiling for a few minutes, and then filter. If the solution was brought to a boil before precipitation, and a good filter-paper is used, there will be no danger of the calcium oxalate running through the filter-paper. Provided magnesia is not present, less ammonium oxalate should be used, and the filtration may be proceeded with as follows: filter, and wash the precipitate out of the beaker on to the filter-paper with boiling water, then wash the precipitate on the filter-paper with boiling water until the washings no longer give a reaction for oxalic acid. Remove the filter and contents from the funnel, and spread out on a watch-glass somewhat larger than the paper. Wash into a beaker with hot water from a wash-bottle with a fine jet, and after all the precipitate is removed from the paper, or all that can be in this way, wash the paper with some dilute sulphuric acid, transferring the washings to the beaker. Sometimes it is difficult to remove the last traces of calcium oxalate from the paper with sulphuric acid. In such a case a few drops of dilute hydrochloric acid may be added to the paper. The contents of the beaker are now diluted with warm water to about 100 cc., 15 cc. sulphuric acid added, and the solution heated to about 70° C. The solution is now ready for titration with a standard solution of potassium permanganate. This titration is performed in the same manner as described for the determination of the standard of the permanganate solution by means of oxalic acid (see Chapter XVI). If magnesia is present it is always safest, and is in fact absolutely necessary where an accurate determination is to be made, to dissolve the first precipitate of calcium oxalate in hydrochloric acid, and reprecipitate, on account of the magnesia which has been carried down with the first precipitate. To do this wash the precipitate into a beaker as before (such care in washing the precipitate as before is not necessary; in fact, it need only be filtered), and dissolve in as little hot dilute hydrochloric acid as possible. Dilute to about 50 cc. with boiling water, make alkaline with ammonia, add 20 cc. of ammonium-oxalate solution, and heat nearly to boiling. Then filter, wash, and determine the lime as above.

The second filtrate is to be combined with the first for the determination of magnesia. (See Chapter XXIV.)

If desirable the lime can be determined gravimetrically, as described below, although the experience of the writer is that the volumetric determination gives fully as accurate results, and is more rapid.

Clays, Cements, Feldspar, etc.—Treat the substance as described in Chapter I, and, after combining the filtrate from the insoluble, and the silica by fusion, proceed as above.

Ores.—For the determination of lime in ores the method as given for limestone may be used. In the cases of lead ores it is necessary to first remove the lead.

Slag.—For the determination of the lime in a slag the following method is generally used, and answers all requirements for technical purposes:

The filtrate from the silica (see Chapter I) is heated to boiling, made alkaline with a slight excess of ammonia, and acidified with a slight excess of a saturated solution of oxalic acid. Ammonia is then added until the solution is slightly alkaline, and then a solution of oxalic acid until the iron precipitate is dissolved. The solution is then heated to boiling, filtered and washed, the lime being determined volumetrically as above. The precipitated calcium oxalate should be white, otherwise iron, manganese, etc., have not been dissolved, showing an insufficiency of oxalic acid. Whilst this latter method is not absolutely accurate, it is generally sufficiently accurate for technical purposes, and is extremely rapid; a determination of silica and lime in a slag having frequently been made by the writer in from an hour and fifteen minutes to an hour and a half whilst doing other work.

For the determination of the lime gravimetrically, obtain the precipitate of calcium oxalate as described above. It is necessary to wash all of the precipitate out of the beaker and on to the filter. Some of the precipitate will usually adhere to the sides of the beaker, and can generally be removed by rubbing with a glass rod provided with a rubber on the end. When this treatment fails to remove all of the precipitate from the sides of the beaker, dissolve it in a few drops of hydrochloric acid, add a few cc. of boiling water, making alkaline with ammonia, and precipitate with ammonium oxalate. When all of the precipitate is transferred to the filter, wash until the washings no longer give a reaction for oxalic acid, and finally wash the precipitate down into the point of the filter. Dry the filter-paper and its contents in a hot-air bath, and when thoroughly dry remove from the funnel. Transfer the precipitate to a weighed platinum crucible by inverting the filter-paper over the crucible and gently rolling between the fingers. Roll the filter-paper and the small amount of precipitate adhering to it into a ball, and ignite on the lid of the crucible over the flame of a burner until white. Add the filter-ash to the precipitate in the crucible, and thoroughly moisten the precipitate with strong c. p. sulphuric acid, place the lid on the crucible, and expel the excess of acid by heating over a burner, allowing the flame to touch only the edge of the crucible cover. After expelling all free sulphuric acid, ignite strongly over a blast-lamp or in the muffle, cool, and weigh.

This weight, after deducting the known weights of the crucible and filter-ash, will be the weight of the calcium sulphate. Multiply this weight by 0.41176, and the result will be the weight of the lime.

CHAPTER XXIV.

MAGNESIUM (Mg).

MAGNESIA (MgO) is universally determined by precipitating it as ammonium-magnesium phosphate, converting it into magnesium pyrophosphate ($Mg_2P_2O_7$) by ignition, and weighing as such. The preparation of the solution for the precipitation of the magnesia will depend upon what metals are present. The metals of the sulphuretted-hydrogen group, the ammonium-sulphide group, and barium, strontium, and calcium, should be removed before the precipitation of the magnesia.

The solution should contain ammonium chloride and an excess of free ammonia, and should be cold before adding the hydrodisodium-phosphate solution, which may be prepared by dissolving one part by weight of the salt in ten parts of water. After adding the phosphate solution, agitate by stirring with a glass rod, care being exercised not to touch the sides of the beaker with the rod, as that will cause crystals of ammonium-magnesium phosphate to adhere to the sides of the beaker, and they will be difficult to remove. Cold, and frequent agitation of the solution, facilitate the precipitation, and it is a good plan to set the beaker in a dish containing ice-water or a freezing mixture and stir from time to time. Several hours' (from 2 to 12) standing in the cold are necessary to complete the precipitation, the time depending to a great extent on the amount of magnesia present. After allowing to stand a sufficient length of time, remove a few drops of the clear liquid with a piece of glass tubing, transfer to a test-tube, and add two or three drops of magnesia mixture. This is prepared by dissolving one gramme of magnesium sulphate and one gramme of ammonium chloride in 8 cc. of water and adding 3 cc. of ammonia. If a precipitate forms it shows that sufficient phosphate solution was added. Should no precipitate form add 5 cc. of the phosphate solution, stir, and proceed as before. Provided one gramme of substance was taken, and the magnesia is not over 30 per cent, 30 cc. of the phosphate solution (prepared as above) and added at first will serve to precipitate all of the magnesia. Filter on a small filter and wash with dilute ammonia, prepared by adding two parts of water to one part of ammonia, until the washings no longer show a precipitate upon the addition of a few drops of silver-nitrate solution, after having previously acidified them with c. p. nitric acid. Dry the filter and precipitate as in the case of calcium oxalate (see Chapter XXIII), and when dry transfer the precipitate to a weighed crucible, and ignite the filter on the lid of the crucible until white. Add the filter-ash to the contents of the crucible, and ignite strongly until the contents of the crucible are white or nearly so. Should the precipitate be of a dark color, moisten with a few drops of nitric acid, and, after having carefully evaporated off the excess of acid, ignite again strongly until the precipitate assumes a light-gray color. Now cool and weigh the crucible and its contents. After deducting the known weight of the crucible and filter-ash, the remainder will be the weight of the magnesium pyrophosphate. Multiply this weight by 0.36036, and the result will be the weight of the magnesia (MgO). From this calculate the percentage.

Slags.—As these contain all the impurities of the ores and fluxes from which they were produced, to a more or less large extent, a separation of the metals of the different groups will be necessary before precipitating the magnesia. Dilute the filtrate from the silica obtained as described in Chapter I, with distilled water, to about 200 cc., and pass a rapid current of sulphuretted-hydrogen gas through the solution, filter off the precipitated sulphides, and oxidize the filtrate as described in Chapter XVII. Transfer the solution to a flask of not less than 500 cc. capacity, and add a saturated solution of sodium carbonate until a slight permanent precipitate forms. Dissolve this precipitate in a slight excess of acetic acid, add about 10 grammes of sodium acetate, dilute to about 300 cc., and heat to boiling. Continue to boil for a few minutes, and filter whilst hot, washing thoroughly with hot water.* Boil the filtrate from the precipitated basic acetates, add a few grammes of sodium acetate, and add bromine-water until the solution has a decided yellow color. Continue to boil and add bromine-water for some time, until the bromine no longer produces a precipitate of manganese oxide. Filter out the precipitate of manganese oxide, and, to be sure that the filtrate contains no manganese, neutralize it with sodium carbonate, acidify with acetic acid, boil, and add bromine. If a precipitate forms, proceed as before. When the solution is free from manganese acidify it thoroughly with acetic acid, boil, and while boiling pass a rapid current of sulphuretted-hydrogen gas. The gas should be passed for from 10 to 30 minutes, depending upon the amount of zinc present. By this means the zinc is precipitated as a sulphide, and can be filtered out. Wash with hot water by decantation once or twice, and then wash thoroughly with sulphuretted-hydrogen water. It is best to remove the beaker containing the bulk of the solution from beneath the funnel, and filter into a small beaker, changing the beaker frequently on account of the liability of the zinc sulphide to run through the filter. To the filtrate from the zinc sulphide add 1 cc. of hydrochloric acid, boil, and add bromine-water to oxidize the sulphur. If a precipitate of sulphur forms, filter it out. The solutions now contains lime and magnesia. The lime is precipitated as calcium oxalate in the manner described in Chapter XXIII, the precaution being observed to dissolve the precipitate of calcium oxalate in a little hydrochloric acid and reprecipitate, on account of the magnesia which may be precipitated together with the lime. The filtrate from the calcium oxalate is now ready for the precipitation of the magnesia in the manner described above.

---

* When considerable quantities of iron, alumina, and magnesia are present, it is best to dissolve the precipitate in a little hot dilute hydrochloric acid, and reprecipitate as basic acetates in the manner described, adding the second filtrate to the first.

Silver, Copper, and Lead Ores.—Proceed as above, except that when manganese and zinc are not present the lime can be precipitated in the filtrate from the precipitate of the basic acetates of iron and alumina, the treatment with bromine, and subsequently with sulphuretted hydrogen, being omitted.

Limestones, Clays, Cements, etc.—As these substances seldom contain any of the metals of the sulphuretted-hydrogen group, proceed as in the determination of lime in limestones (see Chapter XXIII), and precipitate the magnesia in the filtrate from the calcium oxalate as above.

The above examples will serve for nearly every case likely to arise.

CHAPTER XXV.

BARIUM (Ba).

BARIUM is universally precipitated as a sulphate and weighed as such ($BaSO_4$).

The following method will serve for all ores and furnace-products:

Dissolve as described in Chapter I, taking the precaution to add a few drops of sulphuric acid in addition to the hydrochloric and nitric acids, to precipitate the barium as sulphate with the silica. Evaporate to dryness, dissolve in hydrochloric acid, boil, add water, filter and wash thoroughly, and ignite. If the silica is to be determined, weigh the insoluble residue and determine the barium as follows: Fuse the insoluble residue with from one to five grammes (depending on its amount) of carbonate of soda (see Chapter I). Dissolve the fusion in hot water and boil. Filter through a small filter, and wash until the washings no longer show a reaction for sulphuric acid, which can be determined by acidifying some of the washings in a test-tube with hydrochloric acid and adding a few drops of barium-chloride solution. Should no precipitate form, the barium carbonate remaining behind on the filter is washed sufficiently. Dissolve the precipitate on the filter in dilute hydrochloric acid, allowing the solution to run into a small beaker. The funnel should be covered with a watch-glass to prevent loss by effervescence when the acid is added. Wash off the watch-glass and sides of the funnel with hot water, and finally drop a few drops of hydrochloric acid around the edges of the filter-paper and wash thoroughly with hot water. The filtrate should be perfectly clear, and should be brought to a boil when it is ready for the precipitation of the barium, which can be accomplished by adding sulphuric acid to the solution. From a few drops to two cc. of dilute sulphuric acid should be added, depending on the amount of barium present. The solution should be allowed to stand for some time until the precipitate partially settles before filtering. If a good filter-paper, such as Schleicher & Schuell's, is used, it is not necessary to allow the solution to stand until the precipitate settles absolutely, as with such a filter it will seldom run through. A good plan is to filter off into a small beaker, changing the beaker frequently, so if any of the precipitate should run through the filter it will not be necessary to refilter such a large amount of solution. The first filtrate should be tested with a few drops of sulphuric acid to determine whether all of the barium has been precipitated. After the solution is all filtered wash what remains in the beaker on to the filter with hot water, and wash the precipitate on the filter once or twice with hot water, finally washing the precipitate down into the point of the filter. Dry, and ignite in the manner described for the precipitate of magnesia pyrophosphate (Chapter XXIV). A small filter-paper should be used, as the carbon of the filter-paper is liable to reduce barium sulphate to a sulphide. When much of the precipitate adheres to the filter-paper moisten its ash, after ignition, with a few drops of nitric acid, and ignite again. The precipitate should be perfectly white, and can be transferred from the crucible to the watch-glass of the balance and weighed directly. This weight, less the known weight of the filter-ash, will be the weight of the barium sulphate. To obtain the weight of the baryta (BaO) multiply this weight by 0.65636.

For the rapid determination of baryta and silica in lead slags the following method answers for technical purposes: Treat 0.5 gm. with water and hydrochloric acid in a casserole, heat, add water, filter, and determine the silica as usual. This insoluble residue may be considered as silica. Treat another portion (0.5 gm.) with water, hydrochloric acid, and a few drops of sulphuric acid. Evaporate to dryness, heat, dissolve in water and hydrochloric acid, and determine the insoluble residue as usual. This insoluble residue may be considered as consisting of silica and barium sulphate.

CHAPTER XXVI.

POTASSIUM (K) AND SODIUM (Na).

ONE of the two following methods will be used, according to whether the substance is decomposed by acids or not:

First Method.—*The Substance is decomposed by Acids.*—Dissolve from 0.5 to 5.0 grammes in hydrochloric acid, add bromine or chlorine water, and heat to boiling. Evaporate to dryness if necessary, and proceed as in the determination of silica (Chapter I). To the filtrate from the silica add ammonia in slight excess (if any members of the sulphuretted-hydrogen group are present they must be removed, as in the case of determination of alumina, Chap. XVII), and ammonium carbonate, and allow to stand for a few hours. Filter, wash, evaporate the filtrate and washings to dryness in a platinum dish, and expel the ammonia salts by igniting to a point just below redness. Dissolve in water, add solution of barium hydrate until the fluid is decidedly alkaline, filter and wash well, and add to the filtrate solution of ammonium carbonate as long as it produces a precipitate; allow the solution to stand for a short time, filter out the barium carbonate, and wash it until the washings do not render silver nitrate turbid. Now add a few drops of hydrochloric acid to the filtrate, and evaporate it to dryness in a weighed platinum dish, ignite to a slight-red heat, cool and weigh the mixed chlorides of sodium and potassium. Where an accurate determination is required, it is best to dissolve the mixed chlorides in water and repeat the treatment with barium hydrate and ammonium carbonate, and again evaporate and weigh.

The weight of sodium and potassium present may now be

determined indirectly as follows: Dissolve the combined chlorides in warm water, add a few drops of a saturated solution of potassium chromate, and add from a burette a standardized solution of silver nitrate until the red color of silver chromate appears. From the number of cc. of standard silver nitrate-solution used calculate the weight of chlorine present, as described below. The weight of chlorine present having been thus determined, the weights of the sodium and potassium present may be calculated as follows: Suppose we have found 1.0 gramme of sodium and potassium chlorides and 0.563 gramme of chlorine present in the combined chlorides.

35.4 (at. wt. Cl) : 74.4 (mol. wt. KCl) : : 0.563 (Cl found) : x.
$$x = 1.18326.$$

If all of the Cl present were combined with K, the weight of the chloride would amount to 1.18326. As the combined chlorides weigh less, NaCl is present, and in a quantity proportional to the difference (dif. = 1.18326 − 1.0 = 0.18326). The difference between the molecular weight of KCl and that of NaCl (16.0) is to the molecular weight of NaCl (58.4) as the difference found is to the NaCl present; or,

16 : 5.84 :: 0.18326 : x (NaCl present).
x (NaCl present) = 0.67015 gms.
KCl present = 1.0 − 0.67015 = 0.32985.

The above illustrates the method of calculating results.

To prepare the standard silver-nitrate solution, dissolve from 17 to 18 grammes of pure nitrate of silver in one litre of distilled water. To standardize the solution, dissolve 1 gramme of pure fused sodium chloride in one litre of water, pour exactly 100 cc. of the solution into a beaker, add three drops of a saturate solution of potassium chromate, and drop in from the burette the silver solution until the red color of silver chromate appears. The known quantity of chlorine, in the 100 cc. of salt solution, divided by the number of cc. of silver solution used, will give the value of 1 cc. of the latter.

In the case of analyses where extreme accuracy is required the potassium may be determined directly as follows, and the sodium by difference: Dissolve the combined chlorides (after having weighed them) in warm water, and if the solution is complete, transfer it to a small casserole, add 3 to 4 drops of hydrochloric acid and a solution of potassium tetrachloride (as much as contains an amount of the salt equal to about four times the weight of the combined chlorides) and evaporate on the water-bath until the mass is pasty. Now add to the casserole about 50 cc. of 85 per cent alcohol, and heat for a few minutes on the water-bath. Then wash into a small flask (which we will designate as A) the contents of the casserole with alcohol (85 per cent), and cork the flask immediately. After the precipitate of potassium platinochloride has entirely settled, and the fluid shows by its yellow color that sufficient platinum tetrachloride has been added, pour off the clear fluid into a small flask marked B, as completely as possible without transferring any of the precipitate, cork it, and allow it to stand long enough for any particles of potassium platinochloride, which may have passed over with the fluid from flask A, to subside. Then pour into flask A 20 or 30 cc. of 85 per cent alcohol, cork it, and after agitating it gently set it aside until the contents of flask B are disposed of. Pour the contents of B into a dish, add about 10 cc. of water, and proceed to evaporate off the alcohol on a water-bath. Should there be any particles of the precipitate in the fluid, first pour off as much as possible into the dish, without disturbing the precipitate and evaporate it as above, and pour the rest, with the precipitate, on a filter. Add this filtrate to the fluid already evaporating. Keep the funnel covered with a glass while filtering. After all the fluid has thus been transferred to the dish for evaporation, pour upon the same filter the contents of flask A, washing the precipitate onto the filter with 85 per cent alcohol. Dry the filter and contents in an air-bath at $100°$ C. Ignite the dry precipitate, rolled up in the filter, in a weighed crucible, applying the heat very gently at first, and keeping the crucible covered until the filter-paper is charred. Then remove the cover and ignite at a higher heat until the filter is entirely consumed. Allow the crucible to cool, add a little oxalic acid, heat gently at first, until the water of crystallization of the oxalic acid is expelled, and then more intensely until the acid is decomposed and all the carbon consumed. Cool the crucible, and wash by decantation with hot water as long as the wash-water becomes turbid from the formation of silver chloride when treated with silver nitrate. By this means the double chloride is decomposed, and all the potassium and chlorine washed out, leaving only spongy platinum. Heat alone fails to decompose the compound completely. After the platinum is sufficiently washed, dry the crucible and contents, and ignite until everything is consumed but spongy platinum. Cool and weigh. This weight, less the known weight of the crucible and filter-ash, will be the weight of the platinum combined with the potassium as potassium-platinic chloride ($PtCl_4, 2KCl$). To obtain the weight of the potassium multiply the weight of the platinum found by 0.39594.

After all the alcohol has been expelled from the original filtrate by evaporation, as directed above, add 1 cc. of platinum-tetrachloride solution and a small quantity of pure sodium chloride; continue the evaporation to pasty consistency, treat with alcohol, and proceed as directed for the treatment of the main precipitate. The sodium chloride has a tendency to prevent the decomposition of the platinum chloride while evaporating.

Should the solution of the combined chlorides be incomplete, filter, and evaporate the filtrate to dryness, as directed; weigh, and dissolve in warm water. Now determine the potassium, as directed above.

Second Method.—*The Substance is not entirely decomposed by Acids.*—The substance can be fused with sodium carbonate and the silica separated as usual (Chap. I), and the determination proceeded with as above; or the method of Prof. J. L. Smith[*] can be adopted. This method is as follows: Treat

---

[*] Am. Jour. Sci. and Arts, Vol. I, p. 269 (1871); Crooks, Select Methods, p. 409.

0.5 to 1.0 gm. of finely pulverized silicate in an agate or glazed porcelain mortar with an equal amount of granular ammonium chloride, rubbing the two together intimately. Add eight parts of pure calcium carbonate in three or four portions, mixing thoroughly after each addition. Transfer the contents of the mortar completely to the crucible, and tap gently until its contents are settled. It is then clasped by a metallic clamp in an inclined position, and the heat of a small Bunsen burner is now brought to bear upon the crucible just above the top of the mixture, and gradually carried toward the lower part, until the ammonium chloride is completely decomposed, which takes about five minutes. The heat is now raised gradually to a bright red, and kept there for about forty minutes. It is best not to have too intense a heat, as that would vitrify the mass too much. The crucible is now cooled, and when cool its contents will be found to be more or less agglomerated, in the form of a semi-fused mass. The mass is now transferred to a small casserole, and what adheres to the crucible is removed with warm distilled water, and sufficient water added to bring the bulk of the solution up to about 75 cc. The contents of the casserole are now brought to the boiling-point, when the mass will begin to slack. After the mass is completely slacked and disintegrated, the analysis is proceeded with as follows: Filter off the contents of the casserole on a good-sized filter, and wash well with distilled water. The filtrate will contain in solution all the alkalies, with some chloride and hydrate of lime. Proceed to determine the potassium and sodium in this filtrate in the manner described in the First Method, by the addition of ammonium carbonate, etc.

PART III.

CHAPTER I.

ASSAY OF BASE BULLION.

FOUR samples (see Fig. 7) are cut from the small sample bar with a cold-chisel. From each of these samples $\frac{1}{2}$ assay-ton is accurately weighed out for cupellation, it being a good plan to pound each sample into a cube before finishing the weighing.

Cupellation.—Each $\frac{1}{2}$ A. T. sample is now cupelled separately. In the case of impure bullion each sample should be scorified with a little borax before cupellation. In case the lead is very impure and contains a good deal of copper, a little test-lead will help the scorification. Some assayers prefer to scorify all samples before cupellation, contending that the loss of silver in scorification is less than the loss in cupellation.

The cupels should weigh about 20 gms. each, and should be heated in the muffle before introducing the sample for cupellation. After dropping the samples into the cupel the door of the muffle should be closed until the samples are melted and cupellation begins. As soon as the samples begin to cupel the door is opened, and the cupellation is continued at the proper temperature until the buttons "brighten." The temperature of cupellation should be properly regulated. The cupels should always show "feather litharge" around the edges, which they will not do if the temperature is too high. On the other hand, the temperature should not be too low, as in this case the loss of silver will be high, and the buttons are apt to "freeze" and ruin the assay. The proper temperature is something which can only be learned by experience. When the bullion is rich and the buttons, consequently, large, it is a good plan to have some cupels in the rear of the muffle, to cover the cupels containing the buttons just after they "brighten." The cupels should be placed in a hot part of the muffle just before "brightening," and should be gradually removed after "brightening," in order to prevent "spitting." A button which has "spit" or "sprouted" should always be rejected. When the cupels are cool the buttons are ready for weighing.

Weighing.—The buttons are best removed from the cupel by means of a pair of pliers, and should be brushed off with a wire-brush to remove any particles of litharge or bone-ash which may adhere to the bottom. The buttons are now ready for weighing on the button-balance, and should agree together closely. The agreement should be within about 0.5 ounces on a bullion of from 200 to 400 ounces. After weighing, the buttons should be flattened out with a few light blows, when they are ready for parting.

Parting.—The parting can be performed in a small porcelain crucible or, preferably, a glass matrass or test-tube. Two of the flattened buttons are introduced into each matrass, and c. p. nitric acid of 20° Baumé added. The matrass is now gradually warmed on an iron plate or sand-bath until the silver is all dissolved. The contents of the matrass are now boiled for a few minutes and then removed from the heat. After shaking gently to bring all the fine particles of gold into one mass, the solution is poured off. Fresh acid of 32° Baumé is now added, and the gold boiled for three minutes. It is again brought into one mass, if necessary, and the acid decanted off. The gold is now washed three times by decantation with distilled water (free from chlorides), the matrass filled with distilled water and inverted in a small porcelain crucible. After the gold has settled to the bottom the matrass is removed and the water poured off, the last drops of water being readily removed by suction, through a small piece of glass tubing drawn to a point at the end. The crucible is dried, and finally ignited at a red heat, when the gold is ready for weighing on the gold balance. The duplicates should agree almost exactly.

Special Method.—In the case of extremely impure bullion, this method may have to be adopted. Prepare the sample as described in Part I, Chapter II, weighing the dross and the bar separately. Weigh out four samples, of $\frac{1}{2}$ A. T. each, of the dross, scorify, cupel, and part, as described above. Determine the gold and silver in the bar as described above.

The manner of calculating the results is best illustrated by an example:

Bar weighs.............................	4.25 lbs.
Dross weighs...........................	1.50 "
Total weight of sample (after melting).	5.75 lbs.

Bar-assays:

Ag.................................	405.00 oz.
Au.................................	1.00 "

Dross-assays:

Ag.................................	806.00 oz.
Au.................................	3.50 "

Then $\qquad \dfrac{4.25}{2000} \times 405 = 0.860625,$

$$\dfrac{1.5}{2000} \times 806 = 0.6045,$$

the total ounces of silver in the bar and dross.

Hence the total ounces of silver in the sample

$$= 0.86025 + 0.6045 = 1.465125.$$

Now $\qquad 1.465125 \times \dfrac{2000}{5.75} = 509.61,$

the ounces of silver, per ton of 2000 pounds, in the sample.

ASSAY OF BASE BULLION.

In the same manner we have for the gold

$$\frac{4.25}{2000} \times 1.0 = 0.002125, \text{ and } \frac{1.5}{2000} \times 3.5 = 0.002625.$$

Hence

$$0.002125 + 0.002625 = 0.00475, \text{ and } 0.00475 \times \frac{2000}{5.75} = 1.65,$$

the assay-value of the sample in ounces gold per ton.

Hence the assay-value of the bullion is:

Ag................................. 509.61
Au................................. 1.65

The results may also be calculated according to the formulæ given in Part III, Chapter VIII, in which case the bullion and dross are weighed in grammes.

CHAPTER II.

ASSAY OF SILVER BULLION.

FOR the determination of silver in silver bullion any of the following methods are applicable, but the first two are the only ones generally used in the United States.

The first method is universal in its application, and is the method generally adopted by our Western metallurgical establishments, although some refiners use the second method, whilst some works use both the first and second methods, using one as a check on the other.

The first method is preferable when the bullion contains mercury, as in the case of retorted bullion from a pan-amalgamation mill.

The second method is the one which has been adopted by the U. S. Government for the determination of the fineness of silver bullion in the U. S. mints and assay-offices.

The fineness or silver and gold contents of the bullion is always reported in thousandths; i.e., so many degrees or parts of silver or gold in one thousand parts of bullion. For example, we say a bullion is 990 silver and 5 gold fine; that is, it contains 99 per cent of silver and 0.5 per cent of gold.

The sample of bullion should always be annealed, and hammered or rolled out thin so that it can be cut readily with a pair of scissors. A small set of rolls, to be kept only for this purpose, will be found very convenient when many assays are to be made.

First Method: By cupellation with pure lead. Fire-assay.

Second Method: Volumetrically by means of a standard solution of sodium chloride. Gay-Lussac's method.

Third Method: Volumetrically by means of a standard solution of potassium sulphocyanide. Volhard's method.

The first and second methods require a preliminary assay to determine the approximate fineness of the bullion, unless this is known. The third method requires no preliminary assay.

Preliminary Assay.—To determine the approximate fineness of the bullion weigh out 0.500 gramme of bullion (the bullion and buttons should be weighed on the button-balance), wrap in from 5.0 to 10.0 grammes of pure lead-foil, and cupel in the muffle-furnace, using a small cupel weighing about 10 to 12 grammes. The cupel should be hot before placing the button in it, and the door of the muffle should be closed until cupellation commences. As soon as cupellation begins the door is opened and the cupel moved to the front of the muffle. The temperature is the most important point in this operation. The assay should run sufficiently cold to allow *feather litharge* to form on the cupel, but not so cold that there will be danger of the button freezing. The proper temperature is something which can only be gauged by experience; after considerable practice with this method the assayer will be able to control the temperature within comparatively narrow limits. Toward the latter part of the cupellation and just before the button brightens the cupel should be moved back in the muffle. After the play of colors on the button has ceased, the button should be covered with a hot cupel; but before covering, it should be allowed to remain for about a minute to remove the last traces of lead. The assay should be gradually removed from the furnace to prevent spitting or sprouting. Should the button sprout, the assay should be discarded. When the cupel is cold the bottom is removed by a pair of pliers, and brushed with a stiff brush to remove adhering particles of bone-ash, etc. The weight of this button gives the amount of pure silver to be taken for the proof- or check-assay if the first method is adopted or the weight of bullion to be taken for assay if the second method is adopted, according to the following table:

Preliminary Assay of 500 mgs. gave Ag, mgs.	Silver to be used in Proof, mgs.	Bullion to be used for Volumetric Assay, gms.	Weight of sheet lead to be used, gms.
475	480	1.042	5
450	455 to 460	1.091	7
425	430 to 435	1.156	8
400	405 to 410	1.227	10
375	380 to 385	1.307	11
350	355 to 360	1.399	12
325	330 to 335	1.504	13
300	305 to 310	1.610	15
250	255 to 260	1.922	17
200	205 to 210	2.380	19
150	155 to 160	3.125	20

First Method.—The check- or proof-assay should not only contain very approximately the same amount of silver which the bullion contains, but approximately the same amount of copper and lead as the bullion. Should the bullion contain much gold, the proof should contain gold in the same proportion. Should the bullion contain much copper, the amount can be quickly ascertained by dissolving 0.5 gramme of bullion in dilute nitric acid, adding a very slight excess of hydrochloric acid to precipitate the silver, filtering off the precipitated silver chloride, and washing the precipitate with hot water. The filtrate is now rendered alkaline with ammonia, and the copper determined by titration with a standard solution of potassium cyanide. (See Part II, Chapter XIII.) Or the copper may be determined quickly by the colorimetric test. (See Part II, Chapter XIII.) In the case of quite fine bullion, as the bullion from the cupellation process, the copper can be disregarded. The method of making up the proof is best illustrated by an example, as follows: Suppose the preliminary assay gave 375 mgs. of silver and showed the bullion to contain 20 per cent copper. The table shows that we would have to weigh out from 380 to 385 mgs. of pure silver, and that 11 gms. of lead would be required for cupellation. To this should be added

100 mgs. of pure copper-foil and 25 mgs. of lead. The whole is wrapped in the 11 gms. of sheet lead when it is ready for cupellation with the regular assay. The reason for making up the proof in this manner is that the loss of silver in cupellation will depend upon the amount of lead and copper present.

The pure silver-foil used can be made by the reduction of the silver chloride obtained in parting, or it can be purchased from dealers.

The regular assay is performed as follows: Two portions of bullion weighing 0.500 gm. each are accurately weighed out on the button-balance and wrapped in the proper amount of lead-foil as shown by the table. The lead-foil can be cut into sheets of the proper weight. The lead-foil should be free from silver; but, if it contains a small amount of silver and its silver contents are uniform, the silver which it contains can be disregarded, as the same amount will be present in the lead used in the proof-assay. The proof is made up as indicated above. Have three hot cupels in the muffle and introduce into each one of the assays, placing the test-assay in the middle. Proceed with the cupellation in the manner described under the preliminary assay, taking care to have the cupellation of all three of the assays start and finish at about the same time; that is, have all three run at about the same temperature. Weigh all three buttons: the loss in silver of the test-assay will represent the loss in cupellation. In the case of fine bullion this loss should be from 4 to 5 mgs. If greater than 5 mgs., the assay has been run too hot or too cold. The buttons should be bright, and should show no evidence of litharge. The loss in the test-assay is added to each of the regular assays when the product of the two assays will give the fineness of the bullion. The two buttons should not differ from each other by more than 1 mg. A greater difference, except in the case of very impure bullion, when a greater number of assays should be run, should not be allowed. Suppose button No. 1 weighs 489 mgs., button No. 2 weighs 488 mgs., and the test shows a loss of 4.5 mgs.; then

$$(489 + 4.5) + (488 + 4.5) = 986 \text{ fine.}$$

The buttons are parted for gold (see assay of Gold Bullion, Part III, Chapter III), and the gold fineness is deducted from the total fineness (Ag and Au) to determine the silver fineness.

Second Method.—This method requires the following solutions: Normal-salt solution, decinormal-salt solution, and decinormal solution of silver nitrate.

The normal-salt solution is a solution of salt in water, 100 cc. of which will precipitate exactly 1.0 gm. of silver as silver chloride.

The decinormal-salt solution is a solution of salt in water, one cc. of which will precipitate exactly 1.0 mg. of silver. This solution is made by diluting one part of the normal solution with nine parts of water. In making up this solution care should be taken to have the temperature of the solution and the water used for dilution the same.

The decime-silver solution is a solution of pure silver in nitric acid, diluted with distilled water. One cc. of this solution contains 1.0 milligramme of silver, consequently 1 cc. is equivalent to 1 cc. of decime-salt solution.

To prepare the normal-salt solution dissolve 5.4167 grammes of pure dry sodium chloride (dried by heating at about 125° C.) in distilled water, and dilute to 1000 cc. Where many assays are to be made, it is usual to prepare a greater quantity of the solution, the above being given simply to indicate the amount of salt to be used. In making up and measuring the solutions care should be exercised to have the temperatures remain the same. A good plan in making up, measuring, and standardizing is to have the solutions at the ordinary temperature of the laboratory. The laboratory in which the solutions are kept and the assays performed should have a nearly constant temperature. A convenient form of apparatus in which to keep the solutions is a carboy or large glass bottle, provided with a rubber stopper perforated with two holes. Into one of these holes is introduced a piece of glass tubing whose lower end reaches nearly to the bottom of the flask. In the other hole introduce a piece of glass tubing bent in the form of a siphon, the end in the bottle reaching nearly to the bottom, whilst the other end is a foot or so below the level of the bottom of the bottle and a convenient height above the work-table. This siphon tube should be provided with a stop-cock, situated at a convenient height, and a piece of rubber tubing on the end, the latter being provided with a pinch-cock. From time to time the solution in the bottle should be shaken, and it should be restandardized every few weeks, as, no matter what precautions are taken, its strength is liable to change.

The decime-salt solution is prepared by drawing off exactly 100 cc. of the normal solution and diluting it to 1000 cc. with distilled water of the same temperature. It is unnecessary to prepare a large quantity of this solution, as it can be readily prepared from time to time, as needed, from the normal solution.

The decime-silver solution is prepared by dissolving 1 gramme of perfectly pure silver in a few cc. of dilute nitric acid, and diluting to 1000 cc. It is best to prepare this solution freshly about once a week, and it should be kept in a green-glass bottle covered with black paper, and provided with a siphon for convenience in drawing off into the burette.

After preparing the salt solutions they must be carefully standardized as follows: Three or four portions of pure silver of exactly 1 gramme each are weighed out, and each portion is introduced into a glass-stoppered flask of about 250 cc. capacity. The silver in each flask is now dissolved in 10 cc. of dilute nitric acid (free from chlorine), placing the flask in an inclined position on the sand-bath to facilitate solution and avoid loss. After the silver is all dissolved dilute the contents of the flask with about 80 cc. of distilled water. Run into a pipette 100 cc. of the normal solution, and add the solution from the pipette to the contents of the flask. Close the flask with the stopper, and agitate violently. After agitation place the flask in a dark place (a box with several holes in the top in which to introduce the flasks is convenient), and allow the precipitate to settle. Repeat the agitation, if necessary, until the solution settles clear, and then add 1 cc. of the decime-salt (prepared for this purpose by drawing off 25 cc. of the normal-salt solution, and diluting with 225 cc. of distilled water) solution from a burette. Should a precipitate appear, agitate and allow to settle as before, and repeat the addition of decime-salt solution until a precipitate fails to appear. The solution should be added slowly at first, and the addition stopped as soon as a precipitate fails to appear. The reading of the burette is now noted, the contents of the flask agitated and allowed to settle. The decime solution of silver nitrate is now added from a burette, adding not more than 1 cc. at a time. This addition is continued, agitating, and allowing the contents of the flask to settle after each addition until the silver nitrate no longer produces a precipitate, when the reading of the burette is noted.

The method of calculation is best illustrated by the following examples:

Suppose 100 cc. of the normal solution was insufficient to precipitate all the silver, and 7 cc. of the decime-salt solution were added. Then 1 cc. of the decime-silver solution is added, resulting in the formation of a precipitate. The addition of a second cc. of the silver solution fails to produce a precipitate. Hence, $100.7 - (.2 - .1) = 100.6$ cc. of the normal-salt solution, which is necessary to precipitate 1 gramme of silver, whilst only 100 cc. should be required. The normal-salt solution is consequently too weak, and the quantity of salt to be added to 1000 cc. may be calculated as follows:

$$(100 - 0.6) : 5.4167 :: 0.6 : x.$$
$$x = 0.0327 \text{ grammes of NaCl.}$$

Suppose 100 cc. of the normal- and 1 cc. of the decime-salt solution were added, the decime solution failing to produce a precipitate. Decime-silver solution was then added to the amount of 8 cc., the last cc. failing to produce a precipitate. Hence, $100.1 - (.8 - .1) = 99.4$ cc., required to precipitate 1 gramme of silver, whilst 100 cc. should be required; consequently the solution contains an excess of salt.

$$1 : 0.006 :: 5.4167 : x.$$
$$x = \text{salt in excess} = 0.0325002 \text{ gm.}$$

The following calculation gives the number of cc. of water to add to each 1000 cc. of solution in order to make it normal:

$$\frac{0.0325002}{5.4167} \times 1000 = 6 \text{ cc.}$$

Salt or water should be added as required, the solution being thoroughly mixed and restandardized. This operation is to be repeated until the solution is brought to the normal point. After a normal solution is obtained a decime solution can be made by diluting 100 cc. of the normal solution with 900 cc. of water.

The use of a normal solution of sodium bromide, rather than sodium chloride, is preferred by some chemists using this method. Sodium bromide is preferable, as silver bromide is practically insoluble in water containing a slight excess of sodium bromide, whilst silver chloride is slightly soluble in water containing a slight excess of sodium chloride. If sodium bromide is used, 9.5370 grammes of the dried salt dissolved in water and diluted to 1000 cc. should produce a normal solution. The solution is standardized, and the assay performed in the same manner as when sodium chloride is used.

The regular assay can now be made as follows: First determine the approximate fineness of the bullion by cupellation, as described above, or by weighing out 0.5 gramme of the bullion, solution in dilute nitric acid, and titration with the standard salt solution, using the normal solution to start with, and the decime solution to finish with. A good plan is to pour off one half of the solution of the bullion into a beaker, and approximately determine the amount of silver in the half remaining in the flask. Now add the solution in the beaker to the flask, and finish the titration. In this manner the amount of normal-salt solution which can be safely added is determined, and the final titration with the decime solution is quickly proceeded with.

Having determined the fineness approximately, the amount of bullion to weigh out for assay (so as to have about 1 gramme of silver present in each assay) can be obtained from the table. It is usual to take at least two portions for assay. Dissolve each portion in a 250-cc. stoppered flask with dilute c. p. nitric acid, and dilute with water to about 80 cc. Add 100 cc. of normal-salt solution, agitate, and proceed as above described. The method of calculating results is best illustrated by an example, as follows: Suppose we have taken 1.01 gramme of bullion, and have used 100 cc. of the normal- and 11 cc. of the decime-salt solution. Having added too much salt solution, we add 2 cc. of the decime-silver solution, and titrate again with the decime-salt solution, drop by drop, using 0.5 cc. altogether, when a precipitate fails to appear.

Salt solution used, 100 cc. normal,   = 1000.00 mgs. Ag.
"   "   "   11.5 cc. decime, =   11.50 "   "
                                           ————————
                                           1011.50 mgs. Ag.
Less decime-silver solution used, 2 cc., =   2.00 "   "
                                           ————————
                                           1009.50 mgs. Ag.

If $x =$ fineness in thousandths, we have

$$1.01 : 1.0095 :: 1000 : x.$$
$$x = 999.5.$$

As this assay cannot be made in a laboratory where fumes of chlorine, bromine, or ammonia are present, it is best to have a separate room for this assay. If a separate room is used it is preferable to have the light admitted through yellow glass, as the rays admitted by yellow glass do not decompose chloride or nitrate of silver. Should the bullion treated contain mercury, sunlight will not blacken the precipitated silver chloride. Should mercury be present, it may be held in solution by the addition of 10 grammes of sodium acetate containing a few drops of free acetic acid.

Should the bullion contain lead, it can be precipitated, before titration with the salt solution, by the addition of a few cc. of sulphuric acid.

Third Method.—By this method the silver is determined in the same manner as the determination of the silver present in the precipitate of silver arseniate, as described in the determination of arsenic volumetrically by means of a standard solution of potassium sulphocyanide.* A normal solution (1 cc. = 10 mgs. Ag) and a decinormal solution (1 cc. = 1 mg. Ag) of potassium sulphocyanide should be prepared. The titration should begin by the use of the normal solution, and the final reaction should be obtained by the decime solution.

A preliminary assay, either by cupellation or by titration with the normal solution, will be found of advantage.

The assays should be made in duplicate.

---
* Chapter X, page 145.

CHAPTER III.

THE ASSAY OF GOLD BULLION.

THE process of assaying, which is essentially one of refining, requires the removal of both the base metals and the silver. To effect this two operations are necessary:

First. The base metals are removed by cupellation. Weigh out 0.500 gm. on a delicate balance, wrap in 5 gms. of pure sheet lead, and cupel (see Chapter II: Assay of Silver Bullion). Lead under the action of the heat and air forms litharge, which dissolves the oxides of the base metals and carries them into the cupel, leaving behind, when the operation is completed, which is shown by the brightening of the button, pure silver and gold. The button of silver and gold is weighed, and the difference between this weight and the 0.500 gm. taken represents the weight of the base metal.

Second. The silver is removed from the gold by solution in nitric acid, the gold remaining behind in an insoluble state. In order that the silver be entirely removed, it is necessary that there be present at least twice as much silver as gold. A preliminary assay is run by weighing out 0.500 gm. of bullion, adding 1.0 gm. of pure silver, wrapping in 5 gms. of sheet lead, and cupelling. The resulting button is detached from the cupel, brushed and weighed, and then flattened out under a hammer, the weight being noted. It is then heated to redness in a clay annealing-cup and passed through a small set of rolls, which draw it out to about 4 inches in length. It is again annealed, and when cold is rolled into a spiral coil called a cornet. It is now ready for the acid. For this purpose a platinum dish about 3 inches in diameter and 2 inches deep is used. This is nearly filled with c. p. nitric acid of 32° Baumé and heated to boiling. The cornets are placed in a small platinum crate, with a separate compartment for each cornet. This crate is now lowered into the boiling acid and allowed to boil for 10 minutes, as shown by an electric indicator. The acid is now poured off, the dish filled with fresh acid of the same strength, and again boiled for 10 minutes. The crate containing the cornets is now lifted out and washed with pure distilled water. After drying slowly, the platinum crate and cornets are exposed for a few minutes to a strong red heat, which condenses and anneals them. When cool, the cornets are weighed and the number of milligrammes which they weigh is noted. Suppose this preliminary assay shows 0.380 gm. of gold and 0.010 gm. of silver, then twice 0.380 = 0.760, and 0.760 − 5 (half the silver present) = 0.755 gm. of silver, which it is necessary to add to the regular assay in order that there be twice as much silver present as gold.

For the regular assay 0.500 gm. of bullion is weighed out on a delicate balance. This weight is marked 1000. All the lesser weights used are decimal divisions of this weight, down to one ten-thousandth part. From the preliminary assay the amount of silver necessary to add is calculated. The bullion and the added silver are wrapped in 5 gms. of sheet lead and cupelled, the regular assay being performed exactly as above. In practice it is not general to take as much care with the preliminary assay as with the regular assay.

As the process is subject to error from a number of causes, but principally owing to the losses of the precious metals from volatilization and absorption while on the cupel, and from imperfect extraction of the silver by the acid, it is necessary to make a test assay with each set of assays. This assay is made from chemically pure gold, and is made up as nearly like the bullion under examination as possible. This is passed through the same processes as the samples of bullion under assay, and side by side with them. It is evident that, if the process were a perfect one, we would recover from the test-assay exactly the amount of gold taken. If, however, from any cause, it is found to differ from the weight taken, and therefore found to require a correction, it is assumed that the same correction should be made to the regular assays; and this is done. The weights of the cornets with this correction give the true fineness in gold.

The gold fineness being known, and also the fineness in silver and gold, the silver fineness is determined by difference. In practice the fineness of unparted, or Doré, bars is reported to the half-thousandth.

While the method as described is essentially that adopted by some of the government offices, in practice the author uses the following modifications:

A preliminary assay is seldom necessary, as after considerable experience the assayer will be able to judge very approximately the fineness of the bullion by simple eye inspection, and from the manner in which the bullion cuts with the shears after rolling into a ribbon. These estimates are generally sufficiently close where two and one half parts of silver (to one part gold) are used in alloying. Where the proportion of two to one is adopted a preliminary assay is necessary, as in this case so wide a variation is not permissible. For this reason the author has adopted the proportion of two and a half parts silver in alloying.

As the proportion of silver to gold is increased the strength of the first acid must be decreased. Where the proportion of two and one half is adopted the first acid should have a strength of 25° Baumé ($=$ 1.20 sp. gr.). The cornets are boiled in this acid until all action of the acid has ceased. This generally requires about ten minutes' boiling. The acid is now poured off, and fresh acid of 32° Baumé ($=$ 1.27 sp. gr.) is added. The cornets are boiled in the second acid for exactly ten minutes.

Where a proof or blank assay is run with each set of assays (the use of a proof has been generally adopted) care should be exercised that the proof is run under exactly the same conditions as the bullion under examination. For this reason the platinum parting apparatus is preferable to the flasks. Care should also be exercised to have each cornet of exactly the same thickness after passing through the rolls.

As the surcharge of silver (silver remaining with the gold after parting) depends upon the thickness of the cornets, the strength of the first and second acids and the time of boiling, the proportions of alloy, the strength of acid, the thickness of cornets, and time of boiling should be the same in all assays.

The correction for the loss of silver in cupellation of the base-metal assay is generally made by running a proof assay, the proof being made up of pure gold and silver, and as nearly like the bullion under examination as possible (see the fire-assay of silver bullion, Part III, Chapter II). Where gas furnaces are used for cupelling the temperature can be controlled within quite narrow limits. In such a case the silver losses may be determined on bullion of different fineness, and corresponding corrections can be made in subsequent assays.

The following table gives the proportions of silver and lead used by the author for the gold determination on the average bullion carrying silver, and on coppery bullion such as jewellers' melts:

Ordinary Bullion.			Coppery Bullion.			
Fineness.	Add Silver Mgs.	Add Lead Gms.	Fineness.	Add Silver Mgs.	Add Lead Gms.	Add Lead to Base-metal Assay, Gms.
500	400	5	500	550–600	10	14
550	500	5	550	650–700	10	13
600	575	5½	600	700–750	10	12
650	650	6	650	750–800	10	11
700	750	6	700	850	9	10
750	850	6	750	950	9	10
800	925	6¼	800	1000	8	9
850	1025	6¼	850	1050	8	9
900	1100	7	900	1125	7½	8
950	1175	7	950	1200	7	7
1000	1250	7	1000	1250	7	7

For the base-metal assay of ordinary bullion 7 gms. of lead is usually used.

CHAPTER IV.

SPECIAL METHOD FOR THE DETERMINATION OF SILVER AND GOLD IN COPPER MATTES, ETC.

IN the determination of silver and gold in copper mattes, pig-copper and ores carrying much copper, by the usual method of scorification-assay, the losses of silver and gold are quite large, usually from 2 to 3 per cent of the silver present being lost, owing to the fact that in order to obtain lead buttons which are soft and free from copper repeated scorifications are necessary, and, moreover, it is almost impossible to obtain lead buttons which are entirely free from copper. If the lead button contains copper, silver will be carried into the cupel when the button is cupelled.

Mr. Cabell Whitehead * has proposed a method which overcomes these difficulties and also presents the advantage, in gold determinations, of allowing a large quantity of the substance to be taken for assay. The method is essentially as follows:

Dissolve 1 A. T. to 4 A. T. in a large beaker (500 cc. capacity) by the gradual addition of strong nitric acid; drive off the red fumes by heating on the sand-bath, add 50 cc. of a saturated solution of lead acetate, and stir. Now add 1 cc. of dilute sulphuric acid, and allow the precipitated lead sulphate to settle. The lead sulphate collects and carries with it the finely divided gold, and allows of the solution being readily filtered without danger of the loss of gold. Filter, wash with cold water to remove copper salts, dry in a scorifier, burn the filter-paper, and

---

* Journal of Analytical and Applied Chemistry, Vol. VI, p. 262.

scorify with some test-lead. Finally cupel the lead button, weigh the silver-gold bead, and part for gold in the usual manner.

Dilute the filtrate to 1000 cc., divide in halves of exactly 500 cc. each, cool, and add to each a saturated solution of sodium bromide so long as a precipitate forms. The silver is precipitated as bromide along with the lead. The large precipitate of bromide of lead collects, and envelopes the precipitated silver bromide, so that it can be filtered off at once without danger of loss. Filter off each precipitate, and wash with cold water until all the copper is removed. Dry the filters and precipitates, and when thoroughly dry brush each precipitate from the paper into a small crucible. Mix with about three times its weight of carbonate of soda, and some flour or argol for reducing agent; cover with borax-glass and fuse for lead buttons, cupel the lead buttons, and weigh the silver beads.

By dividing the solution into halves we have a check on the results, which should agree closely. This method is also valuable for the assay of material other than copper mattes, as base metals, arsenical sulphides, etc.

CHAPTER V.

ASSAY OF SILVER SULPHIDES.

IN the ordinary crucible-assay of precipitated silver sulphides from a leaching-works the loss of silver in the slag and in the cupel will vary from 0.2 to 1.5 per cent. There is also an additional loss by volatilization during fusion and cupellation.* The loss in scorification will vary from 0.8 to 1.5 per cent, in addition to the usual loss by volatilization. These losses were determined in the case of high-grade (11,000 to 12,000 ounces silver per ton) sulphides. In the case of low-grade sulphides carrying considerable copper the losses will be greater. Scorification-assay gives the best results.

In consequence of this loss it is usual to determine the silver in these sulphides by "corrected assay." From six to twenty scorification-charges are run on each lot of sulphides, using the following charge: Sulphides, 0.1 A. T., test-lead 55 gms., and borax-glass 5 gms. The lead buttons are extracted from the slag, which is retained, and cupelled separately. The silver buttons are weighed and their average taken as the result, the cupels being retained.

The slag is pulverized, passed through a 20-mesh screen, and assayed by crucible-assay using the following charge: Slag; litharge 20 gms.; sodium carbonate, 15 gms.; argol, 2 gms.; salt cover. The resulting lead buttons are cupelled, the silver buttons are weighed and their average is taken.

The cupels are pulverized, passed through a 30-mesh screen

---

* Transactions of the American Institute of Mining Engineers, Vol. XVI, page 378.

and assayed by crucible-assay using the following charge: Cupel; litharge, 30 gms.; borax-glass, 30 gms.; sodium carbonate, 30 gms.; argol, 2 gms.; salt cover. The resulting lead buttons are cupelled, the silver buttons being weighed and their average taken.

The average amount of silver recovered from the slag and cupel in this manner is added to the average amount obtained by the first scorification-assay, the result being the corrected assay.

The gold is determined by treating from 1 A. T. to 4 A. T., in a beaker, with nitric acid, and proceeding in the manner described in Part III, Chapter IV.

CHAPTER VI.

CHLORINATION-ASSAY OF SILVER ORES.

IN milling silver ores by the Pan-Amalgamation process chlorination-assays are made daily to determine the per cent of chloride of silver in the pulp. These assays are also made as a check on the process in a leaching-works.

The process requires a solution of hyposulphite of soda containing two pounds of hyposulphite to the gallon of water, and a solution of sodium sulphide.

Weigh out two samples of the chloridized pulp of from $\frac{1}{10}$ A. T. to $\frac{1}{4}$ A. T., according to the grade of the ore. Scorify one with about 30 gms. of test-lead for every $\frac{1}{10}$ A. T. taken, and cupel. Place the second sample in a beaker and add some of the hyposulphite solution. Warm, and decant on a filter. Continue to wash with the hyposulphite, finally washing the contents of the beaker onto the filter, until all the chloride of silver has been dissolved and leached out of the pulp. This can be determined by testing the filtrate from time to time with a drop of the sodium-sulphide solution. When a black precipitate or brown coloration no longer forms, the silver chloride is all dissolved and the desired point is reached. Wash the pulp on the filter with warm water, dry, and burn the filter and its contents in a scorifier in the muffle. Mix the ashes with 30 gms. of test lead (for each $\frac{1}{10}$ A. T. taken) and scorify. Cupel the resulting lead button. Having the assay of the pulp before and after leaching, the percentage of chlorination is arrived at as follows:

Pulp-assays before leaching....... 95.00 oz. Ag.
Pulp-assays after leaching .... 9.00 oz. Ag.

Hence, if $x =$ per cent of silver chloride,

$$95 : (95 - 9) :: 100 : x.$$
$$x = 90.5.$$

If the pulp contains sulphate of silver, the per cent of sulphate present can be determined by weighing out a third sample and leaching it with warm water until all the silver sulphate is dissolved. Dry, burn, scorify, and cupel the residue. A calculation similar to the above will give the percentage of silver present as sulphate. To determine the percentage present as chloride deduct this per cent of sulphate from the per cent obtained by leaching with the hyposulphite solution.

To determine the per cent of silver which will be extracted by the Russel Process of Lixiviation, see Trans. of the American Institute of Mining Engineers, Vol. XVI, pages 368–381. Also, "The Lixiviation of Silver Ores," by C. A. Stetafeldt (Scientific Pub. Co.).

CHAPTER VII.

CHLORINATION-ASSAY OF GOLD ORES.

A CHLORINATION-ASSAY of a gold ore is made to determine the probable percentage of gold which may be extracted by the chlorination process.

The percentage of extraction will depend not only upon the per cent of free gold present, but also upon the fineness to to which the ore is pulverized, the amount of chlorine gas generated per ore charge, and the time of agitation. Hence in treating a new ore a series of tests under different conditions will be required.

The general practice in a chlorination-mill is to pulverize the ore to about 40 mesh, and treat in a closed vessel with bleaching-powder and sulphuric acid. The sulphuric acid reacts upon the bleaching-powder and chlorine gas and calcium sulphate are produced. (See Part III, Chapter XIV.) The amount of bleaching-powder used per ton of ore in the mill will vary from about 10 pounds to 60 pounds. The amount of sulphuric acid (66° Baumé) used will vary from about 15 pounds to 70 pounds per ton of ore. The same ratios should be preserved in the laboratory tests.

A convenient piece of apparatus for the laboratory test is a glass-stoppered bottle holding from one to three gallons. From one to ten pounds of the ore is weighed out and introduced into the bottle. The proper amount of warm water is added, the contents of the bottle agitated, and the proper quantity of bleaching-powder is added. The proper quantity of sulphuric acid is now added, the bottle is tightly stoppered, and its contents agitated from four to eight hours. It is generally best to add a portion of the bleaching-powder and sulphuric acid at first, agitate for from three to five hours, and then add the balance. In order to insure perfect chlorination there should always be free chlorine present at the last of the operation. This may be determined by removing the stopper and holding a bottle of ammonia-water to the mouth of the bottle. If free chlorine is present the characteristic fumes of ammonium chloride will be produced.

The pulp is now ready for filtration and washing, which is performed in the usual way. When the washings no longer give a reaction for chlorine, upon testing with silver-nitrate solution, the washing is finished. The pulp is now dried, sampled, and assayed for gold in the usual way.

Having the assay on the ore before and after treatment, the following gives the percentage of extraction: Suppose the ore before treatment assayed 0.77 oz. Au, and after treatment 0.04 oz. Au per ton of 2000 pounds. Then

$0.77 - 0.04 = 0.73 =$ gold extracted, and $0.77 : 0.73 :: 100 : x$;

$x = 94.8 =$ percentage of extraction.

Sulphides must be roasted previous to treatment. The roasting must be carefully conducted, and the ore finally brought to a dead-roast, in order to insure a good percentage of extraction. The roasted ore should not show much over 0.3 per cent of sulphur.

The following table gives the amount in grammes of bleaching-powder or sulphuric acid which correspond to the pounds per ton used in the mill:

3.4	gms.	to	1 lb.	is equivalent to	15	lbs.	per ton.		
4.54	"	"	"	"	"	20	"	"	"
5.67	"	"	"	"	"	25	"	"	"
6.80	"	"	"	"	"	30	"	"	"
7.94	"	"	"	"	"	35	"	"	"
9.07	"	"	"	"	"	40	"	"	"
10.21	"	"	"	"	"	45	"	"	"
11.34	"	"	"	"	"	50	"	"	"
12.37	"	"	"	"	"	55	"	"	"
13.61	"	"	"	"	"	60	"	"	"
14.74	"	"	"	"	"	65	"	"	"
15.88	"	"	"	"	"	70	"	"	"

CHAPTER VIII.

ASSAY OF GOLD AND SILVER ORES CONTAINING METALLIC SCALES.

IF an ore of gold or silver contains coarse metallic particles the sample will consist of pulp which has passed through the sieve and of metallic scales which remain on the sieve.

The pulp is weighed (preferably in grammes) and its assay value in gold and silver determined in the regular manner, either by scorification or crucible-assay. The scales are also weighed (preferably in grammes) and their assay value in gold and silver is determined by scorification- or crucible-assay. If the sample of scales is not large, the whole is taken for assay. If too large, an aliquot portion is carefully taken from the sample for assay.

The results may be calculated in the same manner as in the assay of base bullion (see Part III, Chap. I), or they may be calculated by the following formula :*

Let A = the weight of the pulp in grammes;

B = the weight of the scales in grammes;

C = the assay value of the pulp in ounces of gold or silver per ton of 2000 pounds;

D = the total number of milligrammes of gold or silver in the scales.

Now $\dfrac{A}{29.166}$ = the number of assay-tons in the pulp; and

$\dfrac{AC}{29.166}$ = the number of milligrammes of gold or silver in the pulp.

---

* State School of Mines Scientific Quarterly, Vol. I, No. 2, Sept. 1892.

Hence, $\dfrac{AC}{29.166} + D =$ the number of milligrammes of gold or silver in the whole sample.

Now if we divide the total number of milligrammes of gold or silver in the whole sample by the total number of assay-tons in the whole sample, we will have the assay value of the whole sample in ounces per ton of 2000 pounds. The expresssion $\dfrac{A+B}{29.166}$ equals the total number of assay-tons in the whole sample. Hence, making the division, we obtain the following formula for the assay value of the whole sample:

$$\dfrac{AC + 29.166D}{A + B}.$$

EXAMPLE.—Suppose the pulp weighed 105.23 gms. The scales weighed 8.135 gms. One A.T. of the pulp yielded 10.5 mgs. of Ag and 28.3 mgs. Au. One gramme of the scales upon assay yielded 215.5 mgs. Ag and 682.5 mgs. Au. Now the total number of milligrammes of Ag in the scales equals

$$\dfrac{8.135 \times 215.5}{1} = 1753.09 = D;$$

and

$$\dfrac{105.23 \times 10.5 + 29.166 \times 1753.09}{105.23 + 8.135} = 460.77 \text{ ozs. Ag per ton.}$$

In like manner we obtain for the assay value of the sample in gold per ton 1454.68 ounces.

CHAPTER IX.

AMALGAMATION-ASSAY.

THE amalgamation-assay of gold and silver ores is sometimes made to determine the probable per cent of the gold and silver in the ore which can be extracted by amalgamation. Like all laboratory tests, where only small quantities can be taken, the results will simply serve as a guide to show what may probably be expected on a commercial scale in the mill.

Gold Ores.—Pulverize about three pounds of the ore and pass through an 80-mesh sieve. Sample carefully and assay the sample. Weigh out from one to three pounds of the pulverized ore and wash by panning in the gold pan. The ordinary gold pan is a shallow sheet-iron pan 15 inches in diameter across the top, 11 inches in diameter on the bottom, and 2 inches high. The ore is placed in the pan with water, and panned by giving the pan a vibratory motion as in vanning, the light particles being washed over the sides. An expert panner usually performs the operation under water. When all the light particles of gangue have been washed off, leaving only the gold and heavy material (as black sand) in the pan, the contents of the pan are washed into a wide-necked flask or bottle and a few ounces of mercury added. A cork or stopper is fitted in the neck of the flask and the contents agitated. It is best to use boiling water in the flask, as heat assists the amalgamation. The pulp and mercury in the flask are agitated several times when the contents of the flasks are poured off, except the mercury and amalgam, and washed several times with water. The contents of the flask are finally washed out into the gold pan and the mercury and amalgam further freed from particles of ore by panning. The clean mercury and amalgam are now strained through a clean, tight piece of buckskin, when the amalgam will be left behind in the skin, the mercury passing through. This amalgam is collected in a small porcelain crucible and heated, gradually at first, to drive off the mercury, finally heating to redness. It is now cooled, wrapped in a piece of sheet lead, cupelled, and the resulting button weighed. The weighed button is alloyed with silver, and parted as in the assay of gold bullion. (See Part III, Chapter III.)

The calculation of results is as follows: Suppose the ore assayed 1.0 oz. gold and 2 oz. silver per ton. The button from amalgamation weighed 18 milligrammes. After parting, the button of gold weighed 12 milligrammes. Hence the button contained 6 milligrammes of silver. As we saved 12 mgs. of gold and 6 mgs. of silver from one pound, we would have saved 24 grammes of gold and 12 grammes of silver if one ton of ore were used. As there are 31.1035 grammes in one ounce Troy, we have

$$\frac{24}{31.1035} = 0.7716 \text{ oz. of gold saved per ton,}$$

and

$$\frac{12}{31.1035} = 0.3858 \text{ oz. of silver saved per ton.}$$

Let $x =$ per cent of gold saved and $y =$ per cent of silver saved. Then

$$1.0 : 0.7716 :: 100 : x. \quad x = 77.16\%.$$
$$2.0 : 0.3858 :: 100 : y. \quad y = 19.29\%.$$

Silver Ores.—From one to three pounds of the ore are pulverized, sampled, and assayed as before. One to three pounds are weighed out and placed in a small laboratory grinding-pan together with hot water. The pulp in the pan is then ground from one to three hours. As copper sulphate and salt frequently assist the amalgamation on some ores, they can be added in from 0.5 to 5.0 grammes of each. A few ounces of mercury (according to the amount of silver in the ore) are added with the pulp. After the grinding is finished the contents of the pan are agitated with water and the pulp drawn off, the final washing being performed in the gold pan as before described. The amalgam is collected and treated as before, the calculations being as above.

Another method, and the one which the writer prefers, is to have a small pan, similar to the gold pan but only about 8 inches in diameter, made from sheet copper. The bottom and sides of this pan are then covered with a coating of amalgam. A few ounces of the finely pulverized ore are introduced into the pan, the mass thinned with water, and the pulp thoroughly stirred from 1 to 3 hours with a wooden stick rounded on the end, so as to bring all particles of the pulp in contact with the amalgamated surface of the pan. The pulp is now poured off on to a filter, and all the pulp remaining in the pan washed on to the filter with the aid of a wash-bottle. The filter and its contents having been thoroughly dried, the pulp is sampled and assayed. The difference between the original assay of the ore and the assay of the tailings will be the silver and gold which has been collected by the amalgamated surface of the pan, or the silver and gold in the ore which can be saved by amalgamation. Copper pans the same size and shape as the gold pan can also be obtained. It is only necessary to amalgamate the sides of the pan for a short distance above the bottom.

CHAPTER X.

ANALYSIS OF COAL AND COKE.

MINERAL coal is made up of different kinds of hydrocarbons, with, perhaps, in some cases, free carbon.* Mineral coals may be classified as follows, according to H. M. Chance : †

Anthracite—Volatile matter is usually less than 7 p. c.
Semi-anthracite   "   "   "   "   "   "   10 "
Semi-bituminous "   "   "   "   "   "   18 "
Bituminous—Volatile matter is usually more than 18 "

To this classification should be added the lignites, or brown coals, which carry a high percentage of water, and in which the percentage of volatile matter is always greater than 18.

For practical purposes, an approximate analysis, which consists in the determination of moisture, volatile combustible matter, fixed carbon, sulphur, and ash, is all that is required. In the analysis of coke all that is usually required is the moisture, ash, and sulphur.

Approximate Analysis.—*Determination of the Moisture.*—One gramme of finely pulverized coal is introduced into a previously weighed platinum crucible and dried in an air-bath at a temperature of 115° C., until the weight remains constant or begins to increase owing to the incipient oxidation of the finely divided iron pyrites. The last lowest weight is taken, and the loss equals moisture.

Determination of the Volatile Matter.—Heat the crucible and its contents, after having determined the moisture, over the flame of a Bunsen burner, gradually raising the temperature

---

* Dana's System of Mineralogy, Ed. of 1885, p. 754.
† Geological Survey of Pennsylvania, 1888.

and keeping the crucible closely covered to avoid loss by finely divided particles of carbon being carried off mechanically. Continue this heating until all of the light combustible matter is expelled. This will require 4 to 5 minutes' heating. Now place the crucible over the flame of a blast-lamp and gradually raise the temperature to a bright red, and continue the heat to constant weight or until all of the volatile matter is expelled. This heating will usually take about 10 minutes, and should be carefully conducted in order to avoid loss mechanically, and should not be unduly prolonged, as this would involve loss of fixed carbon by oxidation. A little experience will teach the assayer when the operation is finished, so that not more than two or three weighings need be made. Cool the crucible and its contents in a desiccator, and weigh. The loss equals volatile matter $+ \frac{1}{2}$ the sulphur.

Determination of the Fixed Carbon and Ash.—Heat the crucible and its contents, after having expelled the moisture and volatile matter, over the flame of a blast-lamp or in the muffle-furnace at a gradually increasing temperature, until all of the carbon is oxidized and expelled. It is best to heat for half an hour and weigh. Heat for 10 minutes and weigh again, repeating this operation until the weight remains constant. After a little experience two weighings will generally be sufficient, the second being found to correspond to the first. Loss equals fixed carbon and half the sulphur, and the final weight, less the known weight of the crucible, equals ash.

Whilst this analysis is at best an approximation, especially as regards the determination of volatile matter and fixed carbon, it will be found that after a little practice it will give a very close approximation to the truth, and duplicate analyses made on the same sample will agree almost exactly.

The supposition that half of the sulphur is expelled with the volatile matter and that half is expelled with the fixed carbon is based upon the supposition that all of it is in the form of iron pyrites. Of course this supposition would be almost universally wrong, but, however, for practical purposes it answers all requirements, especially in a coal low in sulphur.

In any case the supposition would be wrong, as, should all of the sulphur exist in the form of iron pyrites, it is extremely improbable that half would be expelled in the treatment given to drive off the volatile matter. For practical purposes it may generally be considered that half of the sulphur in the form of pyrites is driven off with the volatile matter and the other half with the fixed carbon.

If it is necessary to determine the sulphur which exists in the coal as calcium sulphate and pyrites, it may be done as follows: Determine the total sulphur by heating 2 to 5 grammes of coal with nitric acid and potassium chlorate, or by fusion with caustic potash (see Part II, Chapter II), evaporating to dryness, after addition of hydrochloric acid and previous addition of bromine in the case of fusion, boiling with water and hydrochloric acid, filtering, washing, and the addition of barium chloride to the filtrate.

The sulphur existing as calcium sulphate may be determined by boiling 5 grammes of pulverized coal with a solution containing about 5 grammes of c. p. sodium carbonate (free from S), thus decomposing the calcium sulphate into sodium sulphate and calcium carbonate. Filter the solution, wash thoroughly with warm water, acidify the filtrate with hydrochloric acid, and determine sulphur as usual. The difference between the total amount of sulphur and the sulphur found after boiling with sodium carbonate (S as $CaSO_4$) represents the amount as pyrites. The same process is applicable to the determination of iron sulphide and gypsum in coke.

Any phosphorus which the coal may contain will be in the ash. If required, determine it according to Part II, Chapter III. If determined, deduct it from the ash in the report.

The manner of tabulating and calculating results is best illustrated by an example as follows:

Moisture...............................	1.5
Volatile matter $+ \frac{1}{2}$ sulphur.............	27.5
Fixed carbon $+ \frac{1}{2}$ sulphur...............	61.3
Ash, including phosphorus...................	9.7
Sulphur....................................	1.0

When the sulphur is determined, if we deduct half from the volatile matter and half from the fixed carbon, the report would be as follows:

Moisture	1.50
Volatile matter	27.00
Fixed carbon	60.80
Ash, including phosphorus	9.70
Sulphur	1.00
	100.00

Determination of the Specific Gravity.—The specific gravity of a coal is often required. Take a small piece of coal and weigh it on the balance, then in water by suspending it from the arm of the balance by a hair or thin wire. The piece taken should not be too small, and care should be taken that no air-bubbles adhere to it during the weighing. The coal also should be thoroughly soaked, which can be attained by immersing the lump, after attaching the hair or wire to it, in the flask of the filter-pump, and exhausting the air in the apparatus. The temperature of the air and water should be the same, about 60° F.

Let W = the weight of the coal in air;
W' = the weight of the coal in water.

The specific gravity $= \dfrac{W}{W - W'}$.

Determination of the Heating Power.—This determination is sometimes required, but at the most is simply an approximation. Knowing the elementary constitution of the fuel, the heating power may be tested by determining the amount of oxygen required to burn it. Mix 1 gramme of powdered coal and 50 grammes of litharge, or white lead when pure, together in a clay assay-crucible, and cover with about 20 grammes of litharge. Heat in a crucible furnace, with a gradually increasing heat until the fusion is complete, which will require from 10 to 15 minutes. Remove the crucible from the fire, pour, and when cold hammer and weigh the lead button. Pure carbon should reduce 34 times its own weight of lead; hydrogen, 102.7 times its own weight.

One part of pure carbon can raise the temperature of 8080 parts of water 1°; consequently, if the fuel is assumed as carbon, its value in heat-units may be estimated by multiplying $\frac{8080}{34}$ by the weight of the lead button obtained in the assay. As hydrogen is always present in the coal this method necessarily gives low results.

If an elementary analysis of the coal has been made to determine its percentage of carbon and hydrogen, the heating power can be accurately determined.

Elementary Analysis.—An estimation of the total carbon and hydrogen which the fuel contains may be made as follows: The fuel is burned in a stream of oxygen, the resulting CO_2 and H_2O being caught in suitable apparatus and weighed in those combinations. The same apparatus as is used for the determination of carbonic acid and water in white-lead (see Part II, Chap. V, and Part III, Chap. XV), may be used with slight modifications. Take a piece of combustion-tubing about 28 inches long, and about one half an inch internal diameter, fit to each end corks through which are passed tubes of about one-tenth inch internal diameter and 4 inches in length. About 2 inches from the front end of the tube (the end to be attached to the apparatus for absorbing CO_2 and H_2O) place a plug of asbestos which has been previously ignited to remove all moisture and carbonaceous material. Back of this plug place enough freshly-ignited CuO to fill the tube a little more than half, and push down upon this another plug of ignited asbestos. Have at the rear end of the combustion-tube two bottles, with corks and tubes, for drying the oxygen and removing from it any traces of CO_2 it may contain, by bubbling it through the bottles containing, respectively, concentrated H_2SO_4 and strong KOH, having the H_2SO_4 bottle next to the tube. For the front end have a tube filled with neutral calcium chloride in fragments, through which a current of dry CO_2 has passed for some time, followed by a current of dry air. To this attach a U-tube filled with fresh soda-lime for the absorption of the carbonic acid. The coal, from which the moisture has been driven off by previous drying, is weighed out into a platinum boat. Weigh the calcium chloride and the soda-lime tubes. Connect the combustion-tube at the rear end with the sulphuric-acid and potassium-hydrate bottles, and at the front end with the aspirator, heat it to redness, and then draw a current of air through it until cool. Now introduce the platinum boat into the rear end of the tube, replace the cork and connect the calcium-chloride and soda-lime tubes at the front end, connecting the last with the aspirator. Draw a slow current of air through the tube, and heat the front end of the CuO, carrying the heat gradually forward. Arrange it so that the CuO shall be highly heated before the coal begins to burn. Just before the heat reaches the boat attach the tube from the oxygen cylinder, and force a slow current of gas through the tube. Heat the coal moderately so that it will burn slowly and not give off the gases too rapidly. When the coal is completely consumed, disconnect the oxygen cylinder, remove the heat, and draw a current of dry air free from carbonic acid through the apparatus until cool. Detach the tubes and weigh. The increase in the weight of the calcium-chloride tube represents water to be calculated to H, and the increase in weight of the soda-lime tube represents carbon dioxide to be calculated to C.

CHAPTER XI.

ANALYSIS OF GASES.

IN a gas or metallurgical works where a number of analyses of mixtures of gases are required daily it is only possible to do the work with simple apparatus.

The following apparatus for the rapid analysis of gases and the method of using it were first described by A. H. Elliott in the *School of Mines Quarterly* (Vol. III, No. 1, page 15): Whilst this method does not compare with the elaborate methods of Bunsen and others, where very delicate readings and nice precautions are taken, it gives very good results for technical work and answers every purpose in the everyday practice of a gas or metallurgical works.

The great advantages of this method are the rapidity with which an analysis can be made (about forty-five minutes) and the simplicity and inexpensiveness of the necessary apparatus.

The apparatus is shown in the drawing. The tube A is of about 125 cc. capacity, whilst B, although of the same length, holds only 100 cc. from the mark D, or zero, to the mark on the capillary tube at C, and is carefully graduated into $\frac{1}{10}$ cc. The attachments to these tubes below are seen from the drawing, except that the stop-cock I is three-way, with a delivery through its stem. The bottles K and L hold about one pint each. The tubes A and B are connected with each other and with the funnel M by capillary tubing about one millimetre in internal diameter. There is a stop-cock at G and another at F, whilst the funnel M, holding about 60 cc., is ground to fit over the end of F above. At E a piece of rubber tubing unites the ends of the capillary tubes, which are ground off square to make them fit as closely as possible.

In beginning the analysis of a mixture of gases, the stem exit of the cock I is closed by turning it so that L and A are connected through the rubber tubing; the stop-cocks F and G are opened and water is allowed to fill the apparatus from the bottles K and L, which have been previously supplied. When the water rises in the funnel M, and all air-bubbles have been

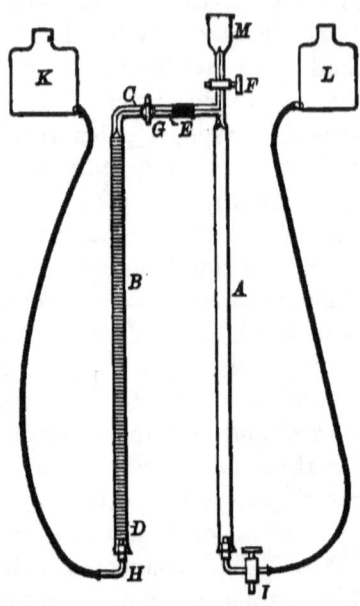

forced out of the tubes, the stop-cocks F and G are closed, the funnel M is removed, and the tube delivering the gas to be tested is attached in its place. By now lowering the bottle L slowly, and simultaneously opening the stop-cock F, the tube A is nearly filled with gas, and the stop-cock F is closed. The tube delivering the gas is now removed, the funnel M replaced, the bottle L raised, the bottle K lowered, and by opening the stop-cock G the gas is transferred to the graduated tube B. By placing the bottle L on a stand at about the level of the water in A, the level in B and in the bottle K can be adjusted to the zero point, and the stop-cock G is closed. The excess of gas in A is expelled by opening the stop-cock F and raising the bottle L. The gas remaining in the capillary tube between C and the vertical part is disregarded, or in very careful work it may be measured and an allowance made in not filling the tube B quite to the zero mark, but usually it is too small to be worth notice.

Having measured the gas to be tested, it is now transferred by means of the bottles K and L into the tube A, and the fluid chemicals added by placing them in the funnel M and allowing them to flow down the sides of the tube slowly, being careful *never* to allow the fluids to run below the level of the top of the vertical tube in the funnel. It is best to have a mark on the outside of the funnel about three quarters of an inch above the top of the level of the vertical tube, and never to draw the fluid down below this point.

Having treated the gas with the chemical, it is transferred by means of the bottles to the tube B, to be measured. Should the chemical get into the horizontal capillary tube, the passage of a little water from the bottle K will remove it, before transferring the gas. When the gas residue is in B, and the fluid in A has been adjusted at the mark C on the horizontal tube, the stop-cock G is closed, the bottle K is lowered till the level of the water in it and that in the tube B are the same, and the reading is made. The tube A is now filled with the chemical just used and water. By turning the stem of the three-way cock I, so that it communicates with A, and also opening the stop-cock F, the contents of the tube can be run out, and water run through the funnel M to clean the tube for a new absorption. When the tube is clean, by turning the stop-cock I, so that A and L communicate, the water is forced into A, and the apparatus is ready to receive the gas for new treatment.

By this means the gas is removed from the action of the water used to wash out the chemicals, and the chemicals are completely removed from any interference with each other when treating a mixture of gases.

In using this apparatus the solutions are added in the following order:

1. *Potassic hydrate*, to absorb carbon dioxide (also hydrogen sulphide and sulphurous oxide if present. If these gases are present in large quantities special methods are necessary for their estimation)..

2. *Potassium pyrogallate*, to absorb oxygen.

3. *Bromine*, to absorb illuminants, like olefiant gas and acetylene, and after the absorption is complete, and the bromine vapors cause an expansion, a little potassium hydrate is added, to absorb these vapors before the gas is transferred and measured.

4. *Cuprous chloride* in concentrated hydrochloric-acid solution, to absorb carbonic oxide. After this absorption is complete, the gas is transferred to the measuring tube, the contents of the tube A run out, the tube washed and filled with water from the bottle L. The gas is now transferred to A, and treated with potassium-hydrate solution, to absorb hydrochloric-acid vapors, before the final reading is made in B.

The treatment up to this point takes from twenty to thirty minutes, according to the amount of practice the operator has had with the apparatus. The gas residue still contains marsh-gas, hydrogen, and nitrogen. By removing the funnel M and attaching in its place a rubber tube communicating with an explosion eudiometer in a deep cylinder of water (both rubber tube and eudiometer being drawn full of water), a portion of the gas residue can be mixed with oxygen, exploded, and the contraction and the carbonic acid determined; the marsh-gas and hydrogen being calculated by the usual formula. The nitrogen is found by the difference of the addition of the other constituents and one hundred. The explosion-tube is a similar tube to A, without the lower attachment and the lateral capillary tube above; the funnel M being retained, and two platinum wires being fused into the glass near the top, to give the spark for ignition. It is only necessary to clamp this tube down upon a piece of cork in a vessel of water during explosion, and adjust the water-level in a tall cylinder of water when making the readings of contraction and absorption of carbon dioxide.

ANALYSIS OF GASES. 273

The water used in the apparatus should be of the same temperature as the room in which the analysis is made, and by careful handling little or none of the chemicals used will get into the bottle L.

When working in a warm place the tube B should be surrounded with a water-jacket, to prevent change of volume in the gas while under treatment.

CHAPTER XII.

ANALYSIS OF WATER.

THE following easy method of analysis will serve for the determination of the value of a water for domestic or manufacturing purposes:

Determination of Total Solids.—Evaporate 500 cc. of the water to dryness in a weighed platinum dish. The evaporation is made either on the water-bath, or the dish may be placed upon a piece of asbestos board and evaporated over the flame of a Bunsen burner, care being exercised to not allow the contents of the dish to boil, as this is liable to result in loss. Now heat the dish and its contents in an air-bath at a temperature of 110° C. to constant weight. This weight will represent the mineral constituents of the water and the organic and volatile matter. This weight in milligrammes multiplied by 0.2 will give the parts in 100,000, and by 0.1166 the grains per U. S. gallon of 231 cubic inches.

Organic and Volatile Matter.—After evaporating and weighing as above, heat the dish and its contents at a low-red heat until all organic matter is consumed and the contents are white or nearly so. Now add about 50 cc. of water saturated with carbon dioxide and evaporate on a water-bath, repeat the treatment with carbon dioxide, and evaporate again. Dry in an air-bath at 110° C. as before, cool, and weigh. The loss in weight approximately expresses the amount of volatile and organic matter in the quantity of water taken.

Analysis of Residue.—The residue obtained as above is now moistened with a few drops of hydrochloric acid, about 50 cc. of hot water is added, and the contents of the dish again evaporated to dryness, and finally heated in an air-bath at 110° C. until there is no longer any odor of chlorine. It is now dissolved in hot water, a few drops of hydrochloric acid added, transferred to a small beaker, and boiled for a few minutes. It is now filtered through a small filter, washed with hot water, and the insoluble residue dried, ignited, and weighed. This weight expresses the amount of silica in the quantity of water taken, the results being calculated as above.

The filtrate from the silica is now boiled for a few minutes, with the addition of a few drops of nitric acid, to insure the oxidation of any ferrous salt which may be present, and made decidedly alkaline with ammonia. It is now boiled to expel the excess of ammonia, and the precipitated hydrates of iron and alumina are filtered off through a small filter and washed until the washings show no reaction for chlorine when tested with a solution of silver nitrate and nitric acid. The precipitate is ignited in a platinum crucible and weighed as Fe_2O_3 and Al_2O_3.

The filtrate from the iron and alumina is now rendered decidedly alkaline with an excess of ammonia, and an excess of a solution of ammonium oxalate added. The solution is boiled for a few minutes and then allowed to cool; when cold it is filtered through a small filter, and the precipitated calcium oxalate is washed thoroughly with hot water. In case the water contains much magnesia it will be necessary to dissolve this precipitate in a little hydrochloric acid and water, and reprecipitate with ammonia and ammonium oxalate. (See Part II, Chap. XXIII and Chap. XXIV.) The calcium oxalate is then ignited over a Bunsen burner, and finally over a blast-lamp to constant weight, and weighed as CaO. The results are calculated by the use of the same factors as above.

The filtrate from the lime is evaporated to about 75 cc., cooled, and 5 cc. of hydrodisodic-phosphate solution added. It is stirred with a glass rod for a few minutes, avoiding allowing the rod to touch the sides of the beaker, and allowed to stand several hours in a cold place. It is filtered onto a small filter and washed, until free from chlorine, with a solution of ammonium nitrate (1 gm. salt in 10 cc. of water). It is dried, ignited, and weighed as $Mg_2P_2O_7$. The weight of the precipitate in milligrammes multiplied by 0.07206 will give the parts by weight of MgO in 100,000 parts of water, and multiplied by 0.042 will give the number of grains of MgO in one U. S. gallon.

In the case of a very pure water, it will be necessary to take a greater quantity of the water than 500 cc., but in most cases a half litre will be sufficient.

Determination of Alkalies.—From $\frac{1}{2}$ to 5 litres of water are evaporated in a platinum dish to about 100 cc. The solution is acidified slightly with hydrochloric acid; a saturated solution of barium hydrate is added until the solution is strongly alkaline; the solution is boiled, the precipitate filtered off and thoroughly washed with hot water until the washings are free from chlorine. To the filtrate ammonium carbonate is added as long as a precipitate is produced, the solution is boiled, and the precipitated barium carbonate filtered off and washed with hot water until the washings no longer give a reaction for chlorine. The filtrate is evaporated to dryness, and heated at a low-red heat, to burn out the ammonium chloride. Take the dry mass up with hot water and repeat the treatment with barium hydrate and ammonium carbonate, to insure the complete removal of the magnesia which may have been held in solution by the alkaline chlorides. Finally, evaporate the filtrate to dryness in a weighed platinum dish, expel all ammonium chloride present by heating to a low-red heat, cool, and weigh the mixed chlorides of potassium and sodium. The potassium and sodium may be separated and determined as described in Part II, Chapter XXVI.

The weight of potassium platinic chloride obtained (in grammes), multiplied by 0.30557, will give the weight of the potassium chloride, which weight subtracted from the weight of the mixed chlorides previously obtained will give the weight of the sodium chloride. The weight (in milligrammes) of the sodium chloride obtained from the treatment of 500 cc. of water, multiplied by 0.0788 and 0.1061, will give the parts of

Na and Na_2O, respectively, in 100,000 parts of water. For the same conversion of potassium chloride the factors are 0.1049 and 0.1263. To convert parts in 100,000 into grains per U. S. gallon, multiply by 0.583.

Determination of Sulphuric Acid.—Acidify 500 cc. of water with about 5 cc. of hydrochloric acid, and evaporate to about 150 cc. Filter, if necessary; boil the solution, and whilst boiling add an excess of a hot solution of barium chloride. Boil for a few minutes and allow to cool. Filter, wash with hot water, dry, ignite, and weigh the $BaSO_4$. The weight of this precipitate in milligrammes multiplied by 0.0687 gives the number of parts of SO_3 in 100,000 parts of water, and multiplied by 0.04 the number of grains of SO_3 in one U. S. gallon.

Determination of Chlorine.—The determination of chlorine is best made volumetrically as follows: Prepare a standard solution of silver nitrate by dissolving 4.788 gms. of c. p. crystallized nitrate of silver in distilled water and diluting to 1000 cc. Each cubic centimetre of this solution should precipitate exactly 1 mg. of chlorine. This solution may be standardized by means of a dilute solution of pure fused sodium chloride. A solution of potassium chromate, made by dissolving 5 gms. of the pure salt in about 100 cc. of water, is used as an indicator.

To determine the chlorine, transfer 100 cc. of the water to be examined to a porcelain evaporating dish, add 2 cc. of the indicator solution, and then run in from the burette the standard solution of silver nitrate until the red precipitate of chromate of silver, which is at first decomposed by the excess of chlorine, is just permanent. The burette reading will give directly the number of parts of chlorine to 100,000 parts of water. To convert this into parts in one U. S. gallon multiply by 0.583.

For domestic purposes the amount of organic matter, free and albuminoid ammonia which the water contains is very important.

Permanganate Test.—This test is made to determine the

amount of oxidizable organic matter in water, and is claimed by some chemists to be quite as valuable as the determination of the albuminoid ammonia. The test requires a solution of oxalic acid and a solution of potassium permanganate, which are prepared as follows: Dissolve 0.7875 gm. of pure crystallized oxalic acid in 1000 cc. of water. One cc. of this solution will be equivalent to one tenth of a milligramme of oxygen, as 0.7875 mgm. of oxalic acid requires 0.1 mgm. of oxygen for conversion to carbonic acid. Dissolve 0.500 gm. of pure potassium permanganate in 1000 cc. of water, and dilute until 1 cc. of the solution exactly oxidizes 1 cc. of the oxalic-acid solution. Then 1 cc. of the potassium-permanganate solution carries one tenth of a milligramme of available oxygen.

To 200 cc. of the water add 3 cc. of dilute sulphuric acid, and then from a burette the permanganate solution until the color produced by it ceases to disappear after allowing to stand three hours. From the number of cc. of permanganate solution used calculate the quantity of oxygen required to oxidize organic matter. It is assumed that the oxygen required multiplied by 8 is equivalent to organic matter.

Free and Albuminoid Ammonia.—The determination of these requires the following solutions:

Nessler's Solution.—Dissolve 50 gms. of potassium iodide in a small quantity of hot water, place the solution on a boiling-water bath; cool, add, with frequent agitation, a strong solution of mercuric chloride (40 gms. of the salt and 300 cc. of water), until the red precipitate just redissolves; filter; add to the filtrate a strong solution of potassium hydrate containing 200 gms. of the salt; filter; dilute to 1000 cc., add 5 cc. of a saturated solution of mercuric chloride, allow the precipitate formed to settle, decant the clear liquid, and keep for use in a tightly stoppered bottle.

Sodium-carbonate Solution.—Add 100 gms. of sodium carbonate to 200 cc. of distilled water free from ammonia, and keep in a well-corked bottle.

Potassium-permanganate Solution.—Dissolve 200 gms. of potassium hydrate and 8 gms. of potassium permanganate in

1000 cc. of distilled water free from ammonia, boil hard for half an hour in a two-litre flask to expel ammonia, and keep in a well-corked bottle.

Ammonium Solution.—Dissolve 0.3883 gm. of ammonium sulphate or 0.315 gm. of ammonium chloride in 1000 cc. of pure distilled water free from ammonia. One cc. of either solution will contain one tenth of a milligramme of ammonia (NH_3). For use dilute to ten volumes, so that each cc. will contain one hundredth of a milligramme of ammonia.

Distilled Water free from Ammonia.—To ordinary distilled water add a little sodium carbonate, and boil, in a large flask, until about one fourth is evaporated, then distil the remainder from a retort holding about 1500 cc. until the distillate gives no reaction for ammonia with Nessler's solution, testing 50 cc. of the distillate at a time. When no more ammonia can be detected, distil off into a large flask 750 cc., and test again to be sure the 750 cc. are free from ammonia. Proceed in this manner until sufficient is prepared, and keep the water in tightly stoppered bottles.

Free Ammonia.—To determine the free ammonia in a water connect a glass retort of at least 1000 cc. capacity with a condenser, and cleanse the apparatus by distilling some clean water. Introduce 200 cc. of clean water and 15 cc. of the sodium-carbonate solution, and distil until the distillate is free from ammonia. Now introduce 500 cc. of the water to be tested, and distil, collecting the distillate in test cylinders. In other cylinders of the same calibre add amounts of the standard ammonia solution containing, respectively, 0.01, 0.02, etc., mgm. NH_3, and dilute each up to 50 cc. with the especially prepared distilled water. When 50 cc. have distilled over, add 1.5 cc. of the Nessler solution to each cylinder. Care should be exercised to always use the same Nessler solution, the same amounts, and to allow it to act as nearly as possible for the same length of time. After allowing the cylinders to stand a few minutes compare the tint of the distillate with those of the comparison cylinders, and thus estimate the amount of ammonia present. Test each succeeding 50 cc. in the same way, and proceed until the last 50 cc. tested contains less than 0.01 gm. of NH_3. The whole amount of ammonia thus determined is the total free ammonia. Should the water contain much ammonia it is safer to thoroughly mix each 50 cc. of the distillate and take out 10 cc., dilute it to 50 cc., and test as above. The remaining four fifths of the distillate may be used to confirm the results thus obtained.

Albuminoid Ammonia.—After having determined the free ammonia as above, add 50 cc. of the permanganate solution to the contents of the retort and distil until the distillate no longer shows the presence of ammonia. Now add 500 cc. of the water to be tested, and distil, testing each 50 cc. of the distillate, as before, until it contains less than 0.01 mg. of NH_3. This gives the total ammonia. The difference between the total and the free gives the albuminoid ammonia.

Nitrates.—The following method is quite simple, and apparently more accurate than the usual method.* Rinse a 100-cc. Nessler tube with the water to be tested, and then fill to the 100-cc. mark with the water to be tested. Drop in 5 to 10 gms. of freshly-prepared sodium amalgam, the amount varying with that of the nitrates presumably present. Enough should be added to keep up the action at ordinary temperatures for at least two hours. Cover with a watch-glass, and allow the tube to stand in an atmosphere free from ammonia vapors, after adding one or two drops of concentrated hydrochloric acid (free from ammonium salt). After two hours the solution should only be faintly acid; if decidedly acid, add more sodium amalgam, and continue the reduction. Finally, filter through a small filter previously freed from all traces of ammonia and Nesslerize 50 cc. of the filtrate in the usual manner. Deduct the free ammonia which the water contains, as determined in a separate portion, and calculate the results as usual.

---

* School of Mines Quarterly, Vol. XV, No. 1, p. 11.

Grouping of the Constituents.—It is impossible to give any exact rule for the proper grouping of the constituents, as determined by the analysis. The following will answer for ordinary water: Combine the sodium with chlorine as sodium chloride. Should there be more sodium than the chlorine will satisfy, combine the excess with sulphuric acid as sodium sulphate. Should there not be sufficient sulphuric acid to satisfy all the sodium, combine the excess with carbonic acid as sodium carbonate. Combine the potassium with sulphuric acid as potassium sulphate. Should there be more sulphuric acid than the potassium and the excess of sodium (over NaCl) will satisfy, combine the excess first with calcium as calcium sulphate, and any further excess with magnesium as magnesium sulphate. Should the water contain a large amount of chlorine (in excess of the amount sufficient to satisfy the sodium), and not sufficient sulphuric acid to satisfy the potassium, combine the excess of potassium with chlorine, and should there be any chlorine still left, combine it first with magnesium, and if there is still an excess, combine it with calcium. Calculate all calcium and magnesium not combined with chlorine and sulphuric acid to carbonates.

CHAPTER XIII.

ACIDIMETRY AND ALKALIMETRY.

ACIDIMETRY and alkalimetry is the determination of the amount of acid or alkali which a solution contains. It is accomplished by means of standard alkali and standard acid solutions and suitable indicators.

Standard Acid Solutions.—The usual solutions employed are solutions of sulphuric, hydrochloric, and nitric acids in water. In addition to these, other acid solutions, as oxalic and acetic, are occasionally employed. The choice of the acid will depend largely upon the character of the substance to be analyzed, certain acids being particularly adapted to certain determinations.

Half-normal Sulphuric Acid.—This solution is prepared so that it will contain exactly 0.04 gm. of SO_4 or 0.049 gm. of H_2SO_4 in each cc. To prepare the solution add 33.3 cc. of c. p. concentrated sulphuric acid to 1000 cc. of water, mix thoroughly, and allow to cool to the normal temperature of the laboratory. Partially fill a burette with the solution, and draw off into beakers two separate portions of exactly 15 cc. each. To each portion add about 50 cc. of water and 30 cc. of a saturated solution of barium chloride, having both the acid solution and the barium-chloride solution at the boiling-point when the addition is made. Filter off the precipitates of barium sulphate, and determine the sulphuric acid as usual. If the precipitates do not differ in weight more than 0.01 gm., take the average and calculate the sulphuric acid in 1 cc. of the solution. Suppose the calculation shows that 1 cc. of the solution contains 0.042 gm. of SO_4 in place of 0.04 gm., then it is too strong and requires dilution. As 1 cc. contains 0.042 gm., 1000 cc. will contain 42 gms. in place of 40 gms., which it should contain; consequently,

$$40 \text{ gms.} : 1000 \text{ cc.} :: 42 \text{ gms.} : 1050 \text{ cc.}$$

Hence 50 cc. of water must be added to each 1000 cc. of the acid solution to make it half normal. To do this fill a dry 1000-cc. flask to the holding mark with the solution, pour the solution from the flask into a clean dry bottle, run into the flask 50 cc. of water, shake well, and pour off into the bottle. Shake the bottle well and pour back into the flask; finally pour back into the bottle, where it is kept for use. The sulphuric acid should be determined in the solution again, and the solution corrected as before.

Normal Nitric Acid.—To prepare this solution add 100 cc. of c. p. nitric acid of 1.32 sp. gr. to 765 cc. of water and thoroughly mix. The best method of determining the strength of this solution is by means of a normal solution of potassium or sodium hydrate which has previously been accurately standardized. One cc. of the acid solution should exactly neutralize 1 cc. of the standard alkali solution. Have two burettes in a stand, and fill one with the acid solution to be tested and the other with the standard alkali solution. Draw off 10 cc. of the acid solution, dilute with 100 cc. of water, add a few drops of a suitable indicator, as litmus solution, and run in the standard alkali solution until the color just changes from red to blue. Take the reading of the burette and run in another 10 cc. of the acid solution, and titrate again with the standard alkali solution. The two readings of the burette should agree closely. Suppose this trial shows that 10 cc. of the acid solution neutralizes 12 cc. of the standard alkali solution, then the acid solution is too strong and requires dilution. In this case every 100 cc. of the acid solution should be diluted to 120 cc. Measure off 800 cc. of the acid solution and add 160 cc. of water, thoroughly mix as in the case of the sulphuric-acid solution, and restandardize, continuing the operation until the acid solution exactly neutralizes the standard alkali solution, cc. for cc. The nitric-acid solution should contain 0.063 gm. of nitric acid in each cc.

Normal Hydrochloric Acid.—The normal hydrochloric acid solution should contain 0.0365 gm. of hydrochloric acid in each cc. To prepare this solution mix 1000 cc. of water with 200 cc. of c. p. hydrochloric acid of 1.12 sp. gr. The amount of hydrochloric acid in each cc. of the thoroughly mixed solution may be determined in several ways. If some standard alkali solution is on hand, its standard may be readily determined by the same method as described above for nitric acid. If it is desired to determine the hydrochloric acid in each cc. directly, the following method is as good as any: Draw off two portions of the acid solution of exactly 10 cc. each into a flask with sloping sides. Dilute with warm water, and precipitate the chlorine completely with a strong solution of nitrate of silver. Shake the flask, fill it completely with warm water, and invert it over a porcelain crucible of suitable size. Allow the precipitate to settle completely into the crucible, remove the flask, and pour off the water from the crucible. Remove the last particles of water from the crucible with a piece of blotting-paper, being careful not to remove any of the precipitate. Evaporate off the last traces of water, and dry the crucible and its contents in a drying-chamber. When thoroughly dry, heat over a low flame until the silver chloride begins to fuse around the edges; cool, and weigh. Deduct from this weight the known weight of the crucible. The remainder will be the weight of the silver chloride. To obtain the weight of the chlorine multiply this weight by $\frac{444}{143}$. From this weight calculate the number of cc. of water or hydrochloric acid to add to a given quantity of the acid solution in order to make it normal. Make the necessary addition, and restandardize as before.

Half-normal Oxalic Acid.—To prepare this solution dissolve 63 gms. of c. p. crystallized oxalic acid in 1000 cc. of water, and standardize by titrating a portion with standard alkali solution; or the oxalic acid may be determined by means of a standard solution of potassium permanganate. (See Part II, Chap. XVI, Iron.)

As the oxalic- and sulphuric-acid solutions are readily and accurately standardized, they are extremely useful in making up different standard acid and alkali solutions. Once having obtained a perfectly normal acid solution, the other solutions are readily obtained by standardizing with the normal or half-normal acid solution.

Standard Alkali Solutions.—The solutions generally employed are normal potassium-hydrate, normal sodium-hydrate, and occasionally half-normal sodium-carbonate solutions.

Normal Potassium Hydrate.—This solution should contain exactly 0.0561 gm. of potassium hydrate, or 0.0471 gm. of potassium oxide (K_2O), in each cc. To prepare the solution dissolve 40 gms. of pure potassium hydrate in 600 cc. of water, and when dissolved mix thoroughly and fill a burette with the solution. Run into a beaker exactly 10 cc. of the standard sulphuric acid (or other standard acid) solution, dilute with water to about 200 cc., add a few drops of the indicator, and run in the potassium hydrate solution, drop by drop towards the last, until the color changes. Note the reading of the burette, and add another 10 cc. of the acid solution and titrate again. Repeat this titration several times, and take the average of the different determinations, provided they do not differ too much. The color imparted to any number of cc. of the acid solution by the indicator should change upon the addition of the same number of cc. of the alkali solution. If it does not, the potassium-hydrate solution should be diluted or strengthened until the two agree. Suppose it only required 9 cc. of the potassium-hydrate solution to neutralize 10 cc. of the half-normal sulphuric acid solution. Then every 9 cc. of the alkali solution requires 1 cc. of water, or 500 cc. of the alkali solution require 55.5 cc. of water.

Normal Sodium Hydrate.—Every cc. of this solution should contain exactly 0.04 gm. of sodium hydrate or 0.031 gm. of sodium oxide (Na_2O). To prepare this solution dissolve 28 gms. of pure sodium hydrate in 600 cc. of water, mix, and titrate as in the case of the potassium-hydrate solution.

Indicators.—This is the name given to the coloring matters used to show when the fluid is acid or alkaline. A great number have been proposed, of which the following are most commonly used :

Litmus.—A solution of litmus is prepared by boiling the coarsely powdered litmus with alcohol of about 80 per cent two or three times, and discarding the liquid so obtained. The litmus is now digested repeatedly with cold water until all the soluble coloring matter is extracted. Allow the mixed washings to settle, decant the clear liquid, and add a few drops of concentrated sulphuric acid until the solution is quite red. Heat to boiling to decompose the alkaline carbonates and convert them into sulphates, and then gradually add baryta-water until the blue color is restored. Allow the precipitated barium sulphate to settle completely, and decant the solution into an open bottle. The solution must be kept in an open bottle, and in a place free from acid or alkaline fumes. It cannot be used in the presence of carbonic acid.

Cochineal.—Take about 3 gms. of powdered cochineal and macerate, frequently shaking, with a mixture of distilled water and alcohol (3 volumes of water and 1 volume of alcohol). Filter into a stoppered bottle. It should be kept tightly corked. It cannot be used in the presence of iron salts, but is not affected by carbonic acid in moderate quantities. The solution is yellow when acid, and carmine when alkaline.

Coralline.—Dissolve some coralline in alcohol and filter if necessary. Keep in a closed bottle. The solution becomes straw color when acid. It is particularly well adapted to the titration of acetic and other organic acids.

Methyl Orange.—This is a very sensitive indicator for mineral acids.

Phenolphthalein.—This is a very sensitive indicator, and is used in the titration of solutions of molybdic acid.

Logwood.—It must be kept unexposed to the light, and cannot be used in the presence of the oxides of the heavy metals. To prepare, boil a few shavings of the logwood with distilled water and mix the concentrated solution with 1 or 2 volumes of alcohol.

These standard solutions have a great number of uses in analytical chemistry. A few of their applications will serve to show the manner of using them.

Determination of Potassium Hydrate in Commercial Caustic Potash.—In order to save time and possible errors in the calculation of results it is best to weigh out an equivalent part. As the molecular weight of caustic potash is 56.1, a one-tenth equivalent would be 5.61 gms. Weigh out this amount, dissolve in a little hot water, filter, and thoroughly wash the residue, filtering into a 100-cc. flask. Bring the bulk of the solution up to exactly 100 cc., and thoroughly mix by pouring from the flask into a dry clean beaker and from the beaker back into the flask, repeating several times. Fill a burette with the solution and draw off exactly 10 c.c. into a beaker. Run in 10 cc. of the half-normal sulphuric acid, dilute to about 50 cc. with water, and add a few drops of the indicator. Now run in normal potassic-hydrate solution until the solution is exactly neutral. Repeat on several other portions of 10 cc. each, and take the average. If the caustic potash contained 100 per cent of KOH, the 10 cc. of acid would have just neutralized the 10 cc. of alkali solution taken. Suppose 2 cc. of the normal potassic-hydrate solution were used: then without calculation we see at once that the commercial alkali contains 80 per cent potassium hydrate.

Analysis of Commercial Acetic Acid.—Weigh out, in a counterpoised beaker, 30 gms. of the acid, wash with water into a 500-cc. flask, and dilute with water to the holding mark. Draw off with a pipette 100 cc., run into a beaker, and add a few drops of a suitable indicator. Coralline is preferable in this case. Now run in normal potassium-hydrate solution until a full alkaline color is obtained. The color should be full alkaline, as neutral alkaline acetates have a slight alkaline reaction. Note the reading of the burette and calculate the per cent of acid. If 30 gms. of acid were taken and diluted to 500 cc., of which solution 100 cc. were taken for titration, each cc. of normal alkali solution will represent 1 per cent of acid.

If it is desired to know the weight of acid in so many gallons of acid, weighing of the solution is unnecessary. In this case measure out a portion of acid, dilute, and take an aliquot portion for titration.

As commercial acetic acid frequently contains both sulphuric and hydrochloric acids, simple titration will not show the percentage of acetic acid in the case of an impure acid. In this case the hydrochloric acid may be determined volumetrically by means of a standard solution of silver nitrate, using potassium chromate as an indicator. The sulphuric acid should be determined by acidifying a weighed portion of the acetic acid with hydrochloric acid, diluting with water, boiling, and precipitation with barium-chloride solution. The weights of hydrochloric acid and sulphuric acid so found are then calculated to their proper equivalents in cc. of normal potassium-hydrate solution, and the corresponding deduction from the total number of cc. of potassium hydrate used is made. The difference will show the per cent of acetic acid present. For example, suppose 3 gms. of acetic acid were taken and the hydrochloric acid found was 0.031 gm. For the determination of sulphuric acid 3 gms. were also taken, the result being .025 gm. sulphuric acid. Now as 6 gms. of acetic acid are taken for titration in each case, we have in the 6 gms. 0.062 gm. of hydrochloric and 0.05 gm. of sulphuric acid. The hydrochloric acid would neutralize 1.7 cc. of the normal alkali solution and the sulphuric acid would neutralize 1 cc. of the normal alkali solution; hence from the total number of cc. of the normal alkali solution used in the titration a deduction of 2.7 cc. should be made for the hydrochloric and sulphuric acids present.

CHAPTER XIV.

CHLORIMETRY.

CHLORIMETRY has for its object the determination of the available chlorine of bleaching-powder.

Bleaching-powder, which is commercially known as chloride of lime, consists of a mixture, or combination, of calcium hypochlorite ($CaCl_2O_2$) and calcium chloride ($CaCl_2$). Its value for commercial and metallurgical purposes will depend upon the amount of chlorine set free (available chlorine) when an acid is added. The reaction which takes place is as follows:

$$Ca(ClO)_2, CaCl_2 + 2H_2SO_4 = 2CaSO_4 + 2H_2O + 4Cl$$

Hence the available chlorine is two atoms of Cl for each atom of O in the hypochlorite.

A number of methods have been proposed for the estimation of the chlorine set free. The following is believed to be as simple and accurate as any:

Weigh out 10 gms. of the bleaching-powder, transfer to a porcelain mortar, add about 50 cc. of water, and rub into a cream. Allow the coarse particles to settle, pour off the turbid fluid into a 1000-cc. flask, add more water, rub again, and pour off into the flask, continuing the operation until all of the powder is transferred to the flask. Fill the flask with water to the holding mark, pour the solution into a dry beaker, mix thoroughly, and draw off 50 cc. for analysis with a pipette.

Weigh out 0.325 gm. of piano-forte wire, dissolve it in a valve flask with about 10 cc. of dilute sulphuric acid (1 part H_2SO and 5 parts H_2O), cool, fill the flask with water, and pour into a beaker. To the solution in the beaker add the 50 cc. of turbid bleaching-powder solution, allowing it to run in slowly from the pipette and stirring constantly. Dilute to about 500 cc., and determine the iron remaining in the ferrous form by means of a standard solution of potassium permanganate. The same solution of permanganate as is used for the determination of iron (see Part II, Chapter XVI) is used for this purpose. Four atoms of iron correspond to four atoms of chlorine, or 56 parts of iron are equivalent to 35.5 parts of chlorine, as is shown by the reaction:

$$4FeSO_4 + Ca(ClO)_2, CaCl_2 + 2H_2SO = 2Fe_2(SO_4)_3 + 2CaCl_2 + 2H_2O.$$

The method of calculating the result is best illustrated by the following example: Suppose 1 cc. of the permanganate solution equals 0.005 gm. of iron, and that 16 cc. of the solution were used in the determination. Hence (.005 × 16 = .08) 0.08 gm. of the 0.324 gm. of the iron taken remained unoxidized by the bleaching-powder used. Then 0.324 − 0.08 = 0.244 gm. of iron which was oxidized by the bleaching-powder. Hence

$$56 : 35.5 :: 0.244 : 0.1547 \text{ gm. available Cl.}$$

Consequently, as 0.5 gm. of bleaching-powder was taken for analysis, the per cent of available chlorine = 30.94.

CHAPTER XV.

ANALYSIS OF WHITE-LEAD.

THE white-lead of commerce, when pure, is a basic carbonate of lead ($2PbCO_3, PbO_2H_2$). Its value, from a chemical standpoint, depends upon the percentages of PbO, CO_2, and H_2O which it contains, and these percentages should correspond pretty closely with the theoretical percentages of the formula.

In a white-lead works manufacturing a pure quality of white-lead all that is generally required is the percentages of PbO, CO_2, and H_2O.

The white-lead of commerce is frequently adulterated, the principal adulterants used being zinc-white (ZnO) and heavy spar ($BaSO_4$). Some white-leads contain lead sulphate ($PbSO_4$).

The best method of determining the water and carbonic acid is by direct weight. The determinations are effected as follows: Weigh out from 1.0 to 2.0 grammes of the white-lead in a porcelain boat, and introduce it into a piece of combustion-tubing. To the right-hand end of the tube a chloride-of-calcium tube, which has been previously filled with fresh, dry calcium chloride, and weighed, is attached. The calcium-chloride tube is attached to a U-tube filled with freshly ignited soda-lime. The U-tube is weighed before connecting up the apparatus. The U-tube is attached to another U-tube filled with pumice saturated with sulphuric acid. (See determination of carbonic acid, Part II, Chap. V.) The last U-tube is connected with an aspirator. The left-hand end of the combustion-tube is connected with a U-tube containing pumice and sulphuric acid and a U-tube containing soda-lime, in order that the air passing through the apparatus shall be dry and free from carbonic acid. After connecting up the apparatus the aspirator is started, and after it has run a few minutes the boat containing the white-lead is gradually heated by the flame of a Bunsen burner. The heat is gradually increased. After 10 to 15 minutes' heating all the water and carbonic acid should be driven off from the lead. The burner is now removed, and the aspirator kept running until the absorption-tubes have cooled. The soda-lime and calcium-chloride tubes are now disconnected and weighed, the increase in weight of the calcium-chloride tube representing the water which the white-lead contained, and the increase in weight of the soda-lime tube representing the carbonic acid which the white-lead contained. Should the lead be pure, the difference between the sum of the percentages of carbonic acid and water and 100 will be the per cent of lead oxide (PbO). As commercial white-lead usually contains some lead acetate, the residue, after treatment as above to drive off water and carbonic acid, is weighed. In pure white-lead this weight may be taken as lead oxide.

In the case of an impure lead, treat 1.0 to 2.0 grammes of the lead with 15 to 30 cc. of pure, strong acetic acid. Warm to effect solution, and when the white-lead is thoroughly decomposed, filter through a small filter and wash thoroughly with warm water. The filtrate will contain all the lead which was combined as carbonate. This may be determined according to Part II, Chapter IX.

Treat the residue with a strong, hot solution of ammonium chloride, and filter. The filtrate will contain the lead combined as sulphate. This may be determined according to Part II, Chapter IX.

The residue will contain the barium sulphate, etc., which may be determined according to Part II, Chapters I and XXV.

To determine the zinc oxide, dissolve 1.0 to 2.0 grammes of the white-lead in dilute hydrochloric acid and determine volumetrically with a standard solution of potassium ferrocyanide. (See Part II, Chapter XXI.)

CHAPTER XVI.

SPECIFIC-GRAVITY DETERMINATIONS.

THE specific gravity of any body is the weight of that body as compared with the weight of an equal volume of another body which is assumed as a standard. The standard taken for solids and liquids is distilled water; for gases and vapors, dry air and occasionally hydrogen.

All determinations of solids and liquids must be made at the same temperature. The temperature usually adopted is 60° Fahrenheit.

Determinations of gases and vapors may be made at any known temperature, and the volumes reduced to what they would be at 60° Fahrenheit.

Solids.—1. The substance is heavier than water and insoluble in water.

Weigh first in the air, suspending the substance from the beam of the balance by a piece of horse-hair, and then in distilled water whose temperature is 60° F. Let $W =$ the weight in air, $W' =$ the weight in water, and Sp. gr. $=$ the specific gravity; then

$$\text{Sp. gr.} = \frac{W}{W - W'}.$$

2. The substance is heavier than water and insoluble in water, but is in fragments.

Fill a specific-gravity bottle* with distilled water whose

---

* If a specific-gravity bottle is not at hand, take a thin-glass flask with a narrow neck and scratch a mark on the neck. The flask is to be filled to this mark in the determinations.

temperature is 60° F., and weigh it. This weight $= W'$. Weigh the substance in the air. This weight $= W$. Now introduce the weighed substance into the flask, fill it with distilled water, and weigh. This weight $= W''$:

$$\text{Sp. gr.} = \frac{W'}{(W + W') - W''}.$$

3. The substance is heavier than water, but soluble in it.

Weigh the substance in the air. This weight $= W$. Now weigh it in some liquid in which it is insoluble and whose specific gravity is known. This weight $= W'$. Hence we have the proportion, the specific gravity of water being 1,

$$\text{Sp. gr. of liquid} : 1 = (W - W') : W'',$$

in which $W'' =$ the weight of water which would have been displaced.

$$\text{Sp. gr.} = \frac{W}{W''}.$$

4. The substance is lighter than water and insoluble in it.

Weigh the substance in air. This weight $= W$. Weigh a piece of lead of suitable size in water. This weight $= W'$. Weigh the substance and the piece of lead together in water. This weight $= W''$.

$$\text{Sp. gr.} = \frac{W}{W - (W' + W'')}.$$

5. The substance is lighter than water and soluble in it.

Weigh the substance in the air. This weight $= W$. Introduce the substance into the flask described in 2, and fill the flask with some liquid in which it is insoluble, and whose specific gravity is known. Weigh. This weight $= W'$. Fill the flask with the liquid alone and weigh. This weight $= W''$. Then the weight of the liquid displaced $= W'' - W' = A$. If $S =$ the specific gravity of the liquid, and $X =$ the corresponding weight of water which would have been displaced, we have

$$S : 1 = A : X, \text{ and } \text{Sp. gr.} = \frac{W}{X}.$$

Liquids.—One of three methods may be employed.

6. Weigh some body, which is insoluble in water and in the liquid, first in air, then in water, and then in the liquid.
Let W = the weight in air;
W' = the weight in water; and
W'' = the weight in the liquid. Then

$$\text{Sp. gr.} = \frac{W'' - W}{W' - W}.$$

7. The specific-gravity bottle is employed, which for liquids is usually provided with a hollow-glass stopper which allows the insertion of a thermometer.
Let W = the weight of the flask empty;
W' = the weight of the flask filled with water;
W'' = the weight of the flask filled with the liquid.

$$\text{Sp. gr.} = \frac{W'' - W}{W' - W}.$$

8. By means of a hydrometer.

The principle upon which the hydrometer depends is that a floating body displaces its own weight of liquid.

Special hydrometers are made, the graduations being for liquids of different specific gravities, as the lactometer for milk and the uriometer for urine.

The Baumé scale of graduation is frequently used in commercial work. It is purely arbitrary. For liquids heavier than water the point to which the hydrometer sinks in a 15-per-cent solution of sodium chloride in water (NaCl 15 parts, H_2O 85 parts) is marked 15°. The point to which it sinks in pure water is marked 0°. For liquids lighter than water the point to which the hydrometer sinks in pure water is marked 10°.

The point to which it sinks in a 10-per-cent sodium-chloride solution (NaCl 10 parts, H_2O 90 parts) is marked 0°.

The observations of Baumé were conducted at 10° R. = 54.5° F.

For liquids heavier than water the degrees Baumé can be converted into specific gravity by the formula

$$\text{Sp. gr.} = \frac{144}{144 - B°}.$$

For liquids lighter than water the degrees Baumé can be converted into specific gravity by the formula

$$\text{Sp. gr.} = \frac{144}{134 + B°}.$$

For specific gravities corresponding to degrees Baumé, see page 297.

Gases.—The specific gravity of a gas or vapor may be determined by Bunsen's method, which consists in weighing a glass globe when filled with air, when filled with the gas, and when exhausted by means of an air-pump. From the data so obtained the specific gravity can be readily calculated. As this method requires a powerful air-pump it is seldom used except for scientific work. (See Watts' Dictionary of Chemistry.)

For commercial work the Schilling effusion method is commonly used. In this method the times of the effusion of equal volumes of gas and air through a fine hole in a thin metallic plate are compared. It depends upon the principle that the specific gravities of two gases passing through such an opening are proportionate to the squares of the times of effusion.

Let A = seconds which the volume of air requires to escape;
  B = seconds which the same volume of gas requires to escape;
  x = the specific gravity of the gas.

If the specific gravity of air = 1, we have

$$1 : x :: A^2 : B^2; \quad \text{or,} \quad x = \frac{B^2}{A^2}.$$

SPECIFIC GRAVITIES OF LIQUIDS HEAVIER THAN WATER.*
Temperature 54.5° F.

Degrees Baumé.	Specific Gravity.	Degrees Baumé.	Specific Gravity.	Degrees Baumé.	Specific Gravity.
0	1.00000	26	1.21129	52	1.53580
1	1.00675	27	1.22122	53	1.55179
2	1.01360	28	1.23131	54	1.56812
3	1.02054	29	1.24156	55	1.58479
4	1.02757	30	1.25199	56	1.60182
5	1.03471	31	1.26260	57	1.61923
6	1.04194	32	1.27338	58	1.63701
7	1.04927	33	1.28436	59	1.65519
8	1.05671	34	1.29552	60	1.67378
9	1.06426	35	1.30688	61	1.69279
10	1.07191	36	1.31844	62	1.71223
11	1.07968	37	1.33021	63	1.73213
12	1.08755	38	1.34218	64	1.75250
13	1.09555	39	1.35438	65	1.77335
14	1.10366	40	1.36680	66	1.79470
15	1.11189	41	1.37945	67	1.81657
16	1.12025	42	1.39234	68	1.83899
17	1.12873	43	1.40547	69	1.86196
18	1.13735	44	1.41885	70	1.88551
19	1.14609	45	1.43248	71	1.90967
20	1.15497	46	1.44638	72	1.93446
21	1.16399	47	1.46056	73	1.95989
22	1.17316	48	1.47501	74	1.98601
23	1.18246	49	1.48975	75	2.01283
24	1.19192	50	1.50479		
25	1.20153	51	1.52014		

SPECIFIC GRAVITIES OF LIQUIDS LIGHTER THAN WATER.†
Temperature 54.5° F.

Degrees Baumé.	Specific Gravity.	Degrees Baumé.	Specific Gravity.	Degrees Baumé.	Specific Gravity.
10	1.00000	35	0.85342	60	0.74432
15	0.96679	40	0.82912	65	0.72577
20	0.93571	45	0.80616	70	0.70811
25	0.90657	50	0.78443	75	0.69130
30	0.87919	55	0.76385		

* "The Baumé Hydrometer," a paper read by Prof. C. F. Chandler before the National Academy of Sciences, at the Philadelphia meeting, 1881.
† Ibid.

CHAPTER XVII.

ANALYSIS OF COMMERCIAL ALUMINIUM.

THE constituents usually required are silicon, iron, copper, and aluminium. The method of decomposition described is due to Rossel.*

Three grammes of the finely-divided metal are gradually introduced into from 30 to 40 cc. of hot caustic potash (30 to 40 per cent solution). The potash should be pure, and free from silica, alumina, etc. The decomposition is best effected in a platinum dish, as the caustic potash attacks glass or porcelain. The metal dissolves, leaving a black flocculent residue. After the decomposition is complete the solution is supersaturated with pure hydrochloric acid and evaporated to dryness. The dusty dry mass is heated at 110° C. to dehydrate the silicic acid, moistened with hydrochloric acid, dissolved in water, and the silica filtered off, washed with hot water, and determined as usual. From the silica, as found, calculate the percentage of silicon.

To the filtrate from the silica add an excess of sulphuric acid, evaporate to drive off the hydrochloric acid, and finally dilute with cold water to 300 cc. Divide into two portions of 100 cc. and 200 cc. each.

In the 100 cc. portion (corresponding to 1 gm. of the original material) determine the aluminium by nearly neutralizing

---

*Chem. Ztg. XXI. 4.

the solution with ammonia, precipitating the iron by electrolysis, and finally determining the aluminium as a phosphate in the manner described in Part II, Chapter XVII.

In the 200-cc. portion (corresponding to 2 gms. of the original material) determine the iron by reduction with pure zinc and titration with a standard solution of potassium permanganate, in the manner described in Part II, Chapter XVI.

For the determination of copper dissolve 1.0 gm. of the metal in 40 cc. of a mixture of hydrochloric acid and water (HCl 33 per cent, H_2O 67 per cent). When solution is effected, boil, dilute with hot water to 250 cc., and pass sulphuretted hydrogen through the solution until it is saturated. The copper sulphide and silicon are filtered off and washed, when the copper may be separated from the silicon and determined electrolytically (see page 157), or by any of the usual methods (Part II, Chap. XIII).

For the analysis of titanium and chromium-aluminium alloys, and for much valuable information in regard to the analysis of commercial aluminium, see an article by Hunt, Clapp, and Handy.*

---

* Jour. of An. and App. Chem., Vol. VI, No. 1, Jan. 1892.

CHAPTER XVIII.

ANALYSIS OF NATURAL PHOSPHATES.

THE value of phosphate rock principally depends upon the percentage of phosphoric acid which it contains. In addition to the phosphoric acid the following substances affect the value of the material in the manner described : Water and insoluble matter, which reduce the percentage of phosphoric acid ; carbonates, which increase the cost of manufacture by neutralizing their equivalent of sulphuric acid ; alumina and ferric oxide, which revert a portion of the soluble phosphoric acid and also have a tendency to render the superphosphates wet and unmanageable ; and fluorine, which, as there are silicates of aluminium otherwise undecomposed by sulphuric acid, which are decomposed in the presence of fluorine, the otherwise inactive alumina assuming an objectionable form.

The following method of analysis is taken from an article by Dr. T. M. Chatard,* and whilst it differs somewhat from the methods of other chemists, it is believed to be as rapid and accurate as any method which we have.

Moisture.—Two grammes are weighed into a tared platinum crucible. This, with its lid, is placed in an air-bath at 105° C., and heated for at least three hours. The lid is then put on, and the crucible is placed in a desiccator and weighed as soon as cold. The loss is the weight in moisture.

---

* Transactions of The American Institute of Mining Engineers, Vol. XXI, page 160.

Combined Water and Organic Matter.—The residue from the moisture determination is gradually heated to full redness over a lamp, and then ignited over the blast-lamp. This operation is repeated to constant weight. The loss (less the percentage of carbonic acid as determined in another portion) may be taken as water and organic matter. This method answers for all technical purposes, but when minerals containing fluorine are strongly ignited, a part of the fluorine is expelled; hence, if more accurate determinations are required, the methods given in Fresenius, etc., should be followed.

Carbonic Acid.—The method by direct weight, using the apparatus described in Part II, Chapter V, may be followed. Many phosphates must be heated with dilute acids to the boiling-point to effect complete decomposition of the carbonates.

Insoluble Matter.—Five grammes of the phosphate are placed in a beaker or casserole; 25 cc. of nitric acid (sp. gr. 1.2) and 12.5 cc. of hydrochloric acid (sp. gr. 1.12) are added; and the vessel, covered with a watch-glass, is placed on the water-bath for thirty minutes. The solution is stirred from time to time, and at the end of the thirty minutes the vessel is removed from the bath, filled with cold water, well stirred, and its contents allowed to settle. The solution is now filtered into a 500-cc. flask, and the residue is thoroughly washed with cold water, partially dried, and finally ignited to constant weight. This weight may be considered as insoluble matter. It will not correctly represent the silica, as the fluorine liberated during solution of the phosphate dissolves a portion of the silica. As the same reaction occurs in the manufacture of a superphosphate from the material, the result may be considered as a fair approximation to commercial practice. The ignited residue should be tested for P_2O_5.

The flask containing the filtrate is filled up to the mark with cold water, and the solution is thoroughly mixed by pouring twice into a dry beaker and returning to the flask.

Phosphoric Acid.—Two portions of 50 cc. each (= 0.5 gm. of original material) are drawn off with a pipette, introduced into beakers, and evaporated until the hydrochloric acid is driven off. To each portion 150 cc. of molybdate solution is added, the solution being well stirred and allowed to stand on a water-bath until quite hot. The beakers are now removed and allowed to stand until the solution is quite cold. It is best to allow the solutions to stand for at least three hours, after which the yellow precipitate is filtered off and well washed with a 20-per-cent solution of ammonium nitrate containing one-thirtieth of its volume of nitric acid. The filtrate should be tested for P_2O_5 by the addition of some molybdate solution and digestion for some time. The funnel, with its contents, is now inclined over the beaker in which the precipitation was effected, and the precipitate washed back into it with a jet of water. Ammonia is now added, and on gently warming complete solution of the precipitate should be effected. Any residue indicates either incomplete washing or, under some circumstances, silica. The solution is filtered through the same filter into a clean beaker, and the first beaker and the filter are thoroughly washed with dilute ammonia water (1 part ammonia and 4 parts water). The solution is now boiled, the beaker is removed from the heat, and magnesia solution is added drop by drop, with continual stirring. The precipitate at first redissolves, but during the continual addition of the magnesia solution the solution becomes cloudy, with a flocculent precipitate, which, as the stirring continues, becomes crystalline and subsides. When further addition of the magnesia solution causes no cloudiness and the *crystalline change is complete*, the beaker is placed in very cold water to chill its contents as rapidly as possible. When perfectly cold it is again tested with a few drops of the magnesia solution, and if the precipitation is found to be complete, about one third of its volume of strong ammonia is added, the solution is stirred and allowed to stand three hours. The precipitate is finally filtered on an asbestos felt in a Gooch* perforated crucible, and washed with the dilute ammonia water. The washing will be completed by the time the precipitate is completely

---

*American Chemical Journal, Vol. I, p. 317.

removed from the sides of the beaker and transferred to the filter. A few drops of a strong solution of ammonium nitrate are poured on the precipitate, which is then carefully dried and gently heated until the fumes of ammonium salts cease to come off. The heat is now increased, and as soon as the glow of the pyrophosphate formation has passed through the whole of the precipitate the crucible is placed in a desiccator and, when cold, weighed. The ignited precipitate is very white, and the difference between the two determinations should not exceed 0.05 per cent for thoroughly satisfactory work.

Should a Gooch crucible not be at hand, the ammonium, magnesium phosphate can be filtered onto a filter-paper, and, after washing, dissolved in dilute nitric acid into a small platinum dish, the solution being evaporated to dryness, carefully ignited, and weighed. A clean mass is thus obtained, whilst, should the precipitate be ignited with the paper, it is difficult to destroy the carbon.

Lime.—Evaporate 100 cc. of the solution (containing 1 gm. of the original substance) in a beaker to about 50 cc., add 10 cc. of sulphuric acid (1 cc. sulphuric acid and 4 cc. water), and evaporate on a water-bath until a considerable crop of gypsum crystals are formed. Cool the solution, when it will generally become pasty owing to the additional separation of gypsum. When cold, 150 cc. of 95-per-cent alcohol are slowly added, with continual stirring, and the whole is allowed to stand for three hours, with occasional stirring. The precipitate is filtered off, with the aid of a filter-pump, into a distillation-flask, and washed with 95-per-cent alcohol. The filter, with the precipitate, is gently removed from the funnel and inverted into a platinum crucible, so that by squeezing the point of the filter the precipitate falls down into the crucible and the paper is pressed down smoothly over it. The crucible is gently heated, and when the alcohol has burned off and the paper is completely destroyed the heat is raised to the full power of the Bunsen burner for a few minutes, after which the crucible is cooled and weighed. From the weight of the $CaSO_4$, as thus determined, the weight of the CaO is calculated. Separate

determinations on the same sample rarely differ more than 0.05 per cent.

Ferric Oxide and Alumina.—The distillation-flask containing the alcoholic filtrate is connected with a condenser and heated until alcohol is no longer distilled over. This distillate, if mixed with a little sodium carbonate and redistilled over quicklime, can be used over and over again. When the distillation is ended, the residue in the flask is washed into a small platinum dish and evaporated as far as possible on the water-bath. It becomes dark brown, owing to the presence of organic matter, which must be destroyed, since it prevents the complete precipitation of the phosphorus in the subsequent operation. To destroy this organic matter, remove the dish from the bath, add a small amount of pure sodium nitrate, and heat carefully over the naked flame, keeping the dish covered with a watch-glass. If care be taken, there will be no loss by spattering; and the mass fuses to a colorless, viscous liquid, cooling to a glass, which is readily soluble in hot water made acid with nitric acid. The solution is transferred to a beaker, made slightly (but distinctly) alkaline with ammonia, then carefully neutralized with acetic acid, then diluted with hot water, brought to a boil, allowed to settle, and filtered. After the precipitate has been completely brought on the filter with hot water, the washing is completed with a solution of ammonium nitrate (made by neutralizing 5 cc. of nitric acid with ammonia and diluting to 250 cc.), and the precipitate is dried, ignited intensely, and weighed. As the determinations are made in pairs, one portion is used for the estimation of phosphoric acid by fusing with a little sodium carbonate, dissolving in dilute nitric acid, and treating with molybdate solution as already described; while the other portion, also fused with sodium carbonate, is dissolved with sulphuric acid, and the iron is reduced and titrated with permanganate. The results should not differ more than 0.1 per cent.

Magnesia.—The filtrate from the aluminium ferric phosphate is evaporated to a small bulk, made strongly ammoniacal, and allowed to stand, when magnesia, if present, will separate as the double salt, and should be treated as usual. If during the evaporation of the filtrate (which should be perfectly clear at first) any flocculent matter separates, it should be filtered off and examined before proceeding with the precipitation of the magnesia.

Fluorine.—Two grammes of the phosphate are intimately mixed in a large platinum crucible with 3 gms. of precipitated silica and 12 gms. of pure sodium carbonate, and the mixture is gradually brought to clear fusion over the blast-lamp. When the fusion is complete, the mass is spread over the walls of the crucible, which is then cooled rapidly. The mass is detached from the crucible and put in a platinum dish, into which whatever remains adhering to the crucible or its lid is also washed with hot water. The contents of the dish are now diluted with hot water, the dish is covered and digested on the water-bath until the mass is thoroughly disintegrated. To hasten this the supernatant liquid may be poured off, the residue being washed into a small porcelain mortar, ground up, returned to the dish, and boiled with fresh water until no hard grains are left. The total liquid is then filtered, and the residue is washed with hot water. The filtrate (which should amount to about 500 cc.) is nearly neutralized with nitric acid (methyl orange being used as an indicator), some pure sodium bicarbonate is at once added, and the solution (in a platinum dish, if one large enough is at hand, otherwise in a beaker) is placed on the water-bath, when it speedily turns turbid through the separation of silica. As soon as the solution is warm it is removed from the bath, stirred, allowed to stand for two or three hours, and then filtered by means of the filter-pump and washed with cold water. The filtrate is concentrated to about 250 cc. and nearly neutralized, as before; some sodium carbonate is added; and the phosphoric acid is precipitated with silver nitrate in excess. The precipitate is filtered off and washed with hot water, and the excess of silver in the filtrate is removed with sodium chloride. The filtrate from the silver chloride (after addition of some sodium bicarbonate) is evaporated to its crystallizing point, then cooled and diluted with cold water; still more sodium bicarbonate is added, and the whole is allowed to stand, when additional silica will separate, and is to be filtered off.

This final solution is nearly neutralized, as before; a little sodium-carbonate solution is added; it is heated to boiling, and an excess of a solution of calcium chloride is added. The precipitate of calcium carbonate and fluoride must be boiled for a few minutes, when it can be easily filtered and washed with hot water. The washed precipitate is washed from the filter into a small platinum dish and evaporated to dryness, while the filter, after being partially dried and used to wipe off any particles of the precipitate adhering to the dish in which it was formed, is burned, and the ash is added to the main precipitate. This, when dry, is ignited, and allowed to cool; dilute acetic acid is added in excess, and the whole is evaporated to dryness, being kept on the water-bath until all odor of acetic acid has disappeared. The residue is now treated with hot water, digested, filtered on a small filter, washed with hot water, partially dried, placed in a crucible, carefully ignited, and weighed as CaF_2. The CaF_2 is then dissolved in sulphuric acid by gently heating and agitating, evaporated to dryness on a radiator, ignited at full red heat, and weighed as $CaSO_4$. From this weight the equivalent weight of CaF_2 should be calculated, and should be very close to that actually found as above, but should never exceed it. The difference (generally about 1 mgm.) is due to silica which is precipitated with the fluoride. The percentage of fluorine is, therefore, always calculated from the weight of the sulphate, and not from that of the original fluoride. The results are very satisfactory.

For other methods, as well as a complete treatise on phosphates, see "The Phosphates of America," by Dr. F. Wyatt.

CHAPTER XIX.

ANALYSIS OF LEAD AND COPPER SLAGS.*

IN the following scheme it is assumed that the slag sample is vitreous, having been suddenly chilled when taken (see Part I, Chapter II, page 18). If such is not the case, a fusion will be necessary in order to effect decomposition of the slag. (See Part II, Chapter I, page 83.)

For technical purposes a partial analysis will be sufficient. Occasionally a careful and more complete analysis may be required.

The constituents of a lead slag most frequently determined are SiO_2, FeO, CaO, Pb, and Ag; MnO and ZnO are frequently important constituents; BaO, MgO, and Al_2O_3 are sometimes important constituents; Na, K, and S, whilst present in all slags, are rarely determined. This is also the case with copper slags, if Cu is substituted for Pb.

Partial Analysis of Lead Slags.—*a*. Determine the silica by treatment of 0.5 gm. with water and hydrochloric acid, boiling the solution for a few minutes to effect solution of all except silica, and filtering as rapidly as possible. (See Part II, Chapter XXV, page 225.)

b. Determine the barium by treatment of 0.5 gm. with water, hydrochloric acid, and a few drops of nitric and sul-

---

* Whilst this scheme is to some extent a repetition of what has already been described in Part II, the chapter has been inserted, as the subject is of the utmost importance to the lead and copper metallurgist ; and the scheme, moreover, illustrates the manner in which a systematic course of analysis may be built up from the methods described in Part II.

phuric acids. Evaporate to dryness, take up with water and hydrochloric acid, filter, wash, dry, ignite, and weigh the combined SiO_2 and $BaSO_4$. The difference between the weight of this precipitate and the weight of the SiO_2, as determined in *a*, will represent the weight of the $BaSO_4$.

c. Determine the lime in the filtrate from the SiO_2 and $BaSO_4$ as obtained in *b*, according to Part II, Chapter XXIII, page 218.

d. Determine the iron in 0.5 gm. according to Part II, Chapter XVI, page 178.

e. Determine the manganese in 1.0 gm. by treatment with water, hydrochloric acid, and a few crystals of potassium chlorate, boiling to effect solution and oxidation of the iron. Treat and determine according to Volhard's Method. (See Part II, Chapter XX, page 198.)

f. Determine the zinc in 1.0 gm. according to Part II, Chapter XIX, page 210.

g. Determine the lead by fire-assay, taking 5 or 10 gms. (see Part II, Chapter IX, page 137). Should the slag be very low in lead (less than 1.0%), it is difficult to find and extract the lead button from the slag. In this case the following method is frequently used: Take 5.0 gms. of slag and weigh out about 0.1 gm. of pure silver, adding it to the charge of slag and lead flux in the crucible. Fuse and pour the charge. The reduced lead will alloy with the silver, giving a button which may readily be found and detached from the slag. The increase in weight of the silver button represents the weight of lead in the 5 gms. of slag taken.

h. Determine the silver in 1 A. T. by crucible fire-assay, adding sufficient litharge and reducing agent to obtain a lead button of about 4 gms., which is cupelled. (Part II, Chapter VII, page 129.)

In the case of copper slags proceed in the same manner, and determining the copper by the colorimetric method. (See Part II, Chapter XIII, page 159.)

Complete Analysis of Lead Slags.—Treat 1.0 gm. of the slag according to *b* and separate the SiO_2, $BaSO_4$, and $PbSO_4$, washing by decantation and leaving as much as possible of the residue in the casserole. Extract the lead with ammonium acetate (see Part II, Chapter I, page 79), and filter off the SiO_2 and $BaSO_4$. After drying, igniting, and weighing this precipitate, fuse it in a platinum crucible with sodium carbonate, and determine the baryta according to Part II, Chapter XXV, page 224. The weight of the $SiO_2 + BaSO_4$, less the weight of the barium sulphate as determined, will equal the weight of the silica. In very accurate work the silica can be determined directly by acidifying the filtrate from the barium carbonate and evaporating it to dryness, the silica being determined as usual.

Nearly neutralize the filtrate from the SiO_2, $BaSO_4$, and $PbSO_4$ with sodium carbonate, add 10 to 15 gms. of sodium acetate, and make a basic-acetate precipitation of the iron and alumina. Filter off this precipitate, wash it with hot water, and dissolve it in a little dilute hydrochloric acid. Reprecipitate the iron and alumina with ammonia as hydroxides (see Part II, Chapter XVII, page 181 and page 184), filter, and wash. Dissolve this precipitate with a little dilute sulphuric acid, and electrolyze, using mercury for the cathode. Determine the iron according to Part II, Chapter XVII, page 187, and the aluminium in the iron-free solution as a phosphate according to Part II, Chapter XVII, page 186.

Combine the filtrates from the basic-acetate precipitate and the precipitate of hydroxides, add a little acetic acid, and boil. Pass a current of sulphuretted hydrogen through the boiling solution for half an hour. Filter off the precipitated zinc sulphide and wash with water containing H_2S. (Should the slag contain Ni or Co—which is unusual except in rare cases of copper-smelting—they will be precipitated with the ZnS as sulphides.) The filtrate from the precipitated zinc sulphide should be tested with H_2S, and should a precipitate form, it should be filtered off and added to the first precipitate. Dissolve the precipitated ZnS with hydrochloric acid, and determine according to Part II, Chapter XIX; or by precipitation as zinc carbonate with a solution of sodium carbonate, filtration, washing thoroughly with hot water, and final ignition of the precipitate to ZnO, weighing as such.

Boil the filtrate from the precipitated zinc sulphide, add an excess of bromine water, and continue to boil for half an hour.

Filter off the precipitated manganese dioxide, wash it thoroughly with hot water, boil the filtrate, and add more bromine water to insure the complete precipitation of the manganese. Dissolve the precipitated manganese dioxide with a little dilute hydrochloric acid, and determine the manganese according to any of the methods described in Part II, Chapter XX; or, the precipitate may be transferred to a beaker and determined by Williams' Method. (See page 196.)

Boil the filtrate from the precipitated manganese dioxide to expel bromine, render it alkaline with an excess of ammonia, and precipitate the lime as an oxalate according to Part II, Chapter XXIII, page 216. The precipitated oxalate should be dissolved in a little dilute hydrochloric acid, the solution is rendered strongly alkaline with ammonia, and the lime is reprecipitated as an oxalate. This is necessary to insure the complete separation of the lime and magnesia. The lime is finally determined according to Part II, Chapter XXIII, pages 217 and 218, either gravimetrically or volumetrically.

The combined filtrates from the precipitated calcium oxalate are rendered strongly alkaline with ammonia, the magnesia is precipitated as ammonium-magnesium phosphate, and determined according to Part II, Chapter XXIV, page 220.

The alkalies are determined in a separate portion of 5 gms., according to Part II, Chapter XXVI, page 230.

The lead is determined in a separate portion of 5 gms. by treatment with water, hydrochloric acid, a few drops of nitric acid, and an excess of sulphuric acid, evaporation to fumes of sulphuric anhydride, and proceeding according to Part II, Chapter IX, page 139.

The sulphur is determined in a separate portion of from 2 to 5 gms., proceeding according to Part II, Chapter II, page 90.

In some cases the slag may contain small amounts of Cu, Bi, Sb, As, and Sn. In such a case it is necessary to precipitate these elements by passing a current of sulphuretted hydrogen through the filtrate from the SiO_2, $BaSO_4$, and $PbSO_4$. The precipitated sulphides are filtered off, the precipitate is washed with water containing H_2S, and the different metals in this precipitate may be separated and determined according to the methods described under the different metals. The filtrate from the precipitated sulphides is boiled, and the sulphur oxidized with bromine or potassium chlorate before proceeding with the analysis.

The same method will answer for copper slags, except that in this case the copper and other metals of the sulphuretted-hydrogen group will have to be precipitated with H_2S, the precipitated sulphides being filtered out before proceeding with the analysis. The precipitated sulphides may be dissolved in nitric acid, and the copper determined colorimetrically according to Part II, Chapter XIII, page 159.

A method preferred by some chemists for slags containing baryta is as follows: Obtain the SiO_2 and $BaSO_4$ by treatment with acids, filtration, etc., as above. Weigh the combined SiO_2 and $BaSO_4$, and then expel the silica as a fluoride by treatment with hydrofluoric and sulphuric acids, repeating the treatment until the weight is constant. The loss in weight equals the silica, and the final weight equals barium sulphate, which should be calculated to baryta (BaO).

PART IV.

CHAPTER I.

THE WRITING OF CHEMICAL EQUATIONS.

IN order to work intelligently and to be able to calculate the results of an analysis by stoichiometry, the chemist should not only thoroughly understand the reactions which take place at each step in the analysis, but should be able to construct the equation which represents the reaction.

A chemical equation is the expression in symbols or formulæ of the changes which elements or chemical compounds undergo when subjected to chemical or physical influences. As all matter is indestructible, these expressions of change must necessarily be equations. A chemical equation differs from a mathematical equation inasmuch as it cannot be accepted as true until verified by experiment; nor can it be treated in the same way as a mathematical equation, as, for example, equal amounts cannot be subtracted from either side of the equation and leave it true.

There are three classes of chemical equations: Synthetical, Analytical, and Metathetical.

Synthetical Equations are those representing the union of elements or compounds:

$$2H + O = H_2O,$$
$$CaO + CO_2 = CaCO_3.$$

THE WRITING OF CHEMICAL EQUATIONS. 313

Analytical Equations are those representing the separation of a compound into its constituents :

$$H_2O + \text{electric spark} = 2H + O,$$
$$CaCO_3 + \text{heat} = CaO + CO_2.$$

Metathetical Equations (equations of interchange) are those representing the interchange of elements or radicals, and the formation of new products :

$$AgNO_3 + HCl = AgCl + HNO_3.$$

The last claim attention most frequently, and of these the equations of oxidation and reduction are the most interesting:

$$3MnO + Mn_2O_7 = 5MnO_2.$$

The laws governing chemical interchange have not been fully determined, but the two following exert an important bearing on the results :

1st. When a compound can be formed which is insoluble in the menstruum present, this compound separates as a precipitate. There are exceptions to this rule.

2d. When a gas can be formed, or any substance which is volatile at the temperature at which the experiment is made, this volatile substance is set free.

The interchange effected is always on terms regulated by the quantivalence of the elements or radicals involved. For example, a monad element or radical can replace another monad element or radical only atom by atom. To effect an exchange between a monad element or radical and a dyad element or radical, two atoms of the monad are required for each atom of the dyad:

$$BaO + 2HCl = BaCl_2 + H_2O.$$

In writing an equation, first place down the symbols or formulæ entering into the equation in the first member of the equation, and write the plus sign between them. Now write the symbols or formulæ of the products resulting from the reaction as the second member of the equation. Now adjust the factors of the symbols or formulæ so that the interchange will result in a true equation. The data for the second member of the equation is either a matter of memory or else must be obtained by actual experiment. Very frequently a knowledge of the conditions which affect an interchange will enable one to predict by equations what products will be formed. The adjustment of the factors is the important point, and is best illustrated by the following examples:

EXAMPLE NO. 1. Required the construction of an equation showing the oxidation of ferrous chloride by potassium bichromate.

The compounds which enter into the reaction are $FeCl_2$, $K_2Cr_2O_7$, and HCl. The compounds formed are Fe_2Cl_6, KCl, Cr_2Cl_6, and H_2O.

As oxidation signifies an increase and reduction signifies a decrease in the quantivalence of an element, the oxidizing agent, in exerting its influence, decreases in quantivalence, whilst the substance oxidized experiences a corresponding increase in its quantivalence. Writing out the equation and leaving spaces for the factors, we have

$$FeCl_2 + K_2Cr_2O_7 + HCl = Fe_2Cl_6 + KCl + Cr_2Cl_6 + H_2O.$$

Now the iron passes from the dyad state to the tetrad state, thus: $2FeO + O = Fe_2O_3$. Hence two Fe require one O.

One $K_2Cr_2O_7$ yields 3O, thus: $Cr_2O_6 = Cr_2O_3 + 3O$. Hence 6 of the ferrous compound need 1 of the bichromate. Making the adjustment, we have

$$6FeCl_2 + K_2Cr_2O_7 + HCl = Fe_2Cl_6 + KCl + Cr_2Cl_6 + H_2O.$$

Now if we arrange the factors for the other compounds according to the prescribed conditions of the solution (acid, alkaline, or neutral), we have

$$6FeCl_2 + K_2Cr_2O_7 + 14HCl = 3Fe_2Cl_6 + 2KCl + Cr_2Cl_6 + 7H_2O.$$

THE WRITING OF CHEMICAL EQUATIONS. 315

Testing to see if this is a true equation, we have

	In the First Member.	In the Second Member.
Fe	6	6
Cl	26	26
Cr	2	2
O	7	7
H	14	14
K	2	2

The factors all balance, and hence the equation is correct.

EXAMPLE NO. 2. Required to construct an equation showing the oxidation of antimonous chloride to antimonic chloride by potassium permanganate.

The compounds which enter into the reaction are Sb_2Cl_6, $K_2Mn_2O_8$, and HCl. The compounds formed are Sb_2Cl_{10}, KCl, $MnCl_2$, and H_2O.

Writing out the equation as before, and leaving spaces for the factors, we have

$$Sb_2Cl_6 + K_2Mn_2O_8 + HCl = Sb_2Cl_{10} + KCl + MnCl_2 + H_2O.$$

Now the antimony passes from the triad to the pentad state, thus:

$$Sb_2O_3 + 2O = Sb_2O_5.$$

One $K_2Mn_2O_8$ yields 5O, thus:

$$Mn_2O_7 = 2MnO + 5O.$$

Hence 1 of the antimonous requires 2O, or 5 of the antimonous requires 10O, or 2 of the $K_2Mn_2O_8$. Making the adjustment, we have

$$5Sb_2Cl_6 + 2K_2Mn_2O_8 + \ HCl =$$
$$5Sb_2Cl_{10} + 4KCl + 4MnCl_2 + \ H_2O.$$

Arranging the factors for the HCl and H_2O, we have

$$5Sb_2Cl_6 + 2K_2Mn_2O_8 + 32HCl =$$
$$5Sb_2Cl_{10} + 4KCl + 4MnCl_2 + 16H_2O.$$

Or the equation may be written

$$5SbCl_3 + K_2Mn_2O_8 + 16HCl = 5SbCl_5 + 2KCl + 2MnCl_2 + 8H_2O.$$

Testing to see if this is a true equation, we have

	In the First Member.	In the Second Member.
Sb	5	5
Cl	31	31
K	2	2
Mn	2	2
O	8	8
H	16	16

The factors all balance, and hence the equation is correct.

This method is due to Prof. Elwyn Waller, and is the method taught by him in the Columbia College School of Mines.

The following excellent method of constructing equations is due to Otis C. Johnson.* According to Mr. Johnson's definition of *bond*, by the bond of an element is meant the amount of oxidation it is capable of sustaining, and hence he defines bond as an oxidizing force. When an element has no oxidizing power it has no bonds. When an element is a reducing agent its bonds are negative.

He gives the following rules for ascertaining the bonds of an element:

1st. Hydrogen in combination has always one bond, and is always positive. (H^I.)

2d. Oxygen always has two bonds, and they are always negative. (O^{-II}.)

3d. Free elements have no bonds; thus metallic iron (Fe^0).

4th. The sum of the bonds of any compound is always equal to zero. Thus

$$H_2^{II} Mn_2^{+XIV} O_8^{-XVI} = O.$$

---

* Negative Bonds and Rules for Balancing Equations, *Chemical News*, 1880, Vol. XLII, p. 51.

5th. Acid radicals are always negative. Thus

$$H^I N^{+V} O_3^{-VI} = O, \quad \text{and} \quad Mg_3{}^{+VI}(PO_4)_2{}^{-VI} = O.$$

6th. Metals in combination are usually positive. The most prominent exceptions to this rule are their compounds with hydrogen. Thus

$$Sb^{-III} H_3{}^{+III} \quad \text{and} \quad As^{-III} H_3{}^{+III}.$$

As the oxidation of one substance involves the reduction of some other substance, the number of bonds gained by the one is lost by the other.

From the above a rule for writing the equations of oxidation and reduction is derived, provided the resulting products are known. The following is the rule:

The number of bonds changed in one molecule of each shows how many molecules of the other must be taken. The words *each* and *other* refer, respectively, to oxidizing and reducing agent.

EXAMPLE NO. 3. Applying this method to the problem

$$FeCl_2 + K_2Cr_2O_7 + HCl = Fe_2Cl_6 + KCl + Cr_2Cl_6 + H_2O,$$

we find that

Cr_2 in the first member has 12 bonds; $(K_2{}^{+II} Cr_2{}^{+XII} O_7{}^{-XIV}.)$
Cr_2 in the second member has 6 bonds. $(Cr_2{}^{+VI} Cl_6{}^{-VI}.)$
        Loss $= 6$. Hence $6FeCl_2$.
Fe in the first member has 2 bonds; $(Fe^{+II} Cl_2{}^{-II}.)$
Fe in the second member has 3 bonds. $(Fe_2{}^{+VI} Cl_6{}^{-VI}.)$
        Gain $= 1$. Hence $1K_2Cr_2O_7$.

EXAMPLE NO. 4. Applying this method to the problem

$$Sb_2Cl_4 + K_2Mn_2O_8 + HCl = Sb_2Cl_{10} + KCl + MnCl_2 + H_2O,$$

we find that

    Mn_2 in the first member has 14 bonds;
    Mn_2 in the second member has 4 bonds.
        Loss $= 10$. Hence $10SbCl_3$ or $5Sb_2Cl_4$.
    Sb in the first member has 3 bonds;
    Sb in the second member has 5 bonds.
        Gain $= 2$. Hence $2K_2Mn_2O_8$.

EXAMPLE No. 5. Required to construct the equation for the oxidation of ferrous sulphate to ferric sulphate by potassium permanganate.

The compounds entering into the reaction are $K_2Mn_2O_8$, $FeSO_4$, and H_2SO_4. The products formed are $Fe_2(SO_4)_3$, K_2SO_4, $MnSO_4$, and H_2O. Writing the equation and leaving spaces for the factors, we have

$FeSO_4 + K_2Mn_2O_8 + H_2SO_4 =$
$\quad\quad\quad\quad Fe_2(SO_4)_3 + K_2SO_4 + MnSO_4 + H_2O.$

Mn_2 in the first member has 14 bonds;
Mn_2 in the second member has 4 bonds.
$\quad$ Loss $= 10$. Hence $10 FeSO_4$.
Fe in the first member has 2 bonds;
Fe in the second member has 3 bonds.
$\quad$ Gain $= 1$. Hence $1 K_2Mn_2O_8$.

Hence for the completed equation we have

$10 FeSO_4 + K_2Mn_2O_8 + 8H_2SO_4 =$
$\quad\quad\quad\quad 5Fe_2(SO_4)_3 + K_2SO_4 + 2MnSO_4 + 8H_2O.$

EXAMPLE No. 6. Required to construct the equation showing the oxidation of oxalic acid to carbonic acid by potassium permanganate.

The compounds entering into the reaction are H_2O, C_2O_3, $K_2Mn_2O_8$ and H_2SO_4. The compounds formed are CO_2, H_2O, $MnSO_4$, and K_2SO_4. Writing the equation and leaving space for the factors, we have

$H_2O, C_2O_3 + K_2Mn_2O_8 + H_2SO_4 =$
$\quad\quad\quad\quad \overline{CO_2} + K_2SO_4 + MnSO_4 + H_2O.$

Mn_2 in the first member has 14 bonds,
Mn_2 in the second member has 4 bonds.
$\quad$ Loss $= 10$. Hence $10 H_2C_2O_4$.
C_2 in the first member has 6 bonds;
C_2 in the second member has 8 bonds.
$\quad$ Gain $= 2$. Hence $2K_2Mn_2O_8$.

Writing the equation and adjusting the factors for the H_2SO_4 and H_2O, we have

$$10H_2C_2O_4 + 2K_2Mn_2O_8 + 6H_2SO_4 =$$
$$20\overline{CO_2} + 2K_2SO_4 + 4MnSO_4 + 16H_2O.$$

Or the equation may be written (dividing the factors of each member by 2),

$$5H_2C_2O_4 + K_2Mn_2O_8 + 3H_2SO_4 =$$
$$10\overline{CO_2} + K_2SO_4 + 2MnSO_4 + 8H_2O.$$

Testing to see if this is a true equation, we have

	In the First Member.	In the Second Member.
H	16	16
C	10	10
O	40	40
K	2	2
Mn	2	2
S	3	3

Hence it is a true equation.

EXAMPLE NO. 7. Required the construction of an equation representing the oxidation of $MnSO_4$ by $K_2Mn_2O_8$. The compounds entering into the first member are $MnSO_4$, $K_2Mn_2O_8$, and H_2O. Those entering into the second member are MnO_2, K_2SO_4, and H_2SO_4. Writing the equation and leaving spaces for the factors, we have

$$MnSO_4 + K_2Mn_2O_8 + H_2O = MnO_2 + K_2SO_4 + H_2SO_4.$$

By the first method we have

$$MnO + O = MnO_2.$$

Hence 1MnO requires 1O.

$$Mn_2O_2 = 2MnO_2 + O_2.$$

Hence $1K_2Mn_2O_8$ yields 3O. Now as $1MnO$ requires 1O and $1K_2Mn_2O_8$ yields 3O, we find that $1K_2Mn_2O_8$ will oxidize $3MnSO_4$. Hence the equation

$$3MnSO_4 + K_2Mn_2O_8 + 2H_2O = 5MnO_2 + K_2SO_4 + 2H_2SO_4.$$

By the second method,
  Mn in the first member has 2 bonds;
  Mn in the second member has 4 bonds.
   Gain = 2. Hence $2K_2Mn_2O_8$.
  Mn_2 in the first member has 14 bonds;
  Mn_2 in the second member has 8 bonds.
   Loss = 6. Hence $6MnSO_4$.

Hence the equation:

$$6MnSO_4 + 2K_2Mn_2O_8 + 4H_2O = 10MnO_2 + 2K_2SO_4 + 4H_2SO_4,$$

which may be written as above.

CHAPTER II.

STOICHIOMETRY.

STOICHIOMETRY is the arithmetic of chemistry. All that is required to solve the different stoichiometrical problems is a knowledge of chemical reactions and the writing of chemical equations, and a knowledge of the principles of arithmetic. Most of the problems which arise in the course of chemical analysis may be solved by simple proportion.

The solution of the different problems is best illustrated by the following examples:

Calculation of Percentage from Weight.—EXAMPLE NO. 1.—Five grammes of lead ore were taken for assay. A lead button weighing 2.466 gms. was obtained. What is the percentage of lead in the ore?

$$5.0 \text{ (weight taken)} : 2.466 \text{ (weight found)} :: 100 : x;$$
$$x = \text{percentage required} = 49.32.$$

EXAMPLE NO. 2. In the assay of a zinc ore 1.521 gms. were taken and 0.3246 gm. of zinc was obtained. What is the percentage of zinc in the ore?

$$1.521 : 0.3246 :: 100 : x; \quad x = 21.34\%$$

Calculation of Percentage Composition from Chemical Formula.—The relation existing between the combining weights and the percentages of the constituents of a chemical compound is best expressed by a simple proportion in which the first two terms are the combining weights of these constituents and the last two terms the corresponding percentages.

EXAMPLE NO. 3. The formula for barium chloride is $BaCl_2, 2H_2O$; required the percentage of Ba.

We have the proportion

$$243.8 : 136.8 :: 100 : x;$$

or, the combining weight of the compound is to the combining weight of the constituent whose percentage is required as 100 per cent is to the percentage required.

In like manner the solution of the following proportions determines the percentages of Cl and H_2O, respectively:

$$243.8 : 71 :: 100 : x;$$
$$243.8 : 36 :: 100 : x.$$

Ans. $Ba = 56.11\%$; $Cl = 29.12\%$; $H_2O = 14.76\%$.

EXAMPLE NO. 4. The formula for magnesium sulphate is $MgSO_4, 7H_2O$; required its percentage composition in MgO, SO_3, and H_2O. We have the following proportions:

$$246 : 40 :: 100 : x; \quad x = MgO\%.$$
$$246 : 80 :: 100 : x; \quad x = SO_3\%.$$
$$246 : 126 :: 100 : x; \quad x = H_2O\%.$$

Ans. $MgO = 16.26\%$; $SO_3 = 32.52\%$; $H_2O = 51.22\%$.

EXAMPLE NO. 5.—In the analysis of a limestone 1.0 gm. was taken for analysis, and a precipitate of $CaSO_4$ weighing 0.812 gm. was obtained. A precipitate of $Mg_2P_2O_7$ weighing 0.385 was also obtained. What is the percentage composition of the limestone in CaO and MgO?

$136 : 56 :: 0.812 : x; \quad x = 0.334254 =$ weight of CaO; and
$1.0 : 0.334254 :: 100 : x; \quad x = 33.43\%$ CaO.
$222 : 80 :: 0.385 : x; \quad x = 0.139 =$ weight of MgO; and
$1.0 : 0.139 :: 100 : x; \quad x = 13.90\%$ MgO.

EXAMPLE NO. 6. Required the percentages of $CaCO_3$ and $MgCO_3$ corresponding to the percentages of CaO and MgO in Example No. 5.

$$56 : 100 :: 33.43 : x; \quad x = 59.69\% \; CaCO_3.$$
$$40 : 84 :: 13.90 : x; \quad x = 29.19\% \; MgCO_3.$$

EXAMPLE NO. 7. How many grammes of oxygen will it take to convert 50 grammes of carbon into carbonic acid gas? As each part of carbon requires two parts of oxygen, we have the equation

$$12 : 32 :: 50 : x; \quad x = 133.33 \; gms.$$

EXAMPLE NO. 8. How many grammes of silver will 5 grammes of sodium bromide precipitate from a solution of silver in nitric acid? From the equation,

$$AgNO_3 + NaBr = AgBr + NaNO_3$$

we see that 1 part of NaBr will precipitate 1 part of silver; hence the proportion

$$103 : 108 :: 5 : x; \quad x = 5.2427 \; gms. \; Ag.$$

The Calculation of Factors.—In gravimetric analysis the substance to be determined is either separated in a state of purity and its weight is obtained directly (see Examples No. 1 and No. 2), or by the operations of the analysis it is obtained and weighed as a constituent of a compound whose formula is known (see Examples No. 5). By the preceding rule the weight of the constituent sought may be calculated. In Part II factors have been given under the different determinations for the calculation of the weight of the constituent sought from the weight of the compound obtained in the analysis. These factors are derived as follows:

EXAMPLE No. 9. Required the factor for the calculation of S in $BaSO_4$.

As in Examples No. 3 and No. 4, we have the equation

$$232.8 : 32 :: 1 : x; \quad x = 0.13745+,$$

which is the factor for S in $BaSO_4$.

EXAMPLE No. 10. Required the factor for the calculation of Sn in SnO_2.

We have the proportion

$$150 : 118 :: 1 : x; \quad x = 0.78667,$$

which is the factor required.

EXAMPLE No. 11. In the course of an analysis nitrogen is converted into $(NH_4Cl)_2PtCl_4$, which precipitate is ignited and the weight of the resulting platinum is obtained. What factor will give the weight of the N?

As one part Pt is combined with 2 parts N, we have the proportion

$$197 : 28 :: 1 : x; \quad x = 0.14213,$$

which is the factor required.

EXAMPLE No. 12.—What are the factors for MgO and P in $Mg_2P_2O_7$? *Ans.* MgO......0.36036.
P......0.27928.

The Calculation of Formulæ.—The deduction of an empirical formula from the percentage composition is the reverse of the process of calculating percentage composition from formulæ.

Three cases may arise.

First Case.—From the percentages of single elements in compounds.

EXAMPLE NO. 13. Upon analysis a substance was found to contain the following parts in 100:

$$H \dots 2.04$$
$$S \dots 32.65$$
$$O \dots 65.31$$

What is the formula of the substance?

Dividing the percentage of each element by its atomic weight and reducing the quotients, we have

$$H \dots 2.04 \div 1 = 2.04 \div 1.02 = 2$$
$$S \dots 32.65 \div 32 = 1.02 \div 1.02 = 1$$
$$O \dots 65.31 \div 16 = 4.08 \div 1.02 = 4$$

Hence the formula is H_2SO_4.

EXAMPLE NO. 14. Upon analysis a compound yielded the following percentages:

$$C \dots 52.20$$
$$H \dots 13.05$$
$$O \dots 35.00$$

What is its formula?

$$C \dots 52.20 \div 12 = 4.35 \div 4.35 = 1$$
$$H \dots 13.05 \div 1 = 13.05 \div 4.35 = 3$$
$$O \dots 35.00 \div 16 = 2.187 \div 4.35 = 0.502$$

Hence, allowing for error in the analysis, the formula is probably C_2H_6O, which is the formula for ethyl alcohol.

Second Case.—From the percentages of groups of elements in compounds, isomorphous constituents being absent.

It is general in the analysis of oxygen salts to calculate the percentages of oxides and water equivalent in quantity to the elements. The results of an analysis being stated in this manner, the percentages of the different elements may readily be computed, and from these percentages the empirical formula may be calculated by the preceding rule. The same result may be attained by the following shorter course.

EXAMPLE NO. 15.—Upon analysis a substance was found to have the following percentage composition:

H_2O 51.20
SO_3 .... 32.53
MgO 16.24

What is its chemical formula?

Dividing each constituent by its molecular weight and reducing the quotients to their simplest relations in whole numbers, we have

H_2O .... 51.20 ÷ 18 = 2.844+ ÷ 0.4006 = 7.09
SO_3 .... 32.53 ÷ 80 = 0.40066+ ÷ 0.4006 = 1.00
MgO ...... 16.24 ÷ 40 = 0.4006 ÷ 0.4006 = 1.00

Hence, allowing for error in the analysis, the probable rational formula is $MgOSO_3,7H_2O$. Rearranging the order in which the symbols of the elements stand, we have the strictly empirical formula $MgSH_{14}O_{11}$.

Having obtained the empirical formula of a compound, its rational formula may be obtained by making any reasonable supposition regarding its chemical constitution and arranging the atoms conformably. For example, in the above case, allowing 1O to the Mg we have 10O remaining and 14H. Assuming that the H is combined with O as water of crystallization we have $7H_2O$, which still leaves 3O to be combined with the S as SO_3. Hence the formula $MgOSO_3,7H_2O$, or $MgSO_4,7H_2O$.

Third Case.—From the percentages of groups of elements in compounds, isomorphous constituents being present.

In the deduction of formula it should be remembered that closely related radicals may replace each other in all proportions. This is especially true of the basic metals. Generally, elements of like valence are found replacing one another; but in some cases equivalent amounts of elements having different valence replace each other.

EXAMPLE NO. 16. Penfield [*] found by analysis of triphylyte the following composition:

$$P_2O_5 \dots\dots 44.76$$
$$FeO \dots\dots 26.40$$
$$MnO \dots\dots 17.84$$
$$CaO \dots\dots 0.24$$
$$MgO \dots\dots 0.47$$
$$Li_2O \dots\dots 9.36$$
$$Na_2O \dots\dots 0.35$$
$$H_2O \dots\dots 0.42$$
$$\overline{99.84}$$

What is the formula for the mineral?

	Molecular Weights.	Mol. Ratio.		Atomic Ratio.	
P_2O_5	$44.76 \div 142 =$	$.315 \times 2 =$	P	.630	
FeO	$26.40 \div 72 =$	$.366$	= Fe	.366	
MnO	$17.84 \div 71 =$	$.251$	= Mn	.251	$= R'' .633$
CaO	$0.24 \div 56 =$	$.004$	= Ca	.004	
MgO	$0.47 \div 40 =$	$.012$	= Mg	.012	
Li_2O	$9.36 \div 30 =$	$.312 \times 2 =$	Li	.624	$= R' .634$
Na_2O	$0.35 \div 62 =$	$.005 \times 2 =$	Na	.010	
H_2O	0.42		O	2.525	

In this case the small amount of water may be disregarded. The atomic ratio column, with the adjoined symbols, is the empirical formula.

As is to be expected, when isomorphous constituents are present, the number of different atoms are not in any simple ratio. Hence it remains to unite the atoms of such elements as are supposed to be capable of mutually replacing each other, and ascertain if the numbers thus obtained are in any simple proportion. For this purpose let R'' represent one atom of any dyad basic metal and R' one atom of any nomad basic

---

[*]Fresenius, Quantitative Chemical Analysis, p. 847.

metal present. The atomic ratio, obtained as above, is expressed by the formula $R''_{632}R'_{634}P_{630}O_{2626}$, or dividing by 630, almost exactly by $R''R'PO_4$, which is equal to

$$(PO)''' {<}^{O}_{O}{>}R'' ,\ O{-}R'$$

anhydrous normal lithium phosphate in which iron is partially replaced by manganese, magnesium, and calcium; and lithium to a slight extent by sodium.

Omitting oxygen from the above calculation, we have $R''R'P$. Referring to the percentage computation, it is seen that two P require five O; two R' one O; one R'' one O. Doubling $R''R'P$ and appending to each constituent the required oxygen atoms, we have $R'''_2O, R'_2OP_2O_5 = R''_2R'_2P_2O_8 = R''R'PO_4$, as before.

EXAMPLE NO. 17. A lead blast-furnace slag upon analysis gave the following percentage composition:

$$SiO_2 \ldots\ldots\ldots 36.0$$
$$FeO \ldots\ldots\ldots 28.8$$
$$CaO \ldots\ldots\ldots 28.0$$
$$Al_2O_3 \ldots\ldots\ldots 7.6$$
$$\overline{100.4}$$

Required a formula which represents the composition?

Molecular Ratio. Atomic Ratio.
$SiO_2 \ldots\ldots 36.0 \div 60 = .6 \quad SiO_2 \ .6$
$FeO \ldots\ldots 28.8 \div 72 = .4 \quad Fe \ .4$ ⎫
$CaO \ldots\ldots 28.0 \div 56 = .5 \quad Ca \ .5$ ⎬ $R'' \ .9$
$Al_2O_3 \ldots\ldots 7.6 \div 102 = .075 \quad Al \ .15 \quad R''' \ .15$ ⎭

Dividing this atomic ratio by 0.15, we obtain the formula $R_6''R_1'''Si_4$, or $(R_2''O_2)_6(R_2'''O_3)(SiO_2)_4 = (R''O)_{12}(R_2'''O_3)(SiO_2)_8$.

Calculations involved in the Making-up and Use of Volumetric Solutions.—EXAMPLE NO. 18. Required the amount of sodium bromide necessary to add to water in order to make a solution of which 1 cc. will exactly precipitate 0.01 gm. of silver?

From the equation

$$AgNO_3 + NaBr = AgBr + NaNO_3$$

we see that 1 atom of Br precipitates 1 atom of Ag. Hence the proportion

$$108 : 103 :: 0.01 : x; \quad x = 0.009537;$$

108 being the atomic weight of Ag and 103 being the molecular weight of NaBr. Consequently if 1000 cc. is the quantity of standard solution required, weigh out 9.537 gms. of pure dry sodium bromide, dissolve, and dilute to 1000 cc. with distilled water.

EXAMPLE NO. 19. Upon trial of the sodium-bromide solution as made up in the preceding example each cc. was found to only precipitate 0.00956 gm. of Ag. Required the amount of the salt which should be added to 1000 cc. so that each cc. will precipitate exactly 0.01 gm. of Ag? As 9.537 gms. of NaBr were taken in making up 1000 cc. of the solution, we have the proportion

$$0.00956 : 0.01 :: 9.537 : x; \quad x = 9.9759 \text{ gms.},$$

which is the amount of sodium bromide which should have been taken. Hence $9.9759 - 9.537 = 0.4389$ gm. of NaBr to be added to each 1000 cc. of the solution to make it normal.

EXAMPLE NO. 20. An acid solution of ferrous sulphate contains 0.215 gm. of iron. How many cc. of a solution of potassium permanganate containing 0.01 gm. of $K_2Mn_2O_8$ in each cc. will be required to convert the ferrous sulphate to ferric sulphate?

By reference to the equation representing the oxidation (see Part IV, Chapter I) we see that 1 molecule of $K_2Mn_2O_8$ will oxidize 10 molecules of ferrous iron. The molecular weight of 10Fe is 560 and the molecular weight of $1K_2Mn_2O$ is 316.2; hence

$$560 : 316.2 :: 0.215 : x; \quad x = 0.1214.$$

Now, as each cc. of the solution contains 0.01 gm. $K_2Mn_2O_8$ and 0.1214 gm. are required, we will require $\dfrac{0.1214}{0.01} = 12.14$ cc. of the solution.

EXAMPLE NO. 21. A solution of potassium permanganate was found to be of such a strength that each cc. was equivalent to (would oxidize) 0.0093 gm. of iron. What is the value of the solution in terms of manganese?

By reference to the equation for the precipitation of manganese by potassium permanganate (see Part IV, Chapter I) we see that 1 molecule of $K_2Mn_2O_8$ will precipitate 3 atoms of Mn, whilst each molecule of $K_2Mn_2O_8$ will oxidize 10 molecules of Fe. Hence the proportion

$$560 : 165 :: 0.0093 : x; \quad x = 0.00274;$$

560 being the molecular weight of 10Fe and 165 being the molecular weight of 3Mn.

EXAMPLE NO. 22. Having prepared and standardized the following solutions, required the equivalent of the iodine solution in terms of sulphur:

A solution of potassium bichromate of which 1 cc. = 0.005 gm. Fe.

As 1 equivalent of $K_2Cr_2O_7$ oxidizes 6 equivalents of Fe, we have the proportion

$$336 : 294.5 :: 0.005 : x; \quad x = 0.004382;$$

or, each cc. of the bichromate solution contains 0.004382 gm. of $K_2Cr_2O_7$.

A solution of iodide of potassium was prepared by dissolving 1 gm. of pure KI in 300 cc. of water and 5 cc. of HCl. To this solution 25 cc. of the bichromate solution was added.

Now, as 294.5 parts of $K_2Cr_2O_7$ will liberate 761.1 equivalents of iodine (see Part II, Chapter II), we have the proportion

$$294.5 : 761.1 :: 0.10955 : x; \quad x = 0.28312;$$

or, the 25 cc. of bichromate will liberate 0.28312 gm. of iodine.

Upon the addition of sodium-hyposulphite solution to this solution containing 0.28312 gm. of free iodine, 24 cc. were required to decolorize the solution. Hence each cc. of the hyposulphite solution contains sufficien $NaHS_2O_3$ to react on 0.0118 gm. of iodine.

Ten cc. of the hyposulphite solution were then drawn off, diluted with water, a few drops of starch solution were added, and the iodine solution to be standardized was run in until the blue color was destroyed, 20 cc. being used.

As 10 cc. of the hyposulphite solution would react on 0.1180 gm. of iodine, each cc. of the iodine solution contains 0.0059 gm. of iodine. From the equation

$$H_2S + 2I = 2HI + S$$

we have the proportion

$$253.7 : 32 :: 0.0059 : x; \quad x = 0.000744;$$

or, each cc. of the iodine solution is equivalent to 0.000744 gm. S.

Calculation of the Results of Indirect Analyses.—EXAMPLE NO. 23. In the analysis of a mineral containing both calcium and strontium the Ca and Sr were separated, converted into $CaCO_3$ and $SrCO_3$, and the mixed carbonates were weighed together. Subsequently the carbonic acid was determined. The weight of the mixed carbonate was 0.935 gm. and the weight of the carbonic acid which the mixed carbonates contained was 0.362 gm. Required the corresponding weights of CaO and SrO.

Mol. Wt. CO_2. Mol. Wt. $SrCO_3$.   Wt. CO_2.
44   :   147.5   ::   0.362   : x; $x = 1.21352$.

If, therefore, the whole of the carbonic acid were combined with strontia, the weight of the carbonate would be 1.21352 gms. The difference (1.21352 − 0.935) = 0.27852 is proportional to the calcium carbonate present, which is calculated as follows:

The difference between the molecular weight of $SrCO_3$ and the molecular weight of $CaCO_3$ (47.5) is to the molecular weight of $CaCO_3$ (100) as the difference found is to the calcium carbonate contained in the mixed salt; or,

$$47.5 : 100 :: 0.27852 : x; \quad x = 0.5864.$$

Therefore the mixture contains 0.5864 gm. $CaCO_3$ and 0.3486 gm. $SrCO_3$.

Calculations involved in the Analysis of Gases.—*Reduction of the Volume to what it would be in the Normal State.*— The tension, and therefore the volume of the gas, depends upon: The pressure; the temperature; the state of moisture.

Gases are measured in their condition at the time at which the measurement is made; that is, at the atmospheric pressure as indicated by the barometer and at the temperature as indicated by the thermometer, and, as the confining liquid is generally water, in a state of complete saturation with moisture. Hence it is necessary to reduce the volume of the gas, as measured under known but varying conditions, to the volume which it would have at the normal barometric pressure of 760 millimetres, at the normal temperature of 0° C., and in the dry state.

According to Boyle's law, the volume of a gas varies inversely as to the pressure to which it is subjected. If

$V_0 = $ the volume at the normal pressure sought;
$V = $ the volume at the barometric pressure B;
$B = $ the state of the barometer at the time of the observation,—we have

$$V_0 = \frac{VB}{760}.$$

The expansion by heat of a gas is $\frac{1}{273}$ of its volume at 0° for each degree C.

Hence, if a gas measures 273 cc. at 0° C., it will measure $273 + t$ cc. at $t°$ C. If

$V_0 =$ the volume of the gas at the normal temperature;
$V =$ the volume of the gas at the temperature t;
$t =$ the temperature at the time of observation,—we have

$$V_0 = V \frac{273}{273 + t}.$$

If a gas is saturated with moisture by contact with water, it always takes up the same quantity of water under the same conditions. This water is itself transformed into the gaseous state, and exerts a certain pressure called *the tension of aqueous vapor*. This tension of the aqueous vapor increases as the temperature increases. This tension has been determined experimentally (see Tables), and must be deducted from the observed barometric pressure in each determination.

If $B - f =$ the corrected barometric pressure, we have the following formula, which embraces all corrections:

$$V_0 = \frac{V \times 273 \times (B - f)}{(273 + t) \times 760}. \quad \ldots \quad \text{(A)}$$

The reduction of the volume of a gas to the normal state may be omitted in cases where only approximate results are required, and also in determinations which are made rapidly, as material changes of pressure and temperature are not to be expected.

To reduce the volume of a gas from the normal state to that which it would occupy at a different pressure and temperature, and in a state of complete saturation with moisture, we have the equation

$$V = \frac{V_0(273 + t)760}{273(B - f)}. \quad \ldots \quad \text{(B)}$$

EXAMPLE NO. 24. A gas measured over water occupied a volume of 100 cc., the barometric pressure being 730 mm. and the temperature being 25° C. What will be its volume at 760 mm. and 0° C.?

Substituting in formula A, we have

$$\frac{100 \times 273 \times (730 - 23.58)}{(273 + 25) \times 760} = 85.15 \text{ cc.}$$

EXAMPLE NO. 25. The volume of a dry gas at 760 mm. pressure and 0° C. was 100 cc. What volume would it occupy if saturated with moisture at a temperature of 40° C. and 740 mm. barometric pressure?

Substituting in formula B, we have

$$\frac{100(273 + 40)760}{273(740 - 55)} = 127.2 \text{ cc.}$$

Calculation of Percentage by Weight from the Volume.—Having measured the volume of the gas and reduced this volume to the normal state (Examples No. 24 and No. 25), its percentage by weight may be obtained by means of Table IV, showing the absolute weight of gases (Tables).

EXAMPLE NO. 26. What is the percentage by weight of nitrogen in a substance of which 1.0 gm. yielded 40 cc. of dry nitrogen gas at 0° C. and 760 mm. barometer?

By Table IV we see that 1000 cc. of dry nitrogen at 0° C. and 760 mm. weighs 1.2562 gms.; hence

$$1000 : 1.2562 :: 40 : x; \quad x = 0.05025 \text{ gms.};$$

and

$$1.0 : 0.05025 :: 100 : x; \quad x = 5.025\% \text{ N.}$$

EXAMPLE NO. 27. One gramme of a substance upon analysis yielded 150 cc. of carbonic-acid gas, the gas being measured at 22° C. and 750 mm. barometer. What is the percentage of carbon in the substance?

Substituting in equation A, we have

$$v_0 = \frac{150(273 \times 730.3)}{(273 + 22)760} = 134.05 \text{ cc.}$$

STOICHIOMETRY.   335

By Table IV we find that 1000 cc. of dry CO_2 in the normal state weighs 1.9663 gms.; hence

$$1000 : 1.9663 :: 134.05 : x; \quad x = 0.2636 \text{ gm.};$$

and

$$1.0 : 0.2636 :: 100 : x; \quad x = 26.36\% \ CO_2;$$

and

$$44 : 12 :: 26.36 : x; \quad x = 7.18\% \ C.$$

When the percentages of the different gases are determined by volume (see Part III, Chapter XI), the calculation will be as follows, no corrections for barometric pressure, temperature, etc., being necessary:

Analysis of Coal Gas.

Volume of Gas employed, 100 cc.

A. *Estimation of the Absorbable Constituents.*

After absorption with caustic potash............	98.6 cc.	
Decrease of volume..................	1.4 "	= 1.4 volume per cent of carbon dioxide.
After absorption by bromine water and removal of the bromine vapor by caustic potash......	94.8 "	
Decrease............................	3.8 "	= 3.8 per cent ethylene, propylene, butylene.
After absorption by fuming nitric acid and removal of the nitrous fumes by caustic potash.	93.8 "	
Decrease............................	1.0 "	= 1.0 per cent benzine vapor.
After absorption by potassium pyrogallate.....	93.5 "	
Decrease........	0.3 "	= 0.3 per cent oxygen.
After absorption by cuprous chloride..........	87.0 "	
Decrease............................	6.5 "	= 6.5 per cent carbon monoxide.
Non-absorbable remainder...................	87.0 "	

B. Estimation of the Hydrogen and Methane.

A portion of the unabsorbable remainder is now drawn off into a eudiometer, mixed with oxygen, and exploded.

Volume of unabsorbable remainder drawn off into
eudiometer (corresponding to 35 cc. of the original gas)... 30.5 cc.
Volume before explosion (57 cc. of oxygen added).. 87.5 "
Volume after explosion............................. 50.0 "
Decrease (H_2O)................................... 37.5 "
Corresponding to hydrogen......................... 25.0 "
Oxygen.. 12.5 "
Volume after absorption of carbon dioxide with
   potassic hydrate................................ 43.0 "
Decrease (CO_2).................................. 7.0 "
Corresponding to carbon............................ 2.33 "
   "   " oxygen................................. 4.66 "
Oxygen added...................................... 57.00 "
Oxygen combined as water and carbon dioxide
   (12.50 + 4.66)................................. 17.16 "
Oxygen remaining after treatment.................. 39.84 "
Volume of oxygen and nitrogen remaining after
   treatment..................................... 43.00 "
Nitrogen (43.00 − 39.84).......................... 3.16 " = 9.03% nitrogen
Carbon calculated to methane (CH_4)............. 11.65 " = 33.28% methane
Total hydrogen .... 25.00 "
Less hydrogen calculated to methane............... 9.32 "
Hydrogen.. 15.68 " = 44.80% hydrogen

CHAPTER III.

THE CALCULATION OF LEAD BLAST-FURNACE CHARGES.

THE calculation of a lead blast-furnace charge is a more or less complex problem, owing to the many different points which have to be taken into consideration. Consideration must be given to the following:

First. The charge must be calculated so as to produce a slag which will be good from both a metallurgical and an economic standpoint. A good metallurgical slag is one which is fusible, is adapted to the ores to be treated, should keep the furnace in good condition, should allow of a good separation of matte and speisse from the slag, and should be low in both lead and silver. An economic slag is one which will fulfil the above conditions and at the same time allow an economic mixture of the ores to be treated and require a minimum amount of costly flux. For example, at the present smelting centres of the West the majority of the ores received are dry silicious ores, and these are the ores in which there is the largest margin of profit. Lead, iron, and lime are necessary fluxes which have to be added to the charge to produce the proper amount of bullion and the proper slag, and these fluxes are more or less costly, as they have to be purchased at a price which allows little or nothing for smelting, and for every pound of flux added to the charge one pound less of ore, in which there is a profit, can be added. The amount of time, fuel, labor, etc., expended in smelting a pound of flux is the same as that expended in smelting a pound of ore. The following table gives the different type slags which are good metallurgical slags.

Slag A is a good slag, which has been used in Utah and elsewhere for several years. It is especially adapted to ores carrying considerable alumina. This slag cannot be successfully made with impure ores having a high percentage of zinc.

Slag B is a favorite slag with Utah smelters, and is one of the best slags which we have, being more fusible and driving faster than A. This slag is not adapted to ores containing high percentages of zinc.

TABLE OF TYPE SLAGS.

Notation.	SiO_2. Per Cent.	FeO. Per Cent.	CaO. Per Cent.	ZnO. Per Cent.
A	35	28	28	
B	34	34	24	
C	34	34	17	7
D	30	40	20	
E	30	48	12	
F	28 to 30	54	6	

Slag C is a favorite type with Colorado smelters, as it runs well with high zinc charges, which is generally the rule in Colorado. As the per cent of zinc on the charge decreases the per cent of lime is raised, the slag more nearly approaching type B in composition. Types B and C really belong to the same general type, and are very similar in many of their physical properties.

Type D is a most excellent slag, generally known as "the half slag." This slag was formerly much used by Colorado and Utah smelters, but owing to the scarcity of iron in the ores of late years it is seldom used now.

Slag E is what is generally known as "the quarter slag," and was much used in the early days of smelting in Utah and Leadville when the ores were generally oxidized ores carrying a high per cent of ferric oxide. It is a most excellent slag, and answers all metallurgical purposes, but can only be run in exceptional cases owing to the prevailing scarcity of iron in the ores.

Slag F is not as good a slag as any of the foregoing, and is only to be recommended in certain rare and isolated places where there is a large excess of iron in the ores, and silicious ores are not available.

In all of the above types the sum of the SiO_2, FeO, and CaO is considered as making about 90 per cent of the slag constituents. This will be found to be the case except when the ores contain much ZnO and Al_2O_3, MnO being considered as FeO and MgO and BaO as CaO. Up to certain limits MnO will satisfactorily replace FeO, and the same may be said of MgO and BaO as regards CaO. Too much MnO (above 7 per cent or 8 per cent) seems to have a tendency to carry silver into the slag and too much MgO or BaO (above 4 per cent or 5 per cent in high lime slags) has a tendency to render the slags more infusible and pasty, and is liable to cause trouble in the furnace.

Second. The charges must be calculated with regard to the ore supply on hand, and what may be expected from the daily receipts of ore; that is, the products of the roasting and fusing furnaces, and the raw smelting ore coming to the works, must be used in about the proportions in which they exist, so as to not have a surplus of certain ores or products on hand. Hence the metallurgist must keep posted as to the condition of the ore market, and the ore-buyer must keep posted as to the requirements of the metallurgist.

Third. The charge must not only be so calculated that we will have a sufficient amount of lead on the charge, but also so that the bullion will be of the proper grade. In the early days of smelting in this country a 20-per-cent lead-charge was not unusual, while at the present time a 12-per-cent charge may be stated as the average charge. As low as a 6-per-cent lead charge has been successfully smelted, but for good work, on fairly high-grade bullion, 10 per cent may be considered as the limit. A charge of over 12 per cent is rarely permissible in the Western smelting centres on account of the scarcity of lead and its high cost as a flux. The grade of the bullion must be taken into account, as, for example, some refiners will not pay for gold in the bullion if it is less than 1 ounce per ton, and gold ores are frequently scarce. The smelters generally pay for 95 per cent of all the gold in ores which assay over 0.1 ounce per ton. Also, on account of freight rates and refining charges many smelters are required to keep the silver contents of the bullion within rather narrow limits, as, for example, not below 250 nor above 300 ounces per ton. Account must also be taken of the silver and lead losses in smelting, the amount of silver and lead which goes into the matte, and the amount of silver and lead which goes into the flue-dust, in determining the amount of bullion which should be produced. No exact rule can be given for determining these points, as they will differ according to the individual practice of the works, and can only be settled by the actual results at any particular works.

Fourth. In addition to the slag and bullion-making elements present in the charge, we have such elements as sulphur and arsenic, part of which elements go to make matte and speisse (a small amount also passing into the bullion), and part are volatilized in the furnace. The composition of pure iron matte is FeS, but as the furnace-matte invariably contains Cu, Ag, Pb, Zn, and other constituents of the charge, its composition is variable. The composition of speisse varies from Fe_4As to Fe_7As when pure; but it almost always contains Cu, Co, Ni, etc. Hence no exact rule can be given for the allowance of iron to be made for the sulphur and arsenic on the charge. Just what the composition of the matte and speisse will be, and what the loss of sulphur and arsenic will be, will depend on the character of the ores under treatment and the working of the furnace. These points can only be determined by actual practice in each individual case. A rule which answers very well (until a more reliable one can be formed based upon the actual results from the working of the furnace) is to allow sufficient iron to convert one half of the sulphur on the charge into FeS. For arsenic allow sufficient iron to convert all the arsenic on the charge into Fe_5As. As the smelting of sulphide and arsenical ores is now usually preceded by roasting, the amount of S or As on the charge will not be very large.

In the case of ores containing copper, which is almost always present, the charge must contain sufficient sulphur to convert all of the copper into matte, as otherwise there will be trouble with the lead-well and hearth of the furnace.

Fifth. The size of the charge and the amount of fuel must be taken into consideration. The size of the charge will depend, to a great extent, upon the size of the furnace. A usual charge is from 700 to 1000 pounds—the latter being a very convenient ore-and-flux charge for a modern, large-sized blast-furnace. In making up a charge, the total weight will frequently run under or over the weight which is desirable, but as the question is simply one of proportion the desired total weight can be obtained by increasing or reducing the weight of each ore, the limestone, etc., by 0.1, 0.2, or whatever proportion will give the desired weight. The weight of fuel to be used will depend upon the character of the charge, the fusibility of the slag, the altitude of the place at which the smelter is situated, the character of the coke and charcoal, and the dimensions of the furnace. The fuel is usually spoken of as such a per cent of fuel, which per cent may vary from 12 to 24. This per cent is such a per cent of the total weight of the ore and flux exclusive of whatever slag, from previous operations, may be on the charge, unless the amount of slag is large, when some fuel must be allowed for it. The amount of sulphur on the charge will affect the fuel-charge, as some of the sulphur will act as a fuel. The amount of lead will also affect the amount of fuel necessary, as high lead-charges will require considerably less fuel than low lead-charges. As an example of the effect of altitude, at Leadville (10,000 feet above sea-level) from 20 to 22 per cent of fuel is necessary, whilst at Denver (5000 feet above sea-level) 15 to 17 per cent is the usual charge, the ores and fuels in both cases being practically the same. The character of the fuel will make a considerable difference, as, if the coke is poor and friable, there will be considerable waste in handling, and in the furnace, for which allowance must be made. The amount of ash which the fuel contains and its composition will also have to be taken into consideration. In the winter, when the coke is apt to be damp from snow and rain, allowance must be made for the moisture by allowing an increased weight of coke.

The above percentages of fuel are based upon a good, hard, dry coke, containing about 10 per cent of ash, which contains from 55 to 65 per cent of silica. High lime-slags, and especially those which contain much baryta, will require a slight increase in the per cent of fuel.

From the above it will be seen that to calculate a charge the first step is to assume the different ores and their amounts which we will have on the charge, due consideration being given to the above points when making this assumption. The second step is to find the total amounts of silica, ferrous oxide, lime, etc., in the weights of ore as assumed, which is accomplished by multiplying the weight of each ore by its per cent of silica, ferrous oxide, etc., and taking the sum of the different weights; a convenient way being to tabulate the results as illustrated in the examples.

If we assume the following notations for the totals and percentages: $A =$ pounds of SiO_2 in the ores (total); $B =$ pounds of FeO in the ores (total); $C =$ pounds of CaO in the ores (total); $d =$ per cent of SiO_2 which the iron ore (iron-flux to be added) contains; $e =$ per cent of SiO_2 which the limestone (lime-flux to be added) contains; $f =$ per cent of FeO in the iron ore; $l =$ per cent of CaO in the limestone; $X =$ pounds of iron-ore required, and $Y =$ pounds of limestone required, we have for slag A

$$\frac{28}{35}(A + Xd + Ye) = B + Xf$$

or

$$\frac{4}{5}(A + Xd + Ye) = B + Xf, \quad \ldots \quad (1)$$

and

$$C + Yl = B + Xf. \quad \ldots \quad (2)$$

CALCULATION OF LEAD BLAST-FURNACE CHARGES. 343

Solving equation (2) with respect to Y, we have

$$Y = \frac{B + Xf - C}{l}. \quad \ldots \ldots \text{(A')}$$

Substituting this value of Y in equation (1), we have

$$\frac{4}{5}\left(A + Xd + \frac{Be + Xef - Ce}{l}\right) = B + Xf.$$

Reducing and transposing, we have

$$5Xfl - 4Xef - 4Xdl = 4Al + 4Be - 4Ce - 5Bl.$$

Solving with respect to X, we have

$$X = \frac{4Al + 4Be - 4Ce - 5Bl}{5fl - 4ef - 4dl}. \quad \ldots \ldots \text{(A)}$$

For slag B we have

$$A + Xd + Ye = B + Xf, \quad \ldots \ldots \text{(1)}$$

$$\frac{24}{34}(B + Xf) = C + Yl. \quad \ldots \ldots \text{(2)}$$

Solving equation (2), with respect to Y, we have

$$Y = \frac{12B + 12Xf - 17C}{17l}. \quad \ldots \quad \text{(B')}$$

Substituting this value for Y in equation (1), reducing and solving, we have

$$X = \frac{17Al + 12Be - 17Ce - 17Bl}{17fl - 12ef - 17dl}. \quad \ldots \text{(B)}$$

In like manner we obtain for slag C

$$X = \frac{2Al + Be - 2Bl - 2Ce}{2fl - ef - 2dl}, \quad \ldots \quad (C)$$

$$Y = \frac{B + Xf - 2C}{2l}; \quad \ldots \quad (C')$$

and in like manner for slag D,

$$X = \frac{4Al + 2Be - 3Bl - 4Ce}{4fl - 2ef - 4dl}, \quad \ldots \quad (D)$$

$$Y = \frac{B + Xf - 2C}{2l}; \quad \ldots \quad (D')$$

and in like manner for slag E,

$$X = \frac{8Al + 2Be - 5Bl - 8Ce}{5fl - 2fe - 8dl}, \quad \ldots \quad (E)$$

$$Y = \frac{B + Xf - 4C}{4l}; \quad \ldots \quad (E')$$

and in like manner for slag F,

$$X = \frac{9Al + Be - 5Bl - 9Ce}{5fl - 9dl - fe}, \quad \ldots \quad (F)$$

$$Y = \frac{B + Xf - 9C}{9l}. \quad \ldots \quad (F')$$

In like manner general equations may be deduced for any type of slag which it is desired to make.

Having obtained the above formulæ it is only necessary to substitute for A, B, C, d, etc., their proper equivalents in the first formula to obtain X. Having obtained X, substitute its value, together with the proper equivalents of $B, f, C,$ and l, in the second formula to obtain Y.

The calculation of a charge is best illustrated by the following examples:

CALCULATION OF LEAD BLAST-FURNACE CHARGES. 345

EXAMPLE NO. 1. We have 50 tons per day of fused ore, 80 tons per day of roasted ore and matte, a bed of 2000 tons of ore which it is desirable to smelt in about two weeks, and a supply of silicious silver ore which it is desirable to smelt as rapidly as possible. In addition we have a regular supply of iron ore, limestone, and coke. The analyses of the ores are as follows:

	Per Ct. SiO_2.	Per Ct. FeO.	Per Ct. CaO.	Per Ct. Al_2O_3.	Per Ct. Zn.	Per Ct. Cu.	Per Ct. Pb.	Per Ct. S.	Oz. per T. Ag.	Oz. perT. Au.
Fused.....	30	30	....	....	8	....	15	3	50.0	1.00
Roasted...	10	30	....	....	8	6	20	5	40.0	0.50
Bed.......	28	21	4	4	5	....	21	2	55.0	0.50
Silver. ...	90	6	....	....	....	....	....	....	100.0	....
Iron Ore..	10	75	....	....	....	....	....	....	....	....
Limestone	5	....	50	....	....	....	....	....	....	....
Coke*.....	5	....	2	3	....	....	....	....	....	....

* Ash = 10 per cent.

Suppose we assume that we will smelt the ores in the same proportions as we have them on hand and smelt 50 pounds of silicious silver ore per charge, and use 150 pounds of coke for a 1000 charge. A convenient method is to tabulate the results as follows:

Ore.	Lbs. per Charge.	Lbs. SiO_2.	Lbs. FeO.	Lbs. CaO.	Lbs. Al_2O_3	Lbs. Zn.	Lbs. Cu.	Lbs. Pb.	Lbs S.	Oz. Ag.	Oz. Au.
Fused......	100	30	30	....	....	8	....	15	3	2.50	0.05
Roasted....	160	16	48	....	....	12.8	9.6	32	8	4.20	0.04
Bed........	300	84	63	12	12	15	....	63	6	8.25	0.045
Silver......	50	45	3	....	....	....	....	....	....	2.50	....
Coke.......	150	7.5	....	3	4.5	....	....	....	....	....	....
Total....	760	182.5	144	15	16.5	35.8	9.6	110	17	17.45	0.135

Calculating one half of the sulphur to Cu_2S and FeS, we have: 126.8 (mol. wt. of 2Cu) : 158.8 (mol. wt. of Cu_2S) :: 9.6 (lbs. Cu) : x (lbs. of Cu_2S); $x = 12$.

Hence $12 - 9.6 = 2.4$ lbs. of S which the Cu present will take up. Now $\frac{1}{2}17 - 2.4 = 6.1$ lbs. S to be taken up by Fe.

Hence 32 (at. wt. S) : 88 (mol. wt. FeS) :: 6.1 : x (lbs. of FeS which will be produced by excess of S); $x = 16.7$. Hence $16.7 - 6.1 = 10.6$ lbs. of Fe necessary to take up excess of S. The following gives the amount of FeO to be deducted from the total pounds of FeO on the charge on account of sulphur, $10.6 \times \frac{9}{7} = 13.6$, and $144.0 - 13.6 = 130.4$ lbs. of FeO available.

From an inspection of the above totals slag "C" appears to be an economical and good slag to make. Substituting in equations (C) and (C') we have

$$X = \frac{(2 \times 182.5 \times .5) + (130.4 \times .05) - (2 \times 130.4 \times .5) - (2 \times 15 \times .05)}{(2 \times .75 \times .5) - (.75 \times .05) - (2 \times .1 \times .5)} = 93.2;$$

$$Y = \frac{130.4 + (93.2 \times .75) - (2 \times 15)}{2 \times .5} = 170.3.$$

As some of the zinc is volatilized, some passes into the bullion and matte, and some goes into the wall accretions of the furnace, it is necessary to assume what amount will pass into the slag. If we assume that 80 per cent of the zinc passes into the slag as ZnO, we will have 35.6 pounds of zinc oxide available as slag-making material. In order to calculate the percentage composition of the slag, which will result from the above charge, it will be necessary to calculate the pounds of SiO_2, FeO, CaO, etc., in the weights of iron ore and limestone on the charge as determined above, and add these weights to the above weights of available SiO_2, FeO, CaO, ZnO, and Al_2O_3 to obtain the total weight of slag-making material on the charge. Making this calculation, we have 200.3 (pounds SiO_2) + 200.3 (pounds FeO) + 100 (pounds CaO) + 35.6 (pounds ZnO) + 16.5 (pounds Al_2O_3) = 552.7. As these elements will not make up the total composition of the slag, it always carrying S, Pb, etc., it will be necessary to assume what proportion of the slag it will make up. If we assume that these elements will make 97 per cent (an assumption which will usually be very near the actual results) we will have

$$SiO_2 = \frac{200.3 \times 97}{552.7} = 35.17 \text{ per cent,}$$

$$\text{FeO} = \frac{200.3 \times 97}{552.7} = 35.17 \text{ per cent,}$$

$$\text{CaO} = \frac{100 \times 97}{552.7} = 17.55 \text{ per cent,}$$

$$\text{ZnO} = \frac{35.6 \times 97}{552.7} = 6.24 \text{ per cent,}$$

$$\text{Al}_2\text{O}_3 = \frac{16.5 \times 97}{552.7} = 2.89 \text{ per cent,}$$

which shows the calculation to be nearly correct for the type of slag chosen. The amount of lead on the charge is usually spoken of as so many per cent, referring to the total ore and flux charge. The following is the calculation of the lead on the above charge:

$$\frac{110 \ (\textit{pounds of lead}) \times 100}{873.5 \ (\textit{pounds of ore and flux})} = 12.6 \text{ per cent.}$$

In order to arrive at the amount of bullion and matte which should be produced and its assay value, it would be necessary to assume the following:

First. The amount of the charge which will pass into the flue-dust. This will depend upon the amount of fine material on the charge, the pressure of the blast, the height of the furnace, and the condition and working of the furnace.

Second. The losses in lead, silver, and gold in smelting (by volatilization and in the slag). These will depend upon the character of the ores and composition of the slag and the working of the furnace.

Third. The amount of lead, silver, and gold which will pass into the matte. These will depend upon the character of the slag, the per cent and character of the fuel, and the working of the furnace.

All of these are variable, and will not only vary at different works, but will vary from time to time at any works, owing to the changes in the ores, the working of the furnaces, etc.

After a works has been in operation some time, reasonably close constants may be deduced for these variables from the actual results obtained in smelting.

In the above example, suppose we assume that 2 per cent of the charge will pass into the flue-dust; that the silver loss in smelting is 3 per cent; that the lead loss in smelting is 8 per cent; that the gold loss in smelting is nothing (it is usually unnecessary to make any allowance for loss in gold, as a works will usually produce more gold than is purchased, owing to the fact that many of the ores contain small quantities of gold which are not taken into account, and other causes); that the matte will carry about 10 per cent of lead, and that the lead passing into the matte will carry with it the same proportion of silver and gold as the lead in the bullion contains. Then, if the Cu_2S, FeS, and Pb make up 90 per cent of the matte, we will have

110 — 9 (loss in smelting) = 101 pounds of lead.

101 — 2 (amount passing into the flue-dust) = 99 pounds of lead.

17.45 — 0.5235 (loss in smelting) = 16.9265 ounces of silver.

16.9265 — 0.3385 (amount passing into the flue-dust) = 16.588 ounces of silver; and 0.135 — 0.0027 = 0.1323 ounces of gold available for matte and bullion.

The composition of the matte will be Cu_2S, 12 pounds; FeS, 16.7 pounds; Pb, 3.6 pounds. Balance (10 per cent), 3.6 pounds. Total = 35.9 pounds.

$$\frac{16.588 \times 3.6}{99} = 0.6032 \text{ ounce Ag in matte};$$

$$\frac{0.1323 \times 3.6}{99} = 0.00481 \text{ ounce Au in matte}.$$

The assay value of the matte in ounces per ton of 2000 pounds will be

$$\frac{0.6032 \times 2000}{35.9} = 33.6 \text{ oz. Ag, and } \frac{0.00481 \times 2000}{35.9} = 0.27 \text{ oz. Au.}$$

The following calculation gives the amount of bullion which should be produced and its assay value:

$$16.588 - 0.6032 = 15.9848 \text{ ounces Ag in bullion,}$$

and

$$0.1323 - 0.00481 = 0.12749 \text{ ounces Au in bullion.}$$

$$(990 - 3.6) + \frac{15.98 + 0.127}{14.58} = 96.51 \text{ lbs. of bullion}$$

which should be produced. The assay value in ounces per ton of 2000 pounds will be

$$\frac{15.9848 \times 2000}{96.51} = 331.2 \text{ oz. Ag,}$$

and

$$\frac{0.12749 \times 2000}{96.51} = 2.64 \text{ oz. Au.}$$

The total pounds of ore and flux on the charge is 873.5. If we desire a 1000-pound charge, this weight is too small by about 15 per cent. Increasing the weight of each ore, the iron ore and limestone by 15 per cent, we have, for the charge, fused ore, 115 pounds; roasted ore, 184 pounds; bed, 345 pounds; silver-ore, 62.5 pounds; iron ore, 107.2 pounds, and limestone, 194.9 pounds.

As it is usual to set the furnace scales only to every 5 pounds difference in weight, the charge would be—

	Pounds.
Fused ore,	115
Roasted ore,	185
Bed,	345
Silver ore,	65
Iron ore,	110
Limestone,	195
	1015
Coke (15 per cent of 1015),	150

As the analyses are made on the dry ore, allowance must be made in making up the charge for the moisture which the ores contain. In the above example the only ores liable to contain sufficient moisture to require allowance for it are the bed and the iron ore. Allowance would be made in the case of these two ores by adding such a number of pounds as the moisture determinations, made from time to time, show to be necessary.

EXAMPLE NO. 2. Suppose we have the following ores:

Ore.	Tons on Hand.	Pr. Ct. SiO_2.	Pr. Ct. FeO.	Pr. Ct. CaO.	Pr. Ct. Al_2O_3	Pr. Ct. ZnO.	Pr. Ct. Pb.	Pr. Ct. S.	Pr. Ct. Cu.	Oz. per T. Ag.	Oz. per T. Au.
A..........	600	25.0	20.9	5.0	5.0	6.0	20.0	3.0		30.0	0.05
B..........	200	90.0	7.9							100.0	0.50
C..........	200	15.0	30.0		3.0	10.0	15.0	6.0	5.0	20.0	0.50
D..........	regular supply	20.0	45.0				15.0			8.0	
Limestone..	"	5.0		50.0							
Iron ore...	"	5.0	80.0								
Coke......	"	6.0			4.0						

If we smelt the ores in the proportions in which we have them on hand and use ore D for iron-flux, we have

Ore.	Lbs per Charge.	Lbs. SiO_2.	Lbs. FeO.	Lbs. CaO.	Lbs. Al_2O_3	Lbs. ZnO.	Lbs. S.	Lbs. Cu.	Lbs. Pb.	Oz. Ag.	Oz. Au.
A....	300	75	62.7	15	15	18	9		60	4.50	0.00750
B....	100	90	7.9							5.00	0.02500
C....	100	15	30.0		3	10	6	5	15	1.00	0.02500
Coke..	150	9			6						
Total......	189	100.6	15	24	28	15	5	75	10.5	0.05750

Calculating one half the sulphur to Cu_2S and FeS, we have 86.2 pounds available FeO. Assuming that 80 per cent of the ZnO passes into the slag and adding this to the CaO, we have for available combined CaO and ZnO 37.4 pounds. Substituting in equations (B) and (B'), we have

$$X = \frac{(17 \times 189 \times 0.5) + (12 \times 86.2 \times 0.05) - (17 \times 37.4 \times 0.05) - (17 \times 86.2 \times 0.5)}{(17 \times 0.45 \times 0.5) - (12 \times 0.05 \times 0.45) - (17 \times 0.2 \times 0.5)} = 480.7$$

$$Y = \frac{(12 \times 86.2) + (12 \times 480.7 \times 0.45) - (17 \times 37.4)}{17 \times 0.5} = 352.2$$

CALCULATION OF LEAD BLAST-FURNACE CHARGES.

From the above we have 10.8 per cent of lead on the charge, and allowing for a 10-per-cent lead loss and a 4-per-cent silver loss in smelting, the bullion should assay about 182.7 ounces of silver and 0.88 ounce of gold per ton of 2000 pounds.

Taking the sum of the pounds of ore and limestone on the charge, we have a total of 1333 pounds, which is about 25 per cent too much if we wish a 1000-pound charge.

Reducing the weights by 25 per cent, we have, for the corrected charge,

	Pounds.
Ore A,	225
Ore B,	75
Ore C,	75
Ore D,	360
Limestone,	265
	1000
Coke,	150

EXAMPLE No. 3. Suppose we have assumed the number of pounds of several ores which we will smelt on a charge, and have figured out the total pounds of SiO_2, FeO, etc. The totals are as follows:

Lbs. SiO_2.	Lbs. FeO.	Lbs. CaO.	Lbs. Al_2O_3.	Lbs. ZnO.	Lbs. Cu.	Lbs. Pb.	Lbs. S.	Oz. Ag.	Oz. Au.
211	177	54.5	30.5	12.	7.5	111	17.5	19.25	0.1075

Assuming that one half of the S passes into the matte as FeS and Cu_2S, we have 161.3 pounds of FeO available for slag. We have, for fluxing, iron ore containing SiO_2 5 per cent, FeO 80 per cent; and limestone containing SiO_2 5 per cent, and CaO 50 per cent. Slags A, B, or D are all good slags for the above charge. If we prefer to run slag A, we have by substitution in equations (A) and (A′)

$$X = \frac{(4 \times 211 \times 0.5)+(4 \times 161.3 \times 0.05)-(4 \times 54.5 \times 0.05)-(5 \times 161.3 \times 0.5)}{(5 \times 0.8 \times 0.5)-(4 \times 0.05 \times 0.8)-(4 \times 0.05 \times 0.5)} = 17.5,$$

$$Y = \frac{161.3 + (17.5 \times 0.8) - 54.5}{0.5} = 241.6.$$

Hence we would require 17.5 pounds of iron ore and 241.6 pounds of limestone to flux the charge.

EXAMPLE NO. 4. We have on a charge, before fluxing, a total of available pounds as follows: SiO_2 200, FeO 160, and CaO 40.

Iron ore containing SiO_2 5 per cent and FeO 75 per cent costs $6 per ton. Limestone containing SiO_2 5 per cent and CaO 50 per cent costs $1.50 per ton. It requires 15 per cent of coke to smelt the charge, and the coke costs $10 per ton of 2000 lbs.

What type of slag would be the most economical?

Substituting in equations (A), (A'), (B), (B'), and (D), (D'), we obtain the following:

Slag A will require 15 pounds of iron ore and 260 pounds of limestone. Hence the flux will cost $0.235 per charge, and the fuel necessary to smelt the flux will cost $0.206. Total cost, $0.44.

Slag B will require 75 pounds of iron ore and 260 pounds of limestone. Hence the flux will cost $0.3862 per charge, and the fuel necessary to smelt the flux will cost $0.225. Total cost $0.61.

Slag D will require 175 pounds of iron ore and 52 pounds of limestone. Hence the cost of flux will be $0.559 per charge, and the fuel necessary to smelt the flux will cost $0.1688. Total cost, $0.73.

With labor and general expense at $1.25 per charge, slag B would have to drive 13 per cent faster than slag A, and slag D would have to drive 9.6 per cent faster than slag B, and 23 per cent faster than slag A to be as economical, other conditions being equal.

TABLES.

TABLE I.
WEIGHTS AND MEASURES.
MEASURES OF CAPACITY.

Gals.	Qts.	Pts.	Fl. Oz.	Fl. Dr.	Grains of Water at 62° F.	Cubic Centimetres.
1 =	4 =	8 =	128 =	1,024 =	58,318.00 =	3,785.200
	1 =	2 =	32 =	256 =	14,579.50 =	946.300
		1 =	16 =	128 =	7,289.75 =	473.150
			1 =	8 =	455.61 =	29.570
				1 =	56.95 =	3.690

1 English imperial gallon = 277.274 cu. in. = 70,000.00 = 4,543.000
1   "   wine or Winchester gal. = 231.000 " = 58,318.00 = 3,785.200
1   "   corn gallon = 268.000 " = 67,861.00 = 4,402.900
1   "   ale   "   = 282.000 " = 71,193.40 = 4,619.200

      1 cu. ft. = 283.15 cc.
      1 cu. in. = 16.38 "
      0.061027 " = 1 "

LINEAR MEASURES.

  1 yd. = 3 ft. = 36 in. = 0.91438 metre.
     1 ft. = 12 in. = 0.30480 "
        1 in. = 0.02540 "
       39.3708 in. = 1.00000 "

TROY WEIGHT.

1 lb. = 12 oz. = 240 dwt. = 5.760 grs. = 373.2419 grammes.
   1 " = 20 " = 480 " = 31.1035 "
      1 " = 24 " = 1.5552 "
         1 " = 0.0648 "

AVOIRDUPOIS WEIGHT.

1 gross ton = 20 cwt. = 2,240 lbs. = 1,016.00 kilogrammes.
     1 " = 112 " = 50.80 "

      Oz. Grs. Troy. Grammes.
    1 lb. = 16 = 7,000.00 = 453.5926
       1 = 437.50 = 28.3495

1 net ton = 2,000 lbs. =   907 kilogrammes.
1 cu. ft. of water at 62° F. = 62.3550 lbs. Av. = 28,315.0000 grammes.
1 cu. in. " " " " = 0.0361 " " = 16.3862 "

APOTHECARIES WEIGHT.

1 lb. = 12 oz. = 96 dr. = 288 scruples = 5,760 grains = 373.2419 grammes.
  1 (℥) = 8 (ʒ) 24   480   31.1035 "
     1 (ʒ) 3   60   3.8879 "
       1 (℈)   20   1.2960 "
0.0022 lb. Av. = 0.03527 oz. Av. = 15.4328 = 1.0000 "

TABLE II.
ATOMIC WEIGHTS.

Name.	Symbol.	Quantivalence.	Atomic Weight.	Name.	Symbol.	Quantivalence.	Atomic Weight
Aluminium....	Al	IV	27.0	Mercury......	Hg	II	200.0
Antimony.....	Sb	V	120.0	Molybdenum..	Mo	VI	96.0
Arsenic.......	As	V	74.9	Nickel........	Ni	VI	59.0
Barium........	Ba	II	136.8	Nitrogen......	N	V	14.0
Bismuth......	Bi	V	210.0	Osmium......	Os	IV	199.0
Boron........	B	III	11.0	Oxygen.......	O	II	16.0
Bromine.....,	Br	I	80.0	Palladium.....	Pd	IV	106.0
Cadmium......	Cd	II	112.0	Phosphorus....	P	V	31.0
Cæsium.......	Cs	I	133.0	Platinum......	Pt	IV	197.0
Calcium.......	Ca	II	40.0	Potassium	K	I	39.1
Carbon........	C	IV	12.0	Rhodium......	Ro	IV	104.0
Cerium........	Ce	III	141.2	Rubidium.....	Rb	I	85.0
Chlorine......	Cl	I	35.5	Ruthenium....	Ru	IV	104.0
Chromium	Cr	VI	52.4	Selenium.	Se	II	79.0
Cobalt........	Co	VI	59.0	Silicon........	Si	IV	28.0
Columbium...	Cb	V	94.0	Silver.........	Ag	I	108.0
Copper...	Cu	II	63.1	Sodium.......	Na	I	23.0
Didymium....	D	III	147.0	Strontium.....	Sr	II	87.5
Erbium........	E	III	169.0	Sulphur.......	S	II	32.0
Fluorine......	F	I	19.0	Tantalum.....	Ta	V	182.0
Gallium.......	Ga	III	69.9	Tellurium.....	Te	II	128.0
Glucinum.....	Gl	II	9.2	Thallium......	Tl	I	204.0
Gold..	Au	III	196.2	Thorium......	Th	IV	231.5
Hydrogen....	H	I	1.0	Tin...........	Sn	IV	118.0
Indium........	In	III	113.4	Titanium......	Ti	IV	50.0
Iodine.... ...	I	I	126.85	Tungsten......	W	IV-VI	184.0
Iron..........	Fe	VI	56.0	Uranium......	U	VI	240.0
Lanthanum....	La	III	139.0	Vanadium	V	V	51.2
Lead..........	Pb	II	207.0	Yttrium.......	Y	III	60.0
Lithium.......	Li	I	7.0	Zinc..........	Zn	II	65.0
Magnesium....	Mg	II	24.0	Zirconium	Zr	IV	90.0
Manganese....	Mn	VI	55.0				

TABLE III.
TENSION OF AQUEOUS VAPOR AT VARIOUS TEMPERATURES.*

Temperature in Degrees C.	Tension of the Aqueous Vapor in Millimetres.	Temperature in Degrees C.	Tension of the Aqueous Vapor in Millimetres.
0	4.525	21	18.505
1	4.867	22	19.675
2	5.231	23	20.909
3	5.619	24	22.211
4	6.032	25	23.582
5	6.471	26	25.026
6	6.939	27	26.547
7	7.436	28	28.148
8	7.964	29	29.832
9	8.525	30	31.602
10	9.126	31	33.464
11	9.751	32	35.419
12	10.421	33	37.473
13	11.130	34	39.630
14	11.882	35	41.893
15	12.677	36	44.268
16	13.519	37	46.758
17	14.409	38	49.368
18	15.351	39	52.103
19	16.345	40	54.969
20	17.396		

* For a more complete table see Winkler's "Technical Gas Analysis."

TABLE IV.
DENSITIES AND LITRE-WEIGHTS OF GASES AND VAPORS.*

Name of the Gas.	Molecular Formula.	Density.	1000 cc. of the Gas in the Normal State weighs, Grammes—
Acetylene	C_2H_2	12.970	1.1621
Air (atmospheric)	....	14.422	1.2922
Ammonia	H_3N	8.510	0.7625
Antimoniuretted hydrogen	H_3Sb	62.545	5.6040
Arseniuretted hydrogen	H_3As	38.960	3.4908
Benzene	C_6H_6	38.910	3.4863
Butylene	C_4H_8	27.940	2.5034
Carbon monoxide	CO	13.965	1.2512
Carbon dioxide	CO_2	21.945	1.9663
Carbon disulphide	CS_2	37.965	3.4017
Carbon oxysulphide	COS	29.955	2.6839
Chlorine	Cl_2	35.370	3.1691
Cyanogen	$(CN)_2$	25.990	2.3287
Ethane	C_2H_6	14.970	1.2413
Ethylene	C_2H_4	13.970	1.2517
Hydrogen	H_2	1.000	0.0896
Hydrogen chloride	HCl	18.185	1.6293
Hydrogen cyanide	HCN	13.495	1.2091
Hydrogen sulphide	H_2S	16.990	1.5223
Methane	CH_4	7.985	0.7154
Nitrogen	N_2	14.020	1.2562
Nitrogen protoxide	N_2O	22.000	1.9712
Nitric oxide	NO	14.990	1.3431
Nitrogen trioxide	N_2O_3	37.960	3.4012
Nitric peroxide	NO_2	22.970	2.0581
Oxygen	O_2	15.960	1.4300
Phosphuretted hydrogen	H_3P	16.980	1.5214
Propylene	C_3H_6	20.955	1.8775
Silicon tetrafluoride	SiF_4	52.055	4.6641
Sulphur dioxide	SO_2	31.950	2.8627
Water	H_2O	8.980	0.8046

* Taken from "Technical Gas Analysis," by Winkler and Lunge, London, 1885.

TABLE V.

FACTORS.

Found.	Required.	Factor.	Found.	Required.	Factor.
$AlPO_4$	Al	0.22131	$Mg_2P_2O_7$	P	0.27928
Al_2O_3	Al	0.52942		P_2O_5	0.63964
Sb_2O_4	Sb	0.78947		MgO	0.36036
Sb_2S_3	Sb	0.71428	MgO	$MgCO_3$	2.10000
$Mg_2As_2O_7$	As	0.48353	Mn	MnO	1.29091
Ag_3AsO_4	As	0.16181	Mn_3O_4	Mn	0.72052
$CaSO_4$	CaO	0.41176	$Mn_2P_2O_7$	Mn	0.38732
	$CaCO_3$	0.73529	$(NH_4)_3 12MoO_3PO_4$	P	0.01630
CaO	$CaCO_3$	1.78571		P_2O_5	0.03735
Cr_2O_3	Cr	0.68586	NiO	Ni	0.78667
CO_2	C	0.27273	K_2PtCl_6	KCl	0.30561
$CoSO_4$	Co	0.38065		K_2O	0.19295
CoO	Co	0.78667	NaCl	Na_2O	0.52991
Cu	CuO	1.25356	SiO_2	Si	0.46667
$BaSO_4$	BaO	0.65636	$BaSO_4$	S	0.13745
Fe_2O_3	Fe	0.70000		SO_3	0.34364
Fe	FeO	1.28571	$PbSO_4$	S	0.10561
	Fe_3O_4	1.38095	SnO_2	Sn	0.78667
$PbSO_4$	Pb	0.68317	TiO_2	Ti	0.60975
PbS	Pb	0.86611	ZnO	Zn	0.80247

Table VI.

THE QUANTITATIVE PRECIPITATION OF VARIOUS METALS BY ELECTROLYSIS.*

Solution.	Au	Pt	Pd	Ag	Hg	Pb	Sb	Sn	Cu
Nitric or sulphuric	—	—	—	—	—	$+a$		—	
Double ammonium oxalate.......			—					—	—.
Double ammonium sulphate.......			—						
Double potassium cyanide.......	—		—						
Sulpho-salt........							—	—	
In glacial phosphoric acid, after $(NH_4)_2CO_3$....								—	

Solution.	Bi	Cd	Tl	Al	Fe	Mn	Zn	Co	Ni
Nitric or sulphuric	—	—	$+b$			$+c$	$-e$		
Double ammonium oxalate........	—	$-f$	—	$+d$		$+ch$	—	—	—
Double ammonium sulphate.......					$-g$	$+cj$	—	—	—
Double potassium cyanide.......		—					—	—	—
Sulpho-salt........									
In glacial phosphoric acid, after $(NH_4)_2CO_3$....	—	—			—	$+$	—	—	—

—. Precipitated at cathode in metallic form.
$-e$.   "   "   "   "   "   " after adding $(NH_4)_2SO_4$.
$-f$.   "   "   "   "   "   " The corresponding potassium salt preferable.
$-g$.   "   "   "   "   "   " after adding $Na_2C_6H_8O_7$ and $H_2C_6H_8O_7$.
$+a$.   "   " anode as PbO_2.
$+b$.   "   "   "   " Tl_2O_3.
$+c$.   "   "   "   " MnO_2.
$+ch$.   "   "   "   "   " incompletely. Completely from corresponding potassium salt.
$+cj$.   "   "   "   "   " incompletely.

* From an article by Kahn and Woodgate in J. S. Chem. Ind., vol. viii. p. 256.

Table VII.

SOLUBILITY, FUSIBILITY, ETC., OF VARIOUS METALS.

Metal.	Color.	Tenacity.	Hardness.	Sp. gr.	Melts at Deg. C.	Best Solvent.
Gold......	yellow	mal.	2.5–3	19–20	1102	aqua regia
Platinum..	whitish to steel-gray	"	4–4.5	16–21	1808	"
Silver.....	white	"	2.5–3	10.5–11	1023	HNO_3
Lead......	bluish	"	1.5	11.45	322	HNO_3
Mercury...	tin-white	liquid	—	13.5	−40*	HNO_3
Bismuth...	silver-white to reddish-wh.	brittle	2–3.5	9.7	258	HNO_3
Copper.....	red	mal.	2.5–3	8.9	1091	HNO_3
Cadmium.	tin-white	"	1	8.6–8.7	320	HNO_3
Arsenic....	lead-gray	brittle	4	5.9	†	aqua regia
Antimony.	bluish-white	"	3–3.5	6.8	432	"
Tin........	white	mal.	4–5	7.28	228	HCl
Iron (cast).	gray	"	4–5	7.1	1530	HCl
Iron (w't).	"	"	4–5	7.6–7.8	1808	HCl
Steel......	"	"	6–7	7.8–7.9	1808	HCl
Aluminum	silver-white	"	2	2.5–2.7	700	HCl
Nickel...	"	"	5–6	8.2–8.7	1537	HNO_3
Cobalt....	steel-gray to reddish	"	5–6	8.5–8.7	1600	HNO_3
Manganese	grayish-white	brittle	9–10	7.1–8	1650	HCl
Zinc.......	bluish-white	mal.	2	6.8–7.2	411	HCl

* Volatilizes at 360° C. † Volatilizes at 356° C.

TABLE

PROPERTIES OF

Element.	Object.	Obtained by or Precipitated with—	Obtained or Precipitated as—	Conditions of Solution.
K	Weighing	Precipitant $PtCl_4$. Precipitate preferably dissolved in hot H_2O and evaporated in a weighed vessel.	K_2PtCl_6	Cold, alcoholic, containing chlorides or HCl. Salts other than NaCl should be absent. Small amounts of Ca or Mg may be present, but are detrimental.
	Weighing	Precipitant $PtCl_4$. .	K_2PtCl_6	As above.
	Weighing	Evaporation and gentle ignition. Volatile at temperatures above a dull red.	KCl	Only chlorides or salts converted into chlorides should be present. Ammonium salts may be present.
	Weighing	Evaporation and ignition. $(NH_4)_2CO_3$ facilitates conversion.	K_2SO_4	Absence of salts forming non-volatile sulphates or containing non-volatile acids (as H_3PO_4).
Na	Weighing	Evaporation and gentle ignition.	NaCl	Same as KCl.
	Weighing	Same as K_2SO_4.	Na_2SO_4	Same as K_2SO_4.
Ca	Weighing	Precipitant $(NH_4)_2C_2O_4$ or $H_2C_2O_4$ in NH_4OH solution.	CaC_2O_4	Hot, strongly ammoniacal and an excess of oxalate.
	Weighing	As above.	CaC_2O_4	As above.
	Separation	Precipitant $(NH_4)_2CO_3$.	$CaCO_3$	Alkaline solution free from large excess of alkaline salts, especially citrates.
Mg	Weighing	Precipitant Na_2HPO_4.	$MgNH_4PO_4$	Cold, containing excess of $NH_4OH + NH_4Cl$. Absence of SiO_2 and bases other than alkalies.
	Separation	Precipitant $Ba(OH)_2$.	$Mg(OH)_2$	Alkaline and moderately concentrated. Free from ammonium salts and organic salts.
Ba	Weighing	Precipitant H_2SO_4. Should be heated before adding.	$BaSO_4$	Hot, containing some free HCl. Absence of SiO_2, large amounts of $(NH_4)_2S$ group and Ca salts.
	Separation	Precipitant $(NH_4)_2CO_3$.	$BaCO_3$	Alkaline, containing NH_4OH and excess of $(NH_4)_2CO_3$.

* Compiled mainly from an article by Prof. E. Waller, entitled

VIII.

PRECIPITATES.*

Soluble in—	Contaminants.	Prepared for Weighing by—	Weighed as—
Slightly soluble in cold, more so in hot, H_2O. Solubility increased by alkali or acid, diminished by $PtCl_4$ or Na_2PtCl_6.	NaCl and other salts (as sulphates) insoluble in alcohol. Removed by washing with $H_2O + NH_4Cl + K_2PtCl_6$.	Drying.	K_2PtCl_6
As above.	As above.	Ignition gently at first. Addition of $H_2C_2O_4$ aids reduction.	Pt
In water. Less in alcohol or strong HCl.	NaCl, and if long exposed to the air, organic dust.	Ignition not above a dull red.	KCl
Moderately in H_2O, much less in alcohol.	Na_2SO_4 or other non-volatile sulphates.	Ignition over an ordinary Bunsen flame.	K_2SO_4
Same as KCl.	KCl and other salts (as sulphates) insoluble in alcohol.	Ignition not above a dull red.	NaCl
Same as K_2SO_4.	K_2SO_4 and other non-volatile sulphates.	Same as K_2SO_4.	Na_2SO_4
Mineral acids. Slightly in $H_2C_2O_4$.	MgC_2O_4, which is removed by solution in HCl and reprecipitation.	Ignition, gently at first, and finally over blast-lamp.	CaO
As above.	As above.	Addition of H_2SO_4, evaporation, and ignition. In presence of C add HNO_3.	$CaSO_4$
H_2O containing CO_2. In acids and in hot solution of NH_4Cl. Insoluble in $H_2O + NH_4OH + (NH_4)_2CO_3$.	$BaCO_3$ and $MgCO_3$, if much are present.		
Acids. Hot solutions, and slightly in cold H_2O. Insoluble in NH_4NO_3.	SiO_2 and $Mg(OH)_2$.	Ignition, gently at first, finally intensely. In presence of C add NH_4NO_3.	$Mg_2P_2O_7$
Acids and ammonium salts. Prevented by organic salts.	Usually unimportant for purposes of separation.		
Conc. H_2SO_4, in strong hot HCl and HNO_3 (dilute). In strong hot Fe_2Cl_6 and in alkaline or alkali-earth nitrates. In citrates.	Alkaline and alkali-earth chlorides, chlorates, sulphates, nitrates, basic, ferric, or aluminic compounds. Repeated boiling in *very* dilute HCl assists in removal, but liable to dissolve some of the precipitate.	Ignition. In the presence of C the addition of HNO_3 is necessary.	$BaSO_4$
H_2O containing CO_2 and acids. In hot NH_4Cl. Insoluble in $NH_4OH + (NH_4)_2CO_3$.	$MgCO_3$ if much is present, and carbonates of the fixed alkalies.		

* "Properties of Precipitates," *School of Mines Quarterly*, vol. xii.

362   A MANUAL OF PRACTICAL ASSAYING.

PROPERTIES OF

Element	Object	Obtained by or Precipitated with—	Obtained or Precipitated as—	Conditions of Solution.
Fe	Weighing	Precipitant NH_4OH. Addition of NH_4Cl aids precipitation.	$Fe_2(OH)_6$	Alkaline, and free from H_2S.
	Separation	As above.	$Fe_2(OH)_6$	As above.
	Separation	Precipitant $NaC_2H_3O_2$. Filtered hot.	$Fe(OH)n(C_2H_3O_2)_{6-n}$	Dilute containing but little free $HC_2H_3O_2$. Hot, but too long boiling should be avoided.
Al	Weighing	Precipitant (usual) NH_4OH. Best precipitated by adding slight excess NH_4OH, boiling, and passing H_2S.	$Al_2(OH)_6$	Neutral or slightly alkaline, containing preferably NH_4Cl.
	Separation	Same as Fe.	$Al_2(OH)n(C_2H_3O_2)_{6-n}$	Same as Fe. No free acetic acid should be present.
Cr	Weighing	Precipitant NH_4OH. Excess removed by boiling.	$Cr_2(OH)_6$	Absence of members of the $(NH_4)_2S$ group, and preferably all non-volatile salts. Solution must be neutral.
Ti	Weighing	Insoluble form by boiling the solution acidified with H_2SO_4.	H_2TiO_3	Dilute containing but little free H_2SO_4. HCl and chlorides must be absent. $HC_2H_3O_2$ facilitates precipitation. Prolonged boiling also.
	Separation	Fusion and leaching until filtrate runs cloudy.	$(x Na_2O, TiO_2)$ Na_2TiO_3	Long fusion with Na_2CO_3 at high temperature.
Zn	Weighing	Precipitant Na_2CO_3.	$2ZnCO_3, Zn(OH)_2$	Absence of caustic and bicarbonate alkalies and ammonium salts.
	Separation	Precipitant H_2S in boiling dilute $HC_2H_3O_2$ solution. NH_4Cl facilitates precipitation.	$ZnS.H_2O$	Alkaline or acid only with weak organic acid. Free mineral acids prevent precipitation (H_2SO_4 least). Fe should be absent.
Mn	Weighing	Precipitant $NaNH_4HPO_4$ in presence of ammonium salts.	$MnNH_4PO_4$	Mn must be entirely in manganous form, and *slightly* alkaline. An excess of phosphate is necessary. Oxalates and excessive amounts of ammonium salts should be absent.
	Separation	Br from acetate solution. $KClO_3$ from boiling nitric-acid solution.	MnO_2	Absence of HCl or other halogen acids. Also lower oxides of nitrogen or reducing agents. Boiling necessary.

PRECIPITATES.

Soluble in—	Contaminants.	Prepared for Weighing by—	Weighed as—
Mineral acids and solutions containing citric, tartaric acids, etc., or organic substances (as sugar).	Basic ferric salts, Cr, P_2O_5, Al, Mn, Zn, Co, Ni, Mg, SiO_2, etc.	Ignition. In presence of C, HNO_3 or NH_4NO_3 should be added. Volatile in presence of chlorides.	Fe_2O_3
As above.	As above.		
In cold mineral acids. Also in citrates and organic substances. Insoluble in hot *very* dilute $HC_2H_3O_2$.	Salts of fixed alkalies; SiO_2, P_2O_5, Al, Cr, Co, Ni, Zn, Mn, Cu, etc. Removed by resolution and reprecipitation.		
Acids and fixed alkalies. Slightly in cold NH_4OH. Tartrates, citrates, sugar, etc., prevent precipitation.	Basic Al salts; SiO_2, P_2O_5, Al, Cr, Co, Ni, Zn, Mn, etc. Removed by resolution and reprecipitation.	Ignition. Slightly volatile in presence of NH_4Cl.	Al_2O_3
Same as Fe, except slightly soluble in hot dilute $HC_2H_3O_2$.	Same as Fe.		
All acids in NaOH, KOH, and slightly in NH_4OH. Tartrates, citrates, sugar, etc., prevent precipitation.	Same as Al.	Ignition.	Cr_2O_3
Soluble form same as $Fe_2(OH)_6$. Insoluble form by fusion with $KHSO_4$ or boiling with conc. HCl or H_2SO_4. Acids. Slightly in H_2O.	Fe_2O_3, Al_2O_3, SiO_2, and P_2O_5. Fe_2O_3 and Al_2O_3 removed by resolution, reduction with SO_2, and reprecipitation in presence of $HC_2H_3O_2$. Fe_2O_3, acid-sodium silicate, alkali-earth carbonates, etc.	Ignition with addition of $(NH_4)_2CO_3$.	TiO_2
Dilute acids, fixed caustic alkalies, bicarbonates, and organic solutions.	Alkaline carbonate removed by repeated washing with hot H_2O. Fe_2O_3, Al_2O_3, and SiO_2 removed by solution and precipitation of the ignited ZnO.	Ignition; absence of C is necessary.	ZnO
Dilute HCl and HNO_3, strong H_2SO_4 when hot. Free NH_4OH retards precipitation.	Mn, Co, and Ni sulphides. Removed by resolution, neutralizing, and reprecipitation. Fe if not previously removed.		
Acids. Slightly in large excess of ammonium salts. The influence of ammonium salts is lessened by large excess of the precipitant.	None if bases forming insoluble phosphates are absent and precipitate is well washed.	Ignition. Gently at first.	$Mn_2P_2O_7$
Dilute mineral acids (especially HCl). Insoluble in strong $HC_2H_3O_2$ and conc. HNO_3.	Salts of fixed alkalies, Fe_2O_3, ZnO.		

A MANUAL OF PRACTICAL ASSAYING.

PROPERTIES OF

Element.	Object.	Obtained by or Precipitated with—	Obtained or Precipitated as—	Conditions of Solution.
Ni	Weighing	Electrolysis. (See Table VI.)	Ni	Absence of all other metals of H_2S and $(NH_4)_2S$ groups. Ni present as oxalate, sulphate, or double ammonium nitrate, and excess of NH_4OH.
	Weighing	Precipitant KOH or NaOH.	$Ni(OH)_2$	Bases other than fixed alkalies should be absent.
	Separation	Precipitant H_2S in weak $HC_2H_3O_2$ solution.	$NiS.HO_2$	Absence of other members of the H_2S or $(NH_4)_2S$ groups. NH_4Cl aids precipitation.
Co	Weighing	Precipitant KNO_2 in solution *slightly* acid with $HC_2H_3O_2$.	$6KNO_2,Co_2(NO_2)_6$	Warm, containing only Co, Ni, and K salts, and nearly saturated with $KC_2H_3O_2$.
	Weighing	Electrolysis. (See Table VI.)	Co	Same as Ni.
	Separation	Same as $NiS.H_2O$.	CoS,H_2O	Same as NiS,H_2O.
Cu	Weighing	Electrolysis. (See Table VI.)	Cu	H_2SO_4 solution containing a few drops of HNO_3 preferable. Organic acids should be absent.
	Separation	Precipitant H_2S in dilute acid solution.	CuS	Moderately strong HCl or H_2SO_4. If HNO_3 is present, the solution must be cold and dilute.
Pb	Weighing	Precipitant H_2SO_4.	$PbSO_4$	Excess of H_2SO_4, and but little HNO_3 or HCl. NH_4 salts and salts of organic acids must be absent.
	Weighing	Precipitant $K_2Cr_2O_7$ in acetic-acid solution.	$PbCrO_4$	Bi, Ag, Fe, and Ba should be absent. Chlorides should be absent, and also alkaline citrates, tartrates, etc.
	Separation	Precipitant H_2S.	PbS	Slightly acid, neutral, or alkaline. Best precipitated in cold H_2SO_4 solution.
Ag	Weighing	Precipitant HCl in very slight excess.	AgCl	Slightly acid with HNO_3 free from chlorides.
	Separation	Precipitant NaBr.	AgBr	Same as AgCl.

PRECIPITATES.

Soluble in—	Contaminants.	Prepared for Weighing by—	Weighed as—
Readily in HNO_3. Slowly in strong $(NH_4)_2C_2O_4$.	Co, Fe, and Zn, unless previously separated. (See Table VI.)	Drying at gentle heat. (See Cu.)	Ni
Mineral acids. In ammonium salts, tartrates, citrates, etc. Precipitation prevented by moderate amounts of free acetic or mineral acids. Soluble in mineral acids and KCN.	Alkalies, Fe_2O_3, Al_2O_3, and SiO_2 from reagents. Sulphides of H_2S and $(NH_4)_2S$ groups, if not previously removed.	Ignition strongly.	NiO
H_2O, acids NH_4 and Na salts. Insoluble in dilute $HC_2H_3O_2$ and alcohol.	Ca and Pb if present. K salts should be removed by careful washing.	Dissolve in dilute H_2SO_4, and evaporate in a weighed vessel. Ignition.	$3K_2SO_4 + 2CoSO_4$
Same as Ni.	Same as Ni.	Same as Ni.	
Same as NiS,H_2O.	Ni and other members of $(NH_4)_2S$ group, if not previously removed by separation.		Co
HNO_3 and HCl. Deposit prevented by Cl, too strong acid, or lower oxides of nitrogen.	As, Sb, or Bi, if HNO_3 is not present. If HNO_3 and Zn are present, Zn will begin to precipitate as soon as Cu is all precipitated. (See Table VI.)	Washing with H_2O and then with alcohol. Drying at a temperature which can be borne by the hand.	Cu
Hot dilute HNO_3 and strong hot HCl.	Other members of the H_2S group.		
Conc. mineral acids; in $Na_2S_2O_3$; in NH_4 salts and especially those of organic acids.	Other sulphates, which are removed by washing with *very* dilute H_2SO_4.	Ignition. If C is present, treat with HNO_3 + H_2SO_4, evaporate, and ignite.	$PbSO_4$
Moderately strong mineral acids; in hot $NH_4C_2H_3O_2$. Insoluble in dilute HNO_3.	Ba, Bi, Hg, and chromates. If much Fe is present, possibly $Fe_2(CrO_4)_3$.	Drying on previously weighed filter.	$PbCrO_4$
Dilute boiling HNO_3; hot conc. HCl. In $Na_2S_2O_3$.	Other members of the H_2S group if present.		
Partially in strong hot HCl or HNO_3. Partially in alkaline and alkaline-earth chlorides. Readily in NH_4OH, KCN, and $Na_2S_2O_3$. Same as AgCl. Insoluble in considerable excess of precipitant.	Chlorides of Pb and Hg if present in the solution.	Ignition until the edges fuse. Volatile at a temperature slightly above dull red.	AgCl

PROPERTIES OF

Element.	Object.	Obtained with or Precipitated by—	Obtained or Precipitated as—	Condition of Solution.
As	Weighing	Precipitant H_2S in HCl solution.	As_2S_3	Acid with mineral acid (preferably HCl).
	Weighing	Precipitant $MgCl_2$ in ammoniacal solution containing alcohol.	$MgNH_4AsO_4$	Alkaline with NH_4OH, containing a minimum of NH_4Cl and 30 per cent of alcohol.
Sb	Weighing	Precipitant H_2S in acid solution, or upon acidifying solutions of sulphantimonite.	Sb_2S_3	Slightly acid and moderately dilute.
Sn	Weighing	Precipitant H_2S in acid solution or upon acidifying solutions of alkaline sulpho-stannate.	SnS_2	Moderately dilute and slightly acid. Precipitation promoted by acetates and interfered with by oxalates or oxalic acid.
P	Weighing	$MgCl_2$ in ammoniacal solution containing NH_4Cl.	$MgNH_4PO_4$	Same as Mg.
	Separation and Titration	Precipitant $(NH_4)_2MoO_4$ in HNO_3 solution heated to 80° C. Agitation facilitates precipitation.	$12MoO_3(NH_4)_3PO_4 +$	Acid with HNO_3, and containing an excess of NH_4NO_3 and precipitant. Chlorides, HCl, reducing agents and organic acids should be absent.
S, SO_2, S_2O_3, SO_3, etc.	Weighing	Precipitant $BaCl_2$ in hot solution containing a little free HCl.	$BaSO_4$	Same as $BaSO_4$.
Cl	Weighing	Precipitant $AgNO_3$.	AgCl	Same as Ag.
Si and SiO_2	Weighing	By evaporation of acid solution to dryness and heating at 115° to 120° C., or by evaporation of H_2SO_4 solution to fumes of SO_3.	$x H_2O, SiO_2$	Should contain HCl. If much HNO_3 is present, should be removed by adding HCl and boiling.
C, CO_2, etc.	Weighing	Absorption with KOH, NaOH, or CaOH + NaOH.	Na_2CO_3, K_2CO_3 or $Na_2CO_3 + CaCO_3$	
N	Weighing	$PtCl_4$	$(NH_4)_2PtCl_6$	Same as K_2PtCl_6.

PRECIPITATES.

Soluble in—	Contaminants.	Prepared for Weighing by—	Weighed as—
Soluble in alkaline hydrates, carbonates, and sulphides. In $KHSO_3$, in aqua regia, and in $H_2O + Cl$ or $H_2O + Br$. In warm acids. In $H_2O + NH_4Cl$. Insoluble in NH_4OH + alcohol.	Other sulphides of H_2S group if present.	Drying. Volatile as As_2S_3 upon ignition.	As_2S_3
	Basic Mg salts, sulphates, and other salts insoluble in NH_4OH + alcohol.	Dissolving the precipitate in HNO_3 into a weighed vessel, evaporating, and igniting slowly at first.	$Mg_2As_2O_7$
Moderately concentrated acids (HCl especially). Tartaric acid assists precipitation. Dissolved by fixed alkalies or alkaline sulphides.	S generally accompanies the precipitate; removed by replacing the H_2O by alcohol, and washing with CS_2.	Mixed with 50 times its weight of HgO, and ignited to dull red.	Sb_2O_4
Moderately strong acids (HCl especially). In boiling solution containing free $H_2C_2O_4$.	Other members of H_2S group, if present. Separated from Sb_2S_3 by adding $H_2C_2O_4$, and boiling.	Heating moderately and slowly with free access of air. Addition of HNO_3 aids conversion.	SnO_2
Same as Mg.	Same as Mg.	Same as Mg.	$Mg_2P_2O_7$
NH_4OH and alkalies. Soluble in HCl and moderately strong H_2SO_4 or HNO_3. In hot H_2O. Insoluble in very dilute HNO_3 containing NH_4NO_3.	Arsenio-molybdate, SiO_2, Fe_2O_3, and TiO_2.	For titration by dissolving in NH_4OH and reducing by Zn + H_2SO_4, or by acidimetry.	
Same as $BaSO_4$.	Same as $BaSO_4$.	Same as $BaSO_4$.	$BaSO_4$
Same as Ag.	Same as Ag.	Same as Ag.	AgCl
Boiling caustic fixed alkalies. By fusion with fixed alkalies (caustic or carbonate). Insoluble in H_2O and acids (HF excepted).	Insoluble sulphates, removed by digestion with conc. H_2SO_4. Also SnO_2, Sb_2O_4, and TiO_2. Sometimes Al_2O_3 and Fe_2O_3. In which case determine by loss.	Ignition after drying. When impurities are present is determined by loss on ignition with HF and H_2SO_4.	SiO_2
	H_2O and CO_2 from the atmosphere. Prevented by suitable absorption apparatus.	Absorption in weighed apparatus containing suitable absorbents.	CO_2
Same as K_2PtCl_6.	Same as K_2PtCl_6.	Ignition to Pt. (See K_2PtCl_6.)	Pt

368 A MANUAL OF PRACTICAL ASSAYING.

TABLE IX.
VOLUMETRIC DETERMINATIONS.

Element.	Reaction.	Condition of Solution.	Standard Solution.	Indicator.
Ag	$AgNO_3 + NaCl = AgCl + NaNO_3$	Silver dissolved in $HNO_3 + H_2O$ should be warm, dilute, slightly acid, and free from Hg, Pb, Cl, and Br.	Normal NaCl	Decime $AgNO_3$ " NaCl
	$AgNO_3 + NaBr = AgBr + NaNO_3$	Same as above.	Normal NaBr	Decime $AgNO_3$ " NaBr
	$AgNO_3 + KCNS = AgCNS + KNO_3$	Same as above.	Normal KCNS or NH_4CNS	$Fe_2(SO_4)_3$
Pb	$5PbC_2O_4 + 8H_2SO_4 + K_2Mn_2O_8 =$ $5PbSO_4 + 10CO_2 + K_2SO_4 + 2MnSO_4 + 8H_2O$	PbC_2O_4 precipitated in acetic-acid solution containing alcohol, and filtered off.	Normal $K_2Mn_2O_8$	Excess of standard
	$Pb(C_2H_3O_2)_2 + (NH_4)_2MoO_4 =$ $PbMoO_4 + 2NH_4C_2H_3O_2$	$PbSO_4$, dissolved in $NH_4C_2H_3O_2$, and acidified slightly with $HC_2H_3O_2$. Warm, moderately dilute.	Normal $(NH_4)_2MoO_4$	Tannin solution
	$2Pb(C_2H_3O_2)_2 + K_2Cr_2O_7 + H_2O =$ $2PbCrO_4 + 2KC_2H_3O_2 + 2HC_2H_3O_2$	Same as above.	Normal $K_2Cr_2O_7$	$AgNO_3$
Cu	$(N_2H_6Cu)O(NH_4NO_2)_2 + 3H_2O +$ $4KCN = (KCN)_2CuC_2N_2 + 2KNO_3 + 4NH_4OH$	Cu dissolved in HNO_3 and an excess of NH_4OH added.	Half-normal KCN	Excess of standard
	$Cu_2I_2 + 2I + Na_2S_2O_3 =$ $Cu_2I_2 + 2NaI + S_2O_3$	The Cu precipitated by KI from a solution of $Cu(C_2H_3O_2)_2$, containing a slight excess of $HC_2H_3O_2$ and the liberated I determined.	Normal $Na_2S_2O_3$	Starch solution

Cd	$2CdCl_2 + K_4FeC_6N_6 =$ $Cd_2FeC_6N_6 + 4KCl$	CdS dissolved in a slight excess of HCl and diluted with H_2O to 180 cc. Cu and Bi must be absent.	Normal $K_4FeC_6N_6$	$U(C_2H_3O_2)_2$
As	$Ag_3AsO_4, 3HNO_3 + 3KCNS =$ $3AgCNS + H_3AsO_4 + 3KNO_3$	The precipitated Ag_3AsO_4 is dissolved in a slight excess of HNO_3 and diluted with warm water.	KCNS, or NH_4CNS	$Fe_2(SO_4)_3$
Fe	$10FeSO_4 + K_2Mn_2O_8 + 8H_2SO_4 =$ $5Fe_2(SO_4)_3 + K_2SO_4 + 2MnSO_4 + 8H_2O$	Fe is dissolved in H_2SO_4 and reduced with Zn or Zn + Pt. Solution must be free from Ti, Cr, As, and Sb, and contain an excess of H_2SO_4.	Normal $K_2Mn_2O_8$	Excess of standard
	$6FeCl_2 + K_2Cr_2O_7 + 14HCl =$ $3Fe_2Cl_6 + 2KCl + Cr_2Cl_6 + 7H_2O$	Fe is dissolved in HCl and reduced with Zn, Zn + Pt or $SnCl_2$. Solution must be free from Ti, Cr, As, and Sb, and contain an excess of HCl.	Normal $K_2Cr_2O_7$	$K_4FeC_6N_6$
Zn	$2ZnCl_2 + K_4FeC_6N_6 =$ $Zn_2FeC_6N_6 + 4KCl$	Zinc solution must be free from Cu, Mn, Cd, and Fe, and contain a slight excess of HCl.	Normal $K_4FeC_6N_6$	$U(C_2H_3O_2)_2$
Mn	$MnO_2 + H_2SO_4 + H_2C_2O_4 =$ $2CO_2 + 2H_2O + MnSO_4$	The precipitated MnO_2 is dissolved in an excess of H_2SO_4 and a known quantity of $H_2C_2O_4$, and the excess of $H_2C_2O_4$ determined by $K_2Mn_2O_8$.	Normal $K_2Mn_2O_8$	Excess of standard
	$3MnSO_4 + K_2Mn_2O_8 + 2H_2O =$ $5MnO_2 + K_2SO_4 + 2H_2SO_4$	The Mn is dissolved in H_2SO_4, the solution is neutralized with an excess of ZnO, and MnO_2 precipitated by titration.	Third-normal $K_2Mn_2O_8$	Excess of standard

VOLUMETRIC DETERMINATIONS—(Continued.)

Element.	Reaction.	Condition of Solution.	Standard Solution.	Indicator.
Ca	$5CaC_2O_4 + 8H_2SO_4 + K_2Mn_2O_8 =$ $5CaSO_4 + 2MnSO_4 + K_2SO_4 + 2CO_2 + 8H_2O$	The precipitated CaC_2O_4 is dissolved in an excess of H_2SO_4, the solution is diluted with hot H_2O, and the combined $H_2C_2O_4$ determined by titration.	Half-normal $K_2Mn_2O_8$	Excess of standard
P	$10Mo_{12}O_{31}+34K_2Mn_2O_8+102H_2SO_4 =$ $120MoO_3 + 68MnSO_4 + 34K_2SO_4 + 102H_2O$	The precipitated $12MoO_3(NH_4)_3\cdot PO_4$ is dissolved in NH_4OH, an excess of H_2SO_4 is added, and the MoO_3 reduced by Zn. The reduced $Mo_{12}O_{31}$ is then determined by titration.	Half-normal $K_2Mn_2O_8$	Excess of standard
	$MoO_3 + 2NaOH = Na_2MoO_4 + H_2O$	The precipitated $12MoO_3(NH_4)_3PO_4$ is treated with an excess of standard NaOH, and the excess of NaOH determined by alkalimetry.	Normal HNO_3	Phenolphthalein
S, SO_3, etc.	$Pb(C_2H_3O_2)_2 + (NH_4)_2MoO_4 =$ $PbMoO_4 + 2NH_4C_2H_3O_2$	The SO_3 is precipitated from a solution slightly acid with HNO_3, by $Pb(NO_3)_2$, and the Pb combined as $PbSO_4$ determined by titration.	Normal $(NH_4)_2MoO_4$	Tannin solution
S	$H_2S + 2I = 2HI + S$	The evolved H_2S is absorbed by an alkaline solution of $CdSO_4$. The S combined as CdS is determined (after solution of the CdS in HCl) by titration.	Normal KI	Starch solution
Cl	$HCl + AgNO_3 = AgCl + HNO_3$	The solution of the chloride should be slightly acid with HNO_3, and moderately dilute.	$AgNO_3$	$K_2Cr_2O_7$

INDEX.

A

	PAGE
Absorbents used in the Analysis of Gases	272
Absorption, Determination of Carbonic Acid by	116
" " " Sulphur by	96, 99
" " " Water by	120
Acetate of Ammonium (Solvent)	70
" " Sodium (Precipitant)	72
Acetic Acid (Solvent)	70
" ", Analysis of Commercial	287
Acid, Citric (Solvent)	70
Acidimetry and Alkalimetry	282
Acid, Hydrochloric (Solvent)	69
", Hydrofluoric (Flux)	67
", Nitric (Oxidizing Reagent)	75
", " (Solvent)	69
", Oxalic (Solvent)	70
", Solutions, Standard	282
", Sulphuric (Precipitant)	72
", " (Solvent)	69
", Tartaric (Solvent)	70
Albuminoid Ammonia in Water, Determination of	280
Alexander's Method for the Determination of Lead	142
Alkalies, see Potassium and Sodium.	
" in Water, Determination of	276
Alkalimetry and Acidimetry	282
Alkali Solutions, Standard	285
Alumina, Determination of	181
" in Iron Ores, Determination of	183
" " Lead Ores, " "	184

371

INDEX.

	PAGE
Alumina in Limestones, Clays, etc., Determination of	184
" " Manganese Ores, " "	184
" " Mattes, " "	184
" " Natural Phosphates, " "	304
" " Slags, " "	184
" " Silver Ores, " "	184
" " Water, " "	275
Aluminium (Precipitant)	73
" , Analysis of Commercial	298
" , Determination of	181
" " " as Alumina	182
" " " as Phosphate	186
" in Commercial Aluminium, Determination of	298
" Phosphate, Composition of	186
" , Test for (Blowpipe)	22
" " " (Qualitative)	39
Amalgamation Assay	260
Ammonia (Precipitant)	71
" (Solvent)	70
" in Water, Determination of	278
Ammonium Acetate (Solvent)	70
" Carbonate (Precipitant)	71
" Chloride (Precipitant)	72
" Nitrate (Oxidizing Reagent)	75
" Oxalate (Precipitant)	71
" Sulphide (Precipitant)	71
" " (Solvent)	70
" , Test for (Blowpipe)	22
Analysis of Bleaching Powder	289
" " Coal and Coke	263
" " Commercial Acetic Acid	287
" " " Caustic Potash	287
" " " Aluminium	298
" " Gases	269
" " Lead and Copper Slags	307
" " Natural Phosphates	300
" " Water	274
" " White-Lead	291
Antimony, Determination of	147
" in Ores containing Iron and Lead, Determination of	150
" " Oxidized Ores, Determination of	149
" " Sulphide Ores, " "	149
" , Test for (Blowpipe)	23
" " " (Qualitative)	39
Apparatus and Operations	49

	PAGE
Apparatus for the Determination of Carbonic Acid by Direct Weight	117
" " " " " Sulphur by Absorption	95
" " " Rapid Analysis of Gases	270
Approximate Analysis of Coal and Coke	263
Aqueous Vapor, Table showing the Tension of	355
Argol (Flux)	68
Arsenic, Determination of	144
" , Test for (Blowpipe)	23
" " " (Qualitative)	39
Assay, Amalgamation	260
" of Base Bullion	232
" " Copper Matte, Special Method for	250
" " Gold and Silver Ores (Crucible)	126
" " " " " " " (Scorification)	123
" " " " " " " containing Metallic Scales	258
" " Gold Bullion	246
" " Silver Bullion by Fire Method	236
" " " " " Gay-Lussac Method	240
" " " " " Volhard's "	245
" " Silver Sulphides	252
Assay-Ton Weights	51
Atomic Weights, Table of	354

B

Balances	51
Barium, Determination of	224
" , Test for (Blowpipe)	24
" " " (Qualitative)	39
" Chloride (Precipitant)	70
Base Bullion Assay	232
" " , Sampling of	14
" " , Special Method for the Assay of Impure	234
Base Metal in Gold Bullion	246
Beakers	61
Bicarbonate of Soda (Flux)	67
Bichromate of Potassium (Oxidizing Reagent)	75
Bismuth, Determination of	163
" , Test for (Blowpipe)	24
" " " (Qualitative)	40
Bisulphate of Potassium (Flux)	66
Black Flux	68
" " Substitute	68
Blowpipe Tests	22

	PAGE
Borax (Flux)..	67
Boron, Test for (Blowpipe)...................................	25
" " " (Qualitative).......................................	40
Bromine (Oxidizing Reagent)..................................	75
" Reagent in Gas Analysis.................................	272
" , Test for (Blowpipe)....................................	25
" " " (Qualitative).......................................	40
Brunton's Sampling Apparatus.................................	12
Bunsen's Method for the Determination of Antimony............	147
Burettes...	63

C

Cadmium, Determination of....................................	165
" " " Zinc in Ores of.......................	210
" , Test for (Blowpipe).............................	25
" " " (Qualitative).............................	40
Calcium, Determination of....................................	215
" " " in Clays..........................	217
" " " " Limestone.......................	215
" " " " Natural Phosphates..............	303
" " " " Ores............................	217
" " " " Slags...........................	218
" " " " Water...........................	275
" , Test for (Blowpipe)..............................	26
" " " (Qualitative).............................	41
Calculation of Factors.......................................	323
" " Formulæ.......................................	324
" " Percentage Composition from Chemical Formula..	321
" " " from Weight..................	321
" " Lead Blast-Furnace Charges....................	337
" " Specific Gravity..............................	293
" " the Results of Analyses, Table of Factors for the	357
" " " " " of Indirect Analysis..................	331
" " " " " of the Amalgamation Assay.............	261
" " " " " " " Assay of an Ore containing Metallic Scales	259
" " " " " " " Analysis of Gases...............	332
" " " " " " " Assay of Gold Bullion...........	248
" " " " " " " " " Silver Bullion............	244
" " " " Percentage of Extraction in the Chlorination Assay of Gold Ores....	257
" " " Percentage of Extraction in the Chlorination Assay of Silver Ores...	254

INDEX. 375

	PAGE
Calculation of the Strength of the Salt Solution used in the Volumetric Assay of Silver Bullion	242
Calculations involved in the Use of Volumetric Solutions	328
Carbonate of Ammonium (Precipitant)	71
" " Potassium (Flux)	66
" " Soda (Flux)	66
" " " (Precipitant)	72
Carbonic Acid, Determination of	116
" " in Natural Phosphates, Determination of	301
" " Test for (Blowpipe)	26
" " " " (Qualitative)	41
Carbon, Determination of	106
" in Coal and Coke, Determination of Fixed	264
" Standards, Eggerz's Mixture for	114
Carnot's Method for the Determination of Antimony	148
Casseroles	61
Characteristic Blowpipe Tests	22
" Qualitative Tests	38
Charcoal (Reducing Flux)	68
Charges for Blast-furnaces, Calculation of	337
Chlorate of Potassium (Oxidizing Reagent)	75
Chloride of Ammonium (Precipitant)	72
" " Barium (Precipitant)	70
" " Silver in Ores, Determination of	254
" " Tin (Reagent)	74
Chlorimetry	289
Chlorination Assay of Gold Ores	256
" " " Silver "	254
Chlorine (Oxidizing Reagent)	75
" Available in Bleaching-powder	289
" in Water, Determination of	277
" , Test for (Blowpipe)	26
" " " (Qualitative)	41
Chromium, Determination of	188
" , Test for (Blowpipe)	26
" " " (Quantitative)	41
Citric Acid (Solvent)	70
Classification of Coals	263
Clays, Determination of Alumina in	184
" " " Calcium in	217
" " " Iron in	177
" " " Magnesia in	223
" " " Silica in	84
Coal, Analysis of	263
Cobalt, Determination of	211

INDEX.

	PAGE
Cobalt, Test for (Blowpipe)	27
" " " Qualitative	41
Coke, Analysis of	263
Colorimetric Determination of Carbon in Iron and Steel	110
" " " Copper	159
" " " Manganese	200
" " " Titanium	190
Combined Carbon in Iron and Steel, Determination of	110
" Water, Determination of	120
Combustion Analysis of Coal and Coke	267
Concentrates, Sampling of	20
Constituents of Water, Grouping of the	281
Copper (Precipitant)	83
" , Determination of	154
" Ingots, Sampling of	14
" Matte, Special Method for the Assay of	250
" Slags, Analysis of	307
" , The Battery Assay for	157
" , The Colorimetric Determination of	159
" , The Volumetric Cyanide-Assay for	154
" " " Iodide " "	161
" , Test for (Blowpipe)	27
" " " (Qualitative)	42
Corrected Assay of Silver Sulphides	252
Crucible-Assay Charges, Table of	129
Crucible Furnace	55
Crucibles	59
Crushing and Pulverizing of Ores, etc	49
Cupellation	128
" of Base Bullion	232
Cupels	61
Cuprous Chloride (Reagent)	272
Cyanide of Potassium (Flux)	68
" " " (Solvent)	70

D

Determination of Alkalies	227
" " " in Water	276
" " Aluminium	181
" " Ammonia in Water	278
" " Antimony	147
" " Arsenic	144
" " Barium	224

INDEX. 377

	PAGE
Determination of Bismuth	163
" Cadmium	165
" Calcium	215
" Carbon	106
" Carbonic Acid	116
" Chlorine in Water	277
" Chromium	188
" Cobalt	211
" Copper	154
" Fixed Carbon in Coal and Coke	264
" Fluorine in Natural Phosphates	305
" Gold and Silver	122
" " " " in Base Bullion	232
" " " " " Copper Matte	250
" " " " " Gold Bullion	246
" " " " " Ores, Slags, etc.	122
" " " " " Silver Bullion	236
" " " " " Silver Sulphides	252
" " Iron	168
" " Lead	136
" " Magnesia	220
" " Manganese	194
" " Mercury	133
" " Moisture	119
" " Nickel	211
" " Nitrates in Water	280
" " Organic Matter in Water	277
" " " and Volatile Matter in Water	274
" " Potassium	227
" " Phosphorus	100
" " Pyrites and Gypsum in Coal and Coke	265
" " Silica and Silicon	77
" " Sodium	227
" " Specific Gravities	293
" " Specific Gravity of Coal and Coke	266
" " Sulphur	88
" " Sulphuric Acid in Water	277
" " the Heating Power of Coal and Coke	266
" " Tin	151
" " Titanium	190
" " Total Solids in Water	274
" " Volatile Matter in Coal	263
" " Water	119
" " Zinc	205
Drown on the Determination of Phosphorus in Iron and Steel	103
Drown's Method for the Separation of Iron and Alumina	185

E

                                                                                 PAGE

Eggerz's Method for the Determination of Combined Carbon in Iron and Steel.. 110
Eggerz's Method for the Determination of Graphite in Iron and Steel..... 109
Eggerz's Mixture for Carbon Standards................................. 114
Electrolytic Determination of Copper................................... 157
     "   "   " Iron... 187
     "   "   " Nickel and Cobalt.............................. 213
     "   Precipitation of Various Metals, Table showing the......... 358
     "   Separation of Iron and Alumina............................ 185
Elementary Analysis of Coal and Coke................................. 267
Elliott's Apparatus for the Rapid Analysis of Gases..................... 270
     " Method for the Determination of Total Carbon................. 106
     "   "   "   " Volumetric Determination of Sulphur............ 97
Emmerton's Method for the Volumetric Determination of Phosphorus.... 100
Equations, The Writing of Chemical.................................... 312
Examination of Ores and Metallurgical Products Preliminary to Assaying. 21

F

Fahlberg-Iles Method for the Determination of Sulphur................. 88
Factors, Calculation of.. 323
     " for the Calculation of Results, Table of......................... 357
Filtration... 61
Filter-paper.. 62–87
Filter-pump... 62
Fire-assay for Gold and Silver Ores (Crucible).......................... 126
    "   "   "   "   "   " (Scorification)............................. 123
    "   " the Determination of Bismuth............................ 164
    "   " "   "   " Lead.................................. 137
    "   " "   "   " Sulphur............................... 91
    "   " "   "   " Tin................................... 152
Fire-assay of Silver Bullion.. 238
Fire-assaying, Fluxes used in.. 67
Fixed Carbon in Coal and Coke, Determination of...................... 264
Flasks.. 63
Flue-dust, Sampling of.. 20
Fluorine in Natural Phosphates, Determination of...................... 305
    " , Test for 28
Fluxes used in Fire-assaying.. 67
    "   "   " Wet Assaying.. 66
Ford's Method for the Determination of Manganese.................... 194

INDEX.

	PAGE
Formulæ, Calculation of	324
" for the Calculation of Lead Blast-furnace Charges	342
" for the Conversion of Degrees Beaumé into Specific Gravity	296
Free Ammonia in Water, Determination of	279
Funnels	61
Furnaces	54
Fused Ore, Determination of Alumina in	184
" " " " Calcium in	218
" " " " Iron in	180
" " " " Manganese in	204
" " " " Silica in	84
" " " " Sulphur in	88
" " " " Zinc in	210

G

Gas Analysis, Calculation of the Results of	332
Gases, Analysis of	269
", Determination of the Specific Gravity of	296
", The Density and Weight of one Litre of Various	356
Gay-Lussac's Method for the Assay of Silver Bullion	240
Gold Bullion, Assay of	246
" " Assay, Calculation of Results of the	248
" ", Sampling of	19
Gold, Determination of	122
" " ", in Base Bullion	233
" " " " Copper Mattes	250
" " " " Ores	122
" " " " Silver Bullion	240
Gold Ores, Amalgamation Assay of	260
" ", Chlorination " "	256
" " containing Metallic Scales, Assay of	258
Graphite in Iron and Steel, Determination of	109
Grouping of the Constituents of Water	281
Gypsum in Coal and Coke, Determination of	265

H

Hand Sampling	6
Handy's Method for the Volumetric Determination of Phosphorus	103
Heating Apparatus	57
" Power of Coal Coke, Determination of	266
Hunt's Remarks on the Colorimetric Determination of Manganese	201

	PAGE
Hunt's Remarks on the Determination of Combined Carbon in Iron and Steel	113
Hydrates of Potassium and Sodium (Fluxes)	67
" " " " " (Precipitants)	72
Hydric Sulphide (Precipitant)	72
" " (Reducing Reagent)	74
Hydrochloric Acid (Solvent)	69
Hydrodisodic Phosphate (Precipitant)	70
Hydrofluoric Acid (Reagent)	67
Hydrogen Peroxide (Oxidizing Reagent)	75
Hyposulphite of Sodium (Solvent)	70

I

Iles' Method for the Determination of Sulphur	88
Indicators	75
" used in Acidimetry and Alkalimetry	285
Indirect Analyses, Calculation of the Results of	331
Iodine, Test for (Blowpipe)	28
Iron (Flux)	69
Iron and Alumina in Water, Determination of	275
Iron, Determination of	168
", Electrolytic Determination of	187
" in Arsenical and Antimonial Ores and Mattes, Determination of	180
" " Clays, Determination of	177
" " Commercial Aluminium, Determination of	299
" " Fused Ores, Determination of	180
" " Iron Ores, Determination of	176
" " Lead and Copper Ores, Determination of	178
" " Limestone, Determination of	177
" " Manganese Ores, Determination of	177
" " Mattes, Determination of	177
" " Natural Phosphates, Determination of	304
" " Pig-iron, Steel, etc., " "	180
" " Silver and Gold Ores, " "	178
" " Slags, Determination of	178
" " Sulphides, Determination of	177
" " Titaniferous Ores, Determination of	193
" Ores, Determination of Alumina in	183
" " " " Chromium in	188
" " " " Iron in	176
" " " " " Titaniferous	193
" " " " Phosphorus in	100
" " " " Silica in	77

INDEX. 381

	PAGE
Iron Ores, Determination of Silica in Titaniferous	192
" " " " Sulphur in	88
", Sampling of Pig-	14
", Test for (Blowpipe)	29
" " " (Qualitative)	42

J

Johnson's Method for the Writing of Chemical Equations 316

K

Knight's Method for the Volumetric Determination of Lead 139

L

Lead (Flux)	69
" (Precipitant)	73
", Comparison of Methods for the Determination of	136
", Determination of	136
" " " by Fire Assay	137
" Flux	68
" Gravimetric Determination of (as Sulphate)	137
" " " " (as Metallic Lead)	139
" Ores, Determination of Alumina in	184
" " " " Calcium in	217
" " " " Iron in	178
" " " " Magnesia in	223
" " " " Manganese in	198
" " " " Silica in	79
" " " " Sulphur in	90
" Slags, Analysis of	307
", Test for (Blowpipe)	30
" " " (Qualitative)	42
Lead, The Volumetric Determination with Potassium Permanganate Solution of	139
Lead, The Volumetric Determination with Molybdate Solution of	142
Lime, see Calcium.	
Limestone, Determination of Alumina in	184
" " " Calcium in	215
" " " Iron in	177
" " " Magnesia in	223
" " " Silica in	84

	PAGE
Litharge (Flux)	67
" , Assay of	128
Lithium, Test for (Blowpipe)	30
" " " (Qualitative)	43
Low's Apparatus for the Electrolytic Determination of Copper	159
" Method for the Determination of Copper	154
" " " " " " Manganese	204

M

Magnesia, Determination of	220
" in Clays, Determination of	223
" " Limestone " "	223
" " Natural Phosphates, Determination of	304
" " Ores, Determination of	223
" " Slags " "	221
" " Water " "	275
" Mixture (Precipitant)	71
Magnesium, Test for (Blowpipe)	31
" " " (Qualitative)	43
Manganese, Determination of	194
" by Ford's Method, Determination of	194
" " Low's Method, " "	204
" " Volhard's Method, " "	198
" " Williams' " " "	196
" in Ores, Determination of	198
" " Iron and Steel, Determination of	194
" " Slags, Determination of	204
" Ores, Determination of Alumina in	184
" " " " Iron in	177
" " " " Silica in	77
" Test for (Blowpipe)	31
" " " (Qualitative)	43
Marguerite's Method for the Volumetric Determination of Iron	169
Mattes, Determination of Alumina in	184
" " " Iron in	177
" " " Silica in	84
Measures and Weights, Table of	353
Mercury, Determination of	133
" , Test for (Blowpipe)	32
" " " (Qualitative)	43
Metallurgical Products, Sampling of	14
Metals, The Characteristic Properties of	359
" " Electrolytic Precipitation of	358

INDEX.

	PAGE
Moisture, Determination of	119
" in Coal and Coke, Determination of	263
" " Natural Phosphates, " "	300
Molybdate Solution (Precipitant)	71
Molybdenum, Test for (Blowpipe)	32
" " " (Qualitative)	43
Moulds used in Assaying	50
Moses, List of Blowpipe Tests by Prof. A. J	22
Muffle Furnace for Coke and Charcoal	57
" " " Soft Coal	56

N

Nickel, Determination of	211
", Test for (Blowpipe)	32
" " " (Qualitative)	43
Nitrate of Ammonium (Oxidizing Reagent)	75
" " Silver (Precipitant)	71
" " Soda (Flux)	67
" " Soda (Oxidizing Reagent)	75
Nitrates in Water, Determination of	280
Nitre (Flux)	68
Nitric Acid (Oxidizing Reagent)	75
" " (Solvent)	69
" ", Test for (Blowpipe)	33
" " " " (Qualitative)	44

O

Operations and Apparatus	49
Ores, Sampling of	6
Organic and Volatile Matter in Water, Determination of	274
Organic Matter in Natural Phosphates, " "	301
Oxalate of Ammonium (Precipitant)	71
Oxalic Acid (Reagent)	70
Oxidizing Reagents	74
Oxygen (Oxidizing Reagent)	74
" consumed by Organic Matter in Water	277

P

Pan for the Amalgamation Assay	262
Parting Buttons from the Assay of Base Bullion	233

Parting Gold and Silver Buttons	131
" Gold Bullion	246
Pearce's Method for the Determination of Arsenic	144
Peeny's Method for the Volumetric Determination of Iron	173
Percentage, Calculation of	321
Permanganate of Potassium (Precipitant)	71
" " " (Oxidizing Reagent)	75
" Test for Organic Matter in Water	277
Peroxide of Hydrogen (Oxidizing Reagent)	75
Phosphate, Hydrodisodic (Precipitant)	70
Phosphates, Analysis of Natural	300
Phosphoric Acid in Natural Phosphates, Determination of	301
Phosphorus, Determination of	100
" , Test for (Blowpipe)	33
" " " (Qualitative)	44
Pig Iron, Determination of Chromium in	189
" " " " Combined Carbon in	110
" " " " Graphite in	109
" " " " Iron in	180
" " " " Phosphorus in	100
" " " " Silicon in	85
" " " " Sulphur in	94
" " " " Total Carbon in	106
Pipettes	63
Platinum Crucibles	60
Porcelain "	60
Potash, Analysis of Commercial	287
Potassium and Sodium, Direct Determination of	229
" " " , Indirect " "	228
" , Determination of	227
" Bichromate (Reagent)	75
" Bisulphate (Flux)	66
" Carbonate (Flux)	66
" Chlorate (Oxidizing Reagent)	75
" Cyanide (Flux)	68
" " (Solvent)	70
" Hydrate (Flux)	67
" " (Precipitant)	72
" " (Reagent in Gas Analysis)	272
" Permanganate (Oxidizing Reagent)	75
" " (Precipitant)	71
" Pyrogallate (Reagent in Gas Analysis)	272
" , Test for (Blowpipe)	33
" " " (Qualitative)	45
Precipitants	70

	PAGE
Precipitates, Table showing the Properties of	360
Preliminary Assay of Silver Bullion	237
" Examination of Ores and Metallurgical Products	21
Properties of Metals, Table of the	359
Proof in the Assay of Silver Bullion	238
Pulverizing	49
Pyrites in Coal and Coke, Determination of	265

Q

Qualitative Tests	38

R

Reagents	66
" used in the Rapid Analysis of Gases	272
Reed on Ore Sampling	14
Rolls	51
Rose Crucible	60
Rose's Method for the Determination of Bismuth	163
" " " " " " Tin	151

S

Salt (Flux)	68
" Solution in the Volumetric Assay for Silver	240
Sampling by Hand (Ores)	6
" , Combined Hand and Mechanical (Ores)	7
" , Mechanical (Ores)	10
" of Base Bullion	14
" " Copper Ingots	20
" " Concentrates	20
" " Flue-dust	20
" " Gold Bullion	19
" " Pig Iron and Steel	14
" " Mattes	20
" " Silver Bullion	18
" " Silver Sulphides	20
" " Slags	18
" " Tailings	20
Scorification	125
" Assay Charges, Table of	124
" Assay for Gold and Silver	123

	PAGE
Scorifiers	61
Selenium, Test for (Blowpipe)	34
" " " (Qualitative)	45
Silica (Flux)	68
", Determination of	77
" in Clays, Determination of	84
" " Copper Furnace Slags, Determination of	84
" " Iron Furnace Slags, Determination of	83
" " Iron Ores, Determination of	77
" " Lead Ores, Determination of	79
" " Limestone, Determination of	84
" " Mattes, Determination of	84
" " Natural Phosphates, Determination of	301
" " Silver and Gold Ores, Determination of	79
" " Slags (Lead), Determination of	80
" " Titaniferous Ores, Determination of	87
" , Test for the Purity of	86
Silicon in Iron and Steel, Determination of	85
" " Commercial Aluminium, Determination of	298
" , Test for (Blowpipe)	34
" " " (Qualitative)	45
Silver Bullion Assay	236
" " , Sampling of	18
" Chloride in Ores, Determination of	254
" Crucibles	60
" , Crucible Assay for	126
" , Determination of	122
" in Base Bullion, Determination of	232
" in Copper Mattes, Determination of	250
" in Ores, Determination of	122
" in Slags, Determination of	129
" Nitrate (Precipitant)	71
" Ores, Amalgamation Assay of	261
" " , Chlorination Assay of	254
" Ores containing Metallic Scales, Assay of	258
" " , Determination of Alumina in	184
" " " " Calcium in	217
" " " " Iron in	178
" " " " Magnesia in	223
" " " " Manganese	198
" " " " Silica in	79
" , Scorification Assay for	123
" Sulphides, Sampling of	20
" " , Assay of	252
" Sulphate in Ores, Determination of	255

INDEX. 387

	PAGE
Silver, Test for (Blowpipe)	34
" " " (Qualitative)	45
Slags, Analysis of	307
" , Sampling of	18
" for Lead Smelting, Table of Type	338
Smith's (J. L.) Method for the Determination of Alkalies	230
Sodium Acetate (Precipitant)	72
" and Potassium, Direct Determination of	229
" " " , Indirect Determination of	228
" Bicarbonate (Flux)	67
" Carbonate (Flux)	66
" " (Precipitant)	72
" Hydrate (Flux)	67
" " (Precipitant)	72
" Hyposulphite (Solvent)	70
" Nitrate (Oxidizing Reagent)	75
" " (Flux)	67
" Sulphide (Precipitant)	72
" Sulphite (Reducing Reagent)	74
" , Test for (Blowpipe)	35
" " " (Qualitative)	46
Solid Matter in Water, Determination of	274
Solvents	69
Specific Gravity and Weight of Gases, Table of the	356
" " Determinations	293
" " of Coal and Coke, Determination of	266
" " of Liquids and Corresponding Degrees Beaumé	297
Split Shovel	9
Standard Acid Solutions	282
" Alkali Solutions	285
Stannous Chloride (Reducing Reagent)	74
Steel, Determination of Combined Carbon in	110
" " " Chromium in	189
" " " Graphite in	109
" " " Iron in	180
" " " Phosphorus in	100
" " " Silicon in	85
" " " Sulphur in	94
" " " Total Carbon in	106
Stoichiometry	321
Strontium, Test for (Blowpipe)	35
" " " (Qualitative)	46
Sulphate of Silver in Ores, Determination of	255
Sulphide of Ammonium (Solvent)	70
" " " (Precipitant)	71

	PAGE
Sulphide of Sodium (Reducing Reagent)	74
Sulphur by Absorption in Alkaline Solution of Cadmium Sulphate, Determination of	96
Sulphur by Absorption in Alkaline Solution of Lead Nitrate, Determination of	99
Sulphur by Fahlberg-Iles Method, Determination of	88
" " Fire Assay, Determination of	91
Sulphur by Oxidation with Potassium Chlorate and Nitric Acid, Determination of	90
Sulphur by Volumetric Method, Determination of	92
Sulphuretted Hydrogen (Reducing Reagent)	74
" " (Precipitant)	72
Sulphuric Acid (Precipitant)	72
" " (Solvent)	69
" " in Water, Determination of	277
Sulphur, Test for (Blowpipe)	35
" " " (Qualitative)	46

T

Table of Atomic Weights	354
" " Crucible Assay Charges	129
" " Factors	357
" " Gramme and Pound Equivalents	257
" " Scorification Assay Charges	124
" " Specific Gravities and Weight of One Litre of Various Gases	356
Table of the Specific Gravities corresponding to Degrees Beaumé of Liquids	297
Table of the Tension of Aqueous Vapor	355
" " Type-lead Slags	338
" " Volumetric Determinations	368
" " Weights and Measures	353
Table of Weights of Lead and Silver to be used in the Assay of Silver Bullion	238
Table showing the Characteristic Properties of Various Metals	359
" " " Electrolytic Precipitation of Various Metals	358
" " " Properties of Precipitates	360
Tartaric Acid (Reagent)	70
Tellurium, Test for (Blowpipe)	36
" " " (Qualitative)	46
Tension of Aqueous Vapor, Table showing the	355
Test-Lead, Assay of	124
Tests, Blowpipe	22
" , Qualitative	38

	PAGE
Tin, Fire-assay for	152
", Determination of	151
", Test for (Blowpipe)	36
" " " (Qualitative)	46
Titaniferous Ores, Determination of Chromium in	189
" " " " Iron "	193
" " " " Silica "	87–192
Titanium, Determination of	190
", Test for (Blowpipe)	37
" " " (Qualitative)	47
Total Carbon, Determination of	106
Tungsten, Test for (Blowpipe)	37
" " " (Qualitative)	47

U

Uranium, Test for (Blowpipe)	37
" " " (Qualitative)	47

V

Vanadium, Test for (Blowpipe)	38
" " " (Qualitative)	48
Volatile Matter in Coal and Coke, Determination of	263
Volhard's Method for the Volumetric Determination of Manganese	198
" " " " " " Silver	245
Volumetric Assay of Silver Bullion, Calculation of the Results of the	244
Volumetric Determination of Arsenic	145
" " " Cadmium	166
" " " Calcium	215
" " " Copper with Cyanide Solution	154
" " " " by the Iodide Method	161
" " " Lead with Molybdate Solution	142
" " " " " Permanganate Solution	139
" " " Manganese by Low's Method	204
" " " " " Volhard's Method	198
" " " " " Williams' Method	197
" " " Phosphorus by Emmerton's Method	100
" " " " " Handy's Method	103
" " " Silver by Gay-Lussac's Method	240
" " " " " Volhard's Method	245
" " " Sulphur	92
" " " " by Elliott's Method	97
" " " Zinc	205
Volumetric Determinations, Table of	368

INDEX.

Volumetric Solutions, Calculations involved in the Preparation and Use of.. 328
Von Schulz and Low's Method for the Determination of Zinc............ 207

W

Waller's Method for the Writing of Chemical Equations................. 314
Water, Distilled (Reagent).. 69
" , Analysis of... 274
" , Determination of.. 119
" in Natural Phosphates, Determination of............................. 301
Weighing.. 51
" Gold and Silver Buttons... 233
Weights... 51
" and Measures, Table of.. 353
" , Table of Atomic... 354
Weller's Colorimetric Method for the Determination of Titanium........ 190
Whitehead's Method for the Determination of Gold and Silver in Copper Matte... 250
White-lead, Analysis of... 291
Williams' Method for the Determination of Manganese................... 196
Wind Furnaces... 55
Writing of Chemical Equations... 312

Z

Zinc (Precipitant).. 72
" , Determination of.. 205
" in Ores containing Cadmium, Determination of........................ 210
" in Slags, Determination of.. 210
" , Test for (Blowpipe)... 38
"   "   " (Qualitative)... 48

www.ingramcontent.com/pod-product-compliance
Lightning Source LLC
Chambersburg PA
CBHW032009220426
43664CB00006B/183